THE MAN VERSUS THE STATE

Herbert Spencer

THE MAN VERSUS THE STATE

With Six Essays on Government, Society, and Freedom

by HERBERT SPENCER

Foreword by Eric Mack
Introduction by Albert Jay Nock

Liberty Fund
Indianapolis

This book is published by Liberty Fund, Inc., a foundation established
to encourage study of the ideal of a society of free and responsible
individuals.

The cuneiform inscription that serves as our logo and as the design motif for
our endpapers is the earliest-known written appearance of the word "freedom" (*amagi*), or "liberty." It is taken from a clay document written about
2300 B.C. in the Sumerian city-state of Lagash.

Introduction by Albert Jay Nock © 1940 by The Caxton Printers, Ltd.,
Caldwell, Idaho.

Frontispiece photograph from The Bettmann Archive, Inc., New York, N.Y.

Library of Congress Cataloging in Publication Data

Spencer, Herbert, 1820-1903.
   The man versus the state.

   Includes index.
   Contents: The man versus the state (1884)—The proper sphere of govern-
ment (1843)—Over-legislation (1853)—Representative government—what is
it good for? (1857)—[etc.]
   1. State, The—Addresses, essays, lectures. 2. Individualism—Addresses,
essays, lectures. 3. Great Britain—Politics and government—1837-1901—
Addresses, essays, lectures. I. Title.
JC571.S75 1981 320.5'1 81-17214
ISBN 0-913966-97-5   AACR2
ISBN 0-913966-98-3 (pbk.)

C 10   9   8   7   6   5   4   3   2
P 10   9   8   7   6

Liberty Fund, Inc.
8335 Allison Pointe Trail, Suite 300
Indianapolis, IN 46250-1684

CONTENTS

PUBLISHER'S NOTE

The Man Versus The State by Herbert Spencer was originally published in 1884 by Williams and Norgate, London and Edinburgh. The book consisted of four articles which had been published in *Contemporary Review* for February, April, May, June, and July of 1884. For collection in book form, Spencer added a Preface and a Postscript. In 1892 the book was reissued with the addition of a few notes in reply to criticism of the first edition.

This Liberty Fund edition contains the entire text of the 1892 edition.

The Man Versus The State was maintained in print for many years in various editions. In 1892 an edition was issued in the United States by D. Appleton and Company. In 1940 one was issued in Great Britain as part of The Thinker's Library.

Two editions have circulated in the United States in the last forty years. In 1940 Caxton Printers, Ltd., of

Caldwell, Idaho, issued an edition with an Introduction by Albert Jay Nock. In this edition, two more essays, "Over-Legislation" and "From Freedom to Bondage," were added to the original four.

In 1969 Penguin Books issued an edition with an Introduction by Donald Macrae. In this edition, "From Freedom to Bondage" was also included along with three other essays, "The Social Organism," "Representative Government—What Is It Good For?," and "Specialized Administration."

For this Liberty Fund edition we have included the Introduction by Nock. In addition, we have printed in a separate section the five essays included in either the Caxton or Penguin editions. Following in the tradition of these earlier publishers we have also added an essay, "The Proper Sphere of Government," which has not, to our knowledge, been reprinted in any book for over one hundred years. Data on original publication are provided at the beginning of each essay.

FOREWORD

Herbert Spencer produced four major works in political philosophy plus numerous additional and important essays. The first of these works, *The Proper Sphere of Government* (1842) is the least well-known. The second is Spencer's most famous systemic treatise in this area, *Social Statics* (1851). *The Man Versus The State* (1884), which is the centerpiece of this volume, is the third major political work. This is a more polemical and quasi-sociological work than either the first two or Spencer's fourth major political study, "Justice," Part IV of *The Principles of Ethics* (1891).

In addition to presenting the first and third of these studies, the present volume makes available two of Spencer's relatively early political essays, "Over-Legislation" (1853) and "Representative Government" (1857); two of his important essays in political sociology, "The Social Organism" (1860) and "Specialized Administration" (1871); and "From Freedom to Bondage"

(1891), which extends the polemical and analytic themes of *The Man Versus The State*.

Herbert Spencer was born in Derby, England on April 27, 1820.[1] He entered a family of dissenting clergymen and teachers in which a long opposition to State-Church ties and solid identification with the rising commercial classes had bred a strong anti-statist individualism. Both his father, George Spencer, and his uncle, the Rev. Thomas Spencer, were supporters of Church disestablishment, the anti-Corn Law Movement and the extention of the franchise. As autodidacts and teachers, Spencer's father and uncles looked to the sciences and their practical applications rather than to the classical tradition. Their anti-statist individualism and their scientifically oriented rationalism were passed on to Herbert Spencer. Spencer himself points to the possible Hussite and Hugenot origins of family as a partial explanation of his own individualism and disregard for authority. And he often recounts how his belief in a universe entirely governed by natural causal law grew out of his father's scientific interests and curiosity about the causes of natural phenomena.

Spencer's education was almost entirely in the hands of his father and, later, his uncles William and Thomas.

---

[1]Two remarkably dry and impersonal accounts of Spencer's life are: *An Autobiography of Herbert Spencer* 2 volumes (New York: D. Appleton and Co., 1904); and D. Duncan's *Life and Letters of Herbert Spencer* 2 volumes (New York: D. Appleton and Co., 1908). D. Wiltshire's *The Social and Political Thought of Herbert Spencer* (Oxford: Oxford University Press, 1978) is the most systematic on the topic. It is personally sympathetic, highly informative, but too conventional in its own theoretical perspective and evaluation.

The focus was on the natural and biological sciences. He gathered plants and insects, performed experiments, sketched and worked out problems in mathematics and attended lectures at the Derby Philosophical Society. When Spencer was in his teens his uncle Thomas sought to broaden his education with classics, languages and history. But his rebellious nephew proved to be relatively immune to such useless and dogmatic pastimes.

In November 1837, just after Victoria ascended to the throne, Spencer joined the engineering staff of the London and Birmingham Railway. Until 1841 and again from 1845 through 1848, working for a number of different firms, Spencer participated in the great expansive phase of railway construction. He appears to have been highly competent and successful at all the engineering tasks undertaken; during these years, and later, Spencer produced a variety of mechanical inventions, and between 1839 and 1842 he published seven articles in the *Civil Engineer's and Architect's Journal.* Only his greater interest in a literary career and, perhaps, the difficulty that this sober and intense young man had in forming warm relations with his colleagues precluded a full-term career in civil engineering. In later years this spectacular growth of the British rail system was continually to serve Spencer as an example of progressive, non-governmental social co-ordination. And just as continually, he used the failure of municipal governments to restrict the noise of trains as an example of the failure of governments to carry out their proper negative functions.

In the Spring of 1842 Spencer began a series of letters to the radical dissenting journal, the *Nonconformist.* Reprinted in pamphlet form *The Proper Sphere of Government* is in some respects his most radical political essay. Spencer maintains that justice construed as respect for natural rights and not any direct pursuit of the "general good" should be the guide for determining the sphere of governmental action. This standard requires of individuals only that they not engage in positive acts of oppression while it requires that the government act only to intervene against such positively oppressive actions.

The publication of *The Proper Sphere of Government* coincided with Spencer's only intense and sustained period of practical political involvement. He served as the secretary of the Derby branch of the Complete Suffrage Union and wrote numerous short tracts for this group as well as for the Anti-State-Church Association. The non-remunerative character of his literary activities during this period explains his return to railway engineering in 1845. In 1848, however, Spencer secured a post as a sub-editor of *The Economist*. At this time *The Economist* was the premier organ for free trade and laissez-faire, and Spencer's submission of a copy of *The Proper Sphere of Government* can hardly have prejudiced his application.

Spencer's five years at *The Economist* were spent at essentially non-ideological ordering of news items, but in *Social Statics* published during the third year, he deepened and systematized the doctrine of *The Proper Sphere of Government*.

The decade following the publication and moderate success of *Social Statics* was devoted to the composition of a number of crucial papers developing Spencer's

Lamarckian-oriented evolutionary perspective and also of a series of important political and sociological essays. Though Spencer's health and finances continued to be in precarious condition, during this period he entered into friendships with many of England's most notable intellectual figures, including George Eliot, Thomas Huxley, George Lewes and John Stuart Mill. Spencer's status as a political heretic during this and succeeding decades should not obscure his broader role as a valued member of the scientific secularist intellectual community. In 1858 Spencer formulated the ambitious outline for his Synthetic Philosophy, on which he was to work, in the face of competing projects and recurring ill-health, for the next thirty-eight years. This scheme included his *First Principles* plus multi-volume works in the Principles of Biology, Psychology, Sociology and Ethics. To fund this project Spencer at first sought the income of some undemanding governmental post in the India administration, as a prison governor, as a postal official or even as a member of the consular service. No suitable posts were available; and, instead, Spencer developed a subscription arrangement to finance his great project. Crucial to this arrangement, as it developed, were the American subscriptions gathered by Spencer's greatest promoter, Edward L. Youmans. When in the mid-sixties this financial construction collapsed due to subscriber's non-payments and Spencer's delays in issuing sections of the Synthetic Philosophy, Mill offered to cover Spencer's immediate losses and to organize a subvention for Spencer's continued work. Spencer refused this charitable aid. However, when Youmans organized a fund among American admirers which would either be paid to Spencer or revert to his American publishers, Spencer "who detested publishers more than he disliked charity, could not refuse."[2]

The political essays of this decade following the publication of *Social Statics* which are reprinted here, "Over-Legislation" and "Representative Government," can easily be read as elaborations upon the doctrine of *Social Statics*. We find a thoroughly general attack on the efficacy of governmental action and a faith that progress will bring the demise of superstitious belief in government omnipotence—albeit, this belief will "die hard." We find a continued expectation that only general suffrage will block class legislation—"only in a general diffusion of political power, is there a safeguard for the general welfare." But effective voter vigilance is possible only when representative government is confined to enforcing the simple and permanent "principles of equity" and not when that government attempts "the complex business of regulating the entire national life."

The two sociological essays reprinted here, "The Social Organism" and "Specialized Administration" represent another, and not entirely compatible, side of Spencer's thought. The relationship between Spencer's political thought and both his general evolutionism and his evolutionary sociology are too intricate and confused to be untangled here—or perhaps anywhere. But a few points can be made with special regard to these two essays. The foremost is that the main purpose of the social

---

[2]Wiltshire, p. 76.

organism metaphor is to emphasize the non-mechanical, non-intentional, yet mutually co-ordinated, character of the processes which give rise to and sustain any given society and its institutions and the pervasiveness, in any complex society, of social orders and structures which are, in Hayek's recent language, the result of human action but not of human design. The metaphor also serves to highlight further parallels between, e.g., the physiological and the economic divisions of labor. It was no part of Spencer's intention to advocate any form of moral or methodological organicism. Thus he asserts that in contrast to biological organisms, "The corporate life [of society] must be subservient to the lives of the parts instead of the lives of the parts being subservient to the corporate life." Yet here too intention and result part company. For, within "The Social Organism," we find Spencer proclaiming that "our Houses of Parliament discharge, in the social economy, functions which are in sundry respects comparable to those discharged by the cerebral masses in a vertebrate animal." Such assertions clearly paved the way for T. H. Huxley to claim in "Administrative Nihilism" that an implication of the organism metaphor was that the economy can and occasionally should be the subject of Parliament's intentional control and manipulation just as a biological organism's body can and usually should be controlled and manipulated by that individual's central nervous system.

Spencer's response in "Specialized Administration" is, unfortunately, both implausible and doctrinally corrosive. He maintains that both the higher biological organism and the higher social organism display systems of passive, negatively regulative, control over inner organs and their interrelations and systems of active, positively regulative, control over outer organs and the relationship of these organs to the external environment. But, in order to maintain the parallelism with respect to inner organs, Spencer must implausibly hold that functional inner parts of biological organisms are merely negatively regulated in accord with something like the principle of equal freedom and the enforcement of contracts. And, in order to maintain the parallelism with respect to outer organs, Spencer must hold that in foreign affairs the state is to go beyond the administration of justice into the realm of positive action. This appears to be inconsistent with Spencer's rejection of offensive war, colonialism and government control of foreign trade. Spencer fails to see the implications of granting the government a positive regulatory function in external affairs because he confuses this significant concession with the truism (applicable to both internal and external affairs) that the government must have positive control over its own apparatus.

Spencer's growing fame and financial security through the 1870s and 1880s was matched neither by happiness nor good health. At least in part the personal tragedy of the second half of Spencer's life was due to his perception of an evolutionary regression after 1850 back toward a mercantilistic and warlike social order of the sort he labeled "militant." Although in one letter he described *The Man Versus The State* as the "finished form" toward which he had been working for forty-two years and as "a positive creed for an advanced party in politics,"[3] for the most part he was deeply pessimistic about stopping the drift to "Communism." By the time this work was composed Spencer no longer saw his task to be charting the course of progress which mankind would be following. Rather it was his duty to oppose the process of "re-barbarization." The essays of *The Man Versus The State* are Spencer's most sustained, brilliant and bitter act of resistance.

"The New Toryism" seeks to define true liberalism and to explain how the Liberal Party had come to advocate a new system of state power. "The Coming Slavery" offers a rich explanation of how increments to state power set in play a dynamic, the ultimate consequences of which are despotism and enslavement. "The Sins of Legislators" attacks legislators' ignorance both of economic laws which co-ordinate people's desires and efforts and evolutionary law which requires that in the course of progress "sufferings must be endured." Here we find an invocation of "the survival of the fittest" though it must be remembered that for Spencer the fittest are those well-adapted to cooperative social life and even those in whom spontaneous sympathy engenders aid to "the unfortunate worthy." "The Great Political Superstition" attacks the doctrine of unlimited governmental sovereignty, whether monarchical or parliamentary, and the associated doctrine that rights are created by the state and may, with equal ease, be abolished by the state. The latter portion of this essay stands as an

[3]Duncan, i, p. 324.

impressive summary of Spencer's political worldview. The present volume closes with "From Freedom to Bondage," one of Spencer's best expositions of his contrast between voluntary, industrial society, the society of contract and compulsory, militant society, the society of status. We find here prophesies as vivid as Bakunin's about the plight of actual workers subordinated to an "army of officials, united by interests common to officialism."

Two of the issues that appear in these later essays operated to further Spencer's defensiveness and isolation. Spencer vehemently attacked Henry George and land-nationalizers and was, in turn, attacked for having abandoned his own belief in the societal ownership of land. George in particular criticized Spencer's alleged apostasy, which seemed to be epitomized by the disappearance of the chapter on "The Right to the Use of the Earth" from the 1892 edition of *Social Statics*. Spencer's angry response was that, in principle, his views had never changed. He continued to believe in the societal ownership of land *and* in just compensation to current landholders—at least for the costs of improvements. Since, however, he had come to realize (on the basis of reasoning that can only be classified as suspect) that society could not afford to pay this just compensation and since the current rampant officialism would translate social ownership into socialism, he rejected explicit social reappropriation under the existing circumstances. And further he declared that the whole issue was moot because everyone, including the author of "The Great Political Superstition," acknowledged Parliament's ultimate

sovereignty over the land. The land question controversy has become one of the test cases for all theories
about Spencer's purported drift to conservatism. Satisfying answers to questions about whether or in what
sense there was such a drift and about how such a drift
might be explained are crucial to a full understanding of
Spencer and are yet to be provided.

In contrast, with the significant exception of Spencer's
sometime acceptance of conscription in defensive war,[4]
Spencer remained clearly and adamantly non-conserv-
ative in his opposition to militarism and imperialism. In
the early 1880s Spencer returned to active politics in
an unsuccessful attempt to build an influential Anti-
Aggression League. It was to these futile efforts plus the
demands of his American tour in the Summer and Fall
of 1882 that Spencer ascribed a further breakdown in
his health. Nevertheless, throughout the 1880s and
1890s Spencer attacked and tried to organize public
opinion against aggressive British involvement abroad.
In "The Sins of Legislators" his greatest ire is directed at
those alleged liberal imperialists who, "though they cannot bear to think of the evils accompanying the struggle
for existence as it is carried on without violence among
individuals in their own society, contemplate with
equanimity such evils in their intense and wholesale
forms, when inflicted by fire and sword on entire communities." For Spencer it was the growth of explicit mil-

---

[4] Cf., *The Principles of Ethics* (Indianapolis: Liberty Fund, 1978) ii, p. 87.
Yet in 1888 Spencer was still attacking conscription as the natural product
of militarism and as an unjust imposition on the "working classes." Duncan, i, pp. 380–391.

itarism which, through numerous channels, was the
underlying cause of the social regression of the last decades of the nineteenth century. As he concludes in
"From Freedom to Bondage," "Everywhere, and at all
times, chronic war generates the militant type of structure, not in the body of soldiers only but throughout the
community at large." The vision of a nation which had
forfeited its historical opportunity and had thereby defeated Spencer's youthful hopes and prophesies domi-
nated Spencer's declining years. The bitterness and the
sadness of this vision show through in Spencer's final
acts of resistance—his essays on "Regimentation," "Re-
Barbarization," and "Imperialism and Slavery" published in 1902. When Herbert Spencer died on December
8, 1903 it was with the conviction that, at least as a political thinker and writer, his life had been in vain.

ERIC MACK

Tulane University

INTRODUCTION

I

In 1851 Herbert Spencer published a treatise called *Social Statics; or, The Conditions Essential to Human Happiness Specified.* Among other specifications, this work established and made clear the fundamental principle that society should be organised on the basis of voluntary cooperation, not on the basis of compulsory cooperation, or under the threat of it. In a word, it established the principle of individualism as against Statism—against the principle underlying all the collectivist doctrines which are everywhere dominant at the present time. It contemplated the reduction of State power over the individual to an absolute minimum, and the raising of social power to its maximum; as against the principle of Statism, which contemplates the precise opposite. Spencer maintained that the State's interventions upon the individual should be confined to punishing those crimes against person or property which are recognised as such by what the Scots philosophers called "the common sense of mankind"*; enforcing the obligations of contract; and making justice costless and easily accessible. Beyond this the State should not go; it should put no further coercive restraint upon the individual. All that the State can do for the best interests of society—all it can do to promote a permanent and stable well-being of society—is by way of these purely negative interventions. Let it go beyond them and attempt the promotion of society's well-being by positive coercive interventions upon the citizen, and whatever apparent and temporary social good may be effected will be greatly at the cost of real and permanent social good.

Spencer's work of 1851 is long out of print and out of currency; a copy of it is extremely hard to find.[1] It should be republished, for it is to the philosophy of individualism what the work of the German idealist philosophers is to the doctrine of Statism, what *Das Kapital* is to Statist economic theory, or what the Pauline Epistles are to the theology of Protestantism.[†] It had no effect, or very little,

---

* These are what the law classifies as *malum in se*, as distinguished from *malum prohibitum*. Thus, murder, arson, robbery, assault, for example, are so classified; the "sense" or judgment of mankind is practically unanimous in regarding them as crimes. On the other hand, selling whiskey, possessing gold, and the planting of certain crops, are examples of the *malum prohibitum*, concerning which there is no such general agreement.

[1] *Social Statics* is now in print again. [Pub.]

†In 1892 Spencer published a revision of *Social Statics*, in which he made some minor changes, and for reasons of his own—reasons which have never been made clear or satisfactorily accounted for—he vacated one position which he held in 1851, and one which is most important to his general doctrine of individualism. It is needless to say that in abandoning a position, for any reason or for no reason, one is quite within one's

on checking the riotous progress of Statism in England; still less in staying the calamitous consequences of that progress. From 1851 down to his death at the end of the century, Spencer wrote occasional essays, partly as running comment on the acceleration of Statism's progress; partly as exposition, by force of illustration and example; and partly as remarkably accurate prophecy of what has since come to pass in consequence of the wholesale substitution of the principle of compulsory coöperation—the Statist principle—for the individualist principle of voluntary cooperation. He reissued four of these essays in 1884, under the title, *The Man Versus The State;* and these four essays, together with two others, called *Overlegislation* and *From Freedom to Bondage,* are now reprinted here under the same general title.[2]

II

The first essay, *The New Toryism*, is of primary importance just now, because it shows the contrast between the aims and methods of early Liberalism and those of modern Liberalism. In these days we hear a great deal

rights; but it must also be observed that the abandonment of a position does not in itself affect the position's validity. It serves merely to raise the previous question whether the position is or is not valid. Galileo's disavowal of Copernican astronomy, for example, does no more, at most, than send one back to a reexamination of the Copernican system. To an unprejudiced mind, Spencer's action in 1892 suggests no more than that the reader should examine afresh the position taken in 1851, and make his own decision about its validity, or lack of validity, on the strength of the evidence offered.

[2] This refers to the Caxton edition for which this Introduction was written. [Pub.]

about Liberalism, Liberal principles and policies, in the conduct of our public life. All sorts and conditions of men put themselves forward on the public stage as Liberals; they call those who oppose them Tories, and get credit with the public thereby. In the public mind, Liberalism is a term of honour, while Toryism—especially "economic Toryism"—is a term of reproach. Needless to say, these terms are never examined; the self-styled Liberal is taken popularly at the face value of his pretensions, and policies which are put forth as Liberal are accepted in the same unreflecting way. This being so, it is useful to see what the historic sense of the term is, and to see how far the aims and methods of latter-day Liberalism can be brought into correspondence with it; and how far, therefore, the latter-day Liberal is entitled to bear that name.

Spencer shows that the early Liberal was consistently for cutting down the State's coercive power over the citizen, wherever this was possible. He was for reducing to a minimum the number of points at which the State might make coercive interventions upon the individual. He was for steadily enlarging the margin of existence within which the citizen might pursue and regulate his own activities as he saw fit, free of State control or State supervision. Liberal policies and measures, as originally conceived, were such as reflected these aims. The Tory, on the other hand, was opposed to these aims, and his policies reflected this opposition. In general terms, the Liberal was consistently inclined towards the individualist philosophy of society, while the Tory was consistently inclined towards the Statist philosophy.

Spencer shows moreover that as a matter of practical policy, the early Liberal proceeded towards the realization of his aims by the method of repeal. He was not for making new laws, but for repealing old ones. It is most important to remember this. Wherever the Liberal saw a law which enhanced the State's coercive power over the citizen, he was for repealing it and leaving its place blank. There were many such laws on the British statute-books, and when Liberalism came into power it repealed an immense grist of them.

Spencer must be left to describe in his own words, as he does in the course of this essay, how in the latter half of the last century British Liberalism went over bodily to the philosophy of Statism, and abjuring the political method of repealing existent coercive measures, proceeded to outdo the Tories in constructing new coercive measures of ever-increasing particularity. This piece of British political history has great value for American readers, because it enables them to see how closely American Liberalism has followed the same course. It enables them to interpret correctly the significance of Liberalism's influence upon the direction of our public life in the last half-century, and to perceive just what it is to which that influence has led, just what the consequences are which that influence has tended to bring about, and just what are the further consequences which may be expected to ensue.

For example, Statism postulates the doctrine that the citizen has no rights which the State is bound to respect; the only rights he has are those which the State grants him, and which the State may attenuate or revoke at its own pleasure. This doctrine is fundamental; without its support, all the various nominal modes or forms of Statism which we see at large in Europe and America—such as are called Socialism, Communism, Naziism, Fascism, etc.,—would collapse at once. The individualism which was professed by the early Liberals, maintained the contrary; it maintained that the citizen has rights which are inviolable by the State or by any other agency. This was fundamental doctrine; without its support, obviously, every formulation of individualism becomes so much waste paper. Moreover, early Liberalism accepted it as not only fundamental, but also as axiomatic, self-evident. We may remember, for example, that our great charter, the Declaration of Independence, takes as its foundation the self-evident truth of this doctrine, asserting that man, in virtue of his birth, is endowed with certain rights which are "unalienable"; and asserting further that it is "to secure these rights" that governments are instituted among men. Political literature will nowhere furnish a more explicit disavowal of the Statist philosophy than is to be found in the primary postulate of the Declaration.

But now, in which direction has latter-day American Liberalism tended? Has it tended towards an expanding *régime* of voluntary cooperation, or one of enforced cooperation? Have its efforts been directed consistently towards repealing existent measures of State coercion, or towards the devising and promotion of new ones? Has it tended steadily to enlarge or to reduce the margin of existence within which the individual may act as he pleases? Has it contemplated State intervention upon the citizen at an ever-increasing number of points, or at an ever-decreasing number? In short, has it consistently exhibited the philosophy of individualism or the philosophy of Statism?

There can be but one answer, and the facts supporting it are so notorious that multiplying examples would be a waste of space. To take but a single one from among the most conspicuous, Liberals worked hard—and successfully—to inject the principle of absolutism into the Constitution by means of the Income-tax Amendment. Under that Amendment it is competent for Congress not only to confiscate the citizen's last penny, but also to levy punitive taxation, discriminatory taxation, taxation for "the equalization of wealth," or for any other purpose it sees fit to promote. Hardly could a single measure be devised which would do more to clear the way for a purely Statist *régime*, than this which puts so formidable a mechanism in the hands of the State, and gives the State *carte blanche* for its employment against the citizen. Again, the present Administration is made up of self-styled Liberals, and its course has been a continuous triumphal advance of Statism. In a preface to these essays, written in 1884, Spencer has a paragraph which sums up with remarkable completeness the political history of the United States during the last six years:

> Dictatorial measures, rapidly multiplied, have tended continually to narrow the liberties of individuals; and have done this in a double way. Regulations have been made in yearly-growing numbers, restraining the citizen in directions where his actions were previously unchecked, and compelling actions which previously he might perform or not as he liked; and at

the same time heavier public burdens, chiefly local, have further restricted his freedom, by lessening that portion of his earnings which he can spend as he pleases, and augmenting the portion taken from him to be spent as public agents please.

Thus closely has the course of American Statism, from 1932 to 1939, followed the course of British Statism from 1860 to 1884. Considering their professions of Liberalism, it would be quite appropriate and by no means inurbane, to ask Mr. Roosevelt and his entourage whether they believe that the citizen has any rights which the State is bound to respect. Would they be willing—*ex animo*, that is, and not for electioneering purposes—to subscribe to the fundamental doctrine of the Declaration? One would be unfeignedly surprised if they were. Yet such an affirmation might go some way to clarify the distinction, if there actually be any, between the "totalitarian" Statism of certain European countries and the "democratic" Statism of Great Britain, France and the United States. It is commonly taken for granted that there is such a distinction, but those who assume this do not trouble themselves to show wherein the distinction consists; and to the disinterested observer the fact of its existence is, to say the least, not obvious.

Spencer ends *The New Toryism* with a prediction which American readers today will find most interesting, if they bear in mind that it was written fifty-five years ago in England and primarily for English readers. He says:

> The laws made by Liberals are so greatly increasing the compulsions and restraints exercised over citizens, that among Conservatives who suffer from this aggressiveness there is growing up a tendency to resist it. Proof is furnished by the fact

that the "Liberty and Property Defense League" largely consisting of Conservatives, has taken for its motto, "Individualism *versus* Socialism." So that if the present drift of things continues, it may by-and-by really happen that the Tories will be defenders of liberties which the Liberals, in pursuit of what they think popular welfare, trample under foot.

This prophecy has already been fulfilled in the United States.

III

Those essays following *The New Toryism* seem to require no special introduction or explanation. They are largely occupied with the various reasons why rapid social deterioration has ensued upon the progress of Statism, and why, unless that progress be checked, there must ensue a further steady deterioration ending in disintegration. All the American reader need do as he goes through these essays is to draw a continuous parallel with Statism's progress in the United States, and to remark at every page the force and accuracy of Spencer's forecast, as borne out by the unbroken sequence of events since his essays were written. The reader can see plainly what that sequence has run up to in England— a condition in which social power has been so far confiscated and converted into State power that there is now not enough of it left to pay the State's bills; and in which, by necessary consequence, the citizen is on a footing of complete and abject State-slavery. The reader will also perceive what he has no doubt already suspected, that this condition now existing in England is one for which there is apparently no help. Even a successful revolution, if such a thing were conceivable, against the military tyranny which is Statism's last expedient, would accomplish nothing. The people would be as thoroughly indoctrinated with Statism after the revolution as they were before, and therefore the revolution would be no revolution, but *a coup d'Etat*, by which the citizen would gain nothing but a mere change of oppressors. There have been many revolutions in the last twenty-five years, and this has been the sum of their history. They amount to no more than an impressive testimony to the great truth that there can be no right action except there be right thinking behind it. As long as the easy, attractive, superficial philosophy of Statism remains in control of the citizen's mind, no beneficent social change can be effected, whether by revolution or by any other means.

The reader may be left to construct for himself whatever conclusions he sees fit concerning conditions now prevailing in the United States, and to make what inferences he thinks reasonable concerning those to which they would naturally be leading. It seems highly probable that these essays will be of great help to him; greater help, perhaps, than any other single work that could be put before him.

ALBERT JAY NOCK

Narragansett, R. I.
25 October, 1939.

THE MAN VERSUS THE STATE

PREFACE

The *Westminster Review* for April, 1860, contained an article entitled "Parliamentary Reform: the Dangers and the Safeguards." In that article I ventured to predict some results of political changes then proposed.

Reduced to its simplest expression, the thesis maintained was that, unless due precautions were taken, increase of freedom in form would be followed by decrease of freedom in fact. Nothing has occurred to alter the belief I then expressed. The drift of legislation since that time has been of the kind anticipated. Dictatorial measures, rapidly multiplied, have tended continually to narrow the liberties of individuals; and have done this in a double way. Regulations have been made in yearly-growing numbers, restraining the citizen in directions where his actions were previously unchecked, and compelling actions which previously he might perform or not as he liked; and at the same time heavier public burdens, chiefly local, have further restricted his freedom,

3

by lessening that portion of his earnings which he can spend as he pleases, and augmenting the portion taken from him to be spent as public agents please.

The causes of these foretold effects, then in operation, continue in operation—are, indeed, likely to be strengthened, and finding that the conclusions drawn respecting these causes and effects have proved true, I have been prompted to set forth and emphasize kindred conclusions respecting the future, and do what little may be done towards awakening attention to the threatened evils.

For this purpose were written the four following articles, originally published in the *Contemporary Review* for February, April, May, June and July of this year. To meet certain criticisms and to remove some of the objections likely to be raised, I have now added a postscript.

Bayswater, July, 1884

Note—The foregoing preface to the original edition of this work, issued more than seven years ago, serves equally well for the present edition. I have to add only that beyond appending in a note one important illustration, enforcing my argument, I have done nothing to this edition save making various verbal improvements, and a small correction of fact.

Avenue Road, Regent's Park, January, 1892

THE NEW TORYISM

Most of those who now pass as Liberals, are Tories of a new type. This is a paradox which I propose to justify. That I may justify it, I must first point out what the two political parties originally were; and I must then ask the reader to bear with me while I remind him of facts he is familiar with, that I may impress on him the intrinsic natures of Toryism and Liberalism properly so called.

Dating back to an earlier period than their names, the two political parties at first stood respectively for two opposed types of social organization, broadly distinguishable as the militant and the industrial—types which are characterized, the one by the régime of status, almost universal in ancient days, and the other by the régime of contract, which has become general in modern days, chiefly among the Western nations, and especially among ourselves and the Americans. If, instead of using the word "cooperation" in a limited sense, we use it in its widest sense, as signifying the combined activities of citizens under whatever system of regulation; then these two are definable as the system of compulsory cooperation and the system of voluntary cooperation. The typical structure of the one we see in an army formed of conscripts, in which the units in their several grades have to fulfil commands under pain of death, and receive food and clothing and pay, arbitrarily apportioned; while the typical structure of the other we see in a body of producers or distributors, who severally agree to specified payments in return for specified services, and may at will, after due notice, leave the organization if they do not like it.

During social evolution in England, the distinction between these two fundamentally-opposed forms of cooperation, made its appearance gradually; but long before the names Tory and Whig came into use, the parties were becoming traceable, and their connexions with militancy and industrialism respectively, were vaguely shown. The truth is familiar that, here as elsewhere, it was habitually by town-populations, formed of workers and traders accustomed to cooperate under contract, that resistances were made to that coercive rule which characterizes cooperation under status. While, conversely, cooperation under status, arising from, and adjusted to, chronic warfare, was supported in rural districts, originally peopled by military chiefs and their dependents, where the primitive ideas and traditions survived. Moreover, this contrast in political leanings, shown before Whig and Tory principles became clearly distinguished, continued to be shown afterwards. At the period of the Revolution, "while the villages and smaller towns were monopolized by Tories, the larger cities, the manufacturing districts, and the ports of commerce, formed the strongholds of the Whigs." And that, spite of exceptions, the like general relation still exists, needs no proving.

Such were the natures of the two parties as indicated by their origins. Observe, now, how their natures were indicated by their early doctrines and deeds. Whiggism began with resistance to Charles II and his cabal, in their efforts to re-establish unchecked monarchical power. The Whigs "regarded the monarchy as a civil institution, established by the nation for the benefit of all its members"; while with the Tories "the monarch was the delegate of heaven." And these doctrines involved the beliefs, the one that subjection of citizen to ruler was conditional, and the other that it was unconditional. Describing Whig and Tory as conceived at the end of the seventeenth century, some fifty years before he wrote his *Dissertation on Parties*, Bolingbroke says:

> The power and majesty of the people, and original contract, the authority and independency of Parliaments, liberty, resistance, exclusion, abdication, deposition; these were ideas associated, at that time, to the idea of a Whig, and supposed by every Whig to be incommunicable, and inconsistent with the idea of a Tory.
> Divine, hereditary, indefeasible right, lineal succession, passive obedience, prerogative, non-resistance, slavery, nay, and sometimes popery too, were associated in many minds to the idea of a Tory, and deemed incommunicable and inconsistent,

in the same manner, with the idea of Whig.—*Dissertation on Parties*, p. 5.

And if we compare these descriptions, we see that in the one party there was a desire to resist and decrease the coercive power of the ruler over the subject, and in the other party to maintain or increase his coercive power. This distinction in their aims—a distinction which transcends in meaning and importance all other political distinctions—was displayed in their early doings. Whig principles were exemplified in the Habeas Corpus Act, and in the measure by which judges were made independent of the Crown; in defeat of the Non-Resisting Test Bill, which proposed for legislators and officials a compulsory oath that they would in no case resist the king by arms; and, later, they were exemplified in the Bill of Rights, framed to secure subjects against monarchical aggressions. These Acts had the same intrinsic nature. The principle of compulsory cooperation throughout social life was weakened by them, and the principle of voluntary cooperation strengthened. That at a subsequent period the policy of the party had the same general tendency, is well shown by a remark of Mr. Green concerning the period of Whig power after the death of Anne:

> Before the fifty years of their rule had passed, Englishmen had forgotten that it was possible to persecute for differences of religion or to put down the liberty of the press, or to tamper with the administration of justice, or to rule without a Parliament.—*Short History*, p. 705.

And now, passing over the war-period which closed the last century and began this, during which that extension of individual freedom previously gained was lost, and the retrograde movement towards the social type proper to militancy was shown by all kinds of coercive measures, from those which took by force the persons and property of citizens for war-purposes to those which suppressed public meetings and sought to gag the press, let us recall the general characters of those changes effected by Whigs or Liberals after the re-establishment of peace permitted revival of the industrial régime and return to its appropriate type of structure. Under growing Whig influence there came repeal of the laws forbidding combinations among artisans as well as of those which interfered with their freedom of travelling. There was the measure by which, under Whig pressure, Dissenters were allowed to believe as they pleased without suffering certain civil penalties; and there was the Whig measure, carried by Tories under compulsion, which enabled Catholics to profess their religion without losing part of their freedom. The area of liberty was extended by Acts which forbade the buying of negroes and the holding of them in bondage. The East India Company's monopoly was abolished, and trade with the East made open to all. The political serfdom of the unrepresented was narrowed in areas, both by the Reform Bill and the Municipal Reform Bill; so that alike generally and locally, the many were less under the coercion of the few. Dissenters, no longer obliged to submit to the ecclesiastical form of marriage, were made free to wed by a purely civil rite. Later came diminution and removal of restraints on the buying of foreign commodities and the employment of foreign vessels and foreign sailors; and later still the removal of those burdens on the press, which were originally imposed to hinder the diffusion of opinion. And of all these changes it is unquestionable that, whether made or not by Liberals themselves, they were made in conformity with principles professed and urged by Liberals.

But why do I enumerate facts so well known to all? Simply because, as intimated at the outset, it seems needful to remind everybody what Liberalism was in the past, that they may perceive its unlikeness to the so-called Liberalism of the present. It would be inexcusable to name these various measures for the purpose of pointing out the character common to them, were it not that in our day men have forgotten their common character. They do not remember that, in one or other way, all these truly Liberal changes diminished compulsory co-operation throughout social life and increased voluntary cooperation. They have forgotten that, in one direction or other, they diminished the range of governmental authority, and increased the area within which each citizen may act unchecked. They have lost sight of the truth that in past times Liberalism habitually stood for individual freedom *versus* State-coercion.

And now comes the inquiry—How is it that Liberals have lost sight of this? How is it that Liberalism, getting more and more into power, has grown more and more coercive in its legislation? How is it that, either directly through its own majorities or indirectly through aid given in such cases to the majorities of its opponents, Liberalism has to an increasing extent adopted the policy of dictating the actions of citizens, and, by consequence, diminishing the range throughout which their actions

remain free? How are we to explain this spreading confusion of thought which has led it, in pursuit of what
appears to be public good, to invert the method by which
in earlier days it achieved public good?

Unaccountable as at first sight this unconscious
change of policy seems, we shall find that it has arisen
quite naturally. Given the unanalytical thought ordinarily brought to bear on political matters, and, under existing conditions, nothing else was to be expected. To
make this clear some parenthetic explanations are
needful.

From the lowest to the highest creatures, intelligence
progresses by acts of discrimination; and it continues so
to progress among men, from the most ignorant to the
most cultured. To class rightly—to put in the same group
things which are of essentially the same natures, and in
other groups things of natures essentially different—is
the fundamental condition to right guidance of actions.
Beginning with rudimentary vision, which gives warning that some large opaque body is passing near (just as
closed eyes turned to the window, perceiving the shade
caused by a hand put before them, tell us of something
moving in front), the advance is to developed vision,
which, by exactly-appreciated combinations of forms,
colours, and motions, identifies objects at great distances as prey or enemies, and so makes it possible to
improve the adjustments of conduct for securing food or
evading death. That progressing perception of differences and consequent greater correctness of classing,
constitutes, under one of its chief aspects, the growth of

intelligence, is equally seen when we pass from the relatively simple physical vision to the relatively complex intellectual vision—the vision through the agency of which, things previously grouped by certain external resemblances or by certain extrinsic circumstances, come to be more truly grouped in conformity with their intrinsic structures or natures. Undeveloped intellectual vision is just as indiscriminating and erroneous in its classings as undeveloped physical vision. Instance the early arrangement of plants into the groups, trees, shrubs, and herbs: size, the most conspicuous trait, being the ground of distinction; and the assemblages formed being such as united many plants extremely unlike in their natures, and separated others that are near akin. Or still better, take the popular classification which puts together under the same general name, fish and shell-fish, and under the sub-name, shell-fish, puts together crustaceans and molluscs; nay, which goes further, and regards as fish the cetacean mammals. Partly because of the likeness in their modes of life as inhabiting the water, and partly because of some general resemblance in their flavours, creatures that are in their essential natures far more widely separated than a fish is from a bird, are associated in the same class and in the same sub-class.

Now the general truth thus exemplified, holds throughout those higher ranges of intellectual vision concerned with things not presentable to the senses, and, among others, such things as political institutions and political measures. For when thinking of these, too, the results of inadequate intellectual faculty, or inadequate culture of it, or both, are erroneous classings and consequent erroneous conclusions. Indeed, the liability to error is here much greater; since the things with which the intellect is concerned do not admit of examination in the same easy way. You cannot touch or see a political institution: it can be known only by an effort of constructive imagination. Neither can you apprehend by physical perception a political measure: this no less requires a process of mental representation by which its elements are put together in thought, and the essential nature of the combination conceived. Here, therefore, still more than in the cases above named, defective intellectual vision is shown in grouping by external characters, or extrinsic circumstances. How institutions are wrongly classed from this cause, we see in the common notion that the Roman Republic was a popular form of government. Look into the early ideas of the French revolutionists who aimed at an ideal state of freedom, and you find that the political forms and deeds of the Romans were their models; and even now a historian might be named who instances the corruptions of the Roman Republic as showing us what popular government leads to. Yet the resemblance between the institutions of the Romans and free institutions properly so-called, was less than that between a shark and a porpoise—a resemblance of general external form accompanying widely different internal structures. For the Roman Government was that of a small oligarchy within a larger oligarchy: the members of each being unchecked autocrats. A society in which the relatively few men who had political power, and were in a qualified sense free, were so many petty despots, holding not only slaves and dependents but even children in a bondage no less absolute than that in which they held their cattle, was, by its intrinsic nature, more nearly allied to an ordinary despotism than to a society of citizens politically equal.

Passing now to our special question, we may understand the kind of confusion in which Liberalism has lost itself: and the origin of those mistaken classings of political measures which have misled it—classings, as we shall see, by conspicuous external traits instead of by internal natures. For what, in the popular apprehension and in the apprehension of those who effected them, were the changes made by Liberals in the past? They were abolitions of grievances suffered by the people, or by portions of them: this was the common trait they had which most impressed itself on men's minds. They were mitigations of evils which had directly or indirectly been felt by large classes of citizens, as causes to misery or as hindrances to happiness. And since, in the minds of most, a rectified evil is equivalent to an achieved good, these measures came to be thought of as so many positive benefits; and the welfare of the many came to be conceived alike by Liberal statesmen and Liberal voters as the aim of Liberalism. Hence the confusion. The gaining of a popular good, being the external conspicuous trait common to Liberal measures in earlier days (then in each case gained by a relaxation of restraints), it has happened that popular good has come to be sought by Liberals, not as an end to be indirectly gained by relaxations of restraints, but as the end to be directly gained. And seeking to gain it directly, they have used methods intrinsically opposed to those originally used.

And now, having seen how this reversal of policy has arisen (or partial reversal, I should say, for the recent Burials Act and the efforts to remove all remaining religious inequalities, show continuance of the original policy in certain directions), let us proceed to contemplate the extent to which it has been carried during recent times, and the still greater extent to which the future will see it carried if current ideas and feelings continue to predominate.

Before proceeding, it may be well to say that no reflections are intended on the motives which prompted one after another of these various restraints and dictations. These motives were doubtless in nearly all cases good. It must be admitted that the restrictions placed by an Act of 1870, on the employment of women and children in Turkey-red dyeing works, were, in intention, no less philanthropic than those of Edward VI, which prescribed the minimum time for which a journeyman should be retained. Without question, the Seed Supply (Ireland) Act of 1880, which empowered guardians to buy seed for poor tenants, and then to see it properly planted, was moved by a desire for public welfare no less great than that which in 1533 prescribed the number of sheep a tenant might keep, or that of 1597, which commanded that decayed houses of husbandry should be rebuilt. Nobody will dispute that the various measures of late years taken for restricting the sale of intoxicating liquors, have been taken as much with a view to public morals as were the measures taken of old for checking the evils of luxury; as, for instance, in the fourteenth century, when diet as well as dress was restricted. Everyone must see that the edicts issued by Henry VIII to prevent the lower classes from playing dice, cards, bowls, etc., were not more prompted by desire for popular welfare than were the acts passed of late to check gambling.

Further, I do not intend here to question the wisdom of these modern interferences, which Conservatives and Liberals vie with one and other in multiplying, any more than to question the wisdom of those ancient ones which they in many cases resemble. We will not now consider whether the plans of late adopted for preserving the lives of sailors, are or are not more judicious than that sweeping Scotch measure which, in the middle of the fifteenth century, prohibited captains from leaving harbour during the winter. For the present, it shall remain undebated whether there is a better warrant for giving sanitary officers powers to search certain premises for unfit food, than there was for the law of Edward III, under which innkeepers at seaports were sworn to search their guests to prevent the exportation of money or plate. We will assume that there is no less sense in that clause of the Canal-boat Act, which forbids an owner to board gratuitously the children of the boatmen, than there was in the Spitalfields Acts, which, up to 1824, for the benefit of the artisans, forbade the manufacturers to fix their factories more than ten miles from the Royal Exchange. We exclude, then, these questions of philanthropic motive and wise judgment, taking both of them for granted; and have here to concern ourselves solely with the compulsory nature of the measures which, for good or evil as the case may be, have been put in force during periods of Liberal ascendency.

To bring the illustrations within compass, let us commence with 1860, under the second administration of Lord Palmerston. In that year, the restrictions of the Factories Act were extended to bleaching and dyeing works; authority was given to provide analysts of food and drink, to be paid out of local rates; there was an Act providing for inspection of gas-works, as well as for fixing quality of gas and limiting price; there was the Act which, in addition to further mine-inspection, made it penal to employ boys under twelve not attending school and unable to read and write. In 1861 occurred an extension of the compulsory provisions of the Factories Act to lace-works; power was given to poor-law guardians, etc., to enforce vaccination; local boards were authorized to fix rates of hire for horses, ponies, mules, asses, and boats; and certain locally-formed bodies had given to them powers of taxing the locality for rural drainage and irrigation works, and for supplying water to cattle. In 1862 an Act was passed for restricting the employment of women and children in open-air bleaching; and an Act for making illegal a coal-mine with a single shaft, or with shafts separated by less than a specified space; as well as an Act giving the Council of Medical Education the exclusive right to publish a Pharmacopoeia, the price of which is to be fixed by the Treasury. In 1863 came the extension of compulsory vaccination to Scotland, and

also to Ireland; there came the empowering of certain
boards to borrow money repayable from the local rates,
to employ and pay those out of work; there came the
authorizing of town-authorities to take possession of
neglected ornamental spaces, and rate the inhabitants
for their support; there came the Bakehouses Regulation
Act, which, besides specifying minimum age of employés occupied between certain hours, prescribed periodical lime-washing, three coats of paint when
painted, and cleaning with hot water and soap at least
once in six months; and there came also an Act giving a
magistrate authority to decide on the wholesomeness or
unwholesomeness of food brought before him by an inspector. Of compulsory legislation dating from 1864,
may be named an extension of the Factories Act to various additional trades, including regulations for cleans-
ing and ventilation, and specifying of certain employés
in match-works, that they might not take meals on the
premises except in the wood-cutting places. Also there
were passed a Chimney-Sweepers Act, an Act for further
regulating the sale of beer in Ireland, an Act for compulsory testing of cables and anchors, an Act extending
the Public Works Act of 1863, and the Contagious Diseases Act: which last gave the police, in specified places,
powers which, in respect of certain classes of women,
abolished sundry of those safeguards to individual freedom established in past times. The year 1865 witnessed
further provision for the reception and temporary relief
of wanderers at the cost of ratepayers; another public-
house closing Act; and an Act making compulsory regulations for extinguishing fires in London. Then, under

the Ministry of Lord John Russell, in 1866, have to be named an Act to regulate cattle-sheds, etc., in Scotland, giving local authorities powers to inspect sanitary conditions and fix the numbers of cattle; an Act forcing hop-growers to label their bags with the year and place of growth and the true weight, and giving police powers of search; an Act to facilitate the building of lodging-houses in Ireland, and providing for regulation of the inmates; a Public Health Act, under which there is registration of lodging-houses and limitation of occupants, with inspection and directions for lime-washing, etc., and a Public Libraries Act, giving local powers by which a majority can tax a minority for their books.

Passing now to the legislation under the first Ministry of Mr. Gladstone, we have, in 1869, the establishment of State-telegraphy, with the accompanying interdict on telegraphing through any other agency; we have the empowering a Secretary of State to regulate hired conveyances in London; we have further and more stringent regulations to prevent cattle-diseases from spreading, another Beerhouse Regulation Act, and a Sea-birds Preservation Act (ensuring greater mortality of fish). In 1870 we have a law authorizing the Board of Public Works to make advances for landlords' improvements and for purchase by tenants; we have the Act which enables the Education Department to form school-boards which shall purchase sites for schools, and may provide free schools supported by local rates, and enabling school-boards to pay a child's fees, to compel parents to send their children, etc.; we have a further Factories and Workshops Act, making, among other restrictions, some on the employment of women and children in fruit-preserving and fish-curing works. In 1871 we met with an amended Merchant Shipping Act, directing officers of the Board of Trade to record the draught of sea-going vessels leaving port; there is another Factory and Workshops Act, making further restrictions; there is a Pedlars Act, inflicting penalties for hawking without a certificate, and limiting the district within which the certificate holds as well as giving the police power to search pedlars' packs; and there are further measures for enforcing vaccination. The year 1872 had, among other Acts, one which makes it illegal to take for hire more than one child to nurse, unless in a house registered by the authorities, who prescribe the number of infants to be received; it had a Licensing Act, interdicting sale of spirits to those apparently under sixteen; and it had another Merchant Shipping Act, establishing an annual survey of passenger steamers. Then in 1873 was passed the Agricultural Children's Act, which makes it penal for a farmer to employ a child who has neither certificate of elementary education nor of certain prescribed school-attendances; and there was passed a Merchant Shipping Act, requiring on each vessel a scale showing draught and giving the Board of Trade power to fix the numbers of boats and life-saving appliances to be carried.

Turn now to Liberal law-making under the present Ministry. We have, in 1880, a law which forbids conditional advance-notes in payment of sailors' wages; also a law which dictates certain arrangements for the safe carriage of grain-cargoes; also a law increasing local coercion over parents to send their children to school. In 1881 comes legislation to prevent trawling over clam-beds and bait-beds, and an interdict making it impossible to buy a glass of beer on Sunday in Wales. In 1882 the Board of Trade was authorized to grant licences to generate and sell electricity, and municipal bodies were enabled to levy rates for electric-lighting: further exactions from ratepayers were authorized for facilitating more accessible baths and washhouses; and local authorities were empowered to make bye-laws for securing the decent lodging of persons engaged in picking fruit and vegetables. Of such legislation during 1883 may be named the Cheap Trains Act, which, partly by taxing the nation to the extent of £400,000 a year (in the shape of relinquished passenger duty), and partly at the cost of railway-proprietors, still further cheapens travelling for workmen: the Board of Trade, through the Railway Commissioners, being empowered to ensure sufficiently good and frequent accommodation. Again, there is the Act which, under penalty of £10 for disobedience, forbids the payment of wages to workmen at or within public-houses; there is another Factory and Workshops Act, commanding inspection of white lead works (to see that there are provided overalls, respirators, baths, acidulated drinks, etc.) and of bakehouses, regulating times of employment in both, and prescribing in detail some constructions for the last, which are to be kept in a condition satisfactory to the inspectors.

But we are far from forming an adequate conception if we look only at the compulsory legislation which has actually been established of late years. We must look also at that which is advocated, and which threatens to be far

more sweeping in range and stringent in character. We
have lately had a Cabinet Minister, one of the most advanced Liberals, so-called, who pooh-poohs the plans
of the late Government for improving industrial dwellings as so much "tinkering"; and contends for effectual
coercion to be exercised over owners of small houses,
over land-owners, and over ratepayers. Here is another
Cabinet Minister who, addressing his constituents,
speaks slightingly of the doings of philanthropic societies and religious bodies to help the poor, and says that
"the whole of the people of this country ought to look
upon this work as being their own work": that is to say,
some extensive Government measure is called for.
Again, we have a Radical member of Parliament who
leads a large and powerful body, aiming with annually-
increasing promise of success, to enforce sobriety by giving to local majorities powers to prevent freedom of exchange in respect of certain commodities. Regulation of
the hours of labour for certain classes, which has been
made more and more general by successive extensions
of the Factories Acts, is likely now to be made still more
general: a measure is to be proposed bringing the employés in all shops under such regulation. There is a
rising demand, too, that education shall be made gratis
(i.e., tax-supported), for all. The payment of school-fees
is beginning to be denounced as a wrong: the State must
take the whole burden. Moreover, it is proposed by
many that the State, regarded as an undoubtedly competent judge of what constitutes good education for the
poor, shall undertake also to prescribe good education
for the middle classes—shall stamp the children of these,

too, after a State pattern, concerning the goodness of which they have no more doubt than the Chinese had when they fixed theirs. Then there is the "endowment of research," of late energetically urged. Already the Government gives every year the sum of £4,000 for this purpose, to be distributed through the Royal Society; and, in the absence of those who have strong motives for resisting the pressure of the interested, backed by those they easily persuade, it may by-and-by establish that paid "priesthood of science" long ago advocated by Sir David Brewster. Once more, plausible proposals are made that there should be organized a system of compulsory insurance, by which men during their early lives shall be forced to provide for the time when they will be incapacitated.

Nor does enumeration of these further measures of coercive rule, looming on us near at hand or in the distance, complete the account. Nothing more than cursory allusion has yet been made to that accompanying compulsion which takes the form of increased taxation, general and local. Partly for defraying the costs of carrying out these ever-multiplying sets of regulations, each of which requires an additional staff of officers, and partly to meet the outlay for new public institutions, such as board-schools, free libraries, public museums, baths and washhouses, recreation grounds, etc., local rates are year after year increased; as the general taxation is increased by grants for education and to the departments of science and art, etc. Every one of these involves further coercion—restricts still more the freedom of the citizen. For the implied address accompanying every additional exaction is—"Hitherto you have been free to spend this portion of your earnings in any way which pleased you; hereafter you shall not be free so to spend it, but we will spend it for the general benefit." Thus, either directly or indirectly, and in most cases both at once, the citizen is at each further stage in the growth of this compulsory legislation, deprived of some liberty which he previously had.

Such, then, are the doings of the party which claims the name of Liberal; and which calls itself Liberal as being the advocate of extended freedom!

I doubt not that many a member of the party has read the preceding section with impatience: wanting, as he does, to point out an immense oversight which he thinks destroys the validity of the argument. "You forget," he wishes to say, "the fundamental difference between the power which, in the past, established those restraints that Liberalism abolished, and the power which, in the present, establishes the restraints you call anti-Liberal. You forget that the one was an irresponsible power, while the other is a responsible power. You forget that if by the recent legislation of Liberals, people are variously regulated, the body which regulates them is of their own creating, and has their warrant for its acts."

My answer is, that I have not forgotten this difference, but am prepared to contend that the difference is in large measure irrelevant to the issue.

In the first place, the real issue is whether the lives of citizens are more interfered with than they were; not the nature of the agency which interferes with them. Take a simpler case. A member of a trades' union has joined others in establishing an organization of a purely representative character. By it he is compelled to strike if a majority so decide; he is forbidden to accept work save under the conditions they dictate; he is prevented from profiting by his superior ability or energy to the extent he might do were it not for their interdict. He cannot disobey without abandoning those pecuniary benefits of the organization for which he has subscribed, and bringing on himself the persecution, and perhaps violence, of his fellows. Is he any the less coerced because the body coercing him is one which he had an equal voice with the rest in forming?

In the second place, if it be objected that the analogy is faulty, since the governing body of a nation, to which, as protector of the national life and interests, all must submit under penalty of social disorganization, has a far higher authority over citizens than the government of any private organization can have over its members; then the reply is that granting the difference, the answer made continues valid. If men use their liberty in such a way as to surrender their liberty, are they thereafter any the less slaves? If people by a *plebiscite* elect a man despot over them, do they remain free because the despotism was of their own making? Are the coercive edicts issued by him to be regarded as legitimate because they are the ultimate outcome of their own votes? As well might it be argued that the East African, who breaks a spear in another's presence that he may so become bondsman to him, still retains his liberty because he freely chose his master.

Finally if any, not without marks of irritation as I can imagine, repudiate this reasoning, and say that there is no true parallelism between the relation of people to government where an irresponsible single ruler has been permanently elected, and the relation where a responsible representative body is maintained, and from time to time re-elected; then there comes the ultimate reply—an altogether heterodox reply—by which most will be greatly astonished. This reply is, that these multitudinous restraining acts are not defensible on the ground that they proceed from a popularly-chosen body; for that the authority of a popularly-chosen body is no more to be regarded as an unlimited authority than the authority of a monarch; and that as true Liberalism in the past disputed the assumption of a monarch's unlimited authority, so true Liberalism in the present will dispute the assumption of unlimited parliamentary authority. Of this, however, more anon. Here I merely indicate it as an ultimate answer.

Meanwhile it suffices to point out that until recently, just as of old, true Liberalism was shown by its acts to be moving towards the theory of a limited parliamentary authority. All these abolitions of restraints over religious beliefs and observances, over exchange and transit, over trade-combinations and the travelling of artisans, over the publication of opinions, theological or political, etc., were tacit assertions of the desirableness of limitation. In the same way that the abandonment of sumptuary laws, of laws forbidding this or that kind of amusement, of laws dictating modes of farming, and many others of like meddling nature, which took place in early days, was an implied admission that the State ought not to interfere in such matters: so those removals of hindrances to individual activities of one or other kind, which the Liberalism of the last generation effected, were practical confessions that in these directions, too, the sphere of governmental action should be narrowed. And this recognition of the propriety of restricting governmental action was a preparation for restricting it in theory. One of the most familiar political truths is that, in the course of social evolution, usage precedes law; and that when usage has been well established it becomes law by receiving authoritative endorsement and defined form. Manifestly then, Liberalism in the past, by its practice of limitation, was preparing the way for the principle of limitation.

But returning from these more general considerations to the special question, I emphasize the reply that the liberty which a citizen enjoys is to be measured, not by the nature of the governmental machinery he lives under, whether representative or other, but by the relative paucity of the restraints it imposes on him; and that, whether this machinery is or is not one he shared in making, its actions are not of the kind proper to Liberalism if they increase such restraints beyond those which are needful for preventing him from directly or indirectly aggressing on his fellows—needful, that is, for maintaining the liberties of his fellows against his invasions of them: restraints which are, therefore, to be distinguished as negatively coercive, not positively coercive.

Probably, however, the Liberal, and still more the subspecies Radical, who more than any other in these latter days seems under the impression that so long as he has a good end in view he is warranted in exercising over men all the coercion he is able, will continue to protest. Knowing that his aim is popular benefit of some kind, to be achieved in some way, and believing that the Tory is, contrariwise, prompted by class-interest and the desire to maintain class-power, he will regard it as palpably absurd to group him as one of the same genus, and will scorn the reasoning used to prove that he belongs to it.

Perhaps an analogy will help him to see its validity. If, away in the far East, where personal government is the only form of government known, he heard from the inhabitants an account of a struggle by which they had deposed a cruel and vicious despot, and put in his place one whose acts proved his desire for their welfare—if, after listening to their self-gratulations, he told them that they had not essentially changed the nature of their government, he would greatly astonish them; and probably he would have difficulty in making them understand that the substitution of a benevolent despot for a malevolent despot, still left the government a despotism. Similarly with Toryism as rightly conceived. Standing as it does for coercion by the State *versus* the freedom of the individual, Toryism remains Toryism, whether it extends this coercion for selfish or unselfish reasons. As certainly as the despot is still a despot, whether his motives for arbitrary rule are good or bad; so certainly is the Tory still a Tory, whether he has egoistic or altruistic motives for using State-power to restrict the liberty of the citizen, beyond the degree required for maintaining the liberties of other citizens. The altruistic Tory as well as the egoistic

Tory belongs to the genus Tory; though he forms a new species of the genus. And both stand in distinct contrast with the Liberal as defined in the days when Liberals were rightly so called, and when the definition was— "one who advocates greater freedom from restraint, especially in political institutions."

Thus, then, is justified the paradox I set out with. As we have seen, Toryism and Liberalism originally emerged, the one from militancy and the other from industrialism. The one stood for the régime of status and the other for the régime of contract—the one for that system of compulsory cooperation which accompanies the legal inequality of classes, and the other for that voluntary cooperation which accompanies their legal equality; and beyond all question the early acts of the two parties were respectively for the maintenance of agencies which effect this compulsory cooperation, and for the weakening or curbing of them. Manifestly the implication is that, in so far as it has been extending the system of compulsion, what is now called Liberalism is a new form of Toryism.

How truly this is so, we shall see still more clearly on looking at the facts the other side upwards, which we will presently do.

NOTE—By sundry newspapers which noticed this article when it was originally published, the meaning of the above paragraphs was supposed to be that Liberals and Tories have changed places. This, however, is by no means the implication. A new species of Tory may arise without disappearance of the original species. When saying, as on page 16, that in our days "Conservatives and Liberals vie with one another in multiplying" interferences, I clearly implied the belief that while Liberals have taken to coercive legislation, Conservatives have not abandoned it. Nevertheless, it is true that the laws made by Liberals are so greatly increasing the compulsions and restraints exercised over citizens, that among Conservatives who suffer from this aggressiveness there is growing up a tendency to resist it. Proof is furnished by the fact that the "Liberty and Property Defense League," largely consisting of Conservatives, has taken for its motto "Individualism versus Socialism." So that if the present drift of things continues, it may by and by really happen that the Tories will be defenders of liberties which the Liberals, in pursuit of what they think popular welfare, trample under foot.

THE COMING SLAVERY

The kinship of pity to love is shown among other ways in this, that it idealizes its object. Sympathy with one in suffering suppresses, for the time being, remembrance of his transgressions. The feeling which vents itself in "poor fellow!" on seeing one in agony, excludes the thought of "bad fellow," which might at another time arise. Naturally, then, if the wretched are unknown or but vaguely known, all the demerits they may have are ignored; and thus it happens that when the miseries of the poor are dilated upon, they are thought of as the miseries of the deserving poor, instead of being thought of as the miseries of the undeserving poor, which in large measure they should be. Those whose hardships are set forth in pamphlets and proclaimed in sermons and speeches which echo throughout society, are assumed to be all worthy souls, grievously wronged; and none of them are thought of as bearing the penalties of their misdeeds.

On hailing a cab in a London street, it is surprising how frequently the door is officiously opened by one who expects to get something for his trouble. The surprise lessens after counting the many loungers about tavern-doors, or after observing the quickness with which a street-performance, or procession, draws from neighbouring slums and stable-yards a group of idlers. Seeing how numerous they are in every small area, it becomes manifest that tens of thousands of such swarm through London. "They have no work," you say. Say rather that they either refuse work or quickly turn themselves out of it. They are simply good-for-nothings, who in one way or other live on the good-for-somethings—vagrants and sots, criminals and those on the way to crime, youths who are burdens on hard-worked parents, men who appropriate the wages of their wives, fellows who share the gains of prostitutes; and then, less visible and less numerous, there is a corresponding class of women.

Is it natural that happiness should be the lot of such? or is it natural that they should bring unhappiness on themselves and those connected with them? Is it not manifest that there must exist in our midst an immense amount of misery which is a normal result of misconduct, and ought not to be dissociated from it? There is a notion, always more or less prevalent and just now vociferously expressed, that all social suffering is removable, and that it is the duty of somebody or other to remove it. Both these beliefs are false. To separate pain from ill-doing is to fight against the constitution of things, and will be followed by far more pain. Saving men from the natural penalties of dissolute living, eventually necessitates the infliction of artificial penalties in solitary cells, on tread-wheels, and by the lash. I suppose a dictum on which the current creed and the creed of science are at one, may be considered to have as high an authority as can be found. Well, the command "if any would not work neither should he eat," is simply a Christian enunciation of that universal law of Nature under which life has reached its present height—the law that a creature not energetic enough to maintain itself must die: the sole difference being that the law which in the one case is to be artificially enforced, is, in the other case, a natural necessity. And yet this particular tenet of their religion which science so manifestly justifies, is the one which Christians seem least inclined to accept. The current assumption is that there should be no suffering, and that society is to blame for that which exists.

"But surely we are not without responsibilities, even when the suffering is that of the unworthy?"

If the meaning of the word "we" be so expanded as to include with ourselves our ancestors, and especially our ancestral legislators, I agree. I admit that those who made, and modified, and administered, the old Poor Law, were responsible for producing an appalling amount of demoralization, which it will take more than one generation to remove. I admit, too, the partial responsibility of recent and present law-makers for regulations which have brought into being a permanent body of tramps, who ramble from union to union; and also their responsibility for maintaining a constant supply of felons by sending back convicts into society under such conditions that they are almost compelled again to commit crimes. Moreover, I admit that the philanthropic are not without their share of responsibility; since, that they may aid the offspring of the unworthy, they disadvantage the offspring of the worthy through burdening their parents by increased local rates. Nay, I even admit that these swarms of good-for-nothings, fostered and multiplied by public and private agencies, have, by sundry mischievous meddlings, been made to suffer more than they would otherwise have suffered. Are these the responsibilities meant? I suspect not.

But now, leaving the question of responsibilities, however conceived, and considering only the evil itself, what shall we say of its treatment? Let me begin with a fact.

A late uncle of mine, the Rev. Thomas Spencer, for some twenty years incumbent of Hinton Charterhouse, near Bath, no sooner entered on his parish duties than he proved himself anxious for the welfare of the poor, by establishing a school, a library, a clothing club, and land-allotments, besides building some model cottages. Moreover, up to 1833 he was a pauper's friend—always for the pauper against the overseer.

There presently came, however, the debates on the Poor Law, which impressed him with the evils of the system then in force. Though an ardent philanthropist he was not a timid sentimentalist. The result was that, immediately the New Poor Law was passed, he proceeded to carry out its provisions in his parish. Almost universal opposition was encountered by him: not the poor only being his opponents, but even the farmers on whom came the burden of heavy poor-rates. For, strange to say, their interests had become apparently identified with the maintenance of this system which taxed them so largely. The explanation is that there had grown up the practice of paying out of the rates a part of the wages of each farm-servant—"make-wages," as the sum was called. And though the farmers contributed most of the fund from which "make-wages" were paid, yet, since all other ratepayers contributed, the farmers seemed to gain by the arrangement. My uncle, however, not easily deterred, faced all this opposition and enforced the law. The result was that in two years the rates were reduced from £700 a year to £200 a year; while the condition of the parish was greatly improved. "Those who had hitherto loitered at the corners of the streets, or at the doors of the beer-shops, had something else to do, and one after another they obtained employment"; so that out of a population of 800, only 15 had to be sent as incapable paupers to the Bath Union (when that was formed), in place of the 100 who received out-door relief a short time before. If it be said that the £25 telescope which, a few years after, his parishioners presented to my uncle, marked the gratitude of the ratepayers only; then my reply is the fact that when, some years later still, having killed himself by overwork in pursuit of popular welfare, he was taken to Hinton to be buried, the procession which followed him to the grave included not the well-to-do only but the poor.

Several motives have prompted this brief narrative. One is the wish to prove that sympathy with the people and self-sacrificing efforts on their behalf, do not nec-

essarily imply approval of gratuitous aids. Another is
the desire to show that benefit may result, not from multiplication of artificial appliances to mitigate distress,
but, contrariwise, from diminution of them. And a further purpose I have in view is that of preparing the way
for an analogy.

Under another form and in a different sphere, we are
now yearly extending a system which is identical in nature with the system of "make-wages" under the old
Poor Law. Little as politicians recognize the fact, it is
nevertheless demonstrable that these various public appliances for working-class comfort, which they are supplying at the cost of ratepayers, are intrinsically of the
same nature as those which, in past times, treated the
farmer's man as half-labourer and half-pauper. In either
case the worker receives in return for what he does,
money wherewith to buy certain of the things he wants;
while, to procure the rest of them for him, money is
furnished out of a common fund raised by taxes. What
matters it whether the things supplied by ratepayers for
nothing, instead of by the employer in payment, are of
this kind or that kind? The principle is the same. For
sums received let us substitute the commodities and
benefits purchased; and then see how the matter stands.
In old Poor-Law times, the farmer gave for work done
the equivalent, say of house-rent, bread, clothes, and
fire; while the ratepayers practically supplied the man
and his family with their shoes, tea, sugar, candles, a
little bacon, etc. The division is, of course, arbitrary; but
unquestionably the farmer and the ratepayers furnished
these things between them. At the present time the ar-

tisan receives from his employer in wages, the equivalent of the consumable commodities he wants: while from the public comes satisfaction for others of his needs and desires. At the cost of ratepayers he has in some cases, and will presently have in more, a house at less than its commercial value; for of course when, as in Liverpool, a municipality spends nearly £200,000 in pulling down and reconstructing low-class dwellings, and is about to spend as much again, the implication is that in some way the ratepayers supply the poor with more accommodation than the rents they pay would otherwise have brought. The artisan further receives from them, in schooling for his children, much more than he pays for; and there is every probability that he will presently receive it from them gratis. The ratepayers also satisfy what desire he may have for books and newspapers, and comfortable places to read them in. In some cases too, as in Manchester, gymnasia for his children of both sexes, as well as recreation grounds, are provided. That is to say, he obtains from a fund raised by local taxes, certain benefits beyond those which the sum received for his labour enables him to purchase. The sole difference, then, between this system and the old system of "make-wages," is between the kinds of satisfactions obtained; and this difference does not in the least affect the nature of the arrangement.

Moreover, the two are pervaded by substantially the same illusion. In the one case, as in the other, what looks like a gratis benefit is not a gratis benefit. The amount which, under the old Poor Law, the half-pauperized labourer received from the parish to eke out his weekly income, was not really, as it appeared, a bonus; for it was accompanied by a substantially equivalent decrease of his wages, as was quickly proved when the system was abolished and the wages rose. Just so is it with these seeming boons received by working people in towns. I do not refer only to the fact that they unawares pay in part through the raised rents of their dwellings (when they are not actual ratepayers); but I refer to the fact that the wages received by them are, like the wages of the farm-labourer, diminished by these public burdens falling on employers. Read the accounts coming of late from Lancashire concerning the cotton-strikes containing proofs, given by artisans themselves, that the margin of profit is so narrow that the less skilful manufacturers, as well as those with deficient capital, fail, and that the companies of cooperators who compete with them can rarely hold their own; and then consider what is the implication respecting wages. Among the costs of production have to be reckoned taxes, general and local. If, as in our large towns, the local rates now amount to one-third of the rental or more—if the employer has to pay this, not on his private dwelling only, but on his business-premises, factories, warehouses, or the like; it results that the interest on his capital must be diminished by that amount, or the amount must be taken from the wages-fund, or partly one and partly the other. And if competition among capitalists in the same business, and in other businesses, has the effect of so keeping down interest that while some gain others lose, and not a few are ruined—if capital, not getting adequate interest, flows elsewhere and leaves labour unemployed; then it is manifest that the choice for the artisan under such conditions, lies between diminished amount of work and diminished rate of payment for it. Moreover, for kindred reasons these local burdens raise the costs of the things he consumes. The charges made by distributors are, on the average, determined by the current rates of interest on capital used in distributing businesses; and the extra costs of carrying on such businesses have to be paid for by extra prices. So that as in the past the rural worker lost in one way what he gained in another, so in the present does the urban worker: there being, too, in both cases, the loss entailed on him by the cost of administration and the waste accompanying it.

"But what has all this to do with 'the coming slavery'?" will perhaps be asked. Nothing directly, but a good deal indirectly, as we shall see after yet another preliminary section.

It is said that when railways were first opened in Spain, peasants standing on the tracks were not unfrequently run over; and that the blame fell on the engine-drivers for not stopping: rural experiences having yielded no conception of the momentum of a large mass moving at a high velocity.

The incident is recalled to me on contemplating the ideas of the so-called "practical" politician, into whose mind there enters no thought of such a thing as political momentum, still less of a political momentum which, instead of diminishing or remaining constant, increases. The theory on which he daily proceeds is that the change caused by his measure will stop where he intends it to stop. He contemplates intently the things his act will achieve, but thinks little of the remoter issues of the movement his act sets up, and still less its collateral issues. When, in war-time, "food for powder" was to be provided by encouraging population—when Mr. Pitt said, "Let us make relief in cases where there are a number of children a matter of right and honour, instead of a ground for opprobrium and contempt,"[1] it was not expected that the poor-rates would be quadrupled in fifty years, that women with many bastards would be preferred as wives to modest women, because of their incomes from the parish, and that hosts of ratepayers would be pulled down into the ranks of pauperism. Legislators who in 1833 voted £30,000 a year to aid in building school-houses, never supposed that the step they then took would lead to forced contributions, local and general, now amounting to £6,000,000;[2] they did not intend to establish a principle that A should be made responsible for educating B's offspring; they did not dream of a compulsion which would deprive poor widows of the help of their elder children; and still less did they dream that their successors, by requiring impoverished parents to apply to Boards of Guardians to pay the fees which School Boards would not remit, would initiate a habit of applying to Boards of Guardians and so cause pauperization.[3] Neither did those who in 1834 passed an Act regulating the labour of women and children in certain factories, imagine that the system they were begin-

---

[1] Hansard's *Parliamentary History*, 32, p. 710.
[2] Since this was written the sum has risen to £10,000,000; i.e., in 1890.
[3] *Fortnightly Review*, January 1884, p. 17.

ning would end in the restriction and inspection of labour in all kinds of producing establishments where more than fifty people are employed; nor did they conceive that the inspection provided would grow to the extent of requiring that before a "young person" is employed in a factory, authority must be given by a certifying surgeon, who, by personal examination (to which no limit is placed) has satisfied himself that there is no incapacitating disease or bodily infirmity: his verdict determining whether the "young person" shall earn wages or not.[4] Even less, as I say, does the politician who plumes himself on the practicalness of his aims, conceive the indirect results which will follow the direct results of his measures. Thus, to take a case connected with one named above, it was not intended through the system of "payment by results," to do anything more than give teachers an efficient stimulus: it was not supposed that in numerous cases their health would give way under the stimulus; it was not expected that they would be led to adopt a cramming system and to put undue pressure on dull and weak children, often to their great injury; it was not foreseen that in many cases a bodily enfeeblement would be caused which no amount of grammar and geography can compensate for.[5] The licensing of public-houses was simply for maintaining public order: those who devised it never imagined that there would

---

[4] Factories and Workshops Act, 41 and 42 Vic., cap. 16.

[5] Since this was written, these mischiefs have come to be recognized, and the system is in course of abandonment; but not one word is said about the immense injury the Government has inflicted on millions of children during the last 20 years!

result an organized interest powerfully influencing elections in an unwholesome way. Nor did it occur to the "practical" politicians who provided a compulsory load-line for merchant vessels, that the pressure of shipowners' interests would habitually cause the putting of the load-line at the very highest limit, and that from precedent to precedent, tending ever in the same direction, the load-line would gradually rise in the better class of ships; as from good authority I learn that it has already done. Legislators who, some forty years ago, by Act of Parliament compelled railway-companies to supply cheap locomotion, would have ridiculed the belief, had it been expressed, that eventually their Act would punish the companies which improved the supply; and yet this was the result to companies which began to carry third-class passengers by fast trains; since a penalty to the amount of the passenger-duty was inflicted on them for every third-class passenger so carried. To which instance concerning railways, add a far more striking one disclosed by comparing the railway policies of England and France. The law-makers who provided for the ultimate lapsing of French railways to the State, never conceived the possibility that inferior travelling facilities would result—did not foresee that reluctance to depreciate the value of property eventually coming to the State, would negative the authorization of competing lines, and that in the absence of competing lines locomotion would be relatively costly, slow, and infrequent; for, as Sir Thomas Farrer has lately shown, the traveller in England has great advantages over the French traveller in the economy, swiftness, and frequency with which his journeys can be made.

But the "practical" politician who, in spite of such experiences repeated generation after generation, goes on thinking only of proximate results, naturally never thinks of results still more remote, still more general, and still more important than those just exemplified. To repeat the metaphor used above—he never asks whether the political momentum set up by his measure, in some cases decreasing but in other cases greatly increasing, will or will not have the same general direction with other like momenta; and whether it may not join them in presently producing an aggregate energy working changes never thought of. Dwelling only on the effects of his particular stream of legislation, and not observing how such other streams already existing, and still other streams which will follow his initiative, pursue the same average course, it never occurs to him that they may presently unite into a voluminous flood utterly changing the face of things. Or to leave figures for a more literal statement, he is unconscious of the truth that he is helping to form a certain type of social organization, and that kindred measures, effecting kindred changes of organization, tend with ever-increasing force to make that type general; until, passing a certain point, the proclivity towards it becomes irresistible. Just as each society aims when possible to produce in other societies a structure akin to its own—just as among the Greeks, the Spartans and the Athenians struggled to spread their respective political institutions, or as, at the time of the

French Revolution, the European absolute monarchies aimed to re-establish absolute monarchy in France while the Republic encouraged the formation of other republics; so within every society, each species of structure tends to propagate itself. Just as the system of voluntary cooperation by companies, associations, unions, to achieve business ends and other ends, spreads throughout a community; so does the antagonistic system of compulsory cooperation under State-agencies spread; and the larger becomes its extension the more power of spreading it gets. The question of questions for the politician should ever be—"What type of social structure am I tending to produce?" But this is a question he never entertains.

Here we will entertain it for him. Let us now observe the general course of recent changes, with the accompanying current of ideas, and see whither they are carrying us.

The blank form of an inquiry daily made is—"We have already done this; why should we not do that?" And the regard for precedent suggested by it, is ever pushing on regulative legislation. Having had brought within their sphere of operation more and more numerous businesses, the Acts restricting hours of employment and dictating the treatment of workers are now to be made applicable to shops. From inspecting lodging-houses to limit the numbers of occupants and enforce sanitary conditions, we have passed to inspecting all houses below a certain rent in which there are members of more than one family, and are now passing to a kindred inspection

of all small houses.[6] The buying and working of telegraphs by the State is made a reason for urging that the
State should buy and work the railways. Supplying children with food for their minds by public agency is being
followed in some cases by supplying food for their bodies; and after the practice has been made gradually more
general, we may anticipate that the supply, now proposed to be made gratis in the one case, will eventually
be proposed to be made gratis in the other: the argument
that good bodies as well as good minds are needful to
make good citizens, being logically urged as a reason for
the extension.[7] And then, avowedly proceeding on the
precedents furnished by the church, the school, and the
reading-room, all publicly provided, it is contended that
"pleasure, in the sense it is now generally admitted,
needs legislating for and organizing at least as much as
work."[8]

Not precedent only prompts this spread, but also the
necessity which arises for supplementing ineffective
measures, and for dealing with the artificial evils continually caused. Failure does not destroy faith in the agencies employed, but merely suggests more stringent use

---

[6] See letter of Local Government Board, *The Times*, 2 January 1884.

[7] Verification comes more promptly than I expected. This article has been
standing in type since 30 January, and in the interval, namely on 13
March, [the article was published on 1 April], the London School Board
resolved to apply for authority to use local charitable funds for supplying
gratis meals and clothing to indigent children. Presently the definition
of "indigent" will be widened; more children will be included, and more
funds asked for.

[8] *Fortnightly Review*, January 1884, p. 21.

of such agencies or wider ramifications of them. Laws to check intemperance, beginning in early times and coming down to our own times, not having done what was expected, there come demands for more thorough-going laws, locally preventing the sale altogether; and here, as in America, these will doubtless be followed by demands that prevention shall be made universal. All the many appliances for "stamping out" epidemic diseases not having succeeded in preventing outbreaks of smallpox, fevers, and the like, a further remedy is applied for in the shape of police-power to search houses for diseased persons, and authority for medical officers to examine any one they think fit, to see whether he or she is suffering from an infectious or contagious malady. Habits of improvidence having for generations been cultivated by the Poor-Law, and the improvident enabled to multiply, the evils produced by compulsory charity are now proposed to be met by compulsory insurance.

The extension of this policy, causing extension of corresponding ideas, fosters everywhere the tacit assumption that Government should step in whenever anything is not going right. "Surely you would not have this misery continue!" exclaims someone, if you hint a demurrer to much that is now being said and done. Observe what is implied by this exclamation. It takes for granted, first, that all suffering ought to be prevented, which is not true: much of the suffering is curative, and prevention of it is prevention of a remedy. In the second place, it takes for granted that every evil can be removed: the truth being that, with the existing defects of human nature, many evils can only be thrust out of one place or form into another place or form—often being increased by the change. The exclamation also implies the unhesitating belief, here especially concerning us, that evils of all kinds should be dealt with by the State. There does not occur the inquiry whether there are at work other agencies capable of dealing with evils, and whether the evils in question may not be among those which are best dealt with by these other agencies. And obviously, the more numerous governmental interventions become, the more confirmed does this habit of thought grow, and the more loud and perpetual the demands for intervention.

Every extension of the regulative policy involves an addition to the regulative agents—a further growth of officialism and an increasing power of the organization formed of officials. Take a pair of scales with many shot in the one and a few in the other. Lift shot after shot out of the loaded scale and put it into the unloaded scale. Presently you will produce a balance; and if you go on, the position of the scales will be reversed. Suppose the beam to be unequally divided, and let the lightly loaded scale be at the end of a very long arm; then the transfer of each shot, producing a much greater effect, will far sooner bring about a change of position. I use the figure to illustrate what results from transferring one individual after another from the regulated mass of the community to the regulating structures. The transfer weakens the one and strengthens the other in a far greater degree than is implied by the relative change of numbers. A comparatively small body of officials, coherent, having common interests, and acting under central authority, has an immense advantage over an incoherent public which has no settled policy, and can be brought to act unitedly only under strong provocation. Hence an organization of officials, once passing a certain stage of growth, becomes less and less resistible; as we see in the bureaucracies of the Continent.

Not only does the power of resistance of the regulated part decrease in a geometrical ratio as the regulating part increases, but the private interests of many in the regulated part itself, make the change of ratio still more rapid. In every circle conversations show that now, when the passing of competitive examinations renders them eligible for the public service, youths are being educated in such ways that they may pass them and get employment under Government. One consequence is that men who might otherwise reprobate further growth of officialism, are led to look on it with tolerance, if not favourably, as offering possible careers for those dependent on them and those related to them. Any one who remembers the numbers of upper-class and middle-class families anxious to place their children, will see that no small encouragement to the spread of legislative control is now coming from those who, but for the personal interests thus arising, would be hostile to it.

This pressing desire for careers is enforced by the preference for careers which are thought respectable. "Even should his salary be small, his occupation will be that of a gentleman," thinks the father, who wants to get a Government-clerkship for his son. And his relative dignity of State-servant as compared with those occupied in business increases as the administrative organization becomes a larger and more powerful element in society, and tends more and more to fix the standard of honour. The prevalent ambition with a young Frenchman is to get some small official post in his locality, to rise thence to a place in the local centre of government, and finally to reach some head-office in Paris. And in Russia, where that university of State-regulation which characterizes the militant type of society has been carried furthest, we see this ambition pushed to its extreme. Says Mr. Wallace, quoting a passage from a play: "All men, even shopkeepers and cobblers, aim at becoming officers, and the man who has passed his whole life without official rank seems to be not a human being."[9]

These various influences working from above downwards, meet with an increasing response of expectations and solicitations proceeding from below upwards. The hard-worked and over-burdened who form the great majority, and still more the incapables perpetually helped who are ever led to look for more help, are ready supporters of schemes which promise them this or the other benefit of State-agency, and ready believers of those who tell them that such benefits can be given, and ought to be given. They listen with eager faith to all builders of political air-castles, from Oxford graduates down to Irish irreconcilables; and every additional tax-supported appliance for their welfare raises hopes of further ones. Indeed the more numerous public instrumentalities become, the more is there generated in citizens the notion that everything is to be done for them, and

---

[9] *Russia,* p. 422.

nothing by them. Each generation is made less familiar with the attainment of desired ends by individual actions or private combinations, and more familiar with the attainment of them by governmental agencies; until, eventually, governmental agencies come to be thought of as the only available agencies. This result was well shown in the recent Trades-Unions Congress at Paris. The English delegates, reporting to their constituents, said that between themselves and their foreign colleagues "the point of difference was the extent to which the State should be asked to protect labour"; reference being thus made to the fact, conspicuous in the reports of the proceedings, that the French delegates always invoked governmental power as the only means of satisfying their wishes.

The diffusion of education has worked, and will work still more, in the same direction. "We must educate our masters," is the well-known saying of a Liberal who opposed the last extension of the franchise. Yes, if the education were worthy to be so called, and were relevant to the political enlightenment needed, much might be hoped from it. But knowing rules of syntax, being able to add up correctly, having geographical information, and a memory stocked with the dates of kings' accessions and generals' victories, no more implies fitness to form political conclusions than acquirement of skill in drawing implies expertness in telegraphing, or than ability to play cricket implies proficiency on the violin. "Surely," rejoins someone, "facility in reading opens the way to political knowledge." Doubtless; but will the way be followed? Table-talk proves that nine out of ten people read what amuses them rather than what instructs them; and proves, also, that the last thing they read is something which tells them disagreeable truths or dispels groundless hopes. That popular education results in an extensive reading of publications which foster pleasant illusions rather than of those which insist on hard realities, is beyond question. Says "A Mechanic," writing in the *Pall Mall Gazette* of 3 December 1883:

> Improved education instils the desire for culture—culture instils the desire for many things as yet quite beyond working men's reach . . . in the furious competition to which the present age is given up they are utterly impossible to the poorer classes; hence they are discontented with things as they are, and the more educated the more discontented. Hence, too, Mr. Ruskin and Mr. Morris are regarded as true prophets by many of us.

And that the connexion of cause and effect here alleged is a real one, we may see clearly enough in the present state of Germany.

Being possessed of electoral power, as are now the mass of those who are thus led to nurture sanguine anticipations of benefits to be obtained by social reorganization, it results that whoever seeks their votes must at least refrain from exposing their mistaken beliefs; even if he does not yield to the temptation to express agreement with them. Every candidate for Parliament is prompted to propose or support some new piece of *ad captandum* legislation. Nay, even the chiefs of parties—those anxious to retain office and those to wrest it from them—severally aim to get adherents by outbidding one another. Each seeks popularity by promising more than his opponent has promised, as we have lately seen. And then, as divisions in Parliament show us, the traditional loyalty to leaders overrides questions concerning the intrinsic propriety of proposed measures. Representatives are unconscientious enough to vote for Bills which they believe to be wrong in principle, because party-needs and regard for the next election demand it. And thus a vicious policy is strengthened even by those who see its viciousness.

Meanwhile there goes on out-of-doors an active propaganda to which all these influences are ancillary. Communistic theories, partially indorsed by one Act of Parliament after another, and tacitly if not avowedly favoured by numerous public men seeking supporters, are being advocated more and more vociferously by popular leaders, and urged on by organized societies. There is the movement for land-nationalization which, aiming at a system of land-tenure equitable in the abstract, is, as all the world knows, pressed by Mr. George and his friends with avowed disregard for the just claims of existing owners, and as the basis of a scheme going more than half-way to State-socialism. And then there is the thorough-going Democratic Federation of Mr. Hyndman and his adherents. We are told by them that "the handful of marauders who now hold possession [of the land] have and can have no right save brute force against the tens of millions whom they wrong." They exclaim against "the shareholders who have been allowed to lay hands upon (!) our great railway communications." They condemn "above all, the active capitalist class, the loan-mongers, the farmers, the mine exploiters, the contractors, the middlemen, the factory-lords—these, the modern slave drivers" who exact "more and yet more surplus value out of the wage-slaves whom they employ." And they think it "high time" that trade should be "removed from the control of individual greed."[10]

It remains to point out that the tendencies thus variously displayed, are being strengthened by press advocacy, daily more pronounced. Journalists, always chary of saying that which is distasteful to their readers, are some of them going with the stream and adding to its force. Legislative meddlings which they would once have condemned they now pass in silence, if they do not advocate them; and they speak of *laissez-faire* as an exploded doctrine. "People are no longer frightened at the thought of socialism," is the statement which meets us one day. On another day, a town which does not adopt the Free Libraries Act is sneered at as being alarmed by a measure so moderately communistic. And then, along with editorial assertions that this economic evolution is coming and must be accepted, there is prominence given to the contributions of its advocates. Meanwhile those who regard the recent course of legislation as disastrous, and see that its future course is likely to be still more disastrous, are being reduced to silence by the belief that it is useless to reason with people in a state of political intoxication.

See, then, the many concurrent causes which threaten continually to accelerate the transformation now going on. There is that spread of regulation caused by following precedents, which become the more authoritative

---

[10] *Socialism made Plain.* Reeves, 185 Fleet Street.

the further the policy is carried. There is that increasing need for administrative compulsions and restraints, which results from the unforeseen evils and shortcomings of preceding compulsions and restraints. Moreover, every additional State-interference strengthens the tacit assumption that it is the duty of the State to deal with all evils and secure all benefits. Increasing power of a growing administrative organization is accompanied by decreasing power of the rest of the society to resist its further growth and control. The multiplication of careers opened by a developing bureaucracy, tempts members of the classes regulated by it to favour its extension, as adding to the chances of safe and respectable places for their relatives. The people at large, led to look on benefits received through public agencies as gratis benefits, have their hopes continually excited by the prospects of more. A spreading education, furthering the diffusion of pleasing errors rather than of stern truths, renders such hopes both stronger and more general. Worse still, such hopes are ministered to by candidates for public choice, to augment their chances of success; and leading statesmen, in pursuit of party ends, bid for popular favour by countenancing them. Getting repeated justifications from new laws harmonizing with their doctrines, political enthusiasts and unwise philanthropists push their agitations with growing confidence and success. Journalism, ever responsive to popular opinion, daily strengthens it by giving it voice; while counter-opinion, more and more discouraged, finds little utterance.

Thus influences of various kinds conspire to increase corporate action and decrease individual action. And the change is being on all sides aided by schemers, each of whom thinks only of his pet plan and not at all of the general reorganization which his plan, joined with others such, are working out. It is said that the French Revolution devoured its own children. Here, an analogous catastrophe seems not unlikely. The numerous socialistic changes made by Act of Parliament, joined with the numerous others presently to be made, will by-and-by be all merged in State-socialism—swallowed in the vast wave which they have little by little raised.

"But why is this change described as 'the coming slavery'?" is a question which many will still ask. The reply is simple. All socialism involves slavery.

What is essential to the idea of a slave? We primarily think of him as one who is owned by another. To be more than nominal, however, the ownership must be shown by control of the slave's actions—a control which is habitually for the benefit of the controller. That which fundamentally distinguishes the slave is that he labours under coercion to satisfy another's desires. The relation admits of sundry gradations. Remembering that originally the slave is a prisoner whose life is at the mercy of his captor, it suffices here to note that there is a harsh form of slavery in which, treated as an animal, he has to expend his entire effort for his owner's advantage. Under a system less harsh, though occupied chiefly in working for his owner, he is allowed a short time in which to work for himself, and some ground on which to grow extra food. A further amelioration gives him power to sell the produce of his plot and keep the pro-

ceeds. Then we come to the still more moderated form
which commonly arises where, having been a free man
working on his own land, conquest turns him into what
we distinguish as a serf; and he has to give to his owner
each year a fixed amount of labour or produce, or both:
retaining the rest himself. Finally, in some cases, as in
Russia before serfdom was abolished, he is allowed to
leave his owner's estate and work or trade for himself
elsewhere, under the condition that he shall pay an annual sum. What is it which, in these cases, leads us to
qualify our conception of the slavery as more or less
severe? Evidently the greater or smaller extent to which
effort is compulsorily expended for the benefit of another instead of for self-benefit. If all the slave's labour
is for his owner the slavery is heavy, and if but little it is
light. Take now a further step. Suppose an owner dies,
and his estate with its slaves comes into the hands of
trustees; or suppose the estate and everything on it to
be bought by a company; is the condition of the slave
any the better if the amount of his compulsory labour
remains the same? Suppose that for a company we substitute the community; does it make any difference to
the slave if the time he has to work for others is as great,
and the time left for himself is as small, as before? The
essential question is—How much is he compelled to labour for other benefit than his own, and how much can
he labour for his own benefit? The degree of his slavery
varies according to the ratio between that which he is
forced to yield up and that which he is allowed to retain;
and it matters not whether his master is a single person
or a society. If, without option, he has to labour for the

society, and receives from the general stock such portion as the society awards him, he becomes a slave to the society. Socialistic arrangements necessitate an enslavement of this kind; and towards such an enslavement many recent measures, and still more the measures advocated, are carrying us. Let us observe, first, their proximate effects, and then their ultimate effects.

The policy initiated by the Industrial Dwellings Acts admits of development, and will develop. Where municipal bodies turn house-builders, they inevitably lower the values of houses otherwise built, and check the supply of more. Every dictation respecting modes of building and conveniences to be provided, diminishes the builder's profit, and prompts him to use his capital where the profit is not thus diminished. So, too, the owner, already finding that small houses entail much labour and many losses—already subject to troubles of inspection and interference, and to consequent costs, and having his property daily rendered a more undesirable investment, is prompted to sell; and as buyers are for like reasons deterred, he has to sell at a loss. And now these still-multiplying regulations, ending, it may be, as Lord Grey proposes, in one requiring the owner to maintain the salubrity of his houses by evicting dirty tenants, and thus adding to his other responsibilities that of inspector of nuisances, must further prompt sales and further deter purchasers: so necessitating greater depreciation. What must happen? The multiplication of houses, and especially small houses, being increasingly checked, there must come an increasing demand upon the local authority to make up for the deficient supply.

More and more the municipal or kindred body will have
to build houses, or to purchase houses rendered unsaleable to private persons in the way shown—houses
which, greatly lowered in value as they must become,
it will, in many cases, pay to buy rather than to build
new ones. Nay, this process must work in a double way;
since every entailed increase of local taxation still further
depreciates property.[11] And then when in towns this
process has gone so far as to make the local authority the
chief owner of houses, there will be a good precedent
for publicly providing houses for the rural population,
as proposed in the Radical programme,[12] and as urged
by the Democratic Federation; which insists on "the
compulsory construction of healthy artisans' and agricultural labourers' dwellings in proportion to the population." Manifestly, the tendency of that which has
been done, is being done, and is presently to be done,
is to approach the socialistic ideal in which the community is sole house-proprietor.

Such, too, must be the effect of the daily-growing policy on the tenure and utilization of the land. More nu-

---

[11] If any one thinks such fears are groundless, let him contemplate the
fact that from 1867-8 to 1880-1, our annual local expenditure for the
United Kingdom has grown from £36,132,834 to £63,276,283; and that
during the same 13 years, the municipal expenditure in England and
Wales alone, has grown from 13 millions to 30 millions a year! How the
increase of public burdens will join with other causes in bringing about
public ownership, is shown by a statement made by Mr. W. Rathbone,
M.P., to which my attention has been drawn since the above paragraph
was in type. He says, "within my own experience, local taxation in New
York has risen from 12s.6d. per cent. to £2 12s. 6d. per cent. on the capital
of its citizens—a charge which would more than absorb the whole income
of an average English landlord."—*Nineteenth Century*, February 1883.
[12] *Fortnightly Review*, November 1883, pp. 619-20.

merous public benefits, to be achieved by more
numerous public agencies, at the cost of augmented
public burdens, must increasingly deduct from the returns on land; until, as the depreciation in value becomes
greater and greater, the resistance to change of tenure
becomes less and less. Already, as everyone knows,
there is in many places difficulty in obtaining tenants,
even at greatly reduced rents; and land of inferior fertility
in some cases lies idle, or when farmed by the owner is
often farmed at a loss. Clearly the profit on capital invested in land is not such that taxes, local and general,
can be greatly raised to support extended public administrations, without an absorption of it which will prompt
owners to sell, and make the best of what reduced price
they can get by emigrating and buying land not subject
to heavy burdens; as, indeed, some are now doing. This
process, carried far, must have the result of throwing
inferior land out of cultivation; after which there will be
raised more generally the demand made by Mr. Arch,
who, addressing the Radical Association of Brighton
lately, and, contending that existing landlords do not
make their land adequately productive for the public
benefit, said "he should like the present Government to
pass a Compulsory Cultivation Bill": an applauded proposal which he justified by instancing compulsory vaccination (thus illustrating the influence of precedent).
And this demand will be pressed, not only by the need
for making the land productive, but also by the need for
employing the rural population. After the Government
has extended the practice of hiring the unemployed to
work on deserted lands, or lands acquired at nominal
prices, there will be reached a stage whence there is but

a small further step to that arrangement which, in the programme of the Democratic Federation, is to follow nationalization of the land—the "organization of agricultural and industrial armies under State control on co-operative principles."

To one who doubts whether such a revolution may be so reached, facts may be cited showing its likelihood. In Gaul, during the decline of the Roman Empire, "so numerous were the receivers in comparison with the payers, and so enormous the weight of taxation, that the labourer broke down, the plains became deserts, and woods grew where the plough had been."[13] In like manner, when the French Revolution was approaching, the public burdens had become such, that many farms remained uncultivated and many were deserted: one-quarter of the soil was absolutely lying waste; and in some provinces one-half was in heath.[14] Nor have we been without incidents of a kindred nature at home. Besides the facts that under the old Poor Law the rates had in some parishes risen to half the rental, and that in various places farms were lying idle, there is the fact that in one case the rates had absorbed the whole proceeds of the soil.

> At Cholesbury, in Buckinghamshire, in 1832, the poor rate "suddenly ceased in consequence of the impossibility to continue its collection, the landlords have given up their rents, the farmers their tenancies, and the clergyman his glebe and his tithes. The clergyman, Mr. Jeston, states that in October 1832, the parish officers threw up their books, and the poor assem-

---

[13] Lactant, *De M. Persecut.*, cc. 7, 23.
[14] Taine, *L'Ancien Régime*, pp. 337–8 (in the English Translation).

bled in a body before his door while he was in bed, asking for advice and food. Partly from his own small means, partly from the charity of neighbours, and partly by rates in aid, imposed on the neighbouring parishes, they were for some time supported."[15]

And the Commissioners add that "the benevolent rector recommends that the whole of the land should be divided among the able-bodied paupers": hoping that after help afforded for two years they might be able to maintain themselves. These facts, giving colour to the prophecy made in Parliament that continuance of the old Poor Law for another thirty years would throw the land out of cultivation, clearly show that increase of public burdens may end in forced cultivation under public control.

Then, again, comes State-ownership of railways. Already this exists to a large extent on the Continent. Already we have had here a few years ago loud advocacy of it. And now the cry, which was raised by sundry politicians and publicists, is taken up afresh by the Democratic Federation; which proposes "State-appropriation of railways, with or without compensation." Evidently pressure from above joined by pressure from below, is likely to effect this change dictated by the policy everywhere spreading; and with it must come many attendant changes. For railway-proprietors, at first owners and workers of railways only, have become masters of numerous businesses directly or indirectly connected with

---

[15] *Report of Commissioners for Inquiry into the Administration and Practical Operation of the Poor Laws*, p. 37. 20 February 1834.

railways; and these will have to be purchased. Already exclusive letter-carrier, exclusive transmitter of telegrams, and on the way to become exclusive carrier of parcels, the State will not only be exclusive carrier of passengers, goods, and minerals, but will add to its present various trades many other trades. Even now, besides erecting its naval and military establishments and building harbours, docks, break-waters, etc., it does the work of ship-builder, cannon-founder, small-arms maker, manufacturer of ammunition, army-clothier and boot-maker; and when the railways have been appropriated "with or without compensation," as the Democratic Federationists say, it will have to become locomotive-engine-builder, carriage-maker, tarpaulin and grease manufacturer, passenger-vessel owner, coal-miner, stone-quarrier, omnibus proprietor, etc. Meanwhile its local lieutenants, the municipal governments, already in many places suppliers of water, gas-makers, owners and workers of tramways, proprietors of baths, will doubt-less have undertaken various other businesses. And when the State, directly or by proxy, has thus come into possession of, or has established, numerous concerns for wholesale production and for wholesale distribution, there will be good precedents for extending its function to retail distribution: following such an example, say, as is offered by the French Government, which has long been a retail tobacconist.

Evidently then, the changes made, the changes in progress, and the changes urged, will carry us not only towards State-ownership of land and dwellings and means of communication, all to be administered and worked by State-agents, but towards State-usurpation of all industries: the private forms of which, disadvantaged more and more in competition with the State, which can arrange everything for its own convenience, will more and more die away; just as many voluntary schools have, in presence of Board-schools. And so will be brought about the desired ideal of the socialists.

And now when there has been compassed this desired ideal, which "practical" politicians are helping socialists to reach, and which is so tempting on that bright side which socialists contemplate, what must be the accompanying shady side which they do not contemplate? It is a matter of common remark, often made when a marriage is impending, that those possessed by strong hopes habitually dwell on the promised pleasures and think nothing of the accompanying pains. A further exemplification of this truth is supplied by these political enthusiasts and fanatical revolutionists. Impressed with the miseries existing under our present social arrangements, and not regarding these miseries as caused by the ill-working of a human nature but partially adapted to the social state, they imagine them to be forthwith curable by this or that rearrangement. Yet, even did their plans succeed it could only be by substituting one kind of evil for another. A little deliberate thought would show that under their proposed arrangements, their liberties must be surrendered in proportion as their material welfares were cared for.

For no form of cooperation, small or great, can be carried on without regulation, and an implied submission

to the regulating agencies. Even one of their own organizations for effecting social changes yields them proof.
It is compelled to have its councils, its local and general
officers, its authoritative leaders, who must be obeyed
under penalty of confusion and failure. And the experience of those who are loudest in their advocacy of a
new social order under the paternal control of a Government, shows that even in private voluntarily-formed societies, the power of the regulative organization becomes
great, if not irresistible: often, indeed, causing grum-
bling and restiveness among those controlled. Trades-
unions which carry on a kind of industrial war in defence
of workers' interests *versus* employers' interests, find
that subordination almost military in its strictness is
needful to secure efficient action; for divided councils
prove fatal to success. And even in bodies of cooperators, formed for carrying on manufacturing or distributing businesses, and not needing that obedience to
leaders which is required where the aims are offensive
or defensive, it is still found that the administrative
agency gains such supremacy that there arise complaints
about "the tyranny of organization." Judge then what
must happen when, instead of relatively small combinations, to which men may belong or not as they please,
we have a national combination in which each citizen
finds himself incorporated, and from which he cannot
separate himself without leaving the country. Judge
what must under such conditions become the despotism
of a graduated and centralized officialism, holding in its
hands the resources of the community, and having behind it whatever amount of force it finds requisite to

carry out its decrees and maintain what it calls order. Well may Prince Bismarck display leanings towards State-socialism.

And then after recognizing, as they must if they think out their scheme, the power possessed by the regulative agency in the new social system so temptingly pictured, let its advocates ask themselves to what end this power must be used. Not dwelling exclusively, as they habitually do, on the material well-being and the mental gratifications to be provided for them by a beneficent administration, let them dwell a little on the price to be paid. The officials cannot create the needful supplies: they can but distribute among individuals that which the individuals have joined to produce. If the public agency is required to provide for them, it must reciprocally require them to furnish the means. There cannot be, as under our existing system, agreement between employer and employed—this the scheme excludes. There must in place of it be command by local authorities over workers, and acceptance by the workers of that which the authorities assign to them. And this, indeed, is the arrangement distinctly, but as it would seem inadvertently, pointed to by the members of the Democratic Federation. For they propose that production should be carried on by "agricultural and industrial *armies* under State-control": apparently not remembering that armies pre-suppose grades of officers, by whom obedience would have to be insisted upon; since otherwise neither order nor efficient work could be ensured. So that each would stand toward the governing agency in the relation of slave to master.

"But the governing agency would be a master which he and others made and kept constantly in check; and one which therefore would not control him or others more than was needful of the benefit of each and all."

To which reply the first rejoinder is that, even if so, each member of the community as an individual would be a slave to the community as a whole. Such a relation has habitually existed in militant communities, even under quasi-popular forms of government. In ancient Greece the accepted principle was that the citizen belonged neither to himself nor to his family, but belonged to his city—the city being with the Greek equivalent to the community. And this doctrine, proper to a state of constant warfare, is a doctrine which socialism unawares re-introduces into a state intended to be purely industrial. The services of each will belong to the aggregate of all; and for these services, such returns will be given as the authorities think proper. So that even if the administration is of the beneficent kind intended to be secured, slavery, however mild, must be the outcome of the arrangement.

A second rejoinder is that the administration will presently become not of the intended kind, and that the slavery will not be mild. The socialist speculation is vitiated by an assumption like that which vitiates the speculations of the "practical" politician. It is assumed that officialism will work as it is intended to work, which it never does. The machinery of Communism, like existing social machinery, has to be framed out of existing human nature; and the defects of existing human nature will generate in the one the same evils as in the other. The love of power, the selfishness, the injustice, the untruth-fulness, which often in comparatively short times bring private organizations to disaster, will inevitably, where their effects accumulate from generation to generation, work evils far greater and less remediable; since, vast and complex and possessed of all the resources, the ad-ministrative organization once developed and consoli-dated, must become irresistible. And if there needs proof that the periodic exercise of electoral power would fail to prevent this, it suffices to instance the French Gov-ernment, which, purely popular in origin, and subject at short intervals to popular judgement, nevertheless tramples on the freedom of citizens to an extent which the English delegates to the late Trades Unions Congress say "is a disgrace to, and an anomaly in, a Republican nation."

The final result would be a revival of despotism. A disciplined army of civil officials, like an army of military officials, gives supreme power to its head—a power which has often led to usurpation, as in medieval Europe and still more in Japan—nay, has thus so led among our neighbours, within our own times. The recent confes-sions of M. de Maupas have shown how readily a con-stitutional head, elected and trusted by the whole people, may, with the aid of a few unscrupulous confed-erates, paralyse the representative body and make him-self autocrat. That those who rose to power in a socialistic organization would not scruple to carry out their aims at all costs, we have good reason for conclud-ing. When we find that shareholders who, sometimes gaining but often losing, have made that railway-system by which national prosperity has been so greatly increased, are spoken of by the council of the Democratic Federation as having "laid hands" on the means of communication, we may infer that those who directed a socialistic administration might interpret with extreme perversity the claims of individuals and classes under their control. And when, further, we find members of this same council urging that the State should take possession of the railways, "with or without compensation," we may suspect that the heads of the ideal society desired, would be but little deterred by considerations of equity from pursuing whatever policy they thought needful: a policy which would always be one identified with their own supremacy. It would need but a war with an adjacent society, or some internal discontent demanding forcible suppression, to at once transform a socialistic administration into a grinding tyranny like that of ancient Peru; under which the mass of the people, controlled by grades of officials, and leading lives that were inspected out-of-doors and in-doors, laboured for the support of the organization which regulated them, and were left with but a bare subsistence for themselves. And then would be completely revived, under a different form, that régime of status—that system of compulsory cooperation, the decaying tradition of which is represented by the old Toryism, and towards which the new Toryism is carrying us back.

"But we shall be on our guard against all that—we shall take precautions to ward off such disasters," will doubtless say the enthusiasts. Be they "practical" politicians with their new regulative measures, or communists with their schemes for re-organizing labour their reply is ever the same: "It is true that plans of kindred nature have, from unforeseen causes or adverse accidents, or the misdeeds of those concerned, been brought to failure; but this time we shall profit by past experiences and succeed." There seems no getting people to accept the truth, which nevertheless is conspicuous enough, that the welfare of a society and the justice of its arrangements are at bottom dependent on the characters of its members; and that improvement in neither can take place without that improvement in character which results from carrying on peaceful industry under the restraints imposed by an orderly social life. The belief, not only of the socialists but also of those so-called Liberals who are diligently preparing the way for them, is that by due skill an ill-working humanity may be framed into well-working institutions. It is a delusion. The defective natures of citizens will show themselves in the bad acting of whatever social structure they are arranged into. There is no political alchemy by which you can get golden conduct out of leaden instincts.

Note—Two replies by socialists to the foregoing article have appeared since its publication—*Socialism and Slavery* by H. M. Hyndman, and *Herbert Spencer on Socialism* by Frank Fairman. Notice of them here must be limited to saying that, as usual with antagonists, they ascribe to me opinions which I do not hold. Disapproval of socialism does not, as Mr. Hyndman assumes, necessitate approval of existing arrangements. Many things he reprobates I reprobate quite as much; but I dissent from his remedy. The gentleman who writes under the pseudonym of "Frank Fairman," reproaches me with having receded from that sympathetic defence of the labouring-classes which he finds in *Social Statics;* but I am quite unconscious of any such change as he alleges. Looking with a lenient eye upon the irregularities of those whose lives are hard, by no means involves tolerance of good-for-nothings.

THE SINS OF LEGISLATORS

B e it or be it not true that Man is shapen in iniquity
and conceived in sin, it is unquestionably true that
Government is begotten of aggression and by aggression. In small undeveloped societies where for ages complete peace has continued, there exists nothing like what
we call Government: no coercive agency, but mere hon-
orary headship, if any headship at all. In these excep-
tional communities, unaggressive and from special
causes unaggressed upon, there is so little deviation
from the virtues of truthfulness, honesty, justice, and
generosity, that nothing beyond an occasional expression of public opinion by informally-assembled elders is
needful.[1] Conversely, we find proofs that, at first recognized but temporarily during leadership in war, the
authority of a chief is permanently established by con-
tinuity of war; and grows strong where successful war

---

[1] *Political Institutions*, § § 437, 573.

ends in subjection of neighbouring tribes. And thence
onwards, examples furnished by all races put beyond
doubt the truth, that the coercive power of the chief,
developing into king, and king of kings (a frequent title
in the ancient East), becomes great in proportion as conquest becomes habitual and the union of subdued nations extensive.[2] Comparisons disclose a further truth
which should be ever present to us—the truth that the
aggressiveness of the ruling power inside a society increases with its aggressiveness outside the society. As,
to make an efficient army, the soldiers must be subordinate to their commander; so, to make an efficient fighting community, must the citizens be subordinate to their
government. They must furnish recruits to the extent
demanded, and yield up whatever property is required.

An obvious implication is that political ethics, originally identical with the ethics of war, must long remain
akin to them; and can diverge from them only as warlike
activities and preparations become less. Current evidence shows this. At present on the Continent, the citizen is free only when his services as a soldier are not
demanded; and during the rest of his life he is largely
enslaved in supporting the military organization. Even
among ourselves a serious war would, by the necessitated conscription, suspend the liberties of large numbers and trench on the liberties of the rest, by taking
from them through taxes whatever supplies were
needed—that is, forcing them to labour so many days
more for the State. Inevitably the established code of

---

[2] Ibid., § § 471–3.

conduct in the dealings of Governments with citizens, must be allied to their code of conduct in their dealings with one another.

I am not, under the title of this article, about to treat of the trespassers and the revenges for trespasses, accounts of which mainly constitute history; nor to trace the internal inequities which have ever accompanied the external inequities. I do not propose here to catalogue the crimes of irresponsible legislators; beginning with that of King Khufu, the stones of whose vast tomb were laid in the bloody sweat of a hundred thousand slaves toiling through long years under the lash; going on to those committed by conquerors, Egyptian, Assyrian, Persian, Macedonian, Roman, and the rest; and ending with those of Napoleon, whose ambition to set his foot on the neck of the civilized world, cost not less than two million lives.[3] Nor do I propose here to enumerate those sins of responsible legislators seen in the long list of laws made in the interests of dominant classes—a list coming down in our own country to those under which there were long maintained slavery and the slave-trade, torturing nearly 40,000 negroes annually by close packing during a tropical voyage, and killing a large percentage of them, and ending with the corn-laws, by which, says Sir Erskine May, "to ensure high rents, it had been decreed that multitudes should hunger."[4]

Not, indeed, that a presentation of the conspicuous misdeeds of legislators, responsible and irresponsible,

---

[3] Landfrey. See also *Study of Sociology*, p. 42, and Appendix.
[4] *Constitutional History of England*, ii, p. 617.

would be useless. It would have several uses—one of
them relevant to the truth above pointed out. Such a
presentation would make clear how that identity of political ethics with military ethics which necessarily exists
during primitive times, when the army is simply the
mobilized society and the society is the quiescent army,
continues through long stages, and even now affects in
great degrees our law-proceedings and our daily lives.
Having, for instance, shown that in numerous savage
tribes the judicial function of the chief does not exist, or
is nominal, and that very generally during early stages
of European civilization, each man had to defend himself
and rectify his private wrongs as best he might—having
shown that in mediaeval times the right of private war
among members of the military order was brought to an
end, not because the head ruler thought it his duty to
arbitrate, but because private wars interfered with the
efficiency of his army in public wars—having shown that
the administration of justice displayed through subsequent ages a large amount of its primitive nature, in trial
by battle carried on before the king or his deputy as
umpire, and which, among ourselves, continued nominally to be an alternative form of trial down to 1819; it
might then be pointed out that even now there survives
trial by battle under another form: counsel being the
champions and purses the weapons. In civil cases, the
ruling agency cares scarcely more than of old about rec-
tifying the wrongs of the injured; but, practically, its deputy does little less than enforce the rules of the fight: the
result being less a question of equity than a question of
pecuniary ability and forensic skill. Nay, so little concern
for the administration of justice is shown by the ruling

agency, that when, by legal conflict carried on in the presence of its deputy, the combatants have been pecuniarily bled even to the extent of producing prostration, and when, an appeal being made by one of them, the decision is reversed, the beaten combatant is made to pay for the blunders of the deputy, or of a preceding deputy; and not unfrequently the wronged man, who sought protection or restitution, is taken out of court pecuniarily dead.

Adequately done, such a portrayal of governmental misdeeds of commission and omission, proving that the partially-surviving code of ethics arising in, and proper to, a state of war, still vitiates governmental action, might greatly moderate the hopes of those who are anxious to extend governmental control. After observing that along with the still-manifest traits of that primitive political structure which chronic militancy produces, there goes a still-manifest survival of its primitive principles; the reformer and the philanthropist might be less sanguine in their anticipations of good from its all-pervading agency, and might be more inclined to trust agencies of a nongovernmental kind.

But leaving out the greater part of the large topic comprehended under the title of this article, I propose here to deal only with a comparatively small remaining part—those sins of legislators which are not generated by their personal ambitions or class interests, but result from lack of the study by which they are morally bound to prepare themselves.

A druggist's assistant who, after listening to the description of pains which he mistakes for those of colic,

but which are really caused by inflammation of the cae-
cum, prescribes a sharp purgative and kills the patient,
is found guilty of manslaughter. He is not allowed to
excuse himself on the ground that he did not intend
harm but hoped for good. The plea that he simply made
a mistake in his diagnosis is not entertained. He is told
that he had no right to risk disastrous consequences by
meddling in a matter concerning which his knowledge
was so inadequate. The fact that he was ignorant how
great was his ignorance is not accepted in bar of judgement. It is tacitly assumed that the experience common
to all should have taught him that even the skilled, and
much more the unskilled, make mistakes in the identification of disorders and in the appropriate treatment;
and that having disregarded the warning derivable from
common experience, he was answerable for the
consequences.

We measure the responsibilities of legislators for mischiefs they may do, in a much more lenient fashion. In
most cases, so far from thinking of them as deserving
punishment for causing disasters by laws ignorantly enacted, we scarcely think of them as deserving reprobation. It is held that common experience should have
taught the druggist's assistant, untrained as he is, not to
interfere; but it is not held that common experience
should have taught the legislator not to interfere till he
has trained himself. Though multitudinous facts are before him in the recorded legislation of our own country
and of other countries, which should impress on him
the immense evils caused by wrong treatment, he is not
condemned for disregarding these warnings against

rash meddling. Contrariwise, it is thought meritorious in him when—perhaps lately from college, perhaps fresh from keeping a pack of hounds which made him popular in his county, perhaps emerging from a provincial town where he acquired a fortune, perhaps rising from the bar at which he has gained a name as an advocate—he enters Parliament; and forthwith, in quite a light-hearted way, begins to aid or hinder this or that means of operating on the body politic. In this case there is no occasion even to make for him the excuse that he does not know how little he knows; for the public at large agrees with him in thinking it needless that he should know anything more than what the debates on the proposed measures tell him.

And yet the mischiefs wrought by uninstructed law-making, enormous in their amount as compared with those caused by uninstructed medical treatment, are conspicuous to all who do but glance over its history. The reader must pardon me while I recall a few familiar instances. Century after century, statesmen went on enacting usury laws which made worse the condition of the debtor—raising the rate of interest "from five to six when intending to reduce it to four,"[5] as under Louis XV; and indirectly producing undreamt of evils of many kinds, such as preventing the reproductive use of spare capital, and "burdening the small proprietors with a multitude of perpetual services."[6] So too, the endeavours which in England continued through five hundred

---

[5] W. E. H. Lecky, *History of Rationalism*, ii, pp. 293–4.
[6] De Tocqueville, *The State of Society in France before the Revolution*, p. 421.

years to stop forestalling, and which in France, as Arthur Young witnessed, prevented any one from buying "more than two bushels of wheat at market,"[7] went on generation after generation increasing the miseries and mortality due to dearth; for, as everybody now knows, the wholesale dealer, who was in the statue "De Pistoribus" vituperated as "an open oppressor of poor people,"[8] is simply one whose function it is to equalize the supply of a commodity by checking unduly rapid consumption. Of kindred nature was the measure which, in 1315, to diminish the pressure of famine, prescribed the prices of foods, but which was hastily repealed after it had caused entire disappearance of various foods from the markets; and also such measures, more continuously operating, as those which settled by magisterial order "the reasonable gains" of victuallers.[9] Of like spirit and followed by allied mischiefs have been the many endeavours to fix wages, which began with the Statute of Labourers under Edward II, and ceased only sixty years ago; when, having long galvanized in Spitalfields a decaying industry and fostered there a miserable population, Lords and Commons finally gave up fixing silkweavers' earnings by the decisions of magistrates.

Here I imagine an impatient interruption. "We know all that; the story is stale. The mischiefs of interfering with trade have been dinned in our ears till we are weary; and no one needs to be taught the lesson afresh." My

---

[7] Young's *Travels*, i, pp. 128–9.
[8] G. L. Craik's *History of British Commerce*, i, p. 134.
[9] Craik, loc. cit., i, pp. 136–7.

first reply is that by the great majority the lesson was never properly learnt at all, and that many of those who did learn it have forgotten it. For just the same pleas which of old were put in for these dictations, are again put in. In the statute 35 of Edward II, which aimed to keep down the price of herrings (but was soon repealed because it raised the price), it was complained that people "coming to the fair . . . do bargain for herring, and every of them, by malice and envy, increase upon other, and, if one proffer forty shilling, another will proffer ten shillings more, and the third sixty shillings, and so every one surmounteth other in the bargain."[10] And now "the higgling of the market," here condemned and ascribed "to malice and envy," is being again condemned. The evils of competition have all along been the stock cry of the Socialists; and the council of the Democratic Federation denounces the carrying on of exchange under "the control of individual and greed profit." My second reply is that interferences with the law of supply and demand, which a generation ago were admitted to be habitually mischievous, are now being daily made by Acts of Parliament in new fields; and that, as I shall presently show, they are in these new fields increasing the evils to be cured and producing fresh ones, as of old they did in fields no longer intruded upon.

Returning from this parenthesis, I go on to explain that the above Acts are named to remind the reader that uninstructed legislators have in past times continually

---

[10] Ibid., i, p. 137.

increased human suffering in their endeavours to miti-gate it; and I have now to add that if these evils, shown to be legislatively intensified or produced, be multiplied by ten or more, a conception will be formed of the ag-gregate evils caused by law-making unguided by social science. In a paper read to the Statistical Society in May 1873, Mr. Janson, vice-president of the Law Society, stated that from the Statute of Merton (20 Henry III) to the end of 1872, there had been passed 18,110 public Acts; of which he estimated that four-fifths had been wholly or partially repealed. He also stated that the num-ber of public Acts repealed wholly or in part, or amended, during the three years 1870–71–72 had been 3,532, of which 2,579 had been totally repealed. To see whether this state of repeal has continued, I have re-ferred to the annually-issued volumes of "The Public General Statutes" for the last three sessions. Saying nothing of the numerous amended Acts, the result is that in the last three sessions there have been totally repealed, separately or in groups, 650 Acts, *belonging to the present reign*, besides many of preceding reigns. This, of course, is greatly above the average rate; for there has of late been an active purgation of the statute-book. But making every allowance, we must infer that within our own times, repeals have mounted some distance into the thousands. Doubtless a number of them have been of laws that were obsolete; others have been demanded by changes of circumstances (though seeing how many of them are of quite recent Acts, this has not been a large cause); others simply because they were inoperative; and others have been consequent on the consolidations of numerous Acts into single Acts. But unquestionably in multitudinous cases, repeals came because the Acts had proved injurious. We talk glibly of such changes—we think of cancelled legislation with indifference. We forget that before laws are abolished they have generally been inflicting evils more or less serious; some for a few years, some for tens of years, some for centuries. Change your vague idea of a bad law into a definite idea of it as an agency operating on people's lives, and you see that it means so much of pain, so much of illness, so much of mortality. A vicious form of legal procedure, for example, either enacted or tolerated, entails on suitors, costs, or delays, or defeats. What do these imply? Loss of money, often ill-spared; great and prolonged anxiety; frequently consequent bad health; unhappiness of family and dependents; children stinted in food and clothing—all of them miseries which bring after them multiplied remoter miseries. Add to which the far more numerous cases of those who, lacking the means or the courage to enter on lawsuits, and therefore submitting to frauds, are impoverished; and have similarly to bear the pains of body and mind which ensue. Even to say that a law has been simply a hindrance, is to say that it has caused needless loss of time, extra trouble, and additional worry; and among over-burdened people extra trouble and worry imply, here and there, physical and mental prostrations, with their entailed direct and indirect sufferings. Seeing, then, that bad legislation means injury to men's lives, judge what must be the total amount of mental distress, physical pain, and raised mortality, which these thousands of repealed Acts of

Parliament represent! Fully to bring home the truth that law-making unguided by adequate knowledge brings enormous evils, let me take an instance which a question of the day recalls.

Already I have hinted that interferences with the connexion between supply and demand, given up in certain fields after immense mischiefs had been done during many centuries, are now taking place in other fields. This connexion is supposed to hold only where it has been proved to hold by the evils of disregarding it: so feeble is men's belief in it. There appears no suspicion that in cases where it seems to fail, natural causation has been traversed by artificial hindrances. And yet in the case to which I now refer—that of the supply of houses for the poor—it needs but to ask what laws have been doing for a long time past, to see that the terrible evils complained of are mostly law-made.

A generation ago discussion was taking place concerning the inadequacy and badness of industrial dwellings, and I had occasion to deal with the question. Here is a passage then written:

> An architect and surveyor described it [the Building Act] as having worked after the following manner. In those districts of London consisting of inferior houses built in that unsubstantial fashion which the new Building Act was to mend, there obtains an average rent, sufficiently remunerative to landlords whose houses were run up economically before the New Building Act passed. This existing average rent fixes the rent that must be charged in these districts for new houses of the same accommodation—that is the same number of rooms, for the people

they are built for do not appreciate the extra safety of living within walls strengthened with hoop-iron bond. Now it turns out upon trial, that houses built in accordance with the present regulations, and let at this established rate, bring in nothing like a reasonable return. Builders have consequently confined themselves to erecting houses in better districts (where the possibility of a profitable competition with pre-existing houses shows that those pre-existing houses were tolerably substantial), and have ceased to erect dwellings for the masses, except in the suburbs where no pressing sanitary evils exist. Meanwhile, in the inferior districts above described, has resulted an increase of overcrowding—half-a-dozen families in a house, a score lodgers to a room. Nay, more than this has resulted. That state of miserable dilapidation into which these abodes of the poor are allowed to fall, is due to the absence of competition from new houses. Landlords do not find their tenants tempted away by the offer of better accommodation. Repairs, being unnecessary for securing the largest amount of profit, are not made. . . . In fact for a large percentage of the very horrors which our sanitary agitators are trying to cure by law, we have to thank previous agitators of the same school!—*Social Statics,* p. 384 (edition of 1851).

These were not the only law-made causes of such evils. As shown in the following further passage, sundry others were recognized:

Writing before the repeal of the brick duty, the *Builder* says: "It is supposed that one-fourth of the cost of a dwelling which lets for 2s. 6d. or 3s. a week is caused by the expense of the title-deeds and the tax on wood and bricks used in its construction. Of course, the owner of such property must be remunerated, and he therefore charges 7½d. or 9d. a week to cover these burdens." Mr. C. Gatliff, secretary to the Society for Improving the Dwellings of the Working Classes, describing the effect of the window-tax, says: "They are now paying upon their institution in St. Pancras the sum of £162 16s. in window-duties, or 1 per cent per annum upon the original outlay. The average rental paid by the Society's tenants is 5s. 6d. per week, and the window-duty deducts from this 7¼d. per week."—*The Times*, 31 January 1850.—*Social Statics*, p. 385 (edition of 1851).

Neither is this all the evidence which the press of those days afforded. There was published in *The Times* of 7 December 1850 (too late to be used in the above-named work, which I issued in the last week of 1850), a letter dated from the Reform Club, and signed "Architect," which contained the following passages:

> Lord Kinnaird recommends in your paper of yesterday the construction of model lodging-houses by throwing two or three houses into one.
>
> Allow me to suggest to his Lordship, and to his friend Lord Ashley to whom he refers, that if,—
>
> 1. The window tax were repealed,
> 2. The building Act repealed (excepting the clauses enacting that party and external walls shall be fireproof),
> 3. The timber duties either equalized or repealed, and,
> 4. An Act passed to facilitate the transfer of property.
>
> There would be no more necessity for model lodging-houses than there is for model ships, model cotton-mills, or model steam-engines.
>
> The first limits the poor man's house to seven windows,
>
> The second limits the size of the poor man's house to 25 feet by 18 (about the size of a gentleman's dining-room), into which space the builder has to cram a staircase, an entrance passage, a parlour, and a kitchen (walls and partitions included).
>
> The third induces the builder to erect the poor man's house of timber unfit for building purposes, the duty on the good material (Baltic) being fifteen times more than the duty on the bad or injurious article (Canadian). The Government, even, exclude the latter from all their contracts.
>
> The fourth would have considerable influence upon the present miserable state of the dwellings of the poor. Small freeholds might then be transferred as easily as leaseholds. The effect of building leases has been a direct inducement to bad building.

To guard against mis-statements or over-statements, I have taken the precaution to consult a large East-end builder and contractor of forty years' experience, Mr. C. Forrest, Museum Works, 17 Victoria Park Square, Bethnal Green, who, being churchwarden, member of the vestry, and of the board of guardians, adds extensive knowledge of local public affairs to his extensive knowledge of the building business. Mr. Forrest, who authorizes me to give his name, verifies the foregoing statements, with the exception of one which he strengthens. He says that "Architect" understates the evil entailed by the definition of "a fourth-rate house"; since the dimensions are much less than those he gives (perhaps in conformity with the provisions of a more recent Building Act). Mr. Forrest has done more than this. Besides illustrating the bad effects of great increase in ground-rents (in sixty years from £1 to £8 10s. for a fourth-rate house) which, joined with other causes, had obliged him to abandon plans for industrial dwellings he had intended to build—besides agreeing with "Architect" that this evil has been greatly increased by the difficulties of land transfer due to the law-established system of trusts and entails; he pointed out that a further penalty on the building of small houses is inflicted by additions to local burdens ("prohibitory imposts" he called them): one of the instances he named being that to the cost of each new house has to be added the cost of pavement, roadway, and sewerage, which is charged according to length of frontage, and which, consequently, bears a far larger ratio to the value of a small house than to the value of a large one.

From these law-produced mischiefs, which were great

a generation ago, and have since been increasing, let us pass to more recent law-produced mischiefs. The misery, the disease, the mortality, in "rookeries," made continually worse by artificial impediments to the increase of fourth-rate houses, and by the necessitated greater crowding of those which existed, having become a scandal, Government was invoked to remove the evil. It responded by Artisans' Dwellings Acts; giving to local authorities powers to pull down bad houses and provide for the building of good ones. What have been the results? A summary of the operations of the Metropolitan Board of Works, dated 21 December 1883, shows that up to last September it had, at a cost of a million and a quarter to ratepayers, unhoused 21,000 persons and provided houses for 12,000—the remaining 9,000 to be hereafter provided for, being, meanwhile, left houseless. This is not all. Another local lieutenant of the Government, the Commission of Sewers for the City, working on the same lines, has, under legislative compulsion, pulled down in Golden Lane and Petticoat Square, masses of condemned small houses, which, together, accommodated 1,734 poor people; and of the spaces thus cleared five years ago, one has, by State authority, been sold for a railway station, and the other is only now being covered with industrial dwellings which will eventually accommodate one-half of the expelled population: the result up to the present time being that, added to those displaced by the Metropolitan Board of Works, these 1,734 displaced five years ago, form a total of nearly 11,000 artificially made homeless, who have had to find corners for themselves in miserable places that were already overflowing!

See then what legislation has done. By ill-imposed taxes, raising the prices of bricks and timber, it added to the costs of houses; and promoted, for economy's sake, the use of bad materials in scanty quantities. To check the consequent production of wretched dwellings, it established regulations which, in mediaeval fashion, dictated the quality of the commodity produced: there being no perception that by insisting on a higher quality and therefore higher price, it would limit the demand and eventually diminish the supply. By additional local burdens, legislation has of late still further hindered the building of small houses. Finally, having, by successive measures, produced first bad houses and then a deficiency of better ones, it has at length provided for the artificially-increased overflow of poor people by diminishing the house-capacity which already could not contain them!

Where then lies the blame for the miseries of the Eastend? Against whom should be raised "The bitter cry of outcast London"?[11]

---

[11] More recently, Glasgow has furnished a gigantic illustration of the disasters which result from the socialistic meddlings of municipal bodies. The particulars may be found in proceedings of the Glasgow Town Council, reported in the *Glasgow Herald* for 11 September 1891. In the course of the debate it was said that the Glasgow Improvement Trust had for years been pursuing a "course of blundering," and had landed the corporation "in a quagmire." Out of some £2,000,000 taken from the ratepayers to buy and clear 88 acres of bad house property, £1,000,000 had been got back by sale of cleared lands, but the property remaining in the hands of the Corporation, mostly vacant land, has, by successive valuations in 1880, 1884, and 1891, been shown to have gradually depreciated to the extent of £320,000—an admitted depreciation, believed to be far less than the actual depreciation. Moreover, model-blocks built by the Improvement Trust, have proved to be not only financial failures, but also failures philanthropically considered. One which cost £10,000,

The German anthropologist Bastian, tells us that a sick native of Guinea who causes the fetish to lie by not recovering is strangled;[12] and we may reasonably suppose that among the Guinea people, any one audacious enough to call in question the power of the fetish would be promptly sacrificed. In days when Governmental au-

---

and in the first year yielded 5 per cent, brought in the second year 4 per cent, and in the third 2¾ per cent. Another which cost £11,000 yields only 3 per cent. And, as is thus implied, these dwellings, instead of being in demand, have a decreasing number of tenants—a decreasing number, too, notwithstanding the fact that the clearing of so large an area of low-class dwellings has increased the pressure of the working population, made the over-crowding greater in other parts of the city, and intensified the sanitary evils which were to be mitigated. Commenting on the results, as they had become manifest at the close of 1888, Mr. Honeyman, President of the Social Economy Section of the Glasgow Philosophical Society, said that the model-building put up by the Improvement Trust, was one "which no sane builder would dream of initiating, because it would not pay," and that they had "put anything like fair competition entirely out of the question": "driving the ordinary builder from the field." He also pointed out that the building regulations and restrictions imposed by the Improvement Trust, tended "to keep the land belonging to the Corporation vacant, and hinder the erection of dwellings of the humblest class." In like manner, at a meeting of the Kyrle Society, the Lord Provost of Glasgow pointed out that when, with philanthropic motives, they built houses for the working-people at prices which would not pay the ordinary builder, then "immediately the whole of those builders who had hitherto supplied the wants of the working classes would stop, and philanthropy would require to take the whole burden of the provision on itself."

To achieve all these failures and produce all these evils, many thousands of hard-working ratepayers, who have difficulty in making both ends meet, have been taxed and pinched and distressed. See, then, the enormous evils that follow in the train of the baseless belief in the unlimited power of a majority—the miserable superstition that a body elected by the greater number of citizens has the right to take from citizens at large any amount of money for any purpose it pleases!

[12] *Mensch*, iii, p. 225.

thority was enforced by strong measures, there was a kindred danger in saying anything disrespectful of the political fetish. Nowadays, however, the worst punishment to be looked for by one who questions its omnipotence, is that he will be reviled as a reactionary who talks *laissez-faire*. That any facts he may bring forward will appreciably decrease the established faith is not to be expected; for we are daily shown that this faith is proof against all adverse evidence. Let us contemplate a small part of that vast mass of it which passes unheeded.

"A Government-office is like an inverted filter; you send in accounts clear and they come out muddy." Such was the comparison I heard made many years ago by the late Sir Charles Fox, who, in the conduct of his business, had considerable experience of public departments. That his opinion was not a singular one, though his comparison was, all men know. Exposures by the press and criticisms in Parliament, leave no one in ignorance of the vices of red-tape routine. Its delays, perpetually complained of, and which in the time of Mr. Fox Maule went to the extent that "the commissions of officers in the army" were generally "about two years in arrear," is afresh illustrated by the issue of the first volume of the detailed census of 1881, more than two years after the information was collected. If we seek explanations of such delays, we find one origin to be a scarcely credible confusion. In the case of the census returns, the Registrar-General tells us that "the difficulty consists not merely in the vast multitude of different areas that have to be taken into account, but still more in the bewildering complexity of their boundaries": there being 39,000 administrative areas of 22 different kinds which overlap one another—hundreds, parishes, boroughs, wards, petty sessional divisions, lieutenancy divisions, urban and rural sanitary districts, dioceses, registration districts, etc. And then, as Mr. Rathbone, M.P., points out,[13] these many superposed sets of areas with intersecting boundaries, have their respective governing bodies with authorities running into one another's districts. Does any one ask why for each additional administration Parliament has established a fresh set of divisions? The reply which suggests itself is—To preserve consistency of method. For this organized confusion corresponds completely with that organized confusion which Parliament each year increases by throwing on to the heap of its old Acts a hundred new Acts, the provisions of which traverse and qualify in all kinds of ways the provisions of multitudinous Acts on to which they are thrown: the onus of settling what is the law being left to private persons, who lose their property in getting judges' interpretations. And again, this system of putting networks of districts over other networks, with their conflicting authorities, is quite consistent with the method under which the reader of the Public Health Act of 1872, who wishes to know what are the powers exercised over him, is referred to 26 preceding Acts of several classes and numerous dates.[14] So, too, with administrative inertia.

---

[13] *The Nineteenth Century,* February 1883.
[14] "The Statistics of Legislation." By F. H. Janson, Esq., F.L.S., Vice-president of the Incorporated Law Society. [Read before the Statistical Society, May 1873 Pub.]

Continually there occur cases showing the resistance of officialism to improvements; as by the Admiralty when use of the electric telegraph was proposed, and the reply was—"We have a very good semaphore system"; or as by the Post Office, which the late Sir Charles Siemens years ago said had obstructed the employment of improved methods of telegraphing and which since then has impeded the use of the telephone. Other cases akin to the case of industrial dwellings, now and then show how the State with one hand increases evils which with the other hand it tries to diminish; as when it puts a duty on fire-insurances and then makes regulations for the better putting out of fires: dictating, too, certain modes of construction which, as Captain Shaw shows, entail additional dangers.[15] Again, the absurdities of official routine, rigid where it need not be and lax where it should be rigid, occasionally become glaring enough to cause scandals; as when a secret State-document of importance, put into the hands of an ill-paid copying-clerk who was not even in permanent Government employ, was made public by him; or as when the mode of making the Moorsom fuse, which was kept secret even from our highest artillery officers, was taught to them by the Russians, who had been allowed to learn it; or as when a diagram showing the "distances at which British and foreign iron-clads could be perforated by our large guns," communicated by an enterprising *attaché* to his own Government, then became known "to all the Gov-

---

[15] *Fire Surveys; or, a Summary of the Principles to be observed in Estimating the Risk of Buildings.*

ernments of Europe," while English officers remained ignorant of the facts.[16] So, too, with State-supervision. Guaranteeing of quality by inspection has been shown, in the hall-marking of silver, to be superfluous, while the silver trade has been decreased by it;[17] and in other cases it has lowered the quality by establishing a standard which it is useless to exceed: instance the case of the Cork butter-market, where the higher kinds are disadvantaged in not adequately profiting by their better repute;[18] or, instance the case of herring-branding (now optional), the effect of which is to put the many inferior curers who just reach the level of official approval, on a par with the few better ones who rise above it, and so to discourage these. But such lessons pass unlearned. Even where the failure of inspection is most glaring, no notice is taken of it; as instance the terrible catastrophe by which a train full of people was destroyed along with the Tay bridge. Countless denunciations, loud and unsparing, were vented against engineer and contractor; but little, if anything, was said about the Government officer from whom the bridge received State-approval. So, too, with prevention of disease. It matters not that under the management or dictation of State-agents some of the worst evils occur; as when the lives of 87 wives and children of soldiers are sacrificed in the ship *Accrington;*[19] or as when typhoid fever and diphtheria are diffused by a State-ordered drainage system, as in

---

[16] See *The Times*, 6 October 1874, where other instances are given.
[17] Sir Thomas Farrer, *"The State in its Relation to Trade*, p. 147.
[18] Ibid., p. 149.
[19] Hansard, vol. clvi, p. 718, and vol. clviii, p. 4464.

Edinburgh;[20] or as when officially-enforced sanitary appliances, ever getting out of order, increase the evils they were to decrease.[21] Masses of such evidence leave unabated the confidence with which sanitary inspection is invoked—invoked, indeed, more than ever; as is shown in the recent suggestion that all public schools should be under the supervision of health-officers. Nay, even when the State has manifestly caused the mischief complained of, faith in its beneficent agency is not at all diminished; as we see in the fact that, having a generation ago authorized, or rather required, towns to establish drainage systems which delivered sewage into the rivers, and having thus polluted the sources of water-supply, an outcry was raised against the water-companies for the impurities of their water—an outcry which continued after these towns had been compelled, at vast extra cost, to revolutionize their drainage systems. And now, as the only remedy, there follows the demand that the State, by its local proxies, shall undertake the whole business. The State's misdoings become, as in the case of industrial dwellings, reasons for praying it to do more!

This worship of the legislature is, in one respect, in-

---

[20] Letter of an Edinburgh M.D. in *The Times* of 17 January 1876, verifying other testimonies; one of which I had previously cited concerning Windsor, where, as in Edinburgh, there was absolutely no typhoid in the undrained parts, while it was very fatal in the drained parts—*Study of Sociology*, chap. i, notes.

[21] I say this partly from personal knowledge; having now before me memoranda made 25 years ago concerning such results produced under my own observation. Verifying facts have recently been given by Sir Richard Cross in the *Nineteenth Century* for January 1884, p. 155.

deed, less excusable than the fetish-worship to which I
have tacitly compared it. The savage has the defence that
his fetish is silent—does not confess its inability. But the
civilized man persists in ascribing to this idol made with
his own hands, power which in one way or other it con-
fesses it has not got. I do not mean merely that the debates daily tell us of legislative measures which have
done evil instead of good; nor do I mean merely that the
thousands of Acts of Parliament which repeal preceding
Acts, are so many tacit admissions of failure. Neither do
I refer only to such quasi-governmental confessions as
that contained in the report of the Poor Law Commissioners, who said that—"We find, on the one hand, that
there is scarcely one statute connected with the administration of public relief which has produced the effect
designed by the legislature, and that the majority of
them have created new evils, and aggravated those
which they were intended to prevent."[22] I refer rather to
confessions made by statesmen and by State departments. Here, for example, in a memorial addressed to
Mr. Gladstone, and adopted by a highly-influential
meeting held under the chairmanship of the late Lord
Lyttelton, I read:

> We, the undersigned, Peers, Members of the House of Com-
> mons, Ratepayers, and Inhabitants of the Metropolis, feeling
> strongly the truth and force of your statement made in the
> House of Commons, in 1866, that, "there is still a lamentable
> and deplorable state of our whole arrangements with regard to
> public works—vacillation, uncertainty, costliness, extrava-

[22] Sir G. Nicholl's *History of the English Poor Law*, ii, p. 252.

gance, meanness, and all the conflicting vices that could be enumerated, are united in our present system," etc.[23]

Here, again, is an example furnished by a recent minute of the Board of Trade (November, 1883), in which it is said that since "the Shipwreck Committee of 1836 scarcely a session has passed without some Act being passed or some step being taken by the legislature or the Government with this object" [prevention of shipwrecks]; and that "the multiplicity of statutes, which were all consolidated into one Act in 1854, has again become a scandal and a reproach": each measure being passed because previous ones had failed. And then comes presently the confession that "the loss of life and of ships has been greater since 1876 than it was before." Meanwhile, the cost of administration has been raised from £17,000 a year to £73,000 a year.[24]

It is surprising how, spite of better knowledge, the imagination is excited by artificial appliances used in particular ways. We see it all through human history, from the warpaint with which the savage frightens his adversary, down through religious ceremonies and regal processions, to the robes of a Speaker and the wand of an officially-dressed usher. I remember a child who, able to look with tolerable composure on a horrible cadaverous mask while it was held in the hand, ran away

---

[23] See *The Times*, 31 March 1873.

[24] In these paragraphs are contained just a few additional examples. Numbers which I have before given in books and essays, will be found in *Social Statics* (1851); "Over-Legislation" (1853); "Representative Government" (1857); "Specialized Administration" (1871); *Study of Sociology* (1873), and Postscript to ditto (1880); besides cases in smaller essays.

shrieking when his father put it on. A kindred change
of feeling comes over constituencies when, from boroughs and counties, their members pass to the Legislative Chamber. While before them as candidates, they
are, by one or other party, jeered at, lampooned,
"heckled," and in all ways treated with utter disrespect.
But as soon as they assemble at Westminster, those
against whom taunts and invectives, charges of incompetence and folly, had been showered from press and
platform, excite unlimited faith. Judging from the prayers made to them, there is nothing which their wisdom
and their power cannot compass.

The reply to all this will doubtless be that nothing
better than guidance by "collective wisdom" can be
had—that the select men of the nation, led by a re-
selected few, bring their best powers, enlightened by all
the knowledge of the time, to bear on the matters before
them. "What more would you have?" will be the question asked by most.

My answer is that this best knowledge of the time with
which legislators are said to come prepared for their duties is a knowledge of which the greater part is obviously
irrelevant, and that they are blameworthy for not seeing
what is the relevant knowledge. No amount of the lin-
guistic acquirements by which many of them are distinguished will help their judgements in the least; nor will
they be appreciably helped by the literatures these acquirements open to them. Political experiences and speculations coming from small ancient societies, through
philosophers who assume that war is the normal state,

that slavery is alike needful and just, and that women must remain in perpetual tutelage, can yield them but small aid in judging how Acts of Parliament will work in great nations of modern types. They may ponder on the doings of all the great men by whom, according to the Carlylean theory, society is framed, and they may spend years over those accounts of international conflicts, and treacheries, and intrigues, and treaties, which fill historical works, without being much nearer understanding the how and the why of social structures and actions, and the ways in which laws affect them. Nor does such information as is picked up at the factory, on 'Change, or in the justice room, go far towards the required preparation.

That which is really needed is a systematic study of natural causation as displayed among human beings socially aggregated. Though a distinct consciousness of causation is the last trait which intellectual progress brings—though with the savage even a simple mechanical cause is not conceived as such—though even among the Greeks the flight of a spear was thought of as guided by a god—though from their times down almost to our own, epidemics have been habitually regarded as of supernatural origin—and though among social phenomena, the most complex of all, causal relations may be expected to continue longest unrecognized; yet in our days, the existence of such causal relations has become clear enough to force on all who think, the inference that before meddling with them they should be diligently studied. The mere facts, now familiar, that there is a connexion between the number of marriages and the price of corn, and that in the same society during the same generation, the ratio of crime to population varies within narrow limits, should be sufficient to make all see that human desires, using as guide such intellect as is joined with them, act with approximate uniformity. It should be inferred that among social causes, those initiated by legislation, similarly operating with an average regularity, must not only change men's actions, but, by consequence, change their natures—probably in ways not intended. There should be recognition of the fact that social causation, more than all other causation, is a fructifying causation; and it should be seen that indirect and remote effects are no less inevitable than proximate effects. I do not mean that there is denial of these statements and inferences. But there are beliefs and beliefs— some which are held nominally, some which influence conduct in small degrees, some which sway it irresistibly under all circumstances; and unhappily the beliefs of law-makers respecting causation in social affairs, are of the superficial sort. Let us look at some of the truths which all tacitly admit, but which scarcely any take account of in legislation.

There is the indisputable fact that each human being is in a certain degree modifiable, both physically and mentally. Every theory of education, every discipline, from that of the arithmetician to that of the prize-fighter, every proposed reward for virtue or punishment for vice, implies the belief, embodied in sundry proverbs, that the use or disuse of each faculty, bodily or mental, is followed by an adaptive change in it—loss of power or gain of power, according to demand.

There is the fact, also in its broader manifestations universally recognized, that modifications of structure, in one way or other produced, are inheritable. No one denies that by the accumulation of small changes, generation after generation, constitution fits itself to conditions; so that a climate which is fatal to other races is innocuous to the adapted race. No one denies that peoples who belong to the same original stock, but have spread into different habitats where they have led different lives, have acquired in course of time different aptitudes and different tendencies. No one denies that under new conditions new national characters are even now being moulded; as witness the Americans. And if adaptation is everywhere and always going on, then adaptive modifications must be set up by every change of social conditions.

To which there comes the undeniable corollary that every law which serves to alter men's modes of action—compelling, or restraining, or aiding, in new ways—so affects them as to cause, in course of time, fresh adjustments of their natures. Beyond any immediate effect wrought, there is the remote effect, wholly ignored by most—a re-moulding of the average character: a re-moulding which may be of a desirable kind or of an undesirable kind, but which in any case is the most important of the results to be considered.

Other general truths which the citizen, and still more the legislator, ought to contemplate until they become wrought into his intellectual fabric, are disclosed when we ask how social activities are produced; and when we recognize the obvious answer that they are the aggregate results of the desires of individuals who are severally seeking satisfactions, and ordinarily pursuing the ways which, with their pre-existing habits and thoughts, seem the easiest—following the lines of least resistance: the truths of political economy being so many sequences. It needs no proving that social structures and social actions must in some way or other be the outcome of human emotions guided by ideas—either those of ancestors or those of living men. And that the right interpretation of social phenomena is to be found in the cooperation of these factors from generation to generation, follows inevitably.

Such an interpretation soon brings us to the inference that among men's desires seeking gratifications, those which have prompted their private activities and their spontaneous cooperations, have done much more towards social development than those which have worked through governmental agencies. That abundant crops now grow where once only wild berries could be gathered, is due to the pursuit of individual satisfactions through many centuries. The progress from wigwams to good houses has resulted from wishes to increase personal welfare; and towns have arisen under the like promptings. Beginning with traffic at gatherings on occasions of religious festivals, the trading organization, now so extensive and complex, has been produced entirely by men's efforts to achieve their private ends. Perpetually, governments have thwarted and deranged the growth, but have in no way furthered it; save by partially discharging their proper function and maintaining social order. So, too, with those advances of knowledge and those improvements of appliances, by which these structural changes and these increasing activities have been made possible. It is not to the State that we owe the multitudinous useful inventions from the spade to the telephone; it was not the State which made possible extended navigation by a developed astronomy; it was not the State which made the discoveries in physics, chemistry, and the rest, which guide modern manufacturers; it was not the State which devised the machinery for producing fabrics of every kind, for transferring men and things from place to place, and for ministering in a thousand ways to our comforts. The world-wide transactions conducted in merchants' offices, the rush of traffic filling our streets, the retail distributing system which brings everything within easy reach and delivers the necessaries of life daily at our doors, are not of governmental origin. All these are results of the spontaneous activities of citizens, separate or grouped. Nay, to these spontaneous activities governments owe the very means of performing their duties. Divest the political machinery of all those aids which Science and Art have yielded it—leave it with those only which State-officials have invented; and its functions would cease. The very language in which its laws are registered and the orders of its agents daily given, is an instrument not in the remotest degree due to the legislator; but is one which has unawares grown up during men's intercourse while pursuing their personal satisfactions.

And then a truth to which the foregoing one introduces us, is that this spontaneously-formed social organization is so bound together that you cannot act on one part without acting more or less on all parts. We see this unmistakably when a cotton-famine, first paralysing certain manufacturing districts and then affecting the doings of wholesale and retail distributors throughout the kingdom, as well as the people they supply, goes on to affect the makers and distributors, as well as the wearers, of other fabrics—woollen, linen, etc. Or we see it when a rise in the price of coal, besides influencing domestic life everywhere, hinders many of our industries, raises the prices of the commodities produced, alters the consumption of them, and changes the habits of consumers. What we see clearly in these marked cases happens in every case, in sensible or in insensible ways. And manifestly, Acts of Parliament are among those factors which, beyond the effects directly produced, have countless other effects of multitudinous kinds. As I heard remarked by a distinguished professor, whose studies give ample means of judging—"When once you begin to interfere with the order of Nature there is no knowing where the results will end." And if this is true of that sub-human order of Nature to which he referred, still more is it true of that order of Nature existing in the social arrangements of human beings.

And now to carry home the conclusion that the legislator should bring to his business a vivid consciousness of these and other such broad truths concerning the society with which he proposes to deal, let me present somewhat more fully one of them not yet mentioned.

The continuance of every higher species of creature depends on conformity, now to one, now to the other, of two radically-opposed principles. The early lives of its members, and the adult lives of its members, have to be dealt with in contrary ways. We will contemplate them in their natural order.

One of the most familiar facts is that animals of superior types, comparatively slow in reaching maturity, are enabled when they have reached it, to give more aid to their offspring than animals of inferior types. The adults foster their young during periods more or less prolonged, while yet the young are unable to provide for themselves; and it is obvious that maintenance of the species can be secured only by this parental care. It requires no proving that the blind unfledged hedge-bird, or the young puppy even after it has acquired sight, would forthwith die if it had to keep itself warm and obtain its own food. The gratuitous aid must be great in proportion as the young one is of little worth, either to itself or to others; and it may diminish as fast as, by increasing development, the young one acquires worth, at first for self-sustentation, and by-and-by for sustentation of others. That is to say, during immaturity, benefits received must vary inversely as the power or ability of the receiver. Clearly if during this first part of life benefits were proportioned to merits, or rewards to deserts, the species would disappear in a generation.

From this régime of the family-group, let us turn to the régime of that larger group formed by adult members of the species. Ask what happens when the new individual, acquiring complete use of its powers and ceasing to have parental aid, is left to itself. Now there comes into play a principle just the reverse to that above described. Throughout the rest of its life, each adult gets benefit in proportion to merit—reward in proportion to desert: merit and desert in each case being understood as ability to fulfil all the requirements of life—to get food, to find shelter, to escape enemies. Placed in competition with members of its own species and in antagonism with members of other species, it dwindles and gets killed off, or thrives and propagates, according as it is ill-endowed or well-endowed. Manifestly an opposite régime, could it be maintained, would, in course of time, be fatal. If the benefits received by each individual were proportionate to its inferiority—if, as a consequence, multiplication of the inferior was furthered, and multiplication of the superior hindered, progressive degradation would result; and eventually the degenerate species would fail to hold its ground in presence of antagonistic species and competing species.

The broad fact then, here to be noted, is that Nature's modes of treatment inside the family-group and outside the family-group are diametrically opposed to one another; and that the intrusion of either mode into the sphere of the other, would be destructive either immediately or remotely.

Does any one think that the like does not hold of the human species? He cannot deny that within the human family, as within any inferior family, it would be fatal to proportion benefits to merits. Can he assert that outside the family, among adults, there should not be, as throughout the animal world, a proportioning of benefits to merits? Will he contend that no mischief will result if the lowly endowed are enabled to thrive and multiply as much as, or more than, the highly endowed? A society of men, standing towards other societies in relations of either antagonism or competition, may be considered as a species, or, more literally, as a variety of a species; and it must be true of it as of other species or varieties, that it will be unable to hold its own in the struggle with other societies, if it disadvantages its superior units that it may advantage its inferior units. Surely none can fail to see that were the principle of family life to be adopted and fully carried out in social life—were reward always great in proportion as desert was small, fatal results to the society would quickly follow; and if so, then even a partial intrusion of the family régime into the régime of the State, will be slowly followed by fatal results. Society in its corporate capacity, cannot without immediate or remoter disaster interfere with the play of these opposed principles under which every species has reached such fitness for its mode of life as it possesses, and under which it maintains that fitness.

I say advisedly—society in its corporate capacity; not intending to exclude or condemn aid given to the inferior by the superior in their individual capacities. Though when given so indiscriminately as to enable the inferior to multiply, such aid entails mischief; yet in the absence of aid given by society, individual aid, more generally demanded than now, and associated with a greater sense of responsibility, would, on the average, be given with the effect of fostering the unfortunate worthy rather than the innately unworthy: there being always, too, the concomitant social benefit arising from culture of the sympathies. But all this may be admitted while asserting that the radical distinction between family-ethics and State-ethics must be maintained; and that while generosity must be the essential principle of the one, justice must be the essential principle of the other—a rigorous maintenance of those normal relations among citizens under which each gets in return for his labour, skilled or unskilled, bodily or mental, as much as is proved to be its value by the demand for it: such return, therefore, as will enable him to thrive and rear offspring in proportion to the superiorities which make him valuable to himself and others.

And yet, notwithstanding the conspicuousness of these truths, which should strike everyone who leaves his lexicons, and his law-deeds, and his ledgers, and looks abroad into that natural order of things under which we exist, and to which we must conform, there is continual advocacy of paternal government. The intrusion of family-ethics into the ethics of the State, instead of being regarded as socially injurious, is more and more demanded as the only efficient means to social benefit. So far has this delusion now gone, that it vitiates the beliefs of those who might, more than all others, be thought safe from it. In the essay to which the Cobden Club awarded its prize in 1880, there occurs the assertion that "the truth of Free Trade is clouded over by the *laissez-faire* fallacy"; and we are told that "we need a great deal more parental government—that bugbear of the old economists."[25]

Vitally important as is the truth above insisted upon, since acceptance or rejection of it affects the entire fabric

---

[25] *On the Value of Political Economy to Mankind.* By A. N. Cumming, pp. 47, 48.

of political conclusions formed, I may be excused if I emphasize it by here quoting certain passages contained in a work I published in 1851: premising, only, that the reader must not hold me committed to such teleological implications as they contain. After describing "that state of universal warfare maintained throughout the lower creation," and showing that an average of benefit results from it, I have continued thus:

> Note further, that their carnivorous enemies not only remove from herbivorous herds individuals past their prime, but also weed out the sickly; the malformed, and the least fleet or powerful. By the aid of which purifying process, as well as by the fighting so universal in the pairing season, all vitiation of the race through the multiplication of its inferior sample is prevented; and the maintenance of a constitution completely adapted to surrounding conditions, and therefore most productive of happiness, is ensured.
>
> The development of the higher creation is a progress towards a form of being capable of a happiness undiminished by these drawbacks. It is in the human race that the consummation is to be accomplished. Civilization is the last stage of its accomplishment. And the ideal man is the man in whom all the conditions of that accomplishment are fulfilled. Meanwhile, the well-being of existing humanity, and the unfolding of it into this ultimate perfection, are both secured by that same beneficent, though severe discipline, to which the animate creation at large is subject: a discipline which is pitiless in the working out of good: a felicity-pursuing law which never swerves for the avoidance of partial and temporary suffering. The poverty of the incapable, the distresses that come upon the imprudent, the starvation of the idle, and those shoulderings aside of the weak by the strong, which leave so many "in shallows and in miseries," are the decrees of a large, far-seeing benevolence.

To become fit for the social state, man has not only to lose his savageness, but he has to acquire the capacities needful for civilized life. Power of application must be developed; such modification of the intellect as shall qualify it for its new tasks must take place; and, above all, there must be gained the ability to sacrifice a small immediate gratification for a future great one. The state of transition will of course be an unhappy state. Misery inevitably results from incongruity between constitution and conditions. All these evils which afflict us, and seem to the uninitiated the obvious consequences of this or that removable cause, are unavoidable attendants on the adaptation now in progress. Humanity is being pressed against the inexorable necessities of its new position—is being moulded into harmony with them, and has to bear the resulting unhappiness as best it can. The process *must* be undergone, and the sufferings *must* be endured. No power on earth, no cunningly-devised laws of statesmen, no world-rectifying schemes of the humane, no communist panaceas, no reforms that men ever did broach or ever will broach, can diminish them one jot. Intensified they may be, and are; and in preventing their intensification, the philanthropic will find ample scope for exertion. But there is bound up with the change a *normal* amount of suffering, which cannot be lessened without altering the very laws of life.

Of course, in so far as the severity of this process is mitigated by the spontaneous sympathy of men for each other, it is proper that it should be mitigated; albeit there is unquestionably harm done when sympathy is shown, without any regard to ultimate results. But the drawbacks hence arising are nothing like commensurate with the benefits otherwise conferred. Only when this sympathy prompts to a breach of equity—only when it originates an interference forbidden by the law of equal freedom—only when, by so doing, it suspends in some particular department of life the relationship between constitution and conditions, does it work pure evil. Then, however, it defeats its own end. Instead of diminishing suffering, it eventually increases it. It favours the multiplication of those worst fitted for existence, and, by consequence, hinders the multiplication of those best fitted for existence—leaving, as it does, less room for them. It tends to fill the world with those to whom life will bring most pain, and tends to keep out of it those to whom life will bring most pleasure. It inflicts positive misery, and prevents positive happiness.—*Social Statics*, pp. 322–5 and pp. 380–1 (edition of 1851).

The lapse of a third of a century since these passages were published, has brought me no reason for retreating from the position taken up in them. Contrariwise, it has brought a vast amount of evidence strengthening that position. The beneficial results of the survival of the fittest, prove to be immeasurably greater than those above indicated. The process of "natural selection," as Mr. Darwin called it, cooperating with a tendency to variation and to inheritance of variations, he has shown to be a chief cause (though not, I believe, the sole cause) of that evolution through which all living things, beginning with the lowest and diverging and rediverging as they evolved, have reached their present degrees of organization and adaptation to their modes of life. So familiar has this truth become that some apology seems needed for naming it. And yet, strange to say, now that this truth is recognized by most cultivated people—now that the beneficent working of the survival of the fittest has been so impressed on them that, much more than people in past times, they might be expected to hesitate before neutralizing its action—now more than ever before in the history of the world, are they doing all they can to further survival of the unfittest!

But the postulate that men are rational beings, continually leads one to draw inferences which prove to be extremely wide of the mark.[26]

---

[26] The saying of Emerson that most people can understand a principle only when its light falls on a fact, induces me here to cite a fact which may carry home the above principle to those on whom, in its abstract

"Yes truly; your principle is derived from the lives of brutes, and is a brutal principle. You will not persuade me that men are to be under the discipline which animals are under. I care nothing for your natural-history arguments. My conscience shows me that the feeble and the suffering must be helped; and if selfish people won't help them, they must be forced by law to help them. Don't tell me that the milk of human kindness is to be reserved for the relations between individuals, and that Governments must be the administrators of nothing but hard justice. Every man with sympathy in him must feel that hunger and pain and squalor must be prevented; and that if private agencies do not suffice, then public agencies must be established."

Such is the kind of response which I expect to be made by nine out of ten. In some of them it will doubtless result from a fellow-feeling so acute that they cannot contemplate human misery without an impatience which excludes all thought of remote results. Concern-

---

form, it will produce no effect. It rarely happens that the amount of evil caused by fostering the vicious and good-for-nothing can be estimated. But in America, at a meeting of the States Charities Aid Association, held on 18 December 1874, a startling instance was given in detail by Dr. Harris. It was furnished by a county on the Upper Hudson, remarkable for the ratio of crime and poverty to population. Generations ago there had existed a certain "gutter-child," as she would be here called, known as "Margaret," who proved to be the prolific mother of a prolific race. Besides great numbers of idiots, imbeciles, drunkards, lunatics, paupers, and prostitutes, "the county records show two hundred of her descendants who have been criminals." Was it kindness or cruelty which, generation after generation, enabled these to multiply and become an increasing curse to the society around them? [For particulars see *The Jukes: a Study in Crime, Pauperism, Disease and Heredity.* By R. L. Dugdale. New York: Putnams.]

ing the susceptibilities of the rest, we may, however, be somewhat sceptical. Persons who are angry if, to maintain our supposed national "interests" or national "prestige," those in authority do not send out thousands of men to be partially destroyed while destroying other thousands of men because we suspect their intentions, or dislike their institutions, or want their territory, cannot after all be so tender in feeling that contemplating the hardships of the poor is intolerable to them. Little admiration need be felt for the professed sympathies of people who urge on a policy which breaks up progressing societies; and who then look on with cynical indifference at the weltering confusion left behind, with all its entailed suffering and death. Those who, when Boers, asserting their independence, successfully resisted us, were angry because British "honour" was not maintained by fighting to avenge a defeat, at the cost of more mortality and misery to our own soldiers and their antagonists, cannot have so much "enthusiasm of humanity" as the protests like that indicated above would lead one to expect. Indeed, along with this sensitiveness which it seems will not let them look with patience on the pains of "the battle of life" as it quietly goes on around, they appear to have a callousness which not only tolerates but enjoys contemplating the pains of battles of the literal kind; as one sees in the demand for illustrated papers containing scenes of carnage, and in the greediness with which detailed accounts of bloody engagements are read. We may reasonably have our doubts about men whose feelings are such that they cannot bear the thought of hardships borne, mostly by the idle and the improvident, and who, nevertheless, have demanded thirty-one editions of *The Fifteen Decisive Battles of the World,* in which they may revel in accounts of slaughter. Nay, even still more remarkable is the contrast between the professed tender-heartedness and the actual hard-heartedness of those who would reverse the normal course of things that immediate miseries may be prevented, even at the cost of greater miseries hereafter produced. For on other occasions you may hear them, with utter disregard of bloodshed and death, contend that in the interests of humanity at large, it is well that the inferior races should be exterminated and their places occupied by the superior races. So that, marvellous to relate, though they cannot bear to think of the evils accompanying the struggle for existence as it is carried on without violence among individuals in their own society, they contemplate with equanimity such evils in their intense and wholesale forms, when inflicted by fire and sword on entire communities. Not worthy of much respect then, as it seems to me, is this generous consideration of the inferior at home which is accompanied by unscrupulous sacrifice of the inferior abroad.

Still less respectable appears this extreme concern for those of our own blood which goes along with utter unconcern for those of other blood, when we observe its methods. Did it prompt personal effort to relieve the suffering, it would rightly receive approving recognition. Were the many who express this cheap pity like the few who devote large parts of their time to aiding and encouraging, and occasionally amusing, those who, by ill-fortune or incapacity, are brought to lives of hardship, they would be worthy of unqualified admiration. The more there are of men and women who help the poor to help themselves—the more there are of those whose sympathy is exhibited directly and not by proxy, the more we may rejoice. But the immense majority of the persons who wish to mitigate by law the miseries of the unsuccessful and the reckless, propose to do this in small measure at their own cost and mainly at the cost of others—sometimes with their assent but mostly without. More than this is true; for those who are to be forced to do so much for the distressed, often equally or more require something done for them. The deserving poor are among those who are taxed to support the undeserving poor. As, under the old Poor Law, the diligent and provident labourer had to pay that the good-for-nothings might not suffer, until frequently under this extra burden he broke down and himself took refuge in the workhouse—as, at present, the total rates levied in large towns for all public purposes, have reached such a height that they "cannot be exceeded without inflicting great hardship on the small shop-keepers and artisans, who already find it difficult enough to keep themselves free from the pauper taint"[27]; so in all cases, the policy is one which intensifies the pains of those most deserving of pity, that the pains of those least deserving of pity may be mitigated. Men who are so sympathetic that they cannot let the struggle for existence bring on the unworthy the sufferings consequent on their incapacity or misconduct, are so unsympathetic that they can, delib-

---

[27] Mr. J. Chamberlain in *Fortnightly Review*, December 1883, p. 772.

erately, make the struggle for existence harder for the worthy, and inflict on them and their children artificial evils in addition to the natural evils they have to bear!

And here we are brought round to our original topic—the sins of legislators. Here there comes clearly before us the commonest of the transgressions which rulers commit—a transgression so common, and so sanctified by custom, that no one imagines it to be a transgression. Here we see that, as indicated at the outset, Government, begotten of aggression and by aggression, ever continues to betray its original nature by its aggressiveness; and that even what on its nearer face seems beneficence only, shows, on its remoter face, not a little maleficence—kindness at the cost of cruelty. For is it not cruel to increase the sufferings of the better that the sufferings of the worse may be decreased?

It is, indeed, marvellous how readily we let ourselves be deceived by words and phrases which suggest one aspect of the facts while leaving the opposite aspect unsuggested. A good illustration of this, and one germane to the immediate question, is seen in the use of the words "protection" and "protectionist" by the antagonists of free-trade, and in the tacit admission of its propriety by free-traders. While the one party has habitually ignored, the other party has habitually failed to emphasize, the truth that this so-called protection always involves aggression; and that the name aggressionist ought to be substituted for the name protectionist. For nothing can be more certain than that if, to maintain A's profit, B is forbidden to buy of C, or is fined to the extent of the duty if he buys of C, then B is aggressed upon that A may be "protected." Nay, "aggressionists" is a title doubly more applicable to the anti-free-traders than is the euphemistic title "protectionists"; since, that one producer may gain, ten consumers are fleeced.

Now just the like confusion of ideas, caused by looking at one face only of the transaction, may be traced throughout all the legislation which forcibly takes the property of this man for the purpose of giving gratis benefits to that man. Habitually when one of the numerous measures thus characterized is discussed, the dominant thought is concerning the pitiable Jones who is to be protected against some evil; while no thought is given to the hard-working Brown who is aggressed upon, often much more to be pitied. Money is exacted (either directly or through raised rent) from the huckster who only by extreme pinching can pay her way, from the mason thrown out of work by a strike, from the mechanic whose savings are melting away during an illness, from the widow who washes or sews from dawn to dark to feed her fatherless little ones; and all that the dissolute may be saved from hunger, that the children of less impoverished neighbours may have cheap lessons, and that various people, mostly better off, may read newspapers and novels for nothing! The error of nomenclature is, in one respect, more misleading than that which allows aggressionists to be called protectionists; for, as just shown, protection of the vicious poor involves aggression on the virtuous poor. Doubtless it is true that the greater part of the money exacted comes from those who are relatively well-off. But this is no consolation to the ill-off from whom the rest is exacted. Nay, if the comparison be made between the pressures borne by the two classes respectively, it becomes manifest that the case is even worse than at first appears; for while to the well-off the exaction means loss of luxuries, to the ill-off it means loss of necessaries.

And now see the Nemesis which is threatening to follow this chronic sin of legislators. They and their class, in common with all owners of property, are in danger of suffering from a sweeping application of that general principle practically asserted by each of these confiscating Acts of Parliament. For what is the tacit assumption on which such Acts proceed? It is the assumption that no man has any claim to his property, not even to that which he has earned by the sweat of his brow, save by permission of the community; and that the community may cancel the claim to any extent it thinks fit. No defence can be made for this appropriation of A's possessions for the benefit of B, save one which sets out with the postulate that society as a whole has an absolute right over the possessions of each member. And now this doctrine, which has been tacitly assumed, is being openly proclaimed. Mr. George and his friends, Mr. Hyndman and his supporters, are pushing the theory to its logical issue. They have been instructed by examples, yearly increasing in number, that the individual has no rights but what the community may equitably over-ride; and they are now saying—"It shall go hard but we will better the instruction," and abolish individual rights altogether.

Legislative misdeeds of the classes above indicated are in large measure explained, and reprobation of them mitigated, when we look at the matter from afar off. They have their root in the error that society is a manufacture; whereas it is a growth. Neither the culture of past times nor the culture of the present time, has given to any considerable number of people a scientific conception of a society—a conception of it as having a natural structure in which all its institutions, governmental, religious, industrial, commercial, etc., are interdependently bound—a structure which is in a sense organic. Or if such a conception is nominally entertained, it is not entertained in such way as to be operative on conduct. Contrariwise, incorporated humanity is very commonly thought of as though it were like so much dough which the cook can mould as she pleases into pie-crust, or puff, or tartlet. The communist shows us unmistakably that he thinks of the body politic as admitting of being shaped thus or thus at will; and the tacit implication of many Acts of Parliament is that aggregated men, twisted into this or that arrangement, will remain as intended.

It may indeed be said that, even irrespective of this erroneous conception of a society as a plastic mass instead of as an organized body, facts forced on his attention hour by hour should make everyone sceptical as to the success of this or that proposed way of changing a people's actions. Alike to the citizen and to the legislator, home-experiences daily supply proofs that the conduct of human beings baulks calculation. He has given up the thought of managing his wife and lets her manage him. Children on whom he has tried now reprimand, now punishment, now suasion, now reward, do not respond satisfactorily to any method; and no expostulation prevents their mother from treating them in ways he thinks mischievous. So, too, his dealings with his servants, whether by reasoning or by scolding, rarely succeed for long; the falling short of attention, or punctuality, or cleanliness, or sobriety, leads to constant changes. Yet, difficult as he finds it to deal with humanity in detail, he is confident of his ability to deal with embodied humanity. Citizens, not one-thousandth of whom he knows, not one-hundredth of whom he ever saw, and the great mass of whom belong to classes having habits and modes of thought of which he has but dim notions, he feels sure will act in ways he foresees, and fulfil ends he wishes. Is there not a marvellous incongruity between premises and conclusion?

One might have expected that whether they observed the implications of these domestic failures, or whether they contemplated in every newspaper the indications of a social life too vast, too varied, too involved, to be even vaguely pictured in thought, men would have entered on the business of law-making with the greatest hesitation. Yet in this more than anything else do they show a confident readiness. Nowhere is there so astounding a contrast between the difficulty of the task and the unpreparedness of those who undertake it. Unquestionably among monstrous beliefs one of the most monstrous is that while for a simple handicraft, such as shoemaking, a long apprenticeship is needful, the sole thing which needs no apprenticeship is making a nation's laws!

Summing up the results of the discussion, may we not reasonably say that there lie before the legislator several

open secrets, which yet are so open that they ought not
to remain secrets to one who undertakes the vast and
terrible responsibility of dealing with millions upon millions of human beings by measures which, if they do not
conduce to their happiness, will increase their miseries
and accelerate their deaths?

There is first of all the undeniable truth, conspicuous
and yet absolutely ignored, that there are no phenomena
which a society presents but what have their origins in
the phenomena of individual human life, which again
have their roots in vital phenomena at large. And there
is the inevitable implication that unless these vital phenomena, bodily and mental, are chaotic in their relations
(a supposition excluded by the very maintenance of life)
the resulting phenomena cannot be wholly chaotic: there
must be some kind of order in the phenomena which
grow out of them when associated human beings have
to cooperate. Evidently, then, when one who has not
studied such resulting phenomena of social order, undertakes to regulate society, he is pretty certain to work
mischiefs.

In the second place, apart from *a priori* reasoning, this
conclusion should be forced on the legislator by comparisons of societies. It ought to be sufficiently manifest
that before meddling with the details of social organization, inquiry should be made whether social organization has a natural history; and that to answer this
inquiry, it would be well, setting out with the simplest
societies, to see in what respects social structures agree.
Such comparative sociology, pursued to a very small extent, shows a substantial uniformity of genesis. The ha-

bitual existence of chieftainship, and the establishment
of chiefly authority by war; the rise everywhere of the
medicine man and priest; the presence of a cult having
in all places the same fundamental traits; the traces of
division of labour, early displayed, which gradually become more marked; and the various complications, political, ecclesiastical, industrial, which arise as groups are
compounded and re-compounded by war; prove to any
who compare them that, apart from all their special differences, societies have general resemblances in their
modes of origin and development. They present traits
of structure showing that social organization has laws
which over-ride individual wills; and laws the disregard
of which must be fraught with disaster.

And then, in the third place, there is that mass of
guiding information yielded by the records of legislation
in our own country and in other countries, which still
more obviously demands attention. Here and elsewhere, attempts of multitudinous kinds, made by kings
and statesmen, have failed to do the good intended and
have worked unexpected evils. Century after century
new measures like the old ones, and other measures
akin in principle, have again disappointed hopes and
again brought disaster. And yet it is thought neither by
electors nor by those they elect, that there is any need
for systematic study of that law-making which in by-
gone ages went on working the ill-being of the people
when it tried to achieve their well-being. Surely there
can be no fitness for legislative functions without wide
knowledge of those legislative experiences which the
past has bequeathed.

Reverting, then, to the analogy drawn at the outset, we must say that the legislator is morally blameless or morally blameworthy, according as he has or has not acquainted himself with these several classes of facts. A physician who, after years of study, has gained a competent knowledge of physiology, pathology, and therapeutics, is not held criminally responsible if a man dies under his treatment: he has prepared himself as well as he can, and has acted to the best of his judgement. Similarly the legislator whose measures produce evil instead of good, notwithstanding the extensive and methodic inquiries which helped him to decide, cannot be held to have committed more than an error of reasoning. Contrariwise, the legislator who is wholly or in great part uninformed concerning the masses of facts which he must examine before his opinion on a proposed law can be of any value, and who nevertheless helps to pass that law, can no more be absolved if misery and mortality result, than the journeyman druggist can be absolved when death is caused by the medicine he ignorantly prescribes.

THE GREAT POLITICAL SUPERSTITION

The great political superstition of the past was the divine right of kings. The great political superstition of the present is the divine right of parliaments. The oil of anointing seems unawares to have dripped from the head of the one on to the heads of the many, and given sacredness to them also and to their decrees.

However irrational we may think the earlier of these beliefs, we must admit that it was more consistent than is the latter. Whether we go back to times when the king was a god, or to times when he was a descendant of a god, or to times when he was god-appointed, we see good reason for passive obedience to his will. When, as under Louis XIV, theologians like Bossuet taught that kings "are gods, and share in a manner the Divine independence," or when it was thought, as by our own Tory party in old days, that "the monarch was the delegate of heaven"; it is clear that, given the premise, the inevitable conclusion was that no bounds could be set

123

to governmental commands. But for the modern belief such a warrant does not exist. Making no pretention to divine descent or divine appointment, a legislative body can show no supernatural justification for its claim to unlimited authority; and no natural justification has ever been attempted. Hence, belief in its unlimited authority is without that consistency which of old characterized belief in a king's unlimited authority.

It is curious how commonly men continue to hold in fact, doctrines which they have rejected in name—retaining the substance after they have abandoned the form. In Theology an illustration is supplied by Carlyle, who, in his student days, giving up, as he thought, the creed of his fathers, rejected its shell only, keeping the contents; and was proved by his conceptions of the world, and man, and conduct, to be still among the sternest of Scotch Calvinists. Similarly, Science furnishes an instance in one who united naturalism in Geology with supernaturalism in Biology—Sir Charles Lyell. While, as the leading expositor of the uniformitarian theory in Geology, he ignored only the Mosaic cosmogony, he long defended that belief in special creations of organic types, for which no other source than the Mosaic cosmogony could be assigned; and only in the latter part of his life surrendered to the arguments of Mr. Darwin. In Politics, as above implied, we have an analogous case. The tacitly-asserted doctrine, common to Tories, Whigs, and Radicals, that governmental authority is unlimited, dates back to times when the law-giver was supposed to have a warrant from God; and it survives still, though the belief that the law-giver has God's warrant has died out. "Oh, an Act of Parliament can do anything," is the reply made to a citizen who questions the legitimacy of some arbitrary State-interference; and the citizen stands paralysed. It does not occur to him to ask the how, and the when, and the whence, of this asserted omnipotence bounded only by physical impossibilities.

Here we will take leave to question it. In default of the justification, once logically valid, that the ruler on Earth being a deputy of the ruler in Heaven, submission to him in all things is a duty, let us ask what reason there is for asserting the duty of submission in all things to a ruling power, constitutional or republican, which has no Heavenly-derived supremacy. Evidently this inquiry commits us to a criticism of past and present theories concerning political authority. To revive questions supposed to be long since settled, may be thought to need some apology; but there is a sufficient apology in the implication above made clear, that the theory commonly accepted is ill-based or unbased.

The notion of sovereignty is that which first presents itself; and a critical examination of this notion, as entertained by those who do not assume the supernatural origin of sovereignty, carries us back to the arguments of Hobbes.

Let us grant Hobbes's postulate that, "during the time men live without a common power to keep them all in awe, they are in that condition which is called war . . . of every man against every man"[1]; though this is not

---

[1] T. Hobbes, *Collected Works*, vol. iii, pp. 112–13.

true, since there are some small uncivilized societies in which, without any "common power to keep them all in awe," men maintain peace and harmony better than it is maintained in societies where such a power exists. Let us suppose him to be right, too, in assuming that the rise of a ruling man over associated men, results from their desires to preserve order among themselves; though, in fact, it habitually arises from the need for subordination to a leader in war, defensive or offensive, and has originally no necessary, and often no actual, relation to the preservation of order among the combined individuals. Once more, let us admit the indefensible assumption that to escape the evils of chronic conflicts, which must otherwise continue among them, the members of a community enter into a "pact or covenant," by which they all bind themselves to surrender their primitive freedom of action, and subordinate themselves to the will of an autocrat agreed upon:[2] accepting, also, the implication that their descendants for ever are bound by the covenant which remote ancestors made for them. Let us, I say, not object to these data, but pass to the conclusions Hobbes draws. He says:

> For where no covenant hath preceded, there hath no right been transferred, and every man has a right to everything; and consequently, no action can be unjust. But when a covenant is made, then to break it is *unjust:* and the definition of INJUSTICE, is no other than *the not performance of covenant.* . . . Therefore before the names of just and unjust can have place, there must be some coercive power, to compel men equally to the performance of their covenants, by the terror of some punishment,

---

[2] Ibid., p. 159.

greater than the benefit they expect by the breach of their covenant.[3]

Were people's characters in Hobbes's day really so bad as to warrant his assumption that none would perform their covenants in the absence of a coercive power and threatened penalties? In our day "the names of just and unjust can have place" quite apart from recognition of any coercive power. Among my friends I could name several whom I would implicitly trust to perform their covenants without any "terror of such punishment"; and over whom the requirements of justice would be as imperative in the absence of a coercive power as in its presence. Merely noting, however, that this unwarranted assumption vitiates Hobbe's argument for State-authority, and accepting both his premises and conclusion, we have to observe two significant implications. One is that State-authority as thus derived, is a means to an end, and has no validity save as subserving that end: if the end is not subserved, the authority, by the hypothesis, does not exist. The other is that the end for which the authority exists, as thus specified, is the enforcement of justice—the maintenance of equitable relations. The reasoning yields no warrant for other coercion over citizens than that which is required for preventing direct aggressions, and those indirect aggressions constituted by breaches of contract; to which, if we add protection against external enemies, the entire function implied by Hobbes's derivation of sovereign authority is comprehended.

---

[3] Hobbes, *Collected Works*, vol. iii, pp. 130–31.

Hobbes argued in the interests of absolute monarchy. His modern admirer, Austin, had for his aim to drive the authority of law from the unlimited sovereignty of one man, or a number of men, small or large compared with the whole community. Austin was originally in the army; and it has been truly remarked that "the permanent traces left" may be seen in his *Province of Jurisprudence.* When, undeterred by the exasperating pedantries—the endless distinctions and definitions and repetitions—which served but to hide his essential doctrines, we ascertain what these are, it becomes manifest that he assimilates civil authority to military authority; taking for granted that the one, as the other, is above question in respect of both origin and range. To get justification for positive law, he takes us back to the absolute sovereignty of the power imposing it—a monarch, an aristocracy, or that larger body of men who have votes in a democracy; for such a body also, he styles the sovereign, in contast with the remaining portion of the community which, from incapacity or other cause, remains subject. And having affirmed, or rather, taken for granted, the unlimited authority of the body, simple or compound, small or large, which he styles sovereign, he, of course, has no difficulty in deducing the legal validity of its edicts, which he calls positive law. But the problem is simply moved a step further back and there left unsolved. The true question is—Whence the sovereignty? What is the assignable warrant for this unqualified supremacy assumed by one, or by a small number, or by a large number, over the rest? A critic might fitly say—"We will dispense with your process of deriving positive law from unlimited sovereignty: the sequence is obvious enough. But first prove your unlimited sovereignty."

To this demand there is no response. Analyse his assumption, and the doctrine of Austin proves to have no better basis than that of Hobbes. In the absence of admitted divine descent or appointment, neither single-headed ruler nor many-headed ruler can produce such credentials as the claim to unlimited sovereignty implies.

"But surely," will come in deafening chorus the reply, "there is the unquestionable right of the majority, which gives unquestionable right to the parliament it elects."

Yes, now we are coming down to the root of the matter. The divine right of parliaments means the divine right of majorities. The fundamental assumption made by legislators and people alike, is that a majority has powers which have no bounds. This is the current theory which all accept without proof as a self-evident truth. Nevertheless, criticism will, I think, show that this current theory requires a radical modification.

In an essay on "Railway Morals and Railway Policy," published in the *Edinburgh Review* for October, 1854, I had occasion to deal with the question of a majority's powers as exemplified in the conduct of public companies; and I cannot better prepare the way for conclusions presently to be drawn, than by quoting a passage from it:

> Under whatever circumstances, or for whatever ends, a number of men cooperate, it is held that if difference of opinion arises among them, justice requires that the will of the greater number shall be executed rather than that of the smaller num-

ber; and this rule is supposed to be uniformly applicable, be the question at issue what it may. So confirmed is this conviction, and so little have the ethics of the matter been considered, that to most this mere suggestion of a doubt will cause some astonishment. Yet it needs but a brief analysis to show that the opinion is little better than a political superstition. Instances may readily be selected which prove, by *reductio ad absurdum*, that the right of a majority is a purely conditional right, valid only within specific limits. Let us take a few. Suppose that at the general meeting of some philanthropic association, it was resolved that in addition to relieving distress the association should employ home-missionaries to preach down popery. Might the subscriptions of Catholics, who had joined the body with charitable views, be rightfully used for this end? Suppose that of the members of a book-club, the greater number, thinking that under existing circumstances rifle-practice was more important than reading, should decide to change the purpose of their union, and to apply the funds in hand for the purchase of powder, ball, and targets. Would the rest be bound by this decision? Suppose that under the excitement of news from Australia, the majority of a Freehold Land Society should determine, not simply to start in a body for the gold-diggings, but to use their accumulated capital to provide outfits. Would this appropriation of property be just to the minority? and must these join the expedition? Scarcely anyone would venture an affirmative answer even to the first of these questions; much less to the others. And why? Because everyone must perceive that by uniting himself with others, no man can equitably be betrayed into acts utterly foreign to the purpose for which he joined them. Each of these supposed minorities would properly reply to those seeking to coerce them: "We combined with you for a defined object; we gave money and time for the furtherance of that object; on all questions thence arising we tacitly agreed to conform to the will of the greater number; but we did not agree to conform on any other questions. If you induce us to join you by professing a certain end, and then undertake some other end of which we were not apprised, you obtain our support under false pretences; you exceed the expressed or understood compact to which we committed ourselves; and we are no longer bound by your decisions." Clearly this is the only rational interpretation of the matter. The general principle underlying the right government of every incorporated body, is, that its members contract with one another severally to submit to the will of the majority in all matters concerning the fulfilment of the objects for which they are incorporated; but in no others. To this extent only can the contract hold. For as it is implied in the very nature of a contract, that those entering into it must know what they contract to do; and as those who unite with others for a specified object, cannot contemplate all the unspecified objects which it is hypothetically possible for the union to undertake; it follows that the contract entered into cannot extend to such unspecified objects. And if there exists no expressed or understood contract between the union and its members respecting unspecified objects, then for the majority to coerce the minority into undertaking them, is nothing less than gross tyranny.

Naturally, if such a confusion of ideas exists in respect of the powers of a majority where the deed of incorporation tacitly limits those powers, still more must there exist such a confusion where there has been no deed of incorporation. Nevertheless the same principle holds. I again emphasize the proposition that the members of an incorporated body are bound "severally to submit to the will of the majority *in all matters concerning the fulfilment of the objects for which they are incorporated; but in no others.*" And I contend that this holds of an incorporated nation as much as of an incorporated company.

"Yes, but," comes the obvious rejoinder, "as there is no deed by which the members of a nation are incorporated—as there neither is, nor ever was, a specification of purposes for which the union was formed, there exist no limits; and, consequently, the power of the majority is unlimited."

Evidently it must be admitted that the hypothesis of

a social contract, either under the shape assumed by Hobbes or under the shape assumed by Rousseau, is baseless. Nay more, it must be admitted that even had such a contract once been formed, it could not be binding on the posterity of those who formed it. Moreover, if any say that in the absence of those limitations to its powers which a deed of incorporation might imply, there is nothing to prevent a majority from imposing its will on a minority by force, assent must be given—an assent, however, joined with the comment that if the superior force of the majority is its justification, then the superior force of a despot backed by an adequate army, is also justified; the problem lapses. What we here seek is some higher warrant for the subordination of minority to majority than that arising from inability to resist physical coercion. Even Austin, anxious as he is to establish the unquestionable authority of positive law, and assuming, as he does, an absolute sovereignty of some kind, monarchic, aristocratic, constitutional, or popular, as the source of its unquestionable authority, is obliged, in the last resort, to admit a moral limit to its action over the community. While insisting, in pursuance of his rigid theory of sovereignty, that a sovereign body originating from the people "is *legally* free to abridge their political liberty, at its own pleasure or discretion," he allows that "a government may be hindered by *positive morality* from abridging the political liberty which it leaves or grants to its subjects."[4] Hence, we have to find, not a physical justification, but a moral justification, for the supposed absolute power of the majority.

---

[4] *The Province of Jurisprudence Determined.* Second Edition, p. 241.

This will at once draw forth the rejoinder—"Of course, in the absence of any agreement, with its implied limitations, the rule of the majority is unlimited; because it is more just that the majority should have its way than that the minority should have its way." A very reasonable rejoinder this seems until there comes the re-rejoinder. We may oppose to it the equally tenable proposition that, in the absence of an agreement, the supremacy of a majority over a minority does not exist at all. It is cooperation of some kind, from which there arises these powers and obligations of majority and minority; and in the absence of any agreement to cooperate, such powers and obligations are also absent.

Here the argument apparently ends in a deadlock. Under the existing condition of things, no moral origin seems assignable, either for the sovereignty of the majority or for the limitation of its sovereignty. But further consideration reveals a solution of the difficulty. For if, dismissing all thought of any hypothetical agreement to cooperate heretofore made, we ask what would be the agreement into which citizens would now enter with practical unanimity, we get a sufficiently clear answer; and with it a sufficiently clear justification for the rule of the majority inside a certain sphere but not outside that sphere. Let us first observe a few of the limitations which at once become apparent.

Were all Englishmen now asked if they would agree to cooperate for the teaching of religion, and would give the majority power to fix the creed and the forms of worship, there would come a very emphatic "No" from a large part of them. If, in pursuance of a proposal to revive sumptuary laws, the inquiry were made whether they would bind themselves to abide by the will of the majority in respect of the fashions and qualities of their clothes, nearly all of them would refuse. In like manner if (to take an actual question of the day) people were polled to ascertain whether, in respect of the beverages they drank, they would accept the decision of the greater number, certainly half, and probably more than half, would be unwilling. Similarly with respect to many other actions which most men now-a-days regard as of purely private concern. Whatever desire there might be to cooperate for carrying on, or regulating, such actions, would be far from a unanimous desire. Manifestly, then, had social cooperation to be commenced by ourselves, and had its purposes to be specified before consent to cooperate could be obtained, there would be large parts of human conduct in respect of which cooperation would be declined; and in respect of which, consequently, no authority by the majority over the minority could be rightly exercised.

Turn now to the converse question—For what ends would all men agree to cooperate? None will deny that for resisting invasion the agreement would be practically unanimous. Excepting only the Quakers, who, having done highly useful work in their time, are now dying out, all would unite for defensive war (not, however, for offensive war); and they would, by so doing, tacitly bind themselves to conform to the will of the majority in respect of measures directed to that end. There would be practical unanimity, also, in the agreement to cooperate for defence against internal enemies as against external enemies. Omitting criminals, all must wish to have person and property adequately protected. Each citizen desires to preserve his life, to preserve things which conduce to maintenance and enjoyment of his life, and to preserve intact his liberties both of using these things and getting further such. It is obvious to him that he cannot do all this if he acts alone. Against foreign invaders he is powerless unless he combines with his fellows; and the business of protecting himself against domestic invaders, if he did not similarly combine, would be alike onerous, dangerous, and inefficient. In one other cooperation all are interested—use of the territory they inhabit. Did the primitive communal ownership survive, there would survive the primitive communal control of the uses to be made of land by individuals or by groups of them; and decisions of the majority would rightly prevail repecting the terms on which portions of it might be employed for raising food, making means of communication, and for other purposes. Even at present, though the matter has been complicated by the growth of private landownership, yet, since the State is still supreme owner (every landlord being in law a tenant of the Crown) able to resume possession, or authorize compulsory purchase, at a fair price; the implication is that the will of the majority is valid respecting the modes in which, and conditions under which, parts of the surface or subsurface, may be utilized: involving certain agreements made on behalf of the public with private persons and companies.

Details are not needful here; nor is it needful to discuss that border region lying between these two classes of cases, and to say how much is included in the last and how much is excluded with the first. For present purposes, it is sufficient to recognize the undeniable truth that there are numerous kinds of actions in respect of which men would not, if they were asked, agree with anything like unanimity to be bound by the will of the majority; while there are some kinds of actions in respect of which they would almost unanimously agree to be thus bound. Here, then, we find a definite warrant for enforcing the will of the majority within certain limits, and a definite warrant for denying the authority of its will beyond those limits.

But evidently, when analysed, the question resolves itself into the further question—What are the relative claims of the aggregate and of its units? Are the rights of the community universally valid against the individual? or has the individual some rights which are valid against the community? The judgement given on this point underlies the entire fabric of political convictions formed, and more especially those convictions which concern the proper sphere of government. Here, then, I propose to revive a dormant controversy, with the expectation of reaching a different conclusion from that which is fashionable.

Says Professor Jevons, in his work, *The State in Relation to Labour*,—"The first step must be to rid our minds of the idea that there are any such things in social matters as abstract rights." Of like character is the belief expressed by Mr. Matthew Arnold in his article on Copyright: "An author has no natural right to a property in his production. But then neither has he a natural right to anything whatever which he may produce or acquire."[5] So, too, I recently read in a weekly journal of high repute, that "to explain once more that there is no such thing as "natural right" would be a waste of philosophy." And the view expressed in these extracts is commonly uttered by statesmen and lawyers in a way implying that only the unthinking masses hold any other.

One might have expected that utterances to this effect would have been rendered less dogmatic by the knowledge that a whole school of legists on the Continent, maintains a belief diametrically opposed to that maintained by the English school. The idea of *Natur-recht* is the root-idea of German jurisprudence. Now whatever may be the opinion held respecting German philosophy at large, it cannot be characterized as shallow. A doctrine current among a people distinguished above all others as laborious inquiries, and certainly not to be classed with superficial thinkers, should not be dismissed as though it were nothing more than a popular delusion. This, however, by the way. Along with the proposition denied in the above quotations, there goes a counter-proposition affirmed. Let us see what it is; and what results when we go behind it and seek its warrant.

On reverting to Bentham, we find this counter-proposition openly expressed. He tells us that government fulfils its office "by creating rights which it confers upon

---

[5] *Fortnightly Review*, 1880, vol. xxvii, p. 322.

individuals: rights of personal security; rights of protection for honour; rights of property"; etc.[6] Were this doctrine asserted as following from the divine right of kings, there would be nothing in it manifestly incongruous, did it come to us from ancient Peru, where the Ynca "was the source from which everything flowed"[7]; or from Shoa (Abyssinia), where "of their persons and worldly substance he [the King] is absolute master"[8]; or from Dahome, where "all men are slaves to the king"[9]; it would be consistent enough. But Bentham, far from being an absolutist like Hobbes, wrote in the interests of popular rule. In his *Constitutional Code*[10] he fixes the sovereignty in the whole people; arguing that it is best "to give the sovereign power to the largest possible portion of those whose greatest happiness is the proper and chosen object," because "this proportion is more apt than any other that can be proposed" for achievement of that object.

Mark, now, what happens when we put these two doctrines together. The sovereign people jointly appoint representatives, and so create a government; the government thus created, creates rights; and then, having created rights, it confers them on the separate members of the sovereign people by which it was itself created. Here is a marvellous piece of political legerdemain! Mr. Matthew Arnold, contending, in the article above

---

[6] Bentham's Works (Bowring's edition), vol. i, p. 301.
[7] W. H. Prescott, *Conquest of Peru*, bk. i, ch. i.
[8] J. Harris, *Highlands of Æthiopia*, ii, 94.
[9] R. F. Burton, *Mission to Gelele, King of Dahome*, i, p. 226.
[10] Bentham's Works, vol. ix, p. 97.

quoted, that "property is the creation of law," tells us to beware of the "metaphysical phantom of property in itself." Surely, among metaphysical phantoms the most shadowy is this which supposes a thing to be obtained by creating an agent, which creates the thing, and then confers the thing on its own creator!

From whatever point of view we consider it, Bentham's proposition proves to be unthinkable. Government, he says, fulfils its office "by creating rights." Two meanings may be given to the word "creating." It may be supposed to mean the production of something out of nothing; or it may be supposed to mean the giving form and structure to something which already exists. There are many who think that the production of something out of nothing cannot be conceived as effected even by omnipotence; and probably none will assert that the production of something out of nothing is within the competence of a human government. The alternative conception is that a human government creates only in the sense that it shapes something pre-existing. In that case, the question arises—"What is the something pre-existing which it shapes?" Clearly the word "creating" begs the whole question—passes off an illusion on the unwary reader. Bentham was a stickler for definiteness of expression, and in his *Book of Fallacies* has a chapter on "Impostor-terms." It is curious that he should have furnished so striking an illustration of the perverted belief which an impostor-term may generate.

But now let us overlook these various impossibilities of thought, and seek the most defensible interpretation of Bentham's view.

It may be said that the totality of all powers and rights, originally exists as an undivided whole in the sovereign people; and that this undivided whole is given in trust (as Austin would say) to a ruling power, appointed by the sovereign people, for the purpose of distribution. If as we have seen, the proposition that rights are created is simply a figure of speech; then the only intelligible construction of Bentham's view is that a multitude of individuals, who severally wish to satisfy their desires, and have, as an aggregate, possession of all the sources of satisfaction, as well as power over all individual actions, appoint a government, which declares the ways in which, and the conditions under which, individual actions may be carried on and the satisfactions obtained. Let us observe the implications. Each man exists in two capacities. In his private capacity he is subject to the government. In his public capacity he is one of the sovereign people who appoint the government. That is to say, in his private capacity he is one of those to whom rights are given; and in his public capacity he is one of those who, through the government they appoint, give the rights. Turn this abstract statement into a concrete statement, and see what it means. Let the community consist of a million men, who, by the hypothesis, are not only joint possessors of the inhabited region, but joint possessors of all liberties of action and appropriation: the only right recognized being that of the aggregate to everything. What follows? Each person, while not owning any product of his own labour, has, as a unit in the sovereign body, a millionth part of the ownership of the products of all others' labour. This is an unavoidable implication. As the government, in Bentham's view, is but an agent; the rights it confers are rights given to it in trust by the sovereign people. If so, such rights must be possessed *en bloc* by the sovereign people before the government, in fulfilment of its trust, confers them on individuals; and, if so, each individual has a millionth portion of these rights in his public capacity, while he has no rights in his private capacity. These he gets only when all the rest of the million join to endow him with them; while he joins to endow with them every other member of the million!

Thus, in whatever way we interpret it, Bentham's proposition leaves us in a plexus of absurdities.

Even though ignoring the opposite opinion of German and French writers on jurisprudence, and even without an analysis which proves their own opinion to be untenable, Bentham's disciples might have been led to treat less cavalierly the doctrine of natural rights. For sundry groups of social phenomena unite to prove that this doctrine is well warranted, and the doctrine they set against it unwarranted.

Tribes all over the world show us that before definite government arises, conduct is regulated by customs. The Bechuanas are controlled by "long-acknowledged customs."[11] Among the Korranna Hottentots, who only "tolerate their chiefs rather than obey them,"[12] "when ancient usages are not in the way, every man seems to

---

[11] W. J. Burchell, *Travels into the Interior of Southern Africa*, vol. i, p. 544.
[12] Arbousset and Daumas, *Voyage of Exploration*, p. 27.

act as is right in his own eyes."[13] The Araucanians are guided by "nothing more than primordial usages or tacit conventions."[14] Among the Kirghizes the judgements of the elders are based on "universally-recognized customs."[15] Similarly of the Dyaks, Rajah Brooke says that "custom seems simply to have become the law; and breaking custom leads to a fine."[16] So sacred are immemorial customs with the primitive man, that he never dreams of questioning their authority; and when government arises, its power is limited by them. In Madagascar the king's word suffices only "where there is no law, custom, or precedent."[17] Raffles tells us that in Java "the customs of the country"[18] restrain the will of the ruler. In Sumatra, too, the people do not allow their chiefs to "alter their ancient usages."[19] Nay, occasionally, as in Ashantee, "the attempt to change some customs" has caused a king's dethronement.[20] Now, among the customs which we thus find to be pre-governmental, and which subordinate governmental power when it is established, are those which recognize certain individual rights—rights to act in certain ways and possess certain things. Even where the recognition of property is least developed, there is proprietorship of weapons, tools,

---

[13] G. Thompson, *Travels and Adventures in Southern Africa*, vol. ii, p. 30.
[14] G. A. Thompson, *Alcedo's Geographical and Historical Dictionary of America*, vol. i, p. 405.
[15] Alex. Michie, *Siberian Overland Route*, p. 248.
[16] C. Brooke, *Ten Years in Sarawak*, vol. i, p. 129.
[17] W. Ellis, *History of Madagascar*, vol. i, p. 377.
[18] Sir T. S. Raffles, *History of Java*, i, 274.
[19] W. Marsden, *History of Sumatra*, p. 217.
[20] J. Beecham, *Ashantee and the Gold Coast*, p. 90.

and personal ornaments; and, generally, the recognition goes far beyond this. Among such North American Indians as the Snakes, who are without Government, there is private ownership of horses. By the Chippewayans, "who have no regular government," game taken in private traps "is considered as private property."[21] Kindred facts concerning huts, utensils, and other personal belongings, might be brought in evidence from accounts of the Ahts, the Comanches, the Esquimaux, and the Brazilian Indians. Among various uncivilized peoples, custom has established the claim to the crop grown on a cleared plot of ground, though not to the ground itself; and the Todas, who are wholly without political organization, make a like distinction between ownership of cattle and of land. Kolff's statement respecting "the peaceful Arafuras" well sums up the evidence. They "recognize the right of property in the fullest sense of the word, without there being any [other] authority among them than the decisions of their elders, according to the customs of their forefathers."[22] But even without seeking proofs among the uncivilized, sufficient proofs are furnished by early stages of the civilized. Bentham and his followers seem to have forgotten that our own common law is mainly an embodiment of "the customs of the realm." It did not give definite shape to that which it found existing. Thus, the fact and the fiction are exactly opposite to what they allege. The fact is that property was well recognized before law existed; the fiction is that "property is the creation of law." These writers and

---

[21] H. R. Schoolcraft, *Expedition to the Sources of the Mississippi River*, v, 177.
[22] G. W. Earl's *Kolff's Voyage of the Dourga*, p. 161.

statesmen who with so much scorn undertake to instruct the ignorant herd, themselves stand in need of instruction.

Considerations of another class might alone have led them to pause. Were it true, as alleged by Bentham, that Government fulfils its office "by creating rights which it confers on individuals"; then, the implication would be, that there should be nothing approaching to uniformity in the rights conferred by different governments. In the absence of a determining cause over-ruling their decisions, the probabilities would be many to one against considerable correspondence among their decisions. But there is very great correspondence. Look where we may, we find that governments interdict the same kinds of aggressions; and, by implication, recognize the same kinds of claims. They habitually forbid homicide, theft, adultery: thus asserting that citizens may not be trespassed against in certain ways. And as society advances, minor individual claims are protected by giving remedies for breach of contract, libel, false witness, etc. In a word, comparisons show that though codes of law differ in their details as they become elaborated, they agree in their fundamentals. What does this prove? It cannot be by chance that they thus agree. They agree because the alleged creating of rights was nothing else than giving formal sanction and better definition to those assertions of claims and recognitions of claims which naturally originate from the individual desires of men who have to live in presence of one another.

Comparative Sociology discloses another group of facts having the same implication. Along with social progress it becomes in an increasing degree the business of the State, not only to give formal sanction to men's rights, but also to defend them against aggressors. Before permanent government exists, and in many cases after it is considerably developed, the rights of each individual are asserted and maintained by himself, or by his family. Alike among savage tribes at present, among civilized peoples in the past, and even now in unsettled parts of Europe, the punishment for murder is a matter of private concern; "the sacred duty of blood revenge" devolves on some one of a cluster of relatives. Similarly, compensations for aggressions on property and for injuries of other kinds, are in early states of society independently sought by each man or family. But as social organization advances, the central ruling power undertakes more and more to secure to individuals their personal safety, the safety of their possessions, and, to some extent, the enforcement of their claims established by contract. Originally concerned almost exclusively with defence of the society as a whole against other societies, or with conducting its attacks on other societies, Government has come more and more to discharge the function of defending individuals against one another. It needs but to recall the days when men habitually carried weapons, or to bear in mind the greater safety to person and property achieved by improved police-administration during our own time, or to note the facilities now given for recovering small debts, to see that the insuring to each individual the unhindered pursuit of the objects of life, within limits set by others' like pursuits, is increasingly recognized as a duty of the State. In other

words, along with social progress, there goes not only
a fuller recognition of these which we call natural rights,
but also a better enforcement of them by Government:
Government becomes more and more the servant to
these essential pre-requisites for individual welfare.

An allied and still more significant change has accompanied this. In early stages, at the same time that the
State failed to protect the individual against aggression,
it was itself an aggressor in multitudinous ways. Those
ancient societies which advanced far enough to leave
records, having all been conquering societies, show us
everywhere the traits of the militant régime. As, for the
effectual organization of fighting bodies, the soldiers,
absolutely obedient, must act independently only when
commanded to do it; so, for the effectual organization of
fighting societies, citizens must have their individuali-
ties subordinated. Private claims are overridden by public claims; and the subject loses much of his freedom of
action. One result is that the system of regimentation,
pervading the society as well as the army, causes detailed
regulation of conduct. The dictates of the ruler, sanctified
by ascription of them to his divine ancestor, are unres-
trained by any conception of individual liberty; and they
specify men's actions to an unlimited extent—down to
kinds of food eaten, modes of preparing them, shaping
of beard, fringing of dresses, sowing of grain, etc. This
omnipresent control, which the ancient Eastern nations
in general exhibited, was exhibited also in large measure
by the Greeks; and was carried to its greatest pitch in the
most militant city, Sparta. Similarly during mediaeval
days throughout Europe, characterized by chronic war-

fare with its appropriate political forms and ideas, there were scarcely any bounds to Governmental interference: agriculture, manufactures, trades, were regulated in detail; religious beliefs and observances were imposed; and rulers said by whom alone furs might be worn, silver used, books issued, pigeons kept, etc. But along with increase of industrial activities, and implied substitution of the régime of contract for the régime of status, and growth of associated sentiments, there went (until the recent reaction accompanying reversion to militant activity) a decrease of meddling with people's doings. Legislation gradually ceased to regulate the cropping of fields, or dictate the ratio of cattle to acreage, or specify modes of manufacture and materials to be used, or fix wages and prices, or interfere with dresses and games (except where there was gambling), or put bounties and penalties on imports or exports, or prescribe men's beliefs, religious or political, or prevent them from combining as they pleased, or travelling where they liked. That is to say, throughout a large range of conduct, the right of the citizen to uncontrolled action has been made good against the pretensions of the State to control him. While the ruling agency has increasingly helped him to exclude intruders from that private sphere in which he pursues the objects of life, it has itself retreated from that sphere; or, in other words—decreased its intrusions.

Not even yet have we noted all the classes of facts which tell the same story. It is told afresh in the improvements and reforms of law itself; as well as in the admissions and assertions of those who have effected them.

"So early as the fifteenth century," says Professor Pollock, "we find a common-law judge declaring that, as in a case unprovided for by known rules the civilians and canonists devise a new rule according to 'the law of nature which is the ground of all law,' the Courts of Westminster can and will do the like."[23] Again, our system of Equity, introduced and developed as it was to make up for the shortcomings of Common-law, or rectify its inequities, proceeded throughout on a recognition of men's claims considered as existing apart from legal warrant. And the changes of law now from time to time made after resistance, are similarly made in pursuance of current ideas concerning the requirements of justice; ideas which, instead of being derived from the law, are opposed to the law. For example, that recent Act which gives to a married woman a right of property in her own earnings, evidently originated in the consciousness that the natural connexion between labour expended and benefit enjoyed, is one which should be maintained in all cases. The reformed law did not create the right, but recognition of the right created the reformed law.

Thus, historical evidences of five different kinds unite in teaching that, confused as are the popular notions concerning rights, and including, as they do, a great deal which should be excluded, yet they shadow forth a truth.

It remains now to consider the original source of this truth. In a previous paper I have spoken of the open secret, that there can be no social phenomena but what,

---

[23] "The Methods of Jurisprudence: an Introductory Lecture at University College, London," 31 October 1882.

if we analyse them to the bottom, bring us down to the laws of life; and that there can be no true understanding of them without reference to the laws of life. Let us, then, transfer this question of natural rights from the court of politics to the court of science—the science of life. The reader need feel no alarm: the simplest and most obvious facts will suffice. We will contemplate first the general conditions to individual life; and then the general conditions to social life. We shall find that both yield the same verdict.

Animal life involves waste; waste must be met by repair; repair implies nutrition. Again, nutrition presupposes obtainment of food; food cannot be got without powers of prehension, and, usually, of locomotion; and that these powers may achieve their ends, there must be freedom to move about. If you shut up a mammal in a small space, or tie its limbs together, or take from it the food it has procured, you eventually, by persistence in one or other of these courses, cause its death. Passing a certain point, hindrance to the fulfilment of these requirements is fatal. And all this, which holds of the higher animals at large, of course holds of man.

If we adopt pessimism as a creed, and with it accept the implication that life in general being an evil should be put an end to, then there is no ethical warrant for these actions by which life is maintained: the whole question drops. But if we adopt either the optimist view or the meliorist view—if we say that life on the whole yields more pleasure than pain; or that it is on the way to become such that it will yield more pleasure than pain;

then these actions by which life is maintained are justified, and there results a warrant for the freedom to perform them. Those who hold that life is valuable, hold, by implication, that men ought not to be prevented from carrying on life-sustaining activities. In other words, if it is said to be "right" that they should carry them on, then, by permutation, we get the assertion that they "have a right" to carry them on. Clearly the conception of "natural rights" originates in recognition of the truth that if life is justifiable, there must be a justification for the performance of acts essential to its preservation; and, therefore, a justification for those liberties and claims which make such acts possible.

But being true of other creatures as of man, this is a proposition lacking ethical character. Ethical character arises only with the distinction between what the individual *may* do in carrying on his life-sustaining activities, and what he *may not* do. This distinction obviously results from the presence of his fellows. Among those who are in close proximity, or even some distance apart, the doings of each are apt to interfere with the doings of others; and in the absence of proof that some may do what they will without limit, while others may not, mutual limitation is necessitated. The non-ethical form of the right to pursue ends, passes into the ethical form, when there is recognized the difference between acts which can be performed without transgressing the limits, and others which cannot be so performed.

This, which is the *a priori* conclusion, is the conclusion yielded *a posteriori*, when we study the doings of the uncivilized. In its vaguest form, mutual limitation of spheres of action, and the ideas and the sentiments associated with it, are seen in the relations of groups to one another. Habitually there come to be established, certain bounds to the territories within which each tribe obtains its livelihood; and these bounds, when not respected, are defended. Among the Wood-Veddahs, who have no political organization, the small clans have their respective portions of forest; and "these conventional allotments are always honourably recognized."[24] Of the ungoverned tribes of Tasmania, we are told that "their hunting grounds were all determined, and trespassers were liable to attack."[25] And, manifestly, the quarrels caused among tribes by intrusions on one another's territories, tend, in the long run, to fix bounds and to give a certain sanction to them. As with each inhabited area, so with each inhabiting group. A death in one, rightly or wrongly ascribed to somebody in another, prompts "the sacred duty of blood-revenge"; and though retaliations are thus made chronic, some restraint is put on new aggressions. Like causes worked like effects in those early stages of civilized societies, during which families or clans, rather than individuals, were the political units; and during which each family or clan had to maintain itself and its possessions against others such. These mutual restraints, which in the nature of things arise between small communities, similarly arise between individuals in each community; and the ideas and usages appropriate to the one are more or less appropriate to the other. Though within each group there is

---

[24] Sir J. E. Tennant, *Ceylon: an Account of the Island, etc.*, ii, p. 440.
[25] J. Bonwick, *Daily Life and Origin of the Tasmanians*, p. 83.

ever a tendency for the stronger to aggress on the
weaker; yet, in most cases, consciousness of the evils
resulting from aggressive conduct serves to restrain.
Everywhere among primitive peoples, trespasses are
followed by counter-trespasses. Says Turner of the
Tannese, "adultery and some other crimes are kept in
check by the fear of club-law."[26] Fitzroy tells us that the
Patagonian, "if he does not injure or offend his neighbour, is not interfered with by others"[27]: personal vengeance being the penalty for injury. We read of the Uapés
that "they have very little law of any kind; but what they
have is of strict retaliation—an eye for an eye and a tooth
for a tooth."[28] And that the *lex talionis* tends to establish
a distinction between what each member of the community may safely do and what he may not safely do,
and consequently to give sanctions to actions within a
certain range but not beyond that range, is obvious.
Though, says Schoolcraft of the Chippewayans, they
"have no regular government, as every man is lord in
his own family, they are influenced more or less by
certain principles, which conduce to their general benefit"[29]: One of the principles named being recognition of
private property.

How mutual limitation of activities originates the ideas
and sentiments implied by the phrase "natural rights,"
we are shown most distinctly by the few peaceful tribes
which have either nominal governments or none at all.

---

[26] *Nineteen Years in Polynesia*, p. 86.
[27] *Voyages of the Adventure and Beagle*, ii, p. 167.
[28] A. R. Wallace, *Travels on Amazon and Rio Negro*, p. 499.
[29] H. R. Schoolcraft, *Expedition to the Sources of the Mississippi*, v, p. 177.

Beyond those facts which exemplify scrupulous regard for one another's claims among the Todas, Santals, Lepchas, Bodo, Chakmas, Jakuns, Arafuras, etc., we have the fact that the utterly uncivilized Wood-Veddahs, without any social organization at all, "think it perfectly inconceivable that any person should ever take that which does not belong to him, or strike his fellow, or say anything that is untrue."[30] Thus it becomes clear, alike from analysis of causes and observation of facts, that while the positive element in the right to carry on life-sustaining activities, originates from the laws of life, that negative element which gives ethical character to it, originates from the conditions produced by social aggregation.

So alien to the truth, indeed, is the alleged creation of rights by government, that, contrariwise, rights having been established more or less clearly before government arises, become obscured as government develops along with that militant activity which, both by the taking of slaves and the establishment of ranks, produces *status;* and the recognition of rights begins again to get definiteness only as fast as militancy ceases to be chronic and governmental power declines.

When we turn from the life of the individual to the life of the society, the same lesson is taught us.

Though mere love of companionship prompts primitive men to live in groups, yet the chief prompter is experience of the advantages to be derived from coop-

---

[30] B. F. Hartshorne in *Fortnightly Review,* March 1876. See also H. C. Sirr, *Ceylon and Ceylonese,* ii, p. 219.

eration. On what condition only can cooperation arise? Evidently on condition that those who join their efforts severally gain by doing so. If, as in the simplest cases, they unite to achieve something which each by himself cannot achieve, or can achieve less readily, it must be on the tacit understanding, either that they shall share the benefit (as when game is caught by a party of them), or that if one reaps all the benefit now (as in building a hut or clearing a plot), the others shall severally reap equivalent benefits in their turns. When, instead of efforts joined in doing the same thing, different things are effected by them—when division of labour arises, with accompanying barter of products, the arrangement implies that each, in return for something which he has in superfluous quantity, gets an approximate equivalent of something which he wants. If he hands over the one and does not get the other, future proposals to exchange will meet with no response. There will be a reversion to that rudest condition in which each makes everything for himself. Hence the possibility of cooperation depends on fulfilment of contract, tacit or overt.

Now this which we see must hold of the very first step towards that industrial organization by which the life of a society is maintained, must hold more or less fully throughout its development. Though the militant type of organization, with its system of *status* produced by chronic war, greatly obscures these relations of contracts, yet they remain partially in force. They still hold between freemen, and between the heads of those small groups which form the units of early societies; and, in a measure, they still hold within these small groups themselves; since survival of them as groups, implies such recognition of the claims of their members, even when slaves, that in return for their labours they get sufficiencies of food, clothing, and protection. And when, with diminution of warfare and growth of trade, voluntary cooperation more and more replaces compulsory cooperation, and the carrying on of social life by exchange under agreement, partially suspended for a time, gradually re-establishes itself; its re-establishment makes possible that vast elaborate industrial organization by which a great nation is sustained.

For in proportion as contracts are unhindered and the performance of them certain, the growth is great and the social life active. It is not now by one or other of two individuals who contract, that the evil effects of breach of contract are experienced. In an advanced society, they are experienced by entire classes of producers and distributors, which have arisen through division of labour; and, eventually, they are experienced by everybody. Ask on what condition it is that Birmingham devotes itself to manufacturing hardware, or part of Staffordshire to making pottery, or Lancashire to weaving cotton. Ask how the rural people who here grow wheat and there pasture cattle, find it possible to occupy themselves in their special businesses. These groups can severally thus act only if each gets from the others in exchange for its own surplus product, due shares of their surplus products. No longer directly effected by barter, this obtainment of their respective shares of one another's products is indirectly effected by money; and if we ask how each division of producers gets its due amount of the required money, the answer is—by fulfilment of contract. If Leeds makes woollens and does not, by fulfilment of contract, receive the means of obtaining from agricultural districts the needful quantity of food, it must starve, and stop producing woollens. If South Wales melts iron and there comes no equivalent agreed upon, enabling it to get fabrics for clothing, its industry must cease. And so throughout, in general and in detail. That mutual dependence of parts which we see in social organization, as in individual organization, is possible only on condition that while each other part does the particular kind of work it has become adjusted to, it receives its proportion of those materials required for repair and growth, which all the other parts have joined to produce: such proportion being settled by bargaining. Moreover, it is by fulfilment of contract that there is effected a balancing of all the various products to the various needs—the large manufacture of knives and the small manufacture of lancets; the great growth of wheat and the little growth of mustard-seed. The check on undue production of each commodity, results from finding that, after a certain quantity, no one will agree to take any further quantity on terms that yield an adequate money equivalent. And so there is prevented a useless expenditure of labour in producing that which society does not want.

Lastly, we have to note the still more significant fact that the condition under which only any specialized group of workers can grow when the community needs more of its particular kind of work, is that contracts shall be free and fulfilment of them enforced. If when, from lack of material, Lancashire failed to supply the usual quantity of cotton-goods, there had been such interference with the contracts as prevented Yorkshire from asking a greater price for its woollens, which it was enabled to do by the greater demand for them, there would have been no temptation to put more capital into the woollen manufacture, no increase in the amount of machinery and number of artisans employed, and no increase of woollens: the consequence being that the whole community would have suffered from not having deficient cottons replaced by extra woollens. What serious injury may result to a nation if its members are hindered from contracting with one another, was well shown in the contrast between England and France in respect of railways. Here, though obstacles were at first raised by classes predominant in the legislature, the obstacles were not such as prevented capitalists from investing, engineers from furnishing directive skill, or contractors from undertaking works; and the high interest originally obtained on investments, the great profits made by contractors, and the large payments received by engineers, led to that drafting of money, energy, and ability, into railway-making, which rapidly developed our railway-system, to the enormous increase of our national prosperity. But when M. Thiers, then Minister of Public Works, came over to inspect, and having been taken about by Mr. Vignoles, said to him when leaving: "I do not think railways are suited to France,"[31] there resulted, from the consequent policy of hindering free contract,

---

[31] Address of C. B. Vignoles, Esq., F.R.S., on his election as President of the Institution of Civil Engineers, Session 1869–70, p. 53.

a delay of "eight or ten years" in that material progress which France experienced when railways were made.

What do these facts mean? They mean that for the healthful activity and due proportioning of those industries, occupations and professions, which maintain and aid the life of a society, there must, in the first place, be few restrictions on men's liberties to make agreements with one another, and there must, in the second place, be an enforcement of the agreements which they do make. As we have seen, the checks naturally arising to each man's actions when men become associated, are those only which result from mutual limitation; and there consequently can be no resulting check to the contracts they voluntarily make: interference with these is interference with those rights to free action which remain to each when the rights of others are fully recognized. And then, as we have seen, enforcement of their rights implies enforcement of contracts made; since breach of contract is indirect aggression. If, when a customer on one side of the counter asks a shopkeeper on the other for a shilling's worth of his goods, and, while the shopkeeper's back is turned, walks off with the goods without leaving the shilling he tacitly contracted to give, his act differs in no essential way from robbery. In each such case the individual injured is deprived of something he possessed, without receiving the equivalent something bargained for; and is in the state of having expended his labour without getting benefit—has had an essential condition to the maintenance of life infringed.

Thus, then, it results that to recognize and enforce the

rights of individuals, is at the same time to recognize and enforce the conditions to a normal social life. There is one vital requirement for both.

Before turning to those corollaries which have practical applications, let us observe how the special conclusions drawn converge to the one general conclusion originally foreshadowed—glancing at them in reversed order.

We have just found that the pre-requisite to individual life is in a double sense the pre-requisite to social life. The life of a society, in whichever of two senses conceived, depends on maintenance of individual rights. If it is nothing more than the sum of the lives of citizens, this implication is obvious. If it consists of those many unlike activities which citizens carry on in mutual dependence, still this aggregate impersonal life rises or falls according as the rights of individuals are enforced or denied.

Study of men's politico-ethical ideas and sentiments, leads to allied conclusions. Primitive peoples of various types show us that before governments exist, immemorial customs recognize private claims and justify maintenance of them. Codes of law independently evolved by different nations, agree in forbidding certain trespasses on the persons, properties, and liberties of citizens; and their correspondences imply, not an artificial source for individual rights, but a natural source. Along with social development, the formulating in law of the rights pre-established by custom, becomes more definite and elaborate. At the same time, Government

undertakes to an increasing extent the business of enforcing them. While it has been becoming a better protector, Government has been becoming less aggressive—
has more and more diminished its intrusions on men's
spheres of private action. And, lastly, as in past times
laws were avowedly modified to fit better with current
ideas of equity; so now, law-reformers are guided by
ideas of equity which are not derived from law but to
which law has to conform.

Here, then, we have a politico-ethical theory justified
alike by analysis and by history. What have we against
it? A fashionable counter-theory, purely dogmatic,
which proves to be unjustifiable. On the one hand, while
we find that individual life and social life both imply
maintenance of the natural relation between efforts and
benefits; we also find that this natural relation, recognized before Government existed, has been all along asserting and re-asserting itself, and obtaining better
recognition in codes of law and systems of ethics. On
the other hand, those who, denying natural rights, commit themselves to the assertion that rights are artificially
created by law, are not only flatly contradicted by facts,
but their assertion is self-destructive: the endeavour to
substantiate it, when challenged, involves them in manifold absurdities.

Nor is this all. The re-institution of a vague popular
conception in a definite form on a scientific basis, leads
us to a rational view of the relation between the wills of
majorities and minorities. It turns out that those cooperations in which all can voluntarily unite, and in the
carrying on of which the will of the majority is rightly

supreme, are cooperations for maintaining the conditions requisite to individual and social life. Defence of the society as a whole against external invaders, has for its remote end to preserve each citizen in possession of such means as he has for satisfying his desires, and in possession of such liberty as he has for getting further means. And defence of each citizen against internal invaders, from murderers down to those who inflict nuisances on their neighbours, has obviously the like end—an end desired by every one save the criminal and disorderly. Hence it follows that for maintenance of this vital principle, alike of individual life and social life, subordination of minority to majority is legitimate; as implying only such a trenching on the freedom and property of each, as is requisite for the better protecting of his freedom and property. At the same time it follows that such subordination is not legitimate beyond this; since, implying as it does a greater aggression upon the individual than is requisite for protecting him, it involves a breach of the vital principle which is to be maintained.

Thus we come round again to the proposition that the assumed divine right of parliaments, and the implied divine right of majorities, are superstitions. While men have abandoned the old theory respecting the source of State-authority, they have retained a belief in that unlimited extent of State-authority which rightly accompanied the old theory, but does not rightly accompany the new one. Unrestricted power over subjects, rationally ascribed to the ruling man when he was held to be a deputy-god, is now ascribed to the ruling body, the deputy-godhood of which nobody asserts.

Opponents will, possibly, contend that discussions about the origin and limits of governmental authority are mere pedantries. "Government," they may perhaps say, is bound to use all the means it has, or can get, for furthering the general happiness. Its aim must be utility; and it is warranted in employing whatever measures are needful for achieving useful ends. The welfare of the people is the supreme law; and legislators are not to be deterred from obeying that law by questions concerning the source and range of their power." Is there really an escape here? or may this opening be effectually closed?

The essential question raised is the truth of the utilitarian theory as commonly held; and the answer here to be given is that, as commonly held, it is not true. Alike by the statements of utilitarian moralists, and by the acts of politicians knowingly or unknowingly following their lead, it is implied that utility is to be directly determined by simple inspection of the immediate facts and estimation of probable results. Whereas, utilitarianism as rightly understood, implies guidance by the general conclusions which analysis of experience yields. "Good and bad results cannot be accidental, but must be necessary consequences of the constitution of things"; and it is "the business of Moral Science to deduce, from the laws of life and the conditions of existence, what kinds of action necessarily tend to produce happiness, and what kinds to produce unhappiness."[32] Current utilitarian speculation, like current practical politics, shows inadequate consciousness of natural causation. The habitual

---

[32] *Data of Ethics,* § 21. See also § § 56–62.

thought is that, in the absence of some obvious impediment, things can be done this way or that way; and no question is put whether there is either agreement or conflict with the normal working of things.

The foregoing discussions have, I think, shown that the dictates of utility, and, consequently, the proper actions of governments, are not to be settled by inspection of facts on the surface, and acceptance of their *prima facie* meanings; but are to be settled by reference to, and deductions from, fundamental facts. The fundamental facts to which all rational judgements of utility must go back, are the facts that life consists in, and is maintained by, certain activities; and that among men in a society, these activities, necessarily becoming mutually limited, are to be carried on by each within the limits thence arising, and not carried on beyond those limits: the maintenance of the limits becoming, by consequence, the function of the agency which regulates society. If each, having freedom to use his powers up to the bounds fixed by the like freedom of others, obtains from his fellow-men as much for his services as they find them worth in comparison with the services of others—if contracts uniformly fulfilled bring to each the share thus determined, and he is left secure in person and possessions to satisfy his wants with the proceeds; then there is maintained the vital principle alike of individual life and of social life. Further, there is maintained the vital principle of social progress; inasmuch as, under such conditions, the individuals of most worth will prosper and multiply more than those of less worth. So that utility, not as empirically estimated but as rationally determined, enjoins this maintenance of individual rights; and, by implication, negatives any course which traverses them.

Here, then, we reach the ultimate interdict against meddling legislation. Reduced to its lowest terms, every proposal to interfere with citizens' activities further than by enforcing their mutual limitations, is a proposal to improve life by breaking through the fundamental conditions to life. When some are prevented from buying beer that others may be prevented from getting drunk, those who make the law assume that more good than evil will result from interference with the normal relation between conduct and consequences, alike in the few ill-regulated and the many well-regulated. A government which takes fractions of the incomes of multitudinous people, for the purpose of sending to the colonies some who have not prospered here, or for building better industrial dwellings, or for making public libraries and public museums, etc., takes for granted that, not only proximately but ultimately, increased general happiness will result from transgressing the essential requirement to general happiness—the requirement that each shall enjoy all those means to happiness which his actions, carried on without aggression, have brought him. In other cases we do not thus let the immediate blind us to the remote. When asserting the sacredness of property against private transgressors, we do not ask whether the benefit to a hungry man who takes bread from a baker's shop, is or is not greater than the injury inflicted on the baker: we consider, not the special effects, but the general effects which arise if property is insecure. But when the State exacts further amounts from citizens, or further restrains their liberties, we consider only the direct and proximate effects, and ignore the direct and distant effects. We do not see that by accumulated small infractions of them, the vital conditions to life, individual and social, come to be so imperfectly fulfilled that the life decays.

Yet the decay thus caused becomes manifest where the policy is pushed to an extreme. Any one who studies, in the writings of MM. Taine and de Tocqueville, the state of things which preceded the French Revolution, will see that that tremendous catastrophe came about from so excessive a regulation of men's actions in all their details, and such an enormous drafting away of the products of their actions to maintain the regulating organization, that life was fast becoming impracticable. The empirical utilitarianism of that day, like the empirical utilitarianism of our day, differed from rational utilitarianism in this, that in each successive case it contemplated only the effects of particular interferences on the actions of particular classes of men, and ignored the effects produced by a multiplicity of such interferences on the lives of men at large. And if we ask what then made, and what now makes, this error possible, we find it to be the political superstition that governmental power is subject to no restraints.

When that "divinity" which "doth hedge a king," and which has left a glamour around the body inheriting his power, has quite died away—when it begins to be seen clearly that, in a popularly governed nation, the government is simply a committee of management; it will also

be seen that this committee of management has no intrinsic authority. The inevitable conclusion will be that
its authority is given by those appointing it; and has just
such bounds as they choose to impose. Along with this
will go the further conclusion that the laws it passes are
not in themselves sacred; but that whatever sacredness
they have, it is entirely due to the ethical sanction—an
ethical sanction which, as we find, is derivable from the
laws of human life as carried on under social conditions.
And there will come the corollary that when they have
not this ethical sanction they have no sacredness, and
may rightly be challenged.

The function of Liberalism in the past was that of putting a limit to the powers of kings. The function of true
Liberalism in the future will be that of putting a limit to
the powers of Parliaments.

POSTSCRIPT

"Do I expect this doctrine to meet with any considerable acceptance?" I wish I could say, yes; but unhappily various reasons oblige me to conclude that only here and there a solitary citizen may have his political creed modified. Of these reasons there is one from which all the others originate.

This essential reason is that the restriction of governmental power within the limits assigned, is appropriate to the industrial type of society only; and, while wholly incongruous with the militant type of society, is partially incongruous with that semi-militant semi-industrial type, which now characterizes advanced nations. At every stage of social evolution there must exist substantial agreement between practices and beliefs—real beliefs I mean, not nominal ones. Life can be carried on only by the harmonizing of thoughts and acts. Either the conduct required by circumstances must modify the sentiments and ideas to fit it; or else the changed

167

sentiments and ideas must eventually modify the conduct.

Hence if the maintenance of social life under one set of conditions, necessitates extreme subordination to a ruler and entire faith in him, there will be established a theory that the subordination and the faith are proper—nay imperative. Conversely if, under other conditions, great subjection of citizens to government is no longer needful for preservation of the national life—if, contrariwise, the national life becomes larger in amount and higher in quality as fast as citizens gain increased freedom of action; there comes a progressive modification of their political theory, having the result of diminishing their faith in governmental action, increasing their tendency to question governmental authority, and leading them in more numerous cases to resist governmental power: involving, eventually, an established doctrine of limitation.

Thus it is not to be expected that current opinion respecting governmental authority, can at present be modified to any great extent. But let us look at the necessities of the case more closely.

Manifestly the success of an army depends very much on the faith of the soldiers in their general: disbelief in his ability will go far towards paralysing them in battle; while absolute confidence in him will make them fulfil their respective parts with courage and energy. If, as in the normally-developed militant type of society, the leader in war and the ruler in peace are one and the same, this confidence in him extends from military action to civil action; and the society, in large measure identical with the army, willingly accepts his judgements as law-giver. Even where the civil head, ceasing to be the military head, does his generalship by deputy, there still clings to him the traditional faith.

As with faith so with obedience. Other things equal an army of insubordinate soldiers fails before an army of subordinate soldiers. Those whose obedience to their leader is perfect and prompt, are obviously more likely to succeed in battle than are those who disregard the commands issued to them. And as with the army so with the society as a whole; success in war must largely depend on that conformity to the ruler's will which brings men and money when wanted, and adjusts all conduct to his needs.

Thus by survival of the fittest, the militant type of society becomes characterized by profound confidence in the governing power, joined with a loyalty causing submission to it in all matters whatever. And there must tend to be established among those who speculate about political affairs in a militant society, a theory giving form to the needful ideas and feelings; accompanied by assertions that the law-giver if not divine in nature is divinely directed, and that unlimited obedience to him is divinely ordered.

Change in the ideas and feelings which thus become characteristic of the militant form of organization, can take place only where circumstances favour development of the industrial form of organization. Being carried on by voluntary cooperation instead of by compulsory cooperation, industrial life as we know it, habituates men to independent activities, leads them to enforce their own claims while respecting the claims of others, strengthens the consciousness of personal rights, and prompts them to resist excesses of governmental control. But since the circumstances which render war less frequent arise but slowly, and since the modifications of nature caused by the transition from a life predominantly militant to a life predominantly industrial can therefore go on but slowly, it happens that the old sentiments and ideas give place to new ones, by small degrees only. And there are several reasons why the transition not only is, but ought to be, gradual. Here are some of them.

In the primitive man and in man but little civilized, there does not exist the nature required for extensive voluntary cooperations. Efforts willingly united with those of others for a common advantage, imply, if the undertaking is large, a perseverance he does not possess. Moreover, where the benefits to be achieved are distant and unfamiliar, as are many for which men now-a-days combine, there needs a strength of constructive imagination not to be found in the minds of the uncivilized. And yet again, great combinations of a private kind for wholesale production or for large enterprises, require a graduated subordination of the united workers—a graduated subordination such as that which militancy produces. In other words, the way to the developed industrial type as we now know it, is through the militant type; which, by discipline generates in long ages the power of continuous application, the willingness to act under direction (now no longer coercive but agreed to under contract) and the habit of achieving large results by organizations.

The implication is that, during long stages of social evolution there needs, for the management of all matters but the simplest, a governmental power great in degree and wide in range, with a correlative faith in it and obedience to it. Hence the fact that, as the records of early civilizations show us, and as we are shown in the East at present, large undertakings can be achieved only by State-action. And hence the fact that only little by little can voluntary cooperation replace compulsory cooperation, and rightly bring about a correlative decrease of faith in governmental ability and authority.

Chiefly, however, the maintenance of this faith is necessitated by the maintenance of fitness for war. This involves continuance of such confidence in the ruling agency, and such subordination to it, as may enable it to wield all the forces of the society on occasions of attack or defence; and there must survive a political theory justifying the faith and the obedience. While their sentiments and ideas are of kinds which perpetually endanger peace, it is requisite that men should have such belief in the authority of government as shall give it adequate coercive power over them for war purposes—a belief in its authority which inevitably, at the same time, gives it coercive power over them for other purposes.

Thus, as said at first, the fundamental reason for not expecting much acceptance of the doctrine set forth, is that we have at present but partially emerged from the militant régime and have but partially entered on that industrial régime to which this doctrine is proper.

So long as the religion of enmity predominates over the religion of amity, the current political superstition must hold its ground. While throughout Europe, the early culture of the ruling classes is one which every day of the week holds up for admiration those who in ancient times achieved the greatest feats in battle, and only on Sunday repeats the injunction to put up the sword— while these ruling classes are subject to a moral discipline consisting of six-sevenths pagan example and one-seventh Christian precept; there is no likelihood that there will arise such international relations as may make a decline in governmental power practicable, and a corresponding modification of political theory acceptable. While among ourselves the administration of colonial affairs is such that native tribes who retaliate on Englishmen by whom they have been injured, are punished, not on their own savage principle of life for life, but on the improved civilized principle of wholesale massacre in return for single murder, there is little chance that a political doctrine consistent only with unaggressive conduct will gain currency. While the creed men profess is so interpreted that one of them who at home addresses missionary meetings, seeks, when abroad, to foment a quarrel with an adjacent people whom he wishes to subjugate, and then receives public honours after his death, it is not likely that the relations of our society to other societies will become such that there can spread to any extent that doctrine of limited governmental functions which accompanies the diminished governmental authority proper to a peaceful state. A nation which, interested in ecclesiastical squabbles about the ceremonies of its humane cult, cares so little about the essence of that cult that filibustering in its colonies receives applause rather than reprobation, and is not denounced even by the priests of its religion of love, is a nation which must continue to suffer from internal aggressions, alike of all individuals on one another and of the State on individuals. It is impossible to unite the blessings of equity at home with the commission of inequities abroad.

Of course there will arise the question—Why, then, enunciate and emphasize a theory at variance with the theory adapted to our present state?

Beyond the general reply that it is the duty of every one who regards a doctrine as true and important, to do what he can towards diffusing it, leaving the result to be what it may, there are several more special replies, each of which is sufficient.

In the first place an ideal, far in advance of practicability though it may be, is always needful for right guidance. If, amid all those compromises which the circumstances of the times necessitates, or are thought to necessitate, there exist no true conceptions of better and worse in social organizations—if nothing beyond the exigencies of the moment are attended to, and the proximately best is habitually identified with the ultimately best; there cannot be any true progress. However distant may be the goal, and however often intervening obstacles may necessitate deviation in our course towards it, it is obviously requisite to know where-abouts it lies.

Again, while something like the present degree of subjection of the individual to the State, and something like the current political theory adapted to it, may remain needful in presence of existing international relations; it is by no means needful that this subjection should be made greater and the adapted theory strengthened. In our days of active philanthropy, hosts of people eager to achieve benefits for their less fortunate fellows by what seem the shortest methods, are busily occupied in developing administrative arrangements of a kind proper to a lower type of society—are bringing about retrogression while aiming at progression. The normal difficulties in the way of advance are sufficiently great, and it is lamentable that they should be made greater. Hence, something well worth doing may be done, if philanthropists can be shown that they are in many cases insuring the future ill-being of men while eagerly pursuing their present well-being.

Chiefly, however, it is important to press on all the great truth, at present but little recognized, that a society's internal and external policies are so bound together, that there cannot be an essential improvement of the one without an essential improvement of the other. A higher standard of international justice must be habitually acted upon, before there can be conformity to a higher standard of justice in our national arrangements. The conviction that a dependence of this kind exists, could it be diffused among civilized peoples, would greatly check aggressive behaviour towards one another; and, by doing this, would diminish the coerciveness of their governmental systems while appropriately changing their political theories.

Note

[*In some of the criticisms on this work, there has reappeared a mistaken inference several times before drawn, that the doctrine of evolution as applied to social affairs precludes philanthropic effort. How untrue this is, was shown by me in the* Fortnightly Review *for February 1875. Here I reproduce the essential part of that which was there said.*]

I am chiefly concerned, however, to repudiate the conclusion that the "private action of citizens" is needless or unimportant, because the course of social evolution is determined by the natures of citizens, as working under the conditions in which they are placed. To assert that each social change is thus determined, is to assert that all the egoistic and altruistic activities of citizens are factors of the change; and is tacitly to assert that in the absence of any of these—say political aspirations, or the promptings of philanthropy—the change will not be the same. So far from implying that the efforts of each man to achieve that which he thinks best, are unimportant, the doctrine implies that such efforts, severally resulting from the natures of the individuals, are indispensable forces. The correlative duty is thus emphasized in §34 of *First Principles:*

> It is not for nothing that he has in him these sympathies with some principles and repugnance to others. He, with all his

capacities, and aspirations, and beliefs, is not an accident, but a product of the time. He must remember that while he is a descendant of the past, he is a parent of the future; and that his thoughts are as children born to him, which he may not carelessly let die. He, like every other man, may properly consider himself as one of the myriad agencies through whom works the Unknown Cause; and when the Unknown Cause produces in him a certain belief, he is thereby authorized to profess and act out that belief. For, to render in their highest sense the words of the poet,—

> . . . Nature is made better by no mean,
> But nature makes that mean: over that art
> Which you say adds to nature, is an art
> That nature makes.

That there is no retreat from this view in the work Professor Cairnes criticizes, *The Study of Sociology,* is sufficiently shown by its closing paragraph:

Thus, admitting that for the fanatic some wild anticipation is needful as a stimulus, and recognizing the usefulness of this delusion as adapted to his particular nature and his particular function, the man of higher type must be content with greatly-moderated expectations, while he perseveres with undiminished efforts. He has to see how comparatively little can be done, and yet to find it worth while to do that little: so uniting philanthropic energy with philosophic calm.

I do not see how Professor Cairnes reconciles with such passages, his statement that "according to Mr. Spencer, the future of the human race may be safely trusted to the action of motives of a private and personal kind—to motives such as operate in the production and distribution of wealth, or in the development of language." This statement is to the effect that I ignore the "action of motives" of a higher kind; whereas these are not only necessarily included by me in the totality of motives, but repeatedly insisted upon as all-essential. I am the more surprised at this misapprehension because, in the essay on "Specialized Administration," to which Professor Cairnes refers (see *Fortnightly Review,* for December 1871), I have dwelt at considerable length on the altruistic sentiments and the resulting social activities, as not having been duly taken into account by Professor Huxley.

As Professor Cairnes indicates at the close of his first paper, the difficulty lies in recognizing human actions as, under one aspect, voluntary, and under another predetermined. I have said elsewhere all I have to say on this point. Here I wish only to point out that the conclusion he draws from my premises is utterly different from the conclusion I draw. Entering this caveat, I must leave all further elucidations to come in due course.

SIX ESSAYS ON GOVERNMENT, SOCIETY, AND FREEDOM

THE PROPER SPHERE OF GOVERNMENT

Letter I

Things of the first importance—principles influencing all the transactions of a country—principles involving the weal or woe of nations, are very generally taken for granted by society. When a certain line of conduct, however questionable may be its policy—however momentous may be its good or evil results, has been followed by our ancestors, it usually happens that the great masses of mankind continue the same course of action, without ever putting to themselves the question—Is it right? Custom has the enviable power, of coming to conclusions upon most debatable points, without a moment's consideration—of turning propositions of a very doubtful character into axioms—and of setting

---

This series of twelve letters was published in The Nonconformist *in 1842–43. In 1843 the letters were reprinted under the present title by W. Brittain of London and sold for fourpence.*

aside almost self-evident truths as unworthy of consideration.

Of all subjects thus cavalierly treated, the fundamental principles of legislation, are perhaps the most important. Politicians—all members of the community who have the welfare of their fellow-men at heart, have their hopes, opinions, and wishes, centered in the actions of government. It therefore behoves them fully to understand the nature, the intention, the proper sphere of action of a government. Before forming opinions upon the best measures to be adoped by a legislative body, it is necessary that well defined views of the power of that body should be formed; that it be understood how far it can go consistently with its constitution; that it be decided what it may do and what it may not do. And yet, how few men have ever given the matter any serious consideration; how few, even of those who are interested in the affairs of society, ever put to themselves the question—Is there any boundary to the interference of government? and, if so, what is that boundary?

We hear one man proclaiming the advantages that would accrue, if all the turnpike roads in the kingdom were kept in repair by the state; another would saddle the nation with a medical establishment, and preserve the popular health by legislation; and a third party maintains that government should make railways for Ireland, at the public expense. The possibility of there being any impropriety in meddling with these things never suggests itself. Government always *has* exercised the liberty of universal interference, and nobody ever questioned its right to do so. Our ancestors, good people, thought it quite reasonable that the executive should have unlimited power (or probably they never troubled themselves to think about it at all); and as they made no objection, we, in our wise veneration for the "good old times," suppose that all is as it should be. Some few, however, imbued with the more healthy spirit of investigation, are not content with this simple mode of settling such questions, and would rather ground their convictions upon reason, than upon custom. To such are addressed the following considerations.

Everything in nature has its laws. Inorganic matter has its dynamical properties, its chemical affinities; organic matter, more complex, more easily destroyed, has also its governing principles. As with matter in its integral form, so with matter in its aggregate; animate beings have their laws, as well as the material, from which they are derived. Man, as an animate being, has functions to perform, and has organs for performing those functions; he has instincts to be obeyed, and the means of obeying those instincts; and, so long as he performs those functions, as he obeys those instincts, as he bends to the laws of his nature, so long does he remain in health. All disobedience to these dictates, all transgression, produces its own punishment. Nature will be obeyed.

As with man physically, so with man spiritually. Mind has its laws as well as matter. The mental faculties have their individual spheres of action in the great business of life; and upon their proper development, and the due performance of their duties, depend the moral integrity, and the intellectual health, of the individual. Psychical laws must be obeyed as well as physical ones; and disobedience as surely brings its punishment in the one case, as in the other.

As with man individually, so with man socially. Society as certainly has its governing principles as man has. They may not be so easily traced, so readily defined. Their action may be more complicated, and it may be more difficult to obey them; but, nevertheless, analogy shows us that they must exist. We see nothing created but what is subject to invariable regulations given by the Almighty, and why should society be an exception? We see, moreover, that beings having volition, are healthy and happy, so long only as they act in accordance with those regulations; and why should not the same thing be true of man in his collective capacity?

This point conceded, it follows that the well being of a community, depends upon a thorough knowledge of social principles, and an entire obedience to them. It becomes of vital importance to know, what institutions are necessary to the prosperity of nations; to discover what are the duties of those institutions; to trace the boundaries of their action; to take care that they perform their functions properly; and especially to see, that they aim not at duties for which they were not intended, and for which they are not fitted.

The legislature is the most important of all national institutions, and as such, it claims our first attention in the investigation of social laws. An attempt to arrive at its principles, from the analysis of existing governments, with all their complex and unnatural arrangements, would be a work of endless perplexity, and one from which it would be extremely difficult, if not impossible, to educe any satisfactory result. To obtain clear ideas, we must consider the question abstractly; we must suppose society in its primitive condition; we must view circumstances and requirements as they would naturally arise; and we shall then be in a position to judge properly, of the relation which should exist, between a people and a government.

Let us, then, imagine a number of men living together without any recognised laws—without any checks upon their actions, save those imposed by their own fears of consequences—obeying nothing but the impulses of their own passions—what is the result? The weak—those who have the least strength, or the least influence—are oppressed by the more powerful: these, in their turn, experience the tyranny of men still higher in the scale; and even the most influential, are subject to the combined vengeance of those whom they have injured. Every man, therefore, soon comes to the conclusion, that his individual interest as well as that of the community at large, will best be served by entering into some common bond of protection: all agree to become amenable to the decisions of their fellows, and to obey certain general arrangements. Gradually the population increases, their disputes become more numerous, and they find that it will be more convenient to depute this arbitrative power, to one or more individuals, who shall be maintained by the rest, in consideration of their time being devoted to the business of the public. Here we have a government springing naturally out of the requirements of the community. But what are those requirements? Is the government instituted for the purpose of regulating trade—of dictating to each man where he shall buy and where he shall sell? Do the people wish to be told what religion they must believe, what forms and ceremonies they must practice, or how many times they must attend church on a Sunday?[1] Is education the object contemplated? Do they ask instruction in the administration of their charity—to be told to whom they shall give, and how much, and in what manner they shall give it? Do they require their means of communication—their roads and railways—designed and constructed for them? Do they create a supreme power to direct their conduct in domestic affairs—to tell them at what part of the year they shall kill their oxen, and how many servings of meat they shall have at a meal?[2] In short, do they want a government because they see that the Almighty has been so negligent in designing social mechanisms, that everything will go wrong unless they are continually interfering? No; they know, or they ought to know, that the laws of society are of such a character, that natural evils will rectify themselves; that there is in society, as in every other part of creation, that beautiful self-adjusting principle, which will keep all its elements in equilibrium; and, moreover, that as the interference of man in external nature often destroys the just balance, and produces greater evils than those to be remedied, so the attempt to regulate all the actions of a

---

[1] "We remember a religious society which, in its laws, declared that it was instituted to promote the goodness of God; and truly it may be said that enactments against atheism are passed upon the pretence of endeavouring to promote his existence."—*Sidney Smith's Phrenology*, p. 8.

[2] It is said that the statute book still contains enactments on these points.

community by legislation, will entail little else but misery and confusion.

What, then, do they want a government for? Not to regulate commerce; not to educate the people; not to teach religion; not to administer charity; not to make roads and railways; but simply to defend the natural rights of man—to protect person and property—to prevent the aggressions of the powerful upon the weak—in a word, to administer justice. This is the natural, the original, office of a government. It was not intended to do less: it ought not to be allowed to do more.

Letter II

Philosophical politicians usually define government, as a body whose province it is, to provide for the "general good." But this practically amounts to no definition at all, if by a definition is meant a description, in which the limits of the thing described are pointed out. It is necessary to the very nature of a definition, that the words in which it is expressed should have some determinate meaning; but the expression "general good," is of such uncertain character, a thing so entirely a matter of opinion, that there is not an action that a government could perform, which might not be contended to be a fulfilment of its duties. Have not all our laws, whether really enacted for the public benefit or for party aggrandisement, been passed under the plea of promoting the "general good?" And is it probable that any government, however selfish, however tyrannical, would be so barefaced as to pass laws avowedly for any other purpose? If, then, the very term "definition," implies a something intended to mark out the boundaries of the thing defined, that cannot be a definition of the duty of a government, which will allow it to do anything and everything.

It was contended in the preceding letter, that "the administration of justice" was the sole duty of the state. Probably it will be immediately objected, that this definition is no more stringent than the other—that the word "justice" is nearly as uncertain in its signification as the expression "general good"—that one man thinks it but "justice" towards the landowner, that he should be protected from the competition of the foreign corn grower; another maintains that "justice" demands that the labourer's wages should be fixed by legislation, and that since such varied interpretations may be given to the term, the definition falls to the ground. The reply is very simple. The word is not used in its legitimate sense. "Justice" comprehends only the preservation of man's natural rights. Injustice implies a violation of those rights. No man ever thinks of demanding "justice" unless he is prepared to prove that violation; and no body of men can pretend that "justice" requires the enactment of any law, unless they can show that their natural rights would otherwise be infringed. If it be conceded that this is the proper meaning of the word, the objection is invalid, seeing that in the cases above cited, and in all similar ones, it is not applicable in this sense.

Having thus examined the exact meaning of the new definition, and having observed its harmony with the original wants of society, we may at once proceed to consider its practical applications; and, in the first few cases, it may be well, for the sake of showing the different effects of the two principles, to note, at the same time, the results of the doctrine of "general good." First, the great question of the day—the corn laws. Our legislators tell us that we have an enormous national debt; that we have to pay the interest of it; and that a free trade would so change the value of money, that we should not be able to raise the taxes; moreover, that were we to allow a competition, between foreign and home-grown produce, the land must be thrown out of cultivation— our agricultural population would be deprived of employment—and that great distress must be the result. These and sundry other plausible reasons, they bring forward, to show that restrictions upon the importation of corn, are necessary to the "general good." On the other hand, suppose we had free trade. Could our farmer complain that it was an infringement of his natural rights, to allow the consumers to purchase their food from any other parties whose prices were lower? Could he urge that the state was not acting justly towards him, unless it forced the manufacturer to give him a high price for that, which he could get on more advantageous terms elsewhere? No. "Justice" would demand no such interference. It is clear, therefore, that if the "administration of justice" had been recognised as the only duty of government, we should never have had any corn laws; and, as the test may be applied to all other cases of restrictions upon commerce with a similar result, it is equally evident, that upon the same assumption, we should always have had free trade.

Again, our clergy and aristocracy maintain, that it is eminently necessary for the "general good" that we should have an established church. They would have us believe that the Christian religion is of itself powerless—that it will never spread unless nurtured by the *pure* and *virtuous* hand of the state—that the truth is too weak to make its way without the assistance of acts of parliament—and that mankind are still so universally selfish and worldly, that there is no chance of the gospel being taught, unless comfortable salaries are provided for its teachers—practically admitting, that were it not for the emoluments their own ministry would cease, and thus inadvertently confessing, that their interest, in the spiritual welfare of their fellow-creatures, is co-extensive with their pecuniary expectations. But, what says the other definition? Can it be contended, that it is unjust to the community to allow each individual to put what construction he sees best upon the scriptures? Can the man who disputes the authority of learned divines, and dares to think for himself, be charged with oppression? Can it even be maintained, that he who goes so far as to disbelieve the Christian religion altogether, is infringing the privileges of his fellow-man? No. Then it follows, that an established church is not only unnecessary to the preservation of the natural rights of man, but that inasmuch as it denies the subject the "rights of conscience," and compels him to contribute towards the spread of doctrines of which he does not approve, it is absolutely inimical to them. So that a state, in setting up a national religion, stands in the anomalous position of a transgressor of those very rights, that it was instituted to defend. It is evident, therefore, that the restrictive principle, would never have permitted the establishment of a state church.

And now, let us apply the test to that much-disputed question—the poor law. Can any individual, whose wickedness or improvidence has brought him to want, claim relief of his fellow-men as an act of justice? Can even the industrious labourer, whose distresses have not resulted from his own misconduct, complain that his natural rights are infringed, unless the legislature compels his neighbours to subscribe for his relief? Certainly not. Injustice implies a positive act of oppression, and no man or men can be charged with it, when merely maintaining a negative position. To get a clearer view of this, let us again refer to a primitive condition of society, where all start with equal advantages. One part of the community is industrious and prudent, and accumulates property; the other, idle and improvident, or in some cases, perhaps, unfortunate. Can any of the one class fairly demand relief from the other? Can even those, whose poverty is solely the result of misfortune, claim part of the produce of the industry of the others as a right? No. They may seek their commiseration; they may hope for their assistance; but they cannot take their stand upon the ground of justice. What is true of these parties, is true of their descendants; the children of the one class stand in the same relation to those of the other that existed between their parents, and there is no more claim in the fiftieth or sixtieth generation than in the first.

Possibly it may be objected to the assumption that the

different classes started upon equal terms, that it is not only entirely gratuitous, but that it is contrary to fact; as we all know, that the property was seized by the few, while the many were left in poverty without any fault of their own and, that in this circumstance, originates the right in question. I reply, that when it can be shown that the two classes of the present day, are the direct descendants of those alluded to; when it can be shown that our poor are the children of the oppressed, and that those who have to pay poor rates are the children of the oppressors, then, the validity of the objection will be admitted; but that until this is shown to be the truth, or an approach to the truth, the objection may be disregarded. It appears, then, that the proposed definition of the duty of the state, would never have allowed the existence of a poor law.

Letter III

From preceding arguments it was inferred, that if the administration of justice had been recognised as the only duty of the state, a national church would not have existed, that restrictions upon commerce could never have been enacted, and that a poor law would be inadmissible. As the last conclusion will not meet with such general approbation as its predecessors, it is deemed requisite to enter more fully into the evidence that may be adduced in support of it: and the *Nonconformist* being the organ of a political body, who profess to act upon principle and not upon expediency, and who avow their intention to follow up sound doctrine, whether it may lead to odium or popularity, it is hoped that the arguments brought forward, will meet with a candid consideration, apart from all personal or political bias.

The fund provided by the poor law is usually considered as a contribution from the richer orders of the community, for the support of the destitute; and, coming from the pockets of those in easy circumstances, it is supposed to be a great boon to their poorer neighbours. But this is not a correct mode of viewing the case. A political economist would reason thus. Here is an institution which practically divides the community into two great classes—labourers and paupers, the one doing nothing towards the production of the general stock of food and clothing, and the other having to provide for the consumption of both. Hence it is evident, that each member of the producing class, is injured by the appropriation of a portion of the general stock by the non-producing class. But who form the great bulk of the producing class? The working population. Their labour is the chief ingredient in the wealth of the nation; without them land and capital would be useless. It follows, then, that this provision, set apart for the poor, is mainly provided by the labours of the people, and hence that the burden falls chiefly upon them.

Lest this generalizing style of argument should be unsatisfactory, it may be well to adopt another mode of proof. We know that the average cost of any article is determined by the expenses attendant upon its production; that the price at which the manufacturer sells his calico, is dependent upon the amount of labour expended upon it, the cost of his machinery, the value of the raw material, and so forth; and that the price at which the farmer can afford to sell his corn, is governed by the amount of his rent, the cost of cultivation, &c.; and we also know, that if any one of these expenses is increased, a rise in the price of the produce must follow; that if the landlords double their rents, the farmers must charge more for their grain. Now the poor rates, in some of the unions under the present law, are 40 per cent upon the rental, and under the old law they were in some cases 75 and 100 per cent. What does this amount to but a doubling of the rent? It matters not whether both portions are paid to the landlord, or whether one half goes to him, and the other to the parish, the effect upon the cost of the produce is the same, and the consumers of that produce, have to pay a higher price for it, than they would have to do, were no such demand made. But *who* form the great mass of consumers?—The working population. *They* then are the parties from whom the greater part of this additional tax comes. Thus we arrive at the same conclusion as before; that not only do the industrious classes contribute a considerable portion of the poor rates directly, but that the greater part of what apparently comes from the upper ranks, is originally derived from them.

Many poor law advocates build their arguments upon the existence of a corn law. They say that were there no bar to the importation of foreign produce, and no consequent check to the demand for our manufactures, they would not object to the working man being dependent upon his own resources; but that so long as the price of food is unnaturally raised, and the call for labour so uncertain, they must maintain the necessity of a public charity. To this there are two replies.

First, That the argument rests upon a wrong hypothesis, originating as it does in the assumption, that public charity proceeds from the stores of the rich, when, as has been shown, the greater portion of it comes from the toils of the labouring classes. The very parties for whose benefit the fund is raised, are, in virtue of their productive industry, chiefly instrumental in raising it. The fact, therefore, that the industrious population are already suffering from a corn law, affords no reason why one part of them should be still further burdened, by having to provide food and clothing for the other.

Secondly, That the new definition of the duty of a government is not in the least affected by the argument, seeking that free trade is a necessary consequence of the same principle that excludes a poor law; and if so, it follows that those objections which are founded upon the existence of commercial restrictions, are not applicable.

But even admitting that a poor law ameliorates the condition of the labouring classes in times of national distress; still it does not follow that it is either a wise, or, ultimately, a benevolent law. So long as the earth continues to produce, and mankind are willing to labour, an extensive distress must indicate something unnatural in the social arrangements. Such is the present condition of England. Europe and America produce more food than they can consume—our artisans are anxious to work, and yet they are bordering upon starvation, consequently there must be something radically wrong, in our political institutions. Is it better to palliate, or to cure the evil? Is it better to mitigate the distress by the distribution of public charity, or to allow it so to manifest itself, as to demand the discovery and removal of its cause? Which do we consider the kindest physician, the one who alleviates the pain of a disease by continually administering anodynes, or the one who allows his patient to experience a little suffering in the exhibition of the symptoms, that he may discover the seat of the malady, and then provide a speedy remedy? The alternative requires no consideration.

It is surprising that writers who have of late been animadverting upon the national collection scheme, and who have pointed out the mockery of recommending charity, in answer to a call for justice, should not perceive that the case is but a type of the poor law. Both are attempts to mitigate an evil, not to remove it; both are means of quieting the complaints of the nation, and both will tend to retard the attainment of those rights which the people demand. *The Times,* in an article upon the national petition, made an observation to the effect, that the contents of the document were not worthy of notice, but that the fact of its presentation, clearly proved the necessity for a "more generous poor law," to satisfy the complainants. Here is a clear exposition of the policy: we must stop the mouths of the people by charity: we need not enter into the question of their rights, but we must give them more parish pay!

A poor law, however, is not only inexpedient in practice, but it is defective in principle. The chief arguments that are urged against an established religion, may be used with equal force against an established charity. The dissenter submits, that no party has a right to compel him to contribute to the support of doctrines, which do not meet his approbation. The rate-payer may as reasonably argue, that no one is justified in forcing him to subscribe towards the maintenance of persons, whom he does not consider deserving of relief. The advocate of religious freedom, does not acknowledge the right of any council, or bishop, to choose for him what he shall believe, or what he shall reject. So the opponent of a poor law, does not acknowledge the right of any government, or commissioner, to choose for him who are worthy of his charity, and who are not. The dissenter from an established church, maintains that religion will always be more general, and more sincere, when the support of its ministry is not compulsory. The dissenter from a poor law, maintains that charity will always be more extensive, and more beneficial, when it is voluntary. The dissenter from an established church can demonstrate that the intended benefit of a state religion, will always be frustrated by the corruption which the system invariably produces. So the dissenter from a poor law, can show that the proposed advantages of state charity, will always be neutralized by the evils of pauperism, which necessarily follow in its train. The dissenter from an established church, objects that no man has a right to step in between him and his religion. So the dissenter from established charity, objects that no man has a right to step in between him and the *exercise* of his religion.

How is it, that those who are so determined in their endeavours to rid themselves of the domination of a national church—who declare that they do not need the instruction of the state in the proper explanation of the gospel—how is it that these same men, are tamely allowing and even advocating, the interference of the state, in the exercise of one of the most important precepts of that gospel? They deny the right of the legislature to explain the theory, and yet argue the necessity of its direction in the practice. Truly it indicates but little consistency on the part of dissenters, that whilst they defend their independence in the article of *faith,* they have so little confidence in their own principles, that they look for extraneous aid in the department of *works.* The man who sees the inhabitants of a country deficient in spiritual instruction, and hence maintains the necessity of a national religion, is doing no more than the one who finds part of the population wanting in food and clothing, and thence infers the necessity of a national charity.

Again, the moral effect of a poor law upon the rate-paying portion of the community is little considered, although one of its most important features. Here, also, there is an evident analogy between established religion and established charity. It is said, that in a system like that of our national church, in which the visible duties of a communicant, consist chiefly, in attendance upon public worship, reception of the sacraments, payment of tithes, church rates, etc., the form will always be substituted for the reality; that the periodical ceremonies will take the place of the daily practice; that the physical will take the place of the spiritual. It may be said, with equal truth, that a similar effect will follow the establishment of a poor law; the same principles in human nature are acted upon; the payment of poor rates will supplant the exercise of real benevolence, and a fulfilment of the legal form, will supersede the exercise of the moral duty. Forced contributions rarely appeal to the kindly feelings. The man who is called upon for a rate, does not put his hand into his pocket out of pure sympathy for the poor; he looks upon the demand as another tax, and feels annoyance rather than pleasure, in paying it. Nor does the effect end here. The poor labourer or artisan, who is struggling hard with the world to maintain his independence, excites no pity. So long as there is a poor law he cannot starve, and it will be time enough to consider his case when he applies for relief. The beggar who knocks at his door, or the way-worn traveler who accosts him in his walk, is told to go to his parish; there is no need to inquire into his history, and to give him private assistance if found deserving, for there is already a public provision for him. Such is the state of mind encouraged by national charity. When the legal demand is paid, the conscience is satisfied; the party is absolved from all exercise of generosity; charity is administered by proxy; the nobler feelings are never required to gain the victory over the selfish propensities; a dormant condition of those feelings necessarily follows, and a depreciation of the national character is the final result. The payment of poor rates bears the same relation to real charity, that the attention to forms and ceremonies bears to real religion.

But, it may be asked, how are we to know that voluntary benevolence would suffice for the relief of the ordinary distresses of the poor, were there no national provision? A somewhat analogous question is put as an

objection to the extension of the suffrage—how are we
to know that those who are not fitted for the exercise of
the franchise, will become so when it is given to them?
and a similar reply to that so ably employed by the editor
of the *Nonconformist* in that case, will apply here. Men
are not in the habit of preparing for duties they are never
called upon to perform; they are not in the habit of exhibiting virtues which are never needed; moral vigour
cannot co-exist with moral inactivity; and the higher
feelings will ever remain inactive, until circumstances
prompt them to exercise. Hence, while there is a public
provision for poverty, there will be no incentive to the
exercise of benevolence on the part of the rich, and no
stimulus to prudence and economy on the part of the
poor. So long as the one class can point to the pay table,
they will not give; and so long as the other have an
inexhaustible fund to apply to, they will not save. It may
reasonably be concluded, therefore, that were there no
poor law, the rich would be more charitable, and the
poor more provident. The one would give more, and the
other would ask less.

A general view of the arguments shows:

1. That the burden of the poor law fall chiefly upon
the industrious classes.

2. That the existence of commercial restrictions, is,
therefore, no argument for retaining it.

3. That even assuming a poor law to be directly beneficial, it is indirectly injurious, inasmuch as it prolongs
the causes of distress.

4. That established charity is open to many of the

strongest objections that can be urged against established religion.

5. That a poor law discourages the exercise of real benevolence, and lowers the standard of national character.

6. That were there no poor law, the increase of voluntary charity, and the decrease of improvidence, would render one unnecessary.

. From these reasons it is concluded, that the proposed definition of the duty of a government, in excluding a poor law, is only excluding what is intrinsically bad.

Letter IV

My last letter, entering as it did rather deeply into the poor law question, might almost be considered by some of your readers, as a digression from the ostensible object of this essay, although a very necessary one to the establishment of the principle advocated. I must now, however, still further trespass upon their patience, in the endeavour to answer the query proposed to me— "Has not every man a right to a maintenance out of the soil?" for this, after all, is the pith of the question submitted.[3] Before proceeding, it may be observed, that the burden of proof falls rather on the party who assert the right, than on those who deny it. The originator of a proposition is usually required to demonstrate its truth; not his opponent to show its fallacy.

Man *has* a claim to a subsistence derived from the soil.

[3] This refers to some remarks which appeared in the *Nonconformist* upon the previous letter.

It is his natural birth-right—the charter given to him at his creation; and whoever, by iniquitous laws, oppressive taxation, or any other means, puts difficulties in the way of his obtaining that subsistence, is infringing that right. But, the right is conditional—the produce is only promised to him in return for the labour he bestows upon the soil; and if the condition is not fulfilled, the right has no existence. Now the poor law principle recognises this right, as independent of that condition; it acknowledges the claim to a share in the produce, but demands no equivalent labour. "Yes," it will be replied, "and for a very good reason; because there is no direction in which that labour can be profitably employed." Be it so; it cannot be denied that this is to a certain extent true. But what then? Is this a natural state of things? Is this great evil irremediable? Is this want of a field for labour the inevitable result of the constitution of the world? No, no! It is one of the evil consequences of human selfishness—it is one of the many curses flowing from class legislation. We know that were we righteously governed, we should hear no cry for employment. Every man would find something for his hand to do, and the promised sustenance would flow abundantly from his labour. What, then, is our duty? Ought we, because some of our fellow men, have, in the wantonness of their power, made arrangements whereby a great part of the people are prevented from earning their bread by the sweat of their brow—ought we, I ask, calmly to submit, and give the subsistence without the labour? Ought we not rather to destroy the laws that have induced this disordered state; and by restoring the healthy action of society, allow that natural fulfilment of the promise, which a submission to its accompanying commandment would ensure? The Almighty has given to man a privilege to be enjoyed after obeying a certain condition: a human power steps in, and to a certain extent renders obedience to that condition impossible: shall we grant the privilege without any attention to the condition? or shall we take away the obstacles which prevent our fellow men from satisfying it? The answer is self-evident. We come, then, to the conclusion that the *unconditional* right to a maintenance out of the soil, is inconsistent with one of the fundamental principles of our religion.

It may be objected that though employment be ever so abundant, and society in its most prosperous state, there will still be numerous cases of distress and destitution. Granted; but what then? It must not be inferred that there needs any public provision for them. In nine cases out of ten, such miseries result from the transgressions of the individual or his parents: and are we to take away the just punishment of those transgressions? We are told that the sins of the wicked shall be visited upon the children to the third and fourth generation. That visitation may either exhibit itself in mental derangement, bodily disease, or temporal want. The parent may either transmit to the child bad moral tendencies, a constitutional taint, or may leave it in circumstances of great misery. The visitation may comprehend any or all of these. But the poor law steps in and says, "As far as I can, I will annul this law. However great may have been your misconduct, or that of your parents—notwithstanding your destitution may have resulted solely from that misconduct, now that you are in distress you have a just claim upon the property of your fellow-creatures, and I will relieve you."[4] In doing this it not only takes away the punishment, but it also destroys the most powerful incentive to reformation. Adversity is, in many cases, the only efficient school for the transgressor. Perhaps it may be asked, where is the justice, or the advantage, of allowing the child to endure the temporal want resulting from the sins of its parents? There is an advantage, and a great one: The same tendency to immorality which characterised the parent is bequeathed to the offspring—the moral disease requires a cure—under a *healthy social condition* that cure will be found in the poverty which has followed in its train. The malady provides its own remedy—the poor-law right prevents that remedy from being administered.

Let not this be misunderstood: it has no reference to the present distresses of the people; it only applies to the few cases of individual destitution, which would occur in a well-governed country.

A natural right may, usually, be easily defined. Its

---

[4] This must not be construed into a reflection upon voluntary benevolence. If, for the sake of ameliorating, to a certain extent, the miseries of the wicked, the Almighty has seen well to implant in their fellow-creatures, sympathies, which shall induce them to pity and assist, it must be at once concluded that the exercise of those sympathies, is conducive to the general happiness. But, this admission in no way involves the approval of a systematic arrangement, set up by fallible men, for the purpose of doing by wholesale, what the Almighty has only seen fit to do partially. Meanwhile, it is greatly to be wished that the charitable, would use a more judicious discrimination, in the distribution of their gifts, and extend their assistance rather to unfortunate industry, than to suffering wickedness.

boundaries are self-existent. But it is not so with the poor law principle. It says that every man has a right to a maintenance out of the soil. But what is a maintenance? One party says that a bare subsistence is all that is implied. Another, that the applicant can demand all the comforts usually enjoyed by those in his station. Another, that he may as fairly claim the luxuries of life as those above him. And the extreme party will be content with nothing short of the socialist principle, of community of property. Who is to say which of these is the true expression of the right? The gradations are infinite, and how can it be decided where the claim begins and where it ends? Who can tell the rate-payer how much of his property can be justly demanded by his fellow creature? Who can tell the pauper when he asks for more pay, that he receives just as much as he is entitled to? or can explain to him why he has a right to what he already receives, but no right to anything more? And yet, if this were really a right, ought it not to be capable of such a definition?

It is said that property is a conventionalism—that its accumulation by the few, is injurious to the interests of the many—that its very existence is detrimental to those excluded from its enjoyment—and that they have consequently a claim on those possessing it. But is property a conventionalism? Let us investigate this question.

Paley says, "Whatever is expedient is right." This is a startling assertion; but it must be remembered, that the word "expedient" is not used in its ordinary sense. It does not here mean that which will best serve present purposes, but that whose effects, both present and future, direct and collateral, will be most beneficial. He does not defend that expediency which would sacrifice the future welfare of a nation to the interests of the present hour; but, he calls that expedient, the total sum of whose good results, immediate and expectant, is greater than that of its bad ones. When the expression is interpreted in this extended sense, when the evils and benefits that may arise in distant ages, meet with the same consideration as the effects of today, the assertion no longer appears extraordinary. Some moralists have, on the strength of this, accused Paley of setting up a standard of right and wrong, independent of that afforded by the Christian religion. They say that he has first acknowledged that the precepts of the gospel form our only safe guide, and then brings forward a principle in opposition to them. They mistake his position. He brings forward a principle not in opposition to, but in accordance with, those precepts. He holds up to view the grand fundamental law, upon which all the commands of our religion are based. He enunciates the great proposition from which the doctrines of Christianity are so many corollaries. God wills the happiness of man. That happiness depends upon the fulfilment of certain conditions. He gives him laws, by obeying which he satisfies those conditions. He says, "Thou shalt not steal"; and why? Because, although the thief may experience a temporary gratification in the acquisition of stolen property, not only is this counterbalanced by the corresponding annoyance on the part of the loser, but the thief himself, as well as every other member of the community, is in constant fear of similar losses. So that the sorrow of losing, added to the general fear of robbery, far outweighs the individual pleasure of acquirement. It follows, then, that obedience to the command, "Thou shalt not steal," is eminently conducive to the general happiness: that is, it is "expedient." Again, man is told to love his neighbour as himself; and why? Because by so doing, he not only increases the comfort of his fellow-creatures, but he also himself reaps a rich reward, in the pleasure that flows from the exercise of genuine benevolence. And similarly in the analysis of every other case, we find that the general happiness is the great end in view; that the commands of the Almighty are such as will best secure that happiness, and hence, that "expediency" is the primitive law of human governance. If, having admitted the truth of this conclusion, we have certain cases presented to us, on which we have no direct expression of the divine will, our proper course is to appeal to the principle which we discover to be in accordance with the spirit of that will. Let us then apply the test to the question in hand.

First—Is the institution of private property expedient? It is. Man's happiness greatly depends upon the satisfaction of his temporal wants. The fruits of the earth are a necessary means of satisfying those wants. Those fruits can never be produced in abundance without cultivation. That cultivation will never prevail without the stimulus of certain possession. No man will sow when others may reap. We have abundant proof of this, in the history of every savage nation. Moreover, we see that so long as their bodily cravings are unsatisfied, men will make no social progress. Without ample provision of food and clothing, they have no time for becoming civilised. And not becoming civilised, is the same thing as making no moral or intellectual advances. And remaining in mental darkness, involves entire insensibility to the highest pleasures, of which the Creator has made human nature capable. Hence, property greatly promotes the mental and bodily happiness of mankind; that is, it is expedient. It must also be borne in mind, that although the test of expediency has been appealed to, in default of any direct command from the Almighty; the scriptures contain abundance of indirect evidence of his will in this matter. Not only in numerous instances does the bible inculcate duties, in which the institution of private property is virtually recognised, but it has one precept, which is clearly decisive. The single command, "Thou shalt not steal," carries with it a complete charter of the rights of possession. Lastly—if these arguments were inconclusive, the simple fact, that there is implanted in every man, a desire to possess, which desire, by the accumulation of property, may be gratified *without injury to his fellow-creatures*, this fact is in itself ample proof, that individual possession is in accordance with the will of the Creator. It follows, therefore, from the law of expediency directly, from the constitution of man directly, and from the revealed will of God by implication, that property is not a *conventional*, but a *natural*, institution.

Now we must either admit the right of possession entirely, or deny it altogether. We cannot say to a man, "So much of the substance you have acquired by your labour is your own, and so much belongs to your fellow-creatures." We cannot divide the right. Either it is a right, or it is not. There is no medium. We must say yes or no. If then, after a review of the arguments, we allow that property is an institution natural to civilised man: if we admit also, what necessarily follows from this—the right of individual possession—and admit that too, as we must, to its full extent; if we do this, the poor-law right vanishes entirely. The two are totally inconsistent, and cannot co-exist.

To return to the test of expediency. The poor law has already been measured by this principle, and found wanting. It was shown that many and great are the evils, that have flowed, and must flow, from its acknowledgment; that those evils have far more than counterbalanced the benefits; and that all the good results, and none of the bad ones, would follow from the substitution of voluntary charity. If the reasoning was conclusive, the right is rejected, without the necessity of an appeal to any of the preceding arguments.

It is submitted, therefore:

1. That under circumstances like ours, in which the poor man is prevented from earning his subsistence by his labour, it is not our duty to give the subsistence without the labour, but to break down those barriers to productive industry, which selfish legislators have set up, and to place the labourer in his proper position, by restoring society to its natural state.

2. That by allowing the wicked to take advantage of the right held out by the poor law, we not only annul the

just punishment awarded to them, but we also take away the most effectual prompter to repentance and improvement.

3. That a real right usually admits of a clear definition, but that the supposed poor-law does not.

4. That the institution of property, is sanctioned by the law of expediency, by the implied will of God, and by the constitution of man; and that if we acknowledge its rights, we must deny those sought to be established by the poor law.

5. That the admission of a claim to a maintenance out of the soil, is not only inconsistent with the rights of property, but that it is in itself productive of more evil than good; that is, it is inexpedient: and if it is inexpedient it cannot be a right.

Letter V

It will probably be objected to the proposed theory of government, that if the administration of justice were the only duty of the state, it would evidently be out of its power to regulate our relations with other countries, to make treaties with foreign powers, to enter into any kind of international arrangement whatever, or to levy wars that might be absolutely necessary.

So much of the objection as relates to the absence of power to make treaties, may be disregarded. Commerce, or war, are nearly always, directly or indirectly, the subjects of negotiation between governments, and as free trade is presupposed by the definition, it is clear that commercial treaties would never be called for. The whole

of the objection is therefore comprised in its last clause—
viz., the want of power to make war. Instead of viewing
such a result as an evil, we should rather hail it as one
of the greatest benefits that could arise from the recognition of this principle. War has been the source of the
greatest of England's burdens. Our landowners would
probably never have dared to enact the corn laws, had
not the people been intoxicated by the seeming prosperity arising from war. The national debt, with all its
direful consequences, would not have been in existence,
had our rulers been deprived of the power of going to
war. Our country would never have been drained of the
hard earnings of her industrious sons, had not the un-
curbed ambition of the aristocracy involved us in war.
Capital that would have constructed all our railways
many times over—that would have given every facility
to commerce—that would have set it upon a real instead
of a nominal foundation—property, the accumulated labour of generations, the grand national store in time of
need, is gone for ever. Not only does England suffer
from the yearly draught upon its resources demanded
by the national debt, it feels likewise the loss of the property of which that debt is the representative. Not only
has the nation to pay the interest, it has lost the principal
also.

Many entertain the opinion that war is essentially beneficial to the community—that it invigorates the social
organism; and they refer to the commercial energy, exhibited during the late continental campaigns, in proof
of their assertion. But if, on the one hand, they would
bear in mind the accidental influences by which such

state was induced; whilst, on the other, they turned their attention to the sufferings experienced by the lower orders, during that period, rather than to the aggrandisement of the trading classes, perhaps they would come to a different conclusion. And, even admitting that war produces temporary good, it infallibly inflicts a more than equivalent injury. It acts upon a nation, as wine does upon a man. It creates the same unnatural activity—the same appearance of increased strength. In a similar manner does it call forth the supplies of life and energy provided for the future; in like fashion is the excitement followed by a corresponding depression; and so likewise is the strength of the constitution gradually undermined; and the short-sighted politician, who, judging by the apparent prosperity it produces, pronounces war a benefit to a nation, is falling into the same error, as the man who concludes that a spirituous stimulant is permanently strengthening, because he experiences an accession of vigour whilst under its influence.

War has been the nurse of the feudal spirit so long the curse of all nations; and from that spirit has flowed much of the selfish and tyrannical legislation under which we have so long groaned. If, for the last four or five centuries, the civilised world, instead of having been engaged in invasions and conquests, had directed its attention to the real sources of wealth—industry and commerce, science and the arts—long since would our nobility have found that they were mere drones in the hive, and long since would they have ceased to glory in their shame.

When to the political and commercial evils of war, we add the moral ones, when we remember that it is inconsistent with the spirit of Christianity—that it unduly encourages animal passions—that it exalts brute courage into the greatest of human virtues—that it tends greatly to retard the civilisation of the world—that it is the grand bar to the extension of that feeling of universal brotherhood with all nations, so essential to the real prosperity of mankind: when, in addition to these collateral evils, we call to mind the immediate ones—the horrors of battle, and the lamentations of kindred—we shall rather feel, that a principle which of necessity excludes these things, should, on that account alone, earnestly commend itself to our notice.

We are told that the time shall come, when nations "shall beat their swords into ploughshares, and their spears into pruning hooks." That time may be yet afar off, but we are advancing towards it—we shall eventually arrive at it, and that too, we may assure ourselves, not by any sudden revolution, but by a continued moral and intellectual progression. We must not wait for a direct interposition of the Almighty to bring about this change; we must use proper means; we must put our shoulders to the wheel, and then look for the fulfilment of the promise as the result of our obedience to the commands. But what are the means? One of them we have before us. Confine the attention of our rulers to their only duty, the administration of justice; and, as far as we are concerned, the prophecy is fulfilled. Many will ask, "What would be the use of our relinquishing war, unless other nations will agree to do so likewise?" The same parties frequently put a similar question, by way of an excuse for not assisting in the reformation of social

abuses—What can one man do? Need they be told that
men never come unanimously to the same conclusion,
at the same time, and that it is impossible they should
do so? Need they be told that all great changes have
emanated from individuals? Need they be told that what
each leaves to the rest, no one does? Would that every
man would cease such puerile pretences, and stand
boldly forward to do his duty. National evils would then
soon be rectified. What is here true of men individually,
is true of men in masses. Never need we expect to see
all nations abandon war at the same time. One must lead
the way. Let England be that one. Let Britain first hold
up the fair flag of peace. Let our nation act up to the
spirit of its religion, without waiting for others to do the
same. Not only would precept and example induce
neighbouring states to follow, but new influences would
come into play. Steps would quickly be taken to establish
the long-talked-of system of national arbitration. Mankind would open their eyes to the advantages of a peaceful decision of state disputes; appeal to arms would
become less and less frequent, and soon should we cease
to applaud in nations, that litigious and unchristian
spirit, and those barbarous notions of "honour," which
we have learned to despise in individuals.

"But," I am asked, "is there no such thing as a necessary war?" In theory perhaps there may be; but it is
very rarely to be seen in practice. Is our war with China
necessary? Is our war with Afghanistan necessary? Was
our war with Syria necessary? Was our war with France
necessary? Was our war with America necessary? No. In

defending ourselves against an invasion, we might perhaps be said to be engaged in a necessary war, but in no
other case; and England has but little to fear on that
score. Improbable, however, as such an event may be,
let us, for the sake of argument, imagine that we involve
ourselves in a quarrel with some foreign state, which
ends in their attacking us, one of two things must happen. Either we repel the attack, or we do not. Many there
are, who, under such circumstances, would look for an
intervention of providence; others who would trust to
the principle of passive resistance. But, without shelter-
ing under either of these, let us suppose that active defence is necessary. That defence may be conducted in
two ways. Either the nation at large must provide for it
independently of the state, must call together a council
of war, volunteer supplies, and make all other necessary
arrangements; or the government must itself, as heretofore, take the affair into its own hands. The first of
these alternatives may appear impracticable; but it is
questionable whether such impression does not arise
from its disagreement with our preconceived notions,
rather than from any reasonable conviction. The wars of
savage nations have very frequently been carried on
without the guidance of any fixed executive power. We
have instances, too, in civilised countries, of rebellions
in which successful war has been maintained in opposition to the government. How much more, then, might
we expect an efficient resistance in such a highly organised social condition as our own? But admitting the
impracticability of this principle—assuming that the in-

terference of the state would be necessary in such cases, what follows? The insufficiency of the original definition, and the consequent sacrifice of the doctrines propounded? No such thing. Strange as it may seem, the admission of such a necessity is no derogation to the theory before us. The question has hitherto been considered in its application to England only, because the cases brought forward have had exclusive reference to internal policy; but, in the present instance, in which international affairs are involved, we must no longer suppose such a limited sphere of action. Some moral laws cannot receive their perfect development unless universally acknowledged; they do not agree with the present state of things, and they cannot be measured by an arbitrary standard, with which they are professedly inconsistent. To imagine one part of mankind acting upon a certain principle—to perceive that they will be obliged to infringe that principle, in their intercourse with the rest who are acting under other guidance, and thence to infer that the principle is at fault, is anything but logical. We must give the system fair play, allow it a general application; and test it in accordance with its own conditions. Suppose, then, that all nations confined the attention of their governments, to the administration of justice, aggressive war would cease; but when aggressive war ceases, defensive war becomes unnecessary. We see, therefore, that the concession that it might be requisite for the state to interfere in cases of invasion, implies no error in the definition. The exception would result, not from any inherent imperfection in the principle, but from its confined application.

The positions are these:

1. That war is a great evil, and that the fact of its exclusion by a proposed definition, is a powerful argument in favour of that definition.

2. That depriving our rulers of the power to make war, would be one of the most effectual means within our reach, of hastening that period, when "nation shall not lift up sword against nation."

3. That resistance to invasion is the only war that has any claim to the title of necessary, and that we have little need to fear its requisition.

4. That even assuming the occurrence of a descent upon our shores, and allowing that the interference of the state would in that case be necessary; the exception shows no defect in our principle, but merely a want of extension in its practice.

Letter VI

Colonisation may possibly appear to some, to be a stumbling-block in their way to the desirable conclusion, that the administration of justice is the only duty of the state. We may anticipate the question—What would the colonies do without our governance and protection? I think facts will bear me out in replying—Far better than they do with them.

The subject naturally ranges itself under three heads— the interests of the mother country, of the emigrants, and of the aborigines. First, then, the interests of the mother country.

The records of ancient nations have ever, shown that the riches of a community, do not depend upon the acquirement of new territory; our own history bears ample testimony of the same character, and our present experience in every instance confirms that testimony. The well known case of the United States may be cited as an example. Whilst that country was a colony, it was a burden to us; the expenses attending its government were far greater than the profits derived from its trade; but since it has become an independent kingdom, it has been a source of great gain. Canada stands to us in the same position that the United States once did; its distance from us is the same, its commercial advantages are greater, it has the benefit of increased civilisation, and yet, like its prototype, it does not repay the cost of its management. Hindostan may be pointed out as another illustration. The statement of the East India company's profit and loss shows that, in this case also, the balance is against us; and that our enormous oriental possessions have been an injury instead of a benefit. Yet, in spite of these and many similar instances, it is still tacitly assumed that extensive territorial property is synonymous with wealth.

Men argue that, by monopolising the colonial trade, we obtain a more extended market for our produce than we should otherwise have, and that this must needs be a great benefit. The position is a very plausible, but a no less fallacious, one. We monopolise their trade from one of two causes. Either we make the articles they consume at a lower rate than any other nation, or we oblige them to buy those articles from us, though they might obtain

them for less elsewhere. If we can undersell other producers, it is plain that we should still exclusively supply
the market, were the colonies independent. If we cannot
undersell them, it may be made equally clear that we are
indirectly injuring ourselves to a greater extent than we
are benefited by the monopoly. For, if the colonists take
our manufactures, we must take their produce—they
cannot pay us in money. Now, the prices of the articles
which they barter for our manufactures (the demand
remaining constant, as it must) are regulated by the cost
of their production; and the cost of their production,
other things being the same, depends upon the prices of
the commodities which they have to purchase. If two
parties agree to deal exclusively with each other, and one
of them doubles his charges, it is clear that the other
cannot continue to trade with him, unless he advances
his terms in the same ratio. So that by making the colonists pay an extra price for certain merchandise with
which we supply them, we do but cause an equivalent
increase in the cost of the produce which they send in
exchange, and thus entirely neutralise the supposed advantage. Nor is this all. "Each country," says M'Culloch,
"has some natural or acquired capabilities that enable
her to carry on certain branches of industry more advantageously than any one else. But the fact of a country
being undersold in the markets of her colonies, shows
conclusively that, instead of having any superiority, she
labours under a disadvantage, as compared with others,
in the production of the peculiar articles in demand in
them. And hence, in providing a forced market in the
colonies, for articles that we should not otherwise be

able to dispose of, we really engage a portion of the capital and labour of the country in a less advantageous channel than that into which it would naturally have flowed." That system only is beneficial to the world at large, and to each nation individually, under which every commodity is obtained with the least expenditure of time and labour. Were it otherwise, we might as well grow sugar and cotton in English hot-houses, and then flatter ourselves that we were deriving advantage from the encouragement of home-grown instead of foreign produce!

We come, then, to the conclusion that, in this case, as in every other, the country loses by this exclusive dealing. But who are the gainers? The monopolists. And who are the monopolists? The aristocracy. Into their pockets, in the shape of salaries to civil and military officers, dividends of profits, etc., has gone a large part of the enormous revenue of the East India company.[5] Into their pockets goes the great bulk of the extra four millions a year which we pay for Jamaica sugar. Into their pockets has gone the large additional sum annually paid by the nation for coffee and other colonial articles, more than would have been paid but for the protection afforded to West India productions. The colonies, then, do but resolve themselves into another channel, through which the earnings of industry flow into the coffers of idleness. The rich owners of colonial property must have protection, as well as their brethren, the landowners of England—the one their prohibitive duties, the other

---

[5] See "Wealth of Nations," vol. iii, p. 257.

their corn laws; and the resources of the poor, starved, overburdened people must be still further drained, to augment the overflowing wealth of their rulers.

Secondly, the welfare of the emigrants. In considering this part of the subject, the question may arise—Has not every colonist a claim to protection from the mother country? Custom answers, "Yes." Reason says, "No." Viewed philosophically, a community is a body of men associated together for mutual defence. The members of that community are supposed to occupy a certain territory; and it may be fairly assumed that the privileges conferred are only enjoyed by those residing within that territory. The nation cannot be expected to extend protection to its members wherever they may chance to wander. It cannot be called upon to defend the rights of a citizen in whatever corner of the earth he may choose to locate himself. The natural inference is, that when a man leaves such a community he loses his membership, he forfeits his privileges, and he foregoes all claim to civil assistance. It is presumed that he duly considers, on the one hand, the benefits to be derived by his contemplated emigration, and, on the other, the evils attendant on the loss of citizenship; and that the prospective advantages of a change have the preponderence.

But, waiving the question of right, suppose we examine to what extent the admission of this claim, has, in time past, been of use to the emigrant. Let us inquire how far the history of our colonies, bears evidence of the proffered protection. In the declaration of American independence, we have a candid expression of the experience of the settlers on this point; and the document may be referred to, as exhibiting a fair abstract of the effects of home-country governance. Speaking of the king—the personification of the mother country, they say,—

"He has obstructed the administration of justice by refusing his assent to laws for establishing judiciary powers.

He has erected a multitude of new offices, and sent hither swarms of officers to harass our people, and eat out their substance.

He has kept among us in times of peace standing armies, without the consent of our legislatures.

He has combined with others to subject us to a jurisdiction foreign to our constitution, and unacknowledged by our laws; giving his assent to their pretended acts of legislation.

For quartering large bodies of armed troops among us.

For protecting them by a mock trial from punishment for any murders which they should commit on the inhabitants of these states.

For cutting off our trade with all parts of the world.

For imposing taxes upon us without our consent.

For depriving us in many cases of the benefits of trial by jury," etc.

Truly we have here, some admirable specimens of the blessings of mother-country protection! Nor are we without analogous instances in our times. The late outbreak in Canada, is a plain indication, of the existence of a similar state of things, to that once experienced by the Americans. And, it is extremely probable, that were we to put it to the Canadians, whether we should continue to take care of them, they would reply, that if it were the same thing to us, they would much rather take care of themselves! We may turn for another example to the settlements in Australia. A living illustration here presents itself, of the evils resulting from the officious interference of our legislature. Thousands of poor emigrants who have been sent out by government, are now without employment, subsisting upon the contributions of the charitable, and almost in a state of starvation. The distress has arisen from the exportation of large bodies of labourers, whilst there has been no corresponding increase in the number of capitalists. Had this colony been left to itself, labour and capital would have kept pace with each other, as they always have done, and always will do; but a meddling state, must needs attempt to regulate the natural laws of society, and hence the calamitous result. Many similar instances,[6] of the injury inflicted upon emigrants, under the pretence of protection, might be quoted, were not those already mentioned sufficiently conclusive.

Thirdly—the interests of the aborigines. A first glance at the bearings of the question, is sufficient to show, that the natives of colonised countries, will meet with much better treatment, at the hands of those settlers, whose emigration has been gradual and unprotected, than from

---

[6] The East and West Indies, cannot be considered as applicable cases, as far as regards the colonists. The greater number of their European inhabitants, are only temporary residents, and nearly all the remainder are either branches of the aristocracy, or their agents, and these are not legislated for as ordinary emigrants.

those who are aided by a powerful government, and backed by a military force. In the one case, being the weaker party, the colonists are obliged to stand on their good behaviour, and are induced, through fear, to deal justly with the owners of the soil; in the other, acting upon the barbarous maxim that they have a lawful right to whatever territories they can conquer, forcible possession of the new country, is taken—a continued scene of oppression and bloodshed ensues, and the extermination of the injured race, is, in many cases, the consequence. This is no imaginary picture. Our colonial history, to our shame be it spoken, is full of the injustice and cruelty, to which the original possessors of the soil have been subjected. The extinct tribes of the North American Indians, bear witness of the fact; the gradual retreat of the natives of Australia, may be quoted in support of it; and the miserable condition of the inhabitants of the East Indies, speaks volumes, on the inhumanity attendant upon state colonisation. The ryots, or cultivators of the soil, in Hindostan, are taxed to the extent of nearly one-half of what they produce,[7] and that, by a foreign government, in which they have no voice—which is oppressing them in all directions, and apparently views them as beings created only for the purpose of producing revenue. Another portion of the population is induced to aid our troops, in the support of this despotic government, and whole regiments of them have been put to death, for daring to disobey the tyrannical commands of their oppressors. The recent affair in

---

[7] See M'Culloch, Art. East India Company.

Afghanistan, affords a further example. Not satisfied with the immense empire already within their grasp, our Eastern government, like the wolf in the fable, must needs find a pretext for quarreling with a neighbouring nation, with the ultimate intention[8] of obtaining possession of their country. And in that war too, some of its officers have been guilty of treachery, of which many a savage would have been ashamed. Thus it is that we exemplify the sublime principles of Christianity.

Having assigned reasons for condemning the artificial system of colonisation, it only remains to inquire, how far the natural system, may be considered feasible. There will be no occasion to enter into any arguments. We may at once appeal to experience, and that experience is conclusive. Pennsylvania affords an admirable example, of a colony originated, and carried out, solely by private enterprise; a colony in which the claims of all parties were duly respected—where natives met with honourable treatment, where strangers as well as friends could obtain justice; a colony that long stood pre-eminent for its prosperity, and which may even now be said to feel the benefits of the liberal conduct of its founders.

The preceding arguments go to prove:

1. That the riches of a country are not increased by great colonial possessions.

2. That the producing classes, both of the colony and the home country, are necessarily injured by any commercial monopoly.

---

[8] See Sir A. Burns' private and *suppressed* correspondence.

3. That the aristocracy are the only gainers.

4. That emigrants have no claim to protection from the mother country.

5. That where this so-called protection has been given, it has always been converted into an engine for their oppression.

6. That if emigration was carried on by private enterprise, the aborigines, would obviously be less liable to the unjust treatment, which has ever characterised the conduct of civilised settlers towards them.

7. That the case of Pennsylvania, gives ample assurance, of the superiority of the natural system of colonisation.

And hence, that in this case, as well as in those previously discussed, the rejection of legislative interference is eminently desirable.

Letter VII

The question of state interference has been hitherto examined, only in those departments of its application, in which its existing effects are visible—viz., in commerce, religion, charity, war, and colonisation. In all of them that interference has been deprecated. It now remains to consider those social institutions which, though at present prospering in their original unfettered simplicity, are threatened by schemes for legislative supervision. Of these the first in importance stands— education.

It is clear that a system of national instruction is excluded by our definition. It cannot be comprehended under the administration of justice. A man can no more call upon the community to educate his children, than he can demand that it shall feed and clothe them. And he may just as fairly claim a continual supply of material food, for the satisfaction of their bodily wants, as of intellectual food, for the satisfaction of their mental ones. It will be the aim of the succeeding arguments to show the advantages of this exclusion.

Mankind are apt to decide upon the means to be employed in the attainment of an end, without sufficient examination into their fitness. Some great object in contemplation, the most obvious mode of securing it is chosen, without duly considering the extreme importance of discovering whether it is the best mode—without ever inquiring whether its ultimate effects may be as good as its immediate ones—without asking what corruptions the machinery of their institution may be liable to—never putting to themselves the question: Is there any other way of arriving at the desideratum?—and neglecting a host of other considerations of like character. Such is the treatment of the question before us. The education of the people is the end in view; an end fraught with results the most momentous—results more intimately connected with the prosperity and happiness of posterity, than, perhaps, any others that may flow from our conduct—results which may accelerate or retard the advancement of mankind for hundreds, perhaps thousands, of years. Yet are there objections, to the method by which this end is to be compassed, of the utmost consequence, that have been entirely overlooked by its advocates—objections fundamentally affecting the prin-

ciples upon which it rests; and which, if they be admitted
as valid, must completely overthrow the whole scheme.

In the first place, national education assumes that a
uniform system of instruction is desirable. A general
similitude in the kinds of knowledge taught, and the
mode of teaching it, must be necessary features in a
state-training establishment. The question therefore presents itself—Would a universal fixed plan of intellectual
culture be beneficial? After due consideration, I think
the general answer will be—No. Almost all men of enlightened views agree that man is essentially a progressive being—that he was intended to be so by the
Creator—and that there are implanted in him, desires
for improvement, and aspirations after perfection, ultimately tending to produce a higher moral and intellectual condition of the world. The grand facts of history,
both sacred and profane—the great principles and promises of revealed religion—the deductions of abstract reasoning—all go to prove that, notwithstanding the oft-
repeated falling back, in spite of every difficulty that may
be thrown in the way, and in defiance of all apparently
adverse circumstances, still, that the grand and irresistible law of human existence, is progressive improvement. The very obstacles themselves ultimately serve as
stepping stones to a higher condition—the tyranny of
an aristocracy is working out the liberties of the people—
the corruption of an established church has helped to
raise the standard of religious purity—the blindfolding
doctrines of priestcraft produce the more perfect discovery, and the still deeper appreciation of the great principles of Christianity—and, as of old, so in our day, the

opposition to truth, still tends to accelerate its final triumph. If, then, the belief set forth at the commencement of this essay—that as there are laws for the guidance of the inorganic world—laws for the government of the animate creation—laws for the development of individual mind—so there are laws for the social governance of man—if, I say, this belief be received, it may be fairly assumed, that, in accordance with the great design of human progression, the Almighty has given laws to the general mind, which are ever working together for its advancement. It may be fairly assumed that, in this case as in the more tangible ones, the apparently untoward circumstances are, in reality, eminently conducive to the attainment of the object sought after. That all the prejudices, the mental idiosyncrasies, the love of opposition, the tendencies to peculiar views, and a host of other qualities, in their infinitely varied proportions and combinations, are all conspiring to bring about the intellectual, moral, and social perfection of the human race. If it be granted that man was created a progressive being, it must be granted, also, that the constitution, given to him by his Creator, was the one most perfectly adapted to secure his progression. It may be presumed that, if a uniform construction of mind had been best calculated to attain this end, it would have been adopted; but, as the opposite law has been given—so that, instead of finding minds similar, we find no two alike—unlimited variety, instead of uniformity, being the existing order of things—we must infer that this is the arrangement tending, in the greatest degree, to produce perfection. This conclusion may be supported, not only by abstract reasoning, but by experience. Varied mental constitution produces variety of opinion; different minds take different views of the same subject; hence, every question gets examined in all its bearings; and, out of the general mass of argument, urged forward by antagonist parties, may sound principle be elicited. Truth has ever originated from the conflict of mind with mind; it is the bright spark that emanates from the collision of opposing ideas; like a spiritual Venus, the impersonation of moral beauty, it is born from the foam of the clashing waves of public opinion. Discussion and agitation are the necessary agents of its discovery; and, without a universal dissimilitude in the minds of society, discussion and agitation could never exist.

If, then, it be admitted, that infinite variety in the mental conformation of individuals is essential to the advancement of the general human mind, what shall we say to a system which would train the feelings and intellects of a whole nation after one pattern—which hopes to correct all the irregularities implanted by the Creator, and proposes to take the plastic characters of our youth, and press them, as nearly as possible, into one common mould? And yet this must be the manifest tendency of any uniform routine of education. Natures differently constituted must be gradually brought, by its action, into a condition of similarity. The same influences, working upon successive generations, would presently produce an approximation to a national model. All men would begin to think in the same direction—to form similar opinions upon every subject. One universal bias would affect the mind of society; and, instead of a continual approach to the truth, there would be a gradual divergence from it. Under our present condition, the eccentricities and prejudices induced by one course of education, are neutralised by the opposing tendencies implanted by others; and the growth of the great and truthful features only of the national mind ensues. If, on the other hand, an established system were adopted, however judicious its arrangements might be—notwithstanding it might endeavour to promote liberality and independence of thought, it must eventually produce a general one-sidedness and similarity of character; and inasmuch as it did this, it would dry up the grand source of that spirit of agitation and inquiry, so essential as a stimulus to the improvement of the moral and intellectual man. It matters not what provisions might be made to guard against this evil—what varieties in the mode of instruction might be instituted; such is the general longing after uniformity, and such would be the ignorance of its evils, that we may rest assured no national system would long continue without merging into it.

Nor would this be the only disadvantage arising from a sameness of instruction. It must be remembered, that differently constituted as are the minds of men, each possessing its peculiar perfections and defects, the same mode of culture cannot with any propriety be pursued in all cases. Every character requires a course of treatment somewhat modified to suit its particular circumstances, and no such modifications are ever likely to be made under a national system. It is to be hoped that the time will come, when the wisdom of the teacher will be shown, in adapting his instructions, to the peculiarities

of each of his pupils: when it will be his aim to correct
this feeling, and to develop the other faculty, and so to
train and prune the mind of every scholar, as to send
him forth into the world, as perfect a being as possible.
Under our present natural arrangement we may one day
expect to see this. While the master is amenable to public
opinion—while his interests require that he should
adopt the most efficient modes of education, we may
presume that he will be always zealously endeavouring
to improve his methods—ever investigating the principles of his profession, and daily applying the results of
those investigations to practice. But no one would ever
expect the salaried state-teacher, answerable only to
some superior officer, and having no public reputation
at stake to stimulate him—no one would expect that he
should study the character of each of his scholars, and
vary his ordinary routine to suit each case; no one would
expect that he should be continually improving, and
ever endeavouring to perfect his moral machinery. We
may rest assured, that in education as in everything else,
the principle of honourable competition, is the only one
that can give present satisfaction, or hold out promise of
future perfection.

Probably, the existing educational institutions of Prus-
sia and Germany will be appealed to in evidence of the
fallacy of these arguments. It may be urged that the plan
has been there many years in operation—that no such
evils have arisen—that the people are in a comparatively
enlightened condition—and that these results, when
contrasted with our own, show that we have not made
such great advances under the natural system, as they

have under the artificial.[9] Strong as this argument may appear, it will be found when closely considered, to be wholly superficial. The foundations of a palace may be hardly above ground, when an ordinary house is nearly complete; but we do not thence infer that the palace will not ultimately be the most magnificent building. It is not argued that because the hot-house plant outstrips its out-door contemporaries, that it will therefore make the most perfect tree; experience teaches the contrary. We do not conclude that the precocious child will make a better man than his less forward companion; we know that the reverse is generally the case. In the same manner, it must be remembered, that although an established education, may, for a time, stimulate the national mind into a rapid growth, we must not therefore presume, that its results will not be ultimately far surpassed by those of the natural system. It is one of the grand laws of creation, that the more perfect the being, the longer must be the time occupied in its development; and analogy would lead us to suppose, that the same may be true of the general mind of man—that the more noble the standard to which it is to attain, the more gradual must be its advancement—the more distant must be the day when it shall arrive at its climax; that the power which is to lead to its highest pinnacle of perfection,

---

[9] Since this was originally published, works have appeared, containing abundant evidence that the boasted intellectual enlightenment produced by government education on the continent, is more than neutralised, by the moral degradation that has accompanied it, and showing that these state-trained nations, are decidedly inferior to the people of this country, in real manliness. Those who are in love with the Prussian system would do well to read Laing's "Notes of a Traveller."

must have a broad and deep foundation—must root itself in some fundamental, and unchangeable attributes of human nature; and that as its results are to be great, so must its action be slow.

Letter VIII

An overwhelming prejudice in favour of ancient and existing usages has ever been, and probably will long continue to be, one of the most prominent characteristics of humanity. No matter how totally inconsistent with the existing condition of society—no matter how utterly unreasonable, both in principle and practice—no matter how eminently absurd, in every respect, such institutions or customs may be—still, if they have but the countenance of fashion or antiquity—if they have but been patronised and handed down to us by our forefathers—their glaring inconsistencies, defects, and puerilities, are so completely hidden by the radiant halo wherewith a blind veneration has invested them, that it is almost impossible to open the dazzled eyes of the world, to an unprejudiced view of them. They are reverenced as relics of the so-called "good old times"—reason and philosophy are laid prostrate before them—and the attempt to introduce amendment is akin to sacrilege. Classical education affords a suitable illustration of this. During those dreary times of rampant Roman catholicism, when ecclesiastical dominion had attained its full growth, and all Europe, under its deadly shade, slumbered in dark and debasing ignorance, it became the practice amongst the more enlightened, to make themselves acquainted with the ancient languages, for the purpose of gaining access to the knowledge that was written in them; writings in their own tongue they had none—learning had fallen into neglect, and their only path to a condition above that of the common herd, was through the study of Latin and Greek. In process of time, however, great changes were effected. Man was not doomed to remain for ever in a state of spiritual bondage—the social mind awoke with new vigour from its long sleep—ignorance and bigotry were swept away by the returning tide of intelligence—science and philosophy soared far above the height to which they had before attained—and the knowledge of the ancients dwindled into insignificance, when compared with that of the moderns. It might have been presumed that, under these circumstances, the dead languages would gradually have sunk into disuse. But, no! such is the extreme veneration for precedent—such is the determined adherence to the practices of our ancestors, that, notwithstanding the conditions of the case are entirely altered—although the original necessities no longer exist, still is the same custom persevered in. It boots not to tell them that words are but the signs of ideas, and not the ideas themselves—that language is but a channel for the communication of knowledge—a means to an end; and that it is valuable only in so far as it serves that end. It matters not how clearly it may be shown that he who learns a language for its own sake, is like a workman who constructs a set of tools at immense cost of time and labour, and never afterwards uses them; or like a man who spends the best years of his life in making a ladder, for the purpose of gathering a scanty supply of indifferent fruit from the top of a high tree, when other fruit, of superior quality, is hanging in abundance within reach on a neighbouring one. No matter, I say, how clearly this may be shown, so great is the influence of ancient prescription, and so strong the desire to "do as the world does," that even in this enlightened age, men neglect the rich stores of real knowledge within their grasp, to follow fashion over the barren waste of grammars and lexicons.

Here then stands an example of a system, which, in spite of its many and manifest absurdities, has for centuries bid defiance to the general flood of improvement; and stands in the midst of our progressing social institutions, its main features unaltered from their original condition. What may we infer from this? Does it not warn us of the dangerous consequences that may ensue, from the erection of any lasting scheme of education? If a system, not nationally established, but rooted only in the prejudices, and sheltered by the bias of society, has been able thus to withstand for ages, the assaults of reason and common sense, how much more difficult would it be to reform one, which, in addition to these supporting influences, should receive the protection of the law? It may indeed be provided that the power of remodelling such an establishment be placed in the hands of the people, but practically this would amount to nothing. We have abundant evidence of the almost insuperable difficulties attending the modification of existing institutions, even when the people have theoretically the means of altering them; and we have no right to assume, that these difficulties would not, to a great degree, exist in time to come. Take, for instance, the church. The national body of dissenters are of opinion, that many of its ordinances, services, and ceremonies, require amendment; the great mass of its own communicants think the same; its founders themselves contemplated such a revision; there are no class interests at stake; the amendments alluded to would entail no loss upon the ecclesiastical body; yet, with all these circumstances in favour of a re-arrangement, things remain as they were. How much greater, then, would be the obstacles in reforming an institution, where any extensive change, would probably incapacitate many of its officers?

Even allowing, for a moment, that there would be no great difficulty in introducing improvements into a system of national education; the important question yet remains—Would the people see the necessity for those improvements? Analogy would lead us to answer—No. The blinding effects of prejudice in favour of existing modes of instruction has already been pointed out, and every day presents us with cases illustrative of the same influence. Ask the classical scholar his opinion of mathematics; or the mathematician what he thinks of geology, chemistry, or physiology, and both their answers will imply a bias in favour of their own kind of education.

It is argued, therefore, that men would never appreciate the imperfections of a mode of teaching, under which they had been brought up; and that even if they did, it would be extremely difficult for them to make any amendments. Should the truth of these conclusions be admitted, there remains but one ground upon which a state education can be defended; namely, the assump-

tion, that it would never require any reform; which is
the same thing as saying, that we of the present day,
have attained to the pinnacle of mental elevation—that
we have duly determined the relative merits of the various kinds of information, and are prepared to point out
the most complete scheme of intellectual training—that
we are fully competent to decide, not only for ourselves,
but for future generations, what are the most valuable
branches of knowledge, and what are the best modes of
instruction; and that, being perfect masters of the philosophy of mind, we are quite justified in dictating to
our successors. Truly a most sensible supposition!

Presuming that all other considerations were favourable, it still behoves us seriously to inquire—What guarantee have we that the beneficial results intended to be
secured would, in future ages, be realised? How do we
know that the evils and perversions that have never yet
been kept out of social institutions by the most perfect
human arrangements, would not creep in here also, to
the ultimate destruction of the proposed advantages?
No satisfactory answer can be given to these questions.
We may feel fully convinced, that corruptions and
abuses would gradually make their appearance, in defiance of the most carefully regulated provisions for their
exclusion—despite of all our endeavours to ensure good
management. Again may we turn to the church for an
example. Little did our protestant reformers suspect,
that the machinery they were about to employ for the
support of their religion, was destined to become a tool
for political party—an instrument for extortion—a gen-
teel means of gaining a comfortable living—a thing of

outside purity and inward depravity—a mere heap of worldliness. True, they had before their eyes the glaring abominations of the church which they had over-turned; but they intended to provide against the recurrence of such calamities. And how have they succeeded? As with them, so with us. We may depend upon it that, were the scheme of state instruction carried out, ere a century was expired, we should have educational sinecures, pluralities, non-resident tutors, highly-paid master, and half-starved teachers, wealthy inspectors, lay patrons, purchasable livings, and numberless other perversions analogous to those of our national church; whilst the whole institution would resolve itself, like its representative, into a field for aristocratic patronage. Surely, if Christianity, the most powerful of all moral antiseptics, has been unable to keep pure, the apparatus devoted to its own ministration; much less can we anticipate freedom from corruption, where the same temptations would exist unopposed by the like preserving influences. It is of no use saying that the people would never again allow such iniquities to be practised. So, in all probability, thought the founders of our state church. But the people *have* allowed them—they *have* had the power to prevent abuses, and have never used it; and we have no right to assume that they would not be equally negligent in time to come.

Another objection, stronger perhaps than any of the foregoing, still remains. The advocates of national education, if they be men who uphold freedom of conscience—if they do not desire one man to pay towards the support of privileges enjoyed only by others—in a word, if they are friends to civil and religious liberty, must necessarily assume that all members of the community, whether churchmen or dissenters, catholics or jews, tories, whigs, radicals, or republicans, will agree, one and all, to support whatever system may be finally adopted. For, if their education is to be truly a national one, it must be managed by the government, and sustained by state funds; those funds must form part of the revenue; that revenue is raised by taxation; that taxation falls upon every individual—upon him that has no children as well as upon him that has; and the result must be, that all would pay towards the maintenance of such an institution, whether they had need of it or not— whether they approved of it or otherwise. Many would, on principle, dissent from a state education, as they would from a state church. Some men would disapprove of the species of instruction—others of the mode of teaching. This man would dislike the moral training— that the intellectual. Here they would disagree upon details—and there protest against the entire system. Would it then be just, would it be reasonable, to let these men bear the burden of an institution from which they derived no benefit? Surely not. Every argument used by religious nonconformists to show the unfairness of calling upon them to uphold doctrines that they cannot countenance, or subscribe towards a ministration which they do not attend, is equally effective in proving the injustice of compelling men to assist in the maintenance of a plan of instruction inconsistent with their principles; and forcing them to pay for teaching, from which neither they nor their children derive any benefit. In the one case, the spread of religious knowledge is the object aimed at—in the other the spread of secular knowledge; and how this difference could affect the right of dissent it would be difficult to discover.

Before dismissing the subject, it may be as well to remark that, rather than see the people educated by means over which they have no control, our government would, no doubt, be very happy to take the task of instruction into their own hands; and we may pretty accurately anticipate what the tendencies of that instruction would be. Bold and independent reasoning, originality of thought, firmness in defence of principles, and all characteristics of that class, we need little expect to be encouraged. Great veneration for authority, a high respect for superiors, and implicit faith in the opinions of the great and learned, would no doubt be studiously inculcated. As for their religious education, we may predict that such virtues as meekness and humility would occupy so much attention as to leave no time for the rest; and we may be sure that the teachers would take especial care to instil into the minds of their pupils all those important and fundamental principles of our religion, such as—"Let every soul be subject to the higher powers"— "Servants be obedient to your masters"—"Learn to be content in that station of life to which it has pleased God to call you"; and other such appropriate selections.[10] An apt illustration of the species of mental training our rulers would patronise, is afforded by the late parliamen-

---

[10] That such prophecies would be realized may be gathered from Sir James Graham's late education bill, which has run its brief career since these remarks first appeared.

tary grant for teaching singing. Truly, it would be a lucky thing for the aristocracy, if the people could be persuaded to cultivate their voices instead of their understandings. The nation asks for cheap bread. Their rulers reply—No, we cannot give you cheap bread, because we should lose part of our rents; but, never mind, we will put aside part of your own money to give you lessons in music! We will not give you back your food, but we will teach you to sing! O generous legislators!

The objections to national education are:

1. That it necessarily involves a uniform system of moral and intellectual training, from which the destruction of that variety of character, so essential to a national activity of mind, would inevitably result.

2. That it takes away the grand stimulus to exertion and improvement on the part of the teacher, that must ever exist under the natural arrangement.

3. That, considering the improbability of amendments being introduced in future ages, it practically assumes that we are capable of pointing out to our descendants, what kinds of knowledge are the most valuable, and what are the best modes of acquiring them—an assumption which is anything but true.

4. That it would be liable to the same perversions as a national religion, and would, in all probability, become ultimately as corrupt.

5. That, if it is intended to be an equitable institution, it must be necessarily presumed that all men will agree to adopt it—a presumption which can never be borne out.

6. That it would be used by government as a means of blinding the people—of repressing all aspirations after better things—and of keeping them in a state of subserviency.

From abstract reasoning, and from the evident analogy with existing institutions, it is, therefore, concluded, that national education would, in the end, be a curse, rather than a blessing.

Letter IX

"That it is the duty of the state to adopt measures for protecting the health, as well as the property, of its subjects," is the fundamental principle espoused by the Eastern Medical Association of Scotland. The majority of the medical profession hold the same opinion; a respectable portion of the public at large apparently agree with them; and, judging by the enactments that have from time to time been made, the state itself admits the truth of the doctrine. The position is a very plausible one. Some of the arguments urged on its behalf appear, at first sight, decisive. And great seem the evils that might result from the exclusion of legislative control, over matters affecting the sanitary state of the nation. The question, therefore, demands a careful consideration.

An advocate of an established church, may reasonably support this proposition. He maintains that it is one of the duties of a government, to look after the spiritual welfare of the community; that it ought not to permit unauthorised persons to administer to the religious necessities of their fellow-creatures, lest they should instil false doctrines; that without legislative supervision, the moral atmosphere of society would be vitiated by the contagious breath of wickedness; in short, that state superintendence is essential to the spiritual sanity of the nation. Holding these opinions, he may fairly employ similar arguments in reference to the physical condition of the body politic. He may submit that it is improper to allow unqualified persons to administer to the corporeal ailments of the people, lest they should prescribe deleterious medicines, or give dangerous advice; that, in default of legal regulations, the air of our populous towns would become impure from want of ventilation, or be contaminated by the malaria arising from uncleansed sewers, and other sources of corruption; in a word, that government interference is necessary to the preservation of the public health. The analogy between these arguments is obvious. But how stands the dissenter affected towards them? Denying, as he does, their cogency in the one case, he cannot consistently admit it in the other. In the first instance, the spiritual health of the people is the object in view; in the second, their bodily health; and the reasoning that is employed to show that legislation is not required in the one case, will go far to prove its needlessness in the other.

One would have thought that in these anti-monopoly days, when the calamities resulting from selfish legislation have awakened public attention, men would take especial care not to permit anything involving an approach to exclusive privileges, to make its appearance upon the political arena, without raising a vigorous outcry against it. But the expectation is not realised. The doctrine that it is the duty of the state to protect the public health, contains the germ of another gigantic monopoly. Years ago did that germ first show itself, in the shape of an enactment for restricting the prescribing practice of chemists and druggists. Again, is the noxious parasite gathering together its energies, to make another and stronger shoot, under the form of a more stringent law for the same purpose. That object gained, and some greater extension of power will be its aim. Already do the professional publications of the day, contain rumours of medical directors, medical inspectors, and various grades of officers, to be appointed as overseers of the public health. Willingly will the aristocracy come forward and lend a helping hand to so promising a project—one that holds out so inviting a prospect of more berths for their younger sons; and happy will they be to patronise an institution, which shall thus serve as another medium for the absorption of the nation's wealth. In this way, if the people permit, will the system unfold itself, and may, in the lapse of a few generations, finally saddle itself upon the public after the manner of a national church.

It is needless, however, to enter into any arguments to show that medical men are endeavouring to establish a monopoly, for they publicly acknowledge it. They openly avow that they are seeking for protection, and boldly maintain that they have a right to it. But then, it is all done out of a friendly desire to defend the public against quackery! And, in proof of the benefits that the nation is to derive from this exclusive dealing, these patterns of disinterestedness, hold forth upon the danger

of allowing the illiterate to be gulled by unlicensed prac-
titioners. Hear Mr. Wakley. Speaking of a recently revived law relating to chemists and druggists—he says,
"It must have the effect of checking, to a vast extent,
that frightful evil called counter practice, exercised by
unqualified persons, which has so long been a disgrace
to the operation of the laws relating to medicine in this
country, and which, doubtless, has been attended with
a dreadful sacrifice of human life." (*Lancet* for Sept. 11,
1841.) And again, "There is not a chemist and druggist
in the empire who would refuse to prescribe in his own
shop in medical cases, or who would hesitate day by day
to prescribe simple remedies for the ailments of infants
and children." * * * * * "We had previously considered
the evil to be of enormous magnitude, but it is quite clear
that we had under-estimated the extent of the danger to
which the public are exposed." (*Lancet* for Oct. 16, 1841.)
One hardly knows how sufficiently to admire the great
penetration that has discovered this "evil of enormous
magnitude," so completely overlooked by society at
large. Truly, it affords matter for much wonderment, that
the "dreadful sacrifice of human life," resulting from this
"frightful evil," has never yet opened men's eyes to a
sense of the great "danger" of their situation. But would
it not have been more prudent, if this grand discovery
had been made public, and the agitation carried forward
by unprofessional persons? Mr. Wakley should remember, that we are told to avoid the appearance of evil, and
he may discover to his cost, that the world is so suspi-
cious, as to ascribe these seeming fruits of patriotic feeling to some less noble origin. And why does Mr. Wakley

stop short of the full extent of his principle? If it is really the duty of the state to take care of the public health, it is surely bound to adopt the most efficient means of fulfilling that duty. Why not then act upon the old adage, that "prevention is better than cure," endeavour to keep the people always well? Enact a national dietary—prescribe so many meals a day for each individual—fix the quantities and qualities of food, both for men and women, how much animal and how much vegetable— state the proportion of fluids; when to be taken, and of what kind—specify the amount of exercise, and define its character—describe the clothing to be employed— determine the hours of sleep, allowing for the difference of age and sex, and so on with all other particulars, necessary to complete a perfect synopsis, for the daily guidance of the nation. Surely this would be much more efficient than any of these half measures, and, in principle, much about as reasonable. If you insist upon a man getting rid of his ailments according to law, you may as well endeavour to keep him in health by law also.

But seriously, all legislation of the kind desired by Mr. Wakley and his colleagues, virtually, rests upon the assumption, that men are not fitted to take care of themselves. It treats them as so many children. It puts the people into leading strings. Poor things! if we do not look after them, they will be going to ignorant quacks for advice, and, perhaps, get poisoned! Such is practically the language of the state towards its subjects, and the longer they are treated in this manner, the more helpless will they become. If any one foolishly chooses, for the sake of saving a little money, to employ an uneducated empiric he must take the consequences, be they what they may. He has acted under the guidance of his own free will, and, if he suffers, he has no one to blame but himself. Imagine a man to have a watch that wants repairing; and, suppose that, from considerations of economy, he takes it to a blacksmith, who tells him that he can rectify it—the blacksmith spoils it—the man is angry—complains that he has been ill used—enlists a number of the mawkishly benevolent upon his side, and gets them to petition parliament, that all blacksmiths be in future prevented from repairing watches. Who would not laugh at such foolishness? The man was in fault for putting his watch into such hands, and richly deserved the reward of his stupidity. Yet the case is perfectly parallel to the one before us. Instead of his timepiece, he takes himself (a much more complicated machine) to be repaired—he applies to one who knows as little about the human frame, as a blacksmith does about a watch— the ignorant pretender prescribes—the patient gets no better—by and by his constitution is permanently injured, and perhaps he becomes an invalid for life—that is, instead of having his watch spoiled, he has been spoiled himself. But what then? The consequence may be more serious in the one case than in the other, but the man has no greater right to complain. If he had exercised his reason, he might have known, that it was as silly to put his body under the care of one who did not understand its mechanism, as to give a chronometer into the hands of a blacksmith; and there is abstractly no more ground for legislative interference to guard against such imprudence in the one instance than in the other.

A large class of officiously humane people, can never see any social evil, but they propose to pass some law for its future prevention. It never strikes them that the misfortunes of one are lessons for thousands—that the world generally learns more by its mistakes than by its successes—and that it is by the continual endeavour to avoid errors, difficulties, and dangers, that society is to become wiser. It is not for a moment denied that many individuals have been injured by druggists' prescriptions, and quack medicines—some temporarily weakened—others permanently debilitated—and a few perhaps killed outright. But, admitting this, it does not follow that it is not the wisest in the end, to let things take their own course. Such conduct may at first sight appear unkind, but when its effects upon future generations are considered, it will be found to be the reverse. Many arrangements in the animal creation cause much suffering and death, but we do not thence infer that the Almighty is unmerciful. Investigation explains the anomaly, and shows us that these apparent evils are collateral results of laws, ultimately tending to produce the greatest amount of health and happiness, and a careful consideration will satisfy us, that the pains inflicted upon human beings by their own imprudence, are of like character.

There is yet another position from which this question may be considered, and one, perhaps, whence the clearest and most extended view of it can be obtained. All legislation which assists the people in the satisfaction of their natural wants—which provides a fund for their maintenance in illness and old age, educates their children, takes care of their religious instruction, looks after their bodily health, or in any other way does for them what they may be fairly expected to do for themselves, arises from a radically wrong understanding of human existence. It wholly neglects the condition of man's earthly being, and altogether loses sight of one of the great and universal laws of creation.

Every animate creature stands in a specific relation to the external world in which it lives. From the meanest zoophyte, up to the most highly organised of the vertebrata, one and all have certain fixed principles of existence. Each has its varied bodily wants to be satisfied— food to be provided for its proper nourishment—a habitation to be constructed for shelter from the cold, or for defence against enemies—now arrangements to be made for bringing up a brood of young, nests to be built, little ones to be fed and fostered—then a store of provisions to be laid in against winter, and so on, with a variety of other natural desires to be gratified. For the performance of all these operations, every creature has its appropriate organs and instincts—external apparatus and internal faculties; and the health and happiness of each being, are bound up with the perfection and activity of these powers. They, in their turn, are dependent upon the position in which the creature is placed. Surround it with circumstances which preclude the necessity for any one of its faculties, and that faculty will become gradually impaired. Nature provides nothing in vain.

Instincts and organs are only preserved so long as they are required. Place a tribe of animals in a situation where one of their attributes is unnecessary—take away its natural exercise—diminish its activity, and you will gradually destroy its power. Successive generations will see the faculty, or instinct, or whatever it may be, become gradually weaker, and an ultimate degeneracy of the race will inevitably ensue. All this is true of man. He, in like manner, has wants, many and varied—he is provided with moral and intellectual faculties, commensurate with the complexity of his relation to the external world—his happiness essentially depends upon the activity of those faculties; and with him, as with all the rest of the creation, that activity is chiefly influenced by the requirements of his condition. The demands made upon his mental powers by his every day want—by the endeavour to overcome difficulties or avoid dangers, and by the desire to secure a comfortable provision for the decline of life, are so many natural and salutary incentives to the exercise of those powers. Imperious necessity is the grand stimulus to man's physical and mental endowments, and without it he would sink into a state of hopeless torpidity. Establish a poor law to render his forethought and self-denial unnecessary—enact a system of national education to take the care of his children off his hands—set up a national church to look after his religious wants—make laws for the preservation of his health, that he may have less occasion to look after it himself—do all this, and he may then, to a great extent, dispense with the faculties that the Almighty has given to him. Every powerful spring of action is destroyed—

acuteness of intellect is not wanted—force of moral feeling is never called for—the higher powers of his mind are deprived of their natural exercise, and a gradual deterioration of character must ensue. Take away the demand for exertion, and you will ensure inactivity. Induce inactivity, and you will soon have degradation.

The reader will therefore observe:

1. That the dissenter cannot consistently admit that the state should have the care of the bodily health of the people, when he denies that it has anything to do with their spiritual health.

2. That the warmest supporters of this theory of government superintendence, are only making it a blind for another monopoly.

3. That no man has a claim upon the legislature to take that care of his health which he will not take himself.

4. That in this case, as in every other, to do for the people what they are naturally fitted to do for themselves, is to adopt one of the most efficient means of lowering the standard of national character.

Letter X

Had our governors always taken care, duly to perform their original, and all-important functions—had the administration of justice ever stood pre-eminent in their eyes—had it at all times been considered as the one thing needful—and had no other questions ever been entertained at its expense, then might their interference, in matters with which they had no concern, have been more excusable. But it is not so. To the long list of their sins of commission, we have to add the sin of omission; and most grievously has the nation suffered from their neglect, as well as from their officiousness.

Describe to an unbiased arbitrator the relationship existing between a people and a government. Tell him that the legislature is a body deputed by the nation to keep order, to protect person and property, and that these are its most important, if not its only duties. Tell him that every man practically gives in his allegiance to this body—that he annually pays towards its support a considerable portion of his earnings—that he sacrifices to it his personal independence—and that he does these things, in the expectation of receiving from it, the advantages of that protection, which it is presumed to give in return for such deprivations. Explain all this, and then ask him to state, in what manner he should expect the government, to fulfill its part of the contract. He would say that when the subjects had paid their taxes, and submitted themselves to the authorities, they had done all that could be required of them—that it remained with those authorities to carry home to every man the benefits of civil order—that the revenue was subscribed by the people for the express purpose of defraying the charges of this protective establishment—and that, after men had thus prepaid the government, it would be a most unjust proceeding for that government to put them to additional expense whenever it was called upon to perform its duty towards them. From these considerations he would infer that it behoved the state to establish courts of justice, which should be easy of access, speedy in their decisions, and in which every man should be able to obtain the protection of the law, free of cost. Such is the obviously equitable conclusion at which a conscientious umpire would arrive. How widely different from the reality! Our legislators tax the people to a most exorbitant extent; squander the money thus wrested from the toiling artisan in the support of institutions for the benefit of the rich; maintain, by its aid, standing armies to ensure popular subjection; and, when the misused subject demands of the government that it defend him in the exercise of his rights and privileges—when he asks it to fulfill the duties for which it was instituted—when he requests it to do for him that for which he has already paid it so extravagantly—what is its conduct? Does it willingly and efficiently respond to his demand? Does it, without further reward, fully and fairly administer the laws? Does it send forth its officers, commanding them diligently to secure to every one, that protection, which he has sacrificed so much to obtain? Does it take up the cause of the poor man, and defend him against the aggressions of his rich neighbour? No! it does none of these things. It turns over the complainant to the tender mercies of solicitors, attorneys, barristers, and a whole legion of law officers. It drains his purse with charges for writs, briefs, affidavits, subpoenas, fees of all kinds, and expenses innumerable. It involves him in all the mazy intricacies of common courts, chancery courts, suits, counter-suits, and appeals; and thousands of times has it overwhelmed with irretrievable ruin, the man whose person and property it was bound to defend. And this is our "glorious constitution!"

We pity the poor subjects of oriental despotism. We

view their absolute form of government with contempt. We turn from it to contemplate what we call our "free institutions" with pride, and congratulate ourselves upon the superiority of our condition. Yet might these autocrat-ridden people hold up to the world's scorn, the results of our seemingly "free institutions." Many and many a case could they point out in this "land of liberty," of misery and famine, inflicted by the rich man's tyranny—of wrongs endured, because money was wanting wherewith to purchase redress—of rights unclaimed, because contention with the powerful usurper was useless—aye, hundreds upon hurdreds might they find, whose hollow cheeks and tattered clothing, could bear testimony to the delusiveness of English justice. And then, by way of contrast, they could tell of the active and even-handed legislation of many an absolute monarch. Countless examples might they point out, of justice freely and fairly administered by Eastern sultans—instances where the poor and weak could pour their tales of tyranny into the ear of the monarch himself, and obtain assistance—where wealth and interest were not required to secure protection; neither were any shield to the oppressor. Fie upon Englishmen that they should still continue to praise and venerate a mere shadow—to pride and congratulate themselves upon the possession of what is daily demonstrated to be a hollow mockery! How long will men allow themselves to be cheated by an empty name? Not only has our government done those things which it ought not to have done, but it has left undone those things which it ought to have done; and truly may it be said that there is no health in it.

Let us, therefore, bear in mind that, by permitting our

rulers to spend their time and our money in the management of matters over which they ought to have no
control, we not only entail upon ourselves, the evils
arising from their mischievous legislation, but likewise
those resulting from the neglect of their real duties.

Letter XI

A few remarks upon an important collateral topic, in
so far as it is affected by the solution of the question in
hand, may not be here out of place. The enfranchisement
of the working classes is the topic alluded to.

With that large class of men, whose conclusions are
determined by the dictates of expediency, rather than by
the demands of justice, one of the objections to an investment of power in the hands of the people, is this—
"Society is a complicated machine; the interests of its
members are many and various, and so mysteriously
connected and intertwined with each other, that it requires deep sagacity, and clearness of intellect, fully to
comprehend and appreciate their multiplied relations.
Legislation has for one of its objects, the proper regulation of these conflicting interests; and such is the difficulty of keeping everything in equilibrium, that even our
most profound statesmen have been baffled in the attempt. Would it then, be prudent, to give to the uneducated classes, the power of directing the legislature
in matters so difficult to understand, yet so important to
the public welfare?"

Now, if it should turn out that these complex and manifold interests require no regulation at all, but that they

are originally so arranged as to regulate themselves—if it should be discovered that the great difficulties encountered in the management of social concerns, arise from the disturbance of natural laws, and that governments have been foolishly endeavouring to maintain, in a condition of *unstable* equilibrium, things which, if let alone, would of themselves assume a condition of *stable* equilibrium; then must the objection be to a great extent invalidated. That the affairs of the nation are in circumstances of dreadful embarrassment, and that it may take some skill to bring them back to their normal state, is not denied; but, whilst it can be shown that this disastrous effect has resulted—not from want of legislation, but from over legislation—not from any intellectual deficiency on the part of our lawmakers, but from their everlasting selfish interference—the fact can afford no argument against complete suffrage. Take an illustration. Imagine some poor unlucky wight to be persuaded by his doctor that he could never enjoy perfect health without medical superintendence—that his digestion would not go on properly without stimulants—that he must take pectoral pills to keep his lungs in order—that he must swallow, now and then, a sudorific, to sustain the functions of his skin, and so on; and suppose that, in the abundance of his faith, our patient puts himself under the direction of this learned physician; and, in obedience to his orders, gulps down, day by day, one dose of medicine after another—first, an aperient to rectify his digestive organs, and then a tonic to strengthen them—now a vapour bath to augment his perspiration, and again a diuretic to diminish it—this week eats abundance of nourishing food to increase his energies, and the next parts with a few ounces of blood to guard against plethora—and so on, through a long course of medical treatment, taking in their turns, emetics, anodynes, cathartics, opiates, febrifuges, and alteratives, together with a due proportion of topical applications, such as plasters, blisters, liniments, emollients, and so forth. And when, after all this doctoring, the poor fellow has been brought to such a pass, as to be for ever going wrong in some way or other, and is continually requiring the attendance of his physician, to remove this pain and to rectify the other distemper—when he has come to such a state, that he no sooner gets rid of one malady, than he is seized with another, imagine this professor of the healing art to gather round the sick man's bed-side a cluster of country clowns, and begin to harangue them upon the various and complicated functions of the human body, describing to them its numerous organs, and their individual duties, the manifold disorders to which they are liable, and the difficulties of their cure; and then, to add point to his lecture, fancy him turning to his patient, and saying, "See what a difficult thing it is to keep a man in health!" Why, even John Bull, with all his gullibility, would smile at this. And yet, when the same thing is said of society—when the invalid is a nation instead of a man, he believes it. Our state physicians have, from time immemorial, persuaded the people that social affairs would never go right without their interference; that a vigilant supervision was necessary to secure the healthy fulfilment of all the national functions;

and, in accordance with all these notions, they have been for ever doctoring the affairs of the country; now prescribing a lower diet under the name of "restrictive duties," and then letting in a surfeit of food to make up for past privations—at one time administering a stimulus to exercise, styled "encouragement to home manufactures," and at another, raising an outcry for some remedy against over-production—here providing a tonic for the nation's morals, called a "national church," and there creating a war, to prevent those morals acquiring undue strength—on one part of the social body, applying a soothing ointment, in the shape of a "poor law," and on another, inflicting an extensive bleeding, under the form of an "income tax." And when, after all these transcendently skilful operations, the nation has been brought almost to the brink of dissolution—when its debility is showing itself in the most alarming forms—when its constitution is so weakened that it is hardly possible to cure one of its disorders without producing a worse—when, in short, it is in the state in which we now see it, we hear these sage and self-complacent legislators exclaim, "See what a difficult thing it is to govern a country!" If, then, it be admitted that our national misfortunes have not arisen from the difficulties inherent in the nature of government, but from the determination to legislate when no legislation was required, that is, if it be admitted that the administration of justice, is the sole duty of the state, we are at once relieved from one of the greatest objections, to the enfranchisement of the working classes.

Letter XII

A brief review of the arguments that have been set
forth in the foregoing letters may serve to place the general question more distinctly before the mind.

Having shown that the proposed definition of state
duties was in exact accordance with the primitive requirements of society—was, in fact, theoretically derived from them, and that its derivation did not
countenance the universal interference now permitted;
an attempt was made to exhibit some of the chief advantages that would arise out of the restoration of our
various social institutions to their original freedom from
legislative control; in the course of which it was
argued:

1. That all commercial restrictions have been proved,
both by past and present experience, to be eminently
inimical to social prosperity; that necessity is fast forcing
us towards free trade, and that we must ultimately return to the perfect commercial liberty dictated by nature,
from which we should never have diverged, had there
been a proper limitation of state power.

2. That a national church is to be deprecated, not only
as being unnecessary to the spread of religion, but as
opposing, by its worldliness, corruption, and unchari-
tableness, a barrier to its progress; that, on the showing
of its own ministers, it is totally incapable of Christian-
ising the nation, seeing that by the vital importance they
attach to a state-paid priesthood, they practically admit
that they have themselves imbibed so little Christian

spirit that their own ministry would cease were it not for it emoluments; and hence in so far as the definition involves the disseverment of church and state, it is advantageous.

3. That a poor law, though apparently a boon to the working classes, is in reality a burden to them; that it delays the rectification of social abuses; that it discourages the exercise of genuine benevolence; that compulsory relief is degrading alike to the giver and to the receiver; that voluntaryism is equally applicable in the practice of religion as in its ministry; and that the blessings of charity would be secured un-accompanied by the evils of pauperism were the legislature prevented from meddling.

4. That war is universally admitted to be a great evil; that it is our duty as Christians to adopt all feasible means of putting an end to it; and that restricting governments, to the fulfilment of their primitive functions, and thereby depriving them of the power of invasion, would be the most effectual means of preventing it.

5. That artificial colonisation is injurious in each of its several influences; that colonial trade has always been turned into a monopoly for the benefit of the aristocracy; that the pretended protection given to the settlers has generally proved a great curse to them; that the original possessors of the soil have ever been cruelly persecuted in state-established colonies; and that the case of Pennsylvania affords satisfactory evidence of the superiority of that voluntary, unprotected, emigration, that must follow from the recognition of the proposed principle.

6. That a national education would tend to destroy

that variety and originality of mind so essential to social progress; that it would discourage improvement by annihilating healthy competition, and by placing in the way of reform the difficulties of institutional changes, in addition to the obstacles arising from natural prejudice in favour of existing modes of instruction; that we have no guarantee for its future efficiency, and have every reason to believe that it would ultimately become as corrupt as a national religion; that the mode of its support, involving as it must, the taxation of the whole community, consentients and dissentients, would be manifestly unjust; and that a constitution which necessarily excludes it, thereby commends itself to our adoption.

7. That the zealous advocacy, by certain medical men, of enactments for the preservation of the public health, arises from interested motives; that the health of the people is no more a subject for legislation than their religion; that no man can reasonably require the state to take that care of his body which he will not take himself; and that in this case as in every other, to do for the people what the Almighty has intended them to do for themselves, is infallibly to lower them in the scale of creation.

8. That by confining the attention of government to the preservation of order, and the protection of person and property, we should not only avoid the many injuries inflicted on us by its officious interferences, but should likewise secure the proper performance of its all-important, though now neglected duties.

Such are the evidences which have been adduced in favour of the theorem, that the administration of justice is the sole duty of the state. Others might be added, did it seem desirable. It is hoped, however, that those already set forth, if not of themselves sufficient to create in candid minds the conviction of its truth, will at least so far serve to exhibit its probability, as to beget for it a serious examination.

In conclusion, it will be well to remind the reader, that whatever may be the result of his deliberations upon this momentous question—whether he agrees with the arguments that have been brought forward, or dissents from them—whether he acknowledges the legitimacy of the deductions, or decides against them—one thing is certain. A definition of the duty of the state there must be. It needs no argument to prove that there is a boundary beyond which no legislative control should pass—that there are individual and social requirements whose fulfilment will be better secured by moral stimulus and voluntary exertion, than by any artificial regulations—that between the two extremes of its possible power, the *everything* and the *nothing* with which a government might be entrusted, there must be some point which both principle and policy indicate as its proper limitation. This point, this boundary, it behoves every man to fix for himself; and if he disagrees with the definition, as above expressed, consistency demands that he should make one for himself. If he wishes to avoid the imputation of political empiricism, he must ascertain the nature and intent of that national organ called the legislature, ere he seeks to prescribe its actions. Before he ventures to entertain another opinion upon what a government should *do,* he must first settle for himself the question—What is a government *for?*

OVER-LEGISLATION (1853)

I

From time to time there returns on the cautious thinker the conclusion that, considered simply as a question of probabilities, it is unlikely that his views upon any debatable topic are correct. "Here," he reflects, "are thousands around me holding on this or that point opinions differing from mine—wholly in many cases; partially in most others. Each is as confident as I am of the truth of his convictions. Many of them are possessed of great intelligence; and, rank myself high as I may, I must admit that some are my equals—perhaps my superiors. Yet, while every one of us is sure he is right, unquestionably most of us are wrong. Why should not I be among the mistaken? True, I cannot realize the likeli-

---

This essay first appeared in The Westminster Review *for July, 1853 and was reprinted in Spencer's* Essays: Scientific, Political and Speculative *(London and New York, 1892, in three volumes).*

hood that I am so. But this proves nothing; for though the majority of us are necessarily in error, we all labor under the inability to think we are in error. Is it not then foolish thus to trust myself? A like warrant has been felt by men all the world through; and, in nine cases out of ten, has proved a delusive warrant. Is it not then absurd in me to put so much faith in my judgments?"

Barren of practical results as this reflection at first sight appears, it may, and indeed should, influence some of our most important proceedings. Though in daily life we are constantly obliged to act out our inferences, trustless as they may be; though in the house, in the office, in the street, there hourly arise occasions on which we may not hesitate; seeing that if to act is dangerous, never to act at all is fatal; and though consequently, on our private conduct, this abstract doubt as to the worth of our judgments must remain inoperative; yet in our public conduct, we may properly allow it to weigh. Here decision is no longer imperative; while the difficulty of deciding aright is incalculably greater. Clearly as we may think we see how a given measure will work, we may infer, drawing the above induction from human experience, that the chances are many against the truth of our anticipations. Whether in most cases it is not wiser to do nothing, becomes now a rational question. Continuing his self-criticism, the cautious thinker may reason—"If in these personal affairs, where all the conditions of the case were known to me, I have so often miscalculated, how much oftener shall I miscalculate in political affairs, where the conditions are too numerous, too widespread, too complex, too obscure to be understood. Here, doubtless, is a social evil and there a desideratum; and were

I sure of doing no mischief I would forthwith try to cure the one and achieve the other. But when I remember how many of my private schemes have miscarried; how speculations have failed, agents proved dishonest, marriage been a disappointment; how I did but pauperize the relative I sought to help; how my carefully-governed son has turned out worse than most children; how the thing I desperately strove against as a misfortune did me immense good; how while the objects I ardently pursued brought me little happiness when gained, most of my pleasures have come from unexpected sources; when I recall these and hosts of like facts, I am struck with the incompetence of my intellect to prescribe for society. And as the evil is one under which society has not only lived but grown, while the desideratum is one it may spontaneously obtain, as it has most others, in some unforeseen way, I question the propriety of meddling."

II

There is a great want of this practical humility in our political conduct. Though we have less self-confidence than our ancestors, who did not hesitate to organize in law their judgments on all subjects whatever, we have yet far too much. Though we have ceased to assume the infallibility of our theological beliefs and so ceased to enact them, we have not ceased to enact hosts of other beliefs of an equally doubtful kind. Though we no longer presume to coerce men for their *spiritual good*, we still think ourselves called upon to coerce them for their *material good:* not seeing that the one is as useless and as unwarrantable as the other. Innumerable failures seem, so far, powerless to teach this. Take up a daily paper and you will probably find a leader exposing the corruption, negligence, or mismanagement of some State-depart-ment. Cast your eye down the next column, and it is not unlikely that you will read proposals for an extension of State-supervision. Yesterday came a charge of gross care-lessness against the Colonial Office. Today Admiralty bunglings are burlesqued. Tomorrow brings the ques-tion, "Should there not be more coal-mine inspectors?" Now there is a complaint that the Board of Health is useless; and now an outcry for more railway regulation. While your ears are still ringing with denunciations of Chancery abuses, or your cheeks still glowing with in-dignation at some well-exposed iniquity of the Eccle-siastical Courts, you suddenly come upon suggestions for organizing "a priesthood of science." Here is a ve-hement condemnation of the police for stupidly allowing sight-seers to crush each other to death. You look for the corollary that official regulation is not to be trusted; when, instead, *à propos* of a shipwreck, you read an ur-gent demand for government-inspectors to see that ships always have their boats ready for launching. Thus, while every day chronicles a failure, there every day reappears the belief that it needs but an Act of Parliament and a staff of officers to effect any end desired. Nowhere is the perennial faith of mankind better seen. Ever since society existed Disappointment has been preaching, "Put not your trust in legislation"; and yet the trust in legislation seems scarcely diminished.

Did the State fulfil efficiently its unquestionable duties, there would be some excuse for this eagerness to assign it further duties. Were there no complaints of its faulty administration of justice; of its endless delays and untold expenses; of its bringing ruin in place of restitution; of its playing the tyrant where it should have been the protector: did we never hear of its complicated stupidities; its 20,000 statutes, which it assumes all Englishmen to know, and which not one Englishman does know; its multiplied forms, which, in the effort to meet every contingency, open far more loopholes than they provide against: had it not shown its folly in the system of making every petty alteration by a new act, variously affecting innumerable preceding acts; or in its score of successive sets of Chancery rules, which so modify, and limit, and extend, and abolish, and alter each other, that not even Chancery lawyers know what the rules are; were we never astounded by such a fact as that, under the system of land registration in Ireland, £6,000 have been spent in a "negative search" to establish the title of an estate; did we find in its doing no such terrible incongruity as the imprisonment of a hungry vagrant for stealing a turnip, while for the gigantic embezzlements of a railway director it inflicts no punishment; had we, in short, proved its efficiency as judge and defender, instead of having found it treacherous, cruel, and anxiously to be shunned, there would be some encouragement to hope other benefits at its hands.

Or if, while failing in its judicial functions, the State had proved itself a capable agent in some other department—the military for example—there would have been some show of reason for extending its sphere of action.

Suppose that it had rationally equipped its troops, instead of giving them cumbrous and ineffective muskets, barbarous grenadier-caps, absurdly heavy knapsacks and cartouche-boxes, and clothing colored so as admirably to help the enemy's marksmen; suppose that it organized well and economically, instead of salarying an immense superfluity of officers, creating sinecure colonelcies of £4,000 a year, neglecting the meritorious and promoting incapables; to suppose that its soldiers were always well housed instead of being thrust into barracks that invalid hundreds, as at Aden, or that fall on their occupants, as at Loodianah, where ninety-five were thus killed; suppose that, in actual war it had shown due administrative ability, instead of occasionally leaving its regiments to march barefoot, to dress in patches, to capture their own engineering tools, and to fight on empty stomachs, as during the Peninsular campaign; suppose all this, and the wish for more State-control might still have had some warrant.

Even though it has bungled in everything else, yet had it in one case done well—had its naval management alone been efficient—the sanguine would have had a colorable excuse for expecting success in a new field. Grant that the reports about bad ships, ships that will not sail, ships that have to be lengthened, ships with unfit engines, ships that will not carry their guns, ships without stowage, and ships that have to be broken up, are all untrue; assume those to be mere slanderers who say the the *Megæra* took double the time taken by a commercial steamer to reach the Cape; that during the same voyage the *Hydra* was three times on fire, and needed the pumps kept going day and night; that the *Charlotte* troop-ship set out with 75 days' provisions on board, and was three months in reaching her destination; that the *Harpy*, at an imminent risk of life, got home in 110 days from Rio; disregard as calumnies the statements about septuagenarian admirals, dilettante ship building, and "cooked" dockyard accounts; set down the affair of the Goldner preserved meats as a myth, and consider Professor Barlow mistaken when he reported of the Admiralty compasses in store, that "at least one-half were mere lumber"; let all these, we say, be held groundless charges, and there would remain for the advocates of much government some basis for their political air-castles, spite of military and judicial mismanagement.

As it is, however, they seem to have read backwards the parable of the talents. Not to the agent of proved efficiency do they consign further duties, but to the negligent and blundering agent. Private enterprise has done much, and done it well. Private enterprise has cleared, drained, and fertilized the country, and built the towns; has excavated mines, laid out roads, dug canals, and embanked railways; has invented, and brought to perfection ploughs, looms, steam-engines, printing-presses, and machines innumerable; has built our ships, our vast manufactories, our docks; has established banks, insurance societies, and the newspaper press; has covered the sea with lines of steam-vessels, and the land with electric telegraphs. Private enterprise has brought agriculture, manufactures, and commerce to their present height, and is now developing them with increasing rapidity. Therefore, do not trust private enterprise. On the other hand, the State so fulfils its judicial function as to ruin many, delude others, and frighten away those who most need succor; its national defences are so extravagantly and yet inefficiently administered as to call forth almost daily complaint, expostulation, or ridicule; and as the nation's steward, it obtains from some of our vast public estates a minus revenue. Therefore, trust the State. Slight the good and faithful servant, and promote the unprofitable one from one talent to ten.

Seriously, the case, while it may not, in some respects, warrant this parallel, is, in one respect, even stronger. For the new work is not of the same order as the old, but of a more difficult order. Ill as government discharges its true duties, any other duties committed to it are likely to be still worse discharged. To guard its subjects against aggression, either individual or national, is a straightforward and tolerably simple matter; to regulate, directly or indirectly, the personal actions of those subjects is an infinitely complicated matter. It is one thing to secure to each man the unhindered power to pursue his own good; it is a widely different thing to pursue the good for him. To do the first efficiently, the State has merely to look on while its citizens act; to forbid unfairness; to adjudicate when called on; and to enforece restitution for injuries. To do the last efficiently, it must become an ubiquitous worker—must know each man's needs better than he knows them himself—must, in short, possess superhuman power and intelligence. Even, therefore, had the State done well in its proper sphere, no sufficient warrant would have existed for extending that sphere; but seeing how ill it has discharged those simple offices which we cannot help consigning to it, small indeed is the probability that it will discharge well offices of a more complicated nature.

Change the point of view however we may, and this conclusion still presents itself. If we define the primary State-duty to be that of protecting each individual against others, then, all other State-action comes under the definition of protecting each individual against himself—against his own stupidity, his own idleness, his own improvidence, rashness, or other defect—his own incapacity for doing something or other which should be done. There is no questioning this classification. For manifestly all the obstacles that lie between a man's desires and the satisfaction of them are either obstacles arising from other men's counter-desires, or obstacles arising from inability in himself. Such of these counter-desires as are just, have as much claim to satisfaction as his; and may not, therefore, be thwarted. Such of them as are unjust, it is the State's duty to hold in check. The only other possible sphere for it, therefore, is that of saving the individual from the consequences of his nature, or, as we say—protecting him against himself. Making no comment, at present, on the policy of this, and confining ourselves solely to the practicability of it, let us inquire how the proposal looks when reduced to its simplest form. Here are men possessed of instincts, and sentiments, and perceptions, all conspiring to self-preservation. The due action of each brings its quantum of pleasure; the inaction, its more or less of pain. Those provided with these faculties in due proportions prosper and multiply; those ill-provided tend to die out. And the general success of this human organization is seen in the fact that under it the world has been peopled, and by it the complicated appliances and arrangements of civilized life have been developed. It is complained, however, that there are certain directions in which this apparatus of motives works but imperfectly. While it is admitted that men are duly prompted by it to bodily sustenance, to the obtainment of clothing and shelter, to marriage and the care of offspring, and to the establishment of the more important industrial and commercial agencies; it is argued that there are many desiderata, as pure air, more knowledge, good water, safe travelling, and so forth, which it does not duly achieve. And these shortcomings being assumed permanent, it is urged that some supplementary means must be employed. It is therefore proposed that out of the mass of men a certain number, constituting the legislature, shall be instructed to attain these various objects. The legislators thus instructed (all characterized, on the average, by the same defects in this apparatus of motives as men in general), being unable personally to fulfil their tasks, must fulfil them by deputy—must appoint commissions, boards, councils, and staffs of officers; and must construct their agencies of this same defective humanity that acts so ill. Why now should this system of complex deputation succeed where the system of simple deputation does not? The industrial, commercial, and philanthropic agencies, which citizens form spontaneously, are directly deputed agencies; these governmental agencies made by electing legislators who appoint officers are indirectly deputed ones. And it is hoped that, by this process of double deputation, things may be achieved which the process of single deputation will not achieve. What is the rationale of this hope? Is it that legislators, and their *employés*, are made to feel more intensely than the rest these evils they are to remedy, these wants they are to satisfy? Hardly; for by position they are mostly relieved from such evils and wants. Is it, then, that they are to have the primary motive replaced by a secondary motive— the fear of public displeasure, and ultimate removal from office? Why scarcely; for the minor benefits which citizens will not organize to secure *directly*, they will not organize to secure *indirectly*, by turning out inefficient servants: especially if they cannot readily get efficient ones. Is it, then, that these State-agents are to do from a sense of duty, what they would not do from any other motive? Evidently this is the only possibility remaining. The proposition on which the advocates of much government have to fall back is, that things which the people will not unite to effect for personal benefit, a law-appointed portion of them will unite to effect for the benefit of the rest. Public men and functionaries love their neighbors better than themselves! The philanthropy of statesmen is stronger than the selfishness of citizens!

No wonder, then, that every day adds to the list of legislative miscarriages. If colliery explosions increase, notwithstanding the appointment of coal-mine inspectors, why, it is but a natural sequence to these false methods. If Sunderland shipowners complain that, as far as tried, "the Mercantile Marine Act has proved a total failure"; and if, meanwhile, the other class affected by it— the sailors—show their disapprobation by extensive strikes; why, it does but exemplify the folly of trusting a theorizing benevolence rather than an experienced self-interest. On all sides we may expect such facts; and on all sides we find them. Government, turning engineer, appoints its lieutenant, the Sewers' Commission, to drain London. Presently Lambeth sends deputations to say that it pays heavy rates, and gets no benefit. Tired of waiting, Bethnal Green calls meetings to consider "the most effectual means of extending the drainage of the district." From Wandsworth come complainants, who threaten to pay no more until something is done. Camberwell proposes to raise a subscription and do the work itself. Meanwhile, no progress is made towards the purification of the Thames; the weekly returns show an increasing rate of mortality; in Parliament, the friends of the Commission have nothing save good intentions to urge in mitigation of censure; and, at length, despairing ministers gladly seize an excuse for quietly shelving the Commission and its plans altogether. As architectural surveyor, the State has scarcely succeeded better than as engineer; witness the Metropolitan Buildings' Act. New houses still tumble down from time to time. A few months since, two fell at Bayswater, and one more recently near the Pentonville prison: all notwithstanding prescribed thicknesses, and hoop-iron bond, and inspectors. It never struck those who provided these delusive sureties that it was possible to build walls without bonding the two surfaces together, so that the inner layer might be removed after the surveyor's approval. Nor did they foresee that, in dictating a larger *quantity* of bricks than experience proved absolutely needful, they were simply insuring a slow deterioration of *quality* to an equivalent extent. The government guarantee for safe passenger-ships answers no better than its guarantee for safe houses. Though the burning of the *Amazon* arose from either bad construction or bad stowage, she had received the Admiralty certificate before sailing. Notwithstanding official approval, the *Adelaide* was found, on her first voyage, to steer ill, to have useless pumps, ports that let floods of water into the cabins, and coals so near the furnaces that they twice caught fire. The *W. S. Lindsay*, which turned out unfit for sailing, had been passed by the government agent; and, but for the owner, might have gone to sea at a great risk of life. The *Melbourne*—originally a State-built ship—which took twenty-four days to reach Lisbon, and then needed to be docked to undergo a thorough repair, had been duly inspected. And lastly, the notorious *Australian*, before her third futile attempt to proceed on her voyage, had, her owners tell us, received "the full approbation of the government inspector." Neither does the like supervision give security to land-travelling. The iron bridge at Chester, which, breaking, precipitated a train into the Dee, had passed under the official eye. Inspection did not prevent a column on the South-Eastern from being so placed as to kill a man who put his head out of the carriage window. The locomotive that burst at Brighton lately did so notwithstanding a State-approval given but ten days previously. And—to look at the facts in the gross—this system of supervision has not prevented the increase of railway accidents; which, be it remembered, has arisen *since* the system was commenced.

III

"Well; let the State fail. It can but do its best. If it succeed, so much the better; if it do not, where is the harm? Surely it is wiser to act, and take the chance of success, than to do nothing." To this plea the rejoinder is that, unfortunately, the results of legislative intervention are not only negatively bad, but often positively so. Acts of Parliament do not simply fail; they frequently make worse. The familiar truth that persecution aids rather than hinders proscribed doctrines—a truth lately afresh illustrated by the forbidden work of Gervinus—is a part of the general truth that legislation often does indirectly the reverse of that which it directly aims to do. Thus has it been with the Metropolitan Buildings' Act. As was lately agreed unanimously by the delegates from all the parishes in London, and as was stated by them to Sir William Molesworth, this act "has encouraged bad building, and has been the means of covering the suburbs of the metropolis with thousands of wretched hovels, which are a disgrace to a civilized country." Thus, also, has it been in provincial towns. The Nottingham Inclosure Act of 1845, by prescribing the structure of the houses to be built, and the extent of yard or garden to be allotted to each, has rendered it impossible to build working-class dwellings at such moderate rents as to compete with existing ones. It is estimated that, as a consequence, 10,000 of the population are debarred from the new homes they would otherwise have, and are forced to live crowded together in miserable places unfit for human habitation; and so, in its anxiety to insure healthy accommodation for artisans, the law has entailed on them still worse accommodations than before. Thus, too, has it been with the Passengers' Act. The terrible fevers which arose in the Australian emigrant ships a few months since, causing in the *Buorneuf* 83 deaths, in the *Wanota* 39 deaths, in the *Marco Polo* 53 deaths, and in the *Ticonderoga* 104 deaths, arose in vessels sent out by the government; and arose *in consequence* of the close packing which the Passengers' Act authorizes. Thus, moreover, has it been with the safeguards provided by the Mercantile Marine Act. The examinations devised for insuring the efficiency of captains have had the effect of certifying the superficially-clever and unpractised men, and, as we are told by a shipowner, rejecting many of the long-tried and most trustworthy: the general result being that *the ratio of shipwrecks has increased*. Thus also has it happened with Boards of Health, which have, in sundry cases, exacerbated the evils to be removed; as, for instance, at Croydon, where, according to the official report, the measures of the sanitary authorities produced an epidemic, which attacked 1,600 people and killed 70. Thus again has it been with the Joint Stock Companies Registration Act. As was shown by Mr. James Wilson, in his late motion for a select committee on life-assurance asociations, this measure, passed in 1844 to guard the public against bubble schemes, actually facilitated the rascalities of 1845 and subsequent years. The legislative sanction, devised as a guarantee of genuineness, and supposed by the people to be such, clever adventurers have without difficulty obtained for the most worthless projects. Having obtained it, an amount of public confidence has followed which they could never otherwise have gained. In this way literally hundreds of sham enterprises that would not else have seen the light have been fostered into being; and thousands of families have been ruined who would never have been so but for legislative efforts to make them more secure.

Moreover, when these topical remedies applied by statesmen do not exacerbate the evils they were meant to cure, they constantly induce collateral evils; and these often graver than the original ones. It is the vice of this empirical school of politicians that they never look beyond proximate causes and immediate effects. In common with the uneducated masses they habitually regard each phenomenon as involving but one antecedent and one consequent. They do not bear in mind that each phenomenon is a link in an infinite series—is the result of myriads of preceding phenomena, and will have a share in producing myriads of succeeding ones. Hence they overlook the fact that, in disturbing any natural chain of sequences, they are not only modifying the result next in succession, but all the future results into which this will enter as a part-cause. The serial genesis of phenomena, and the interaction of each series upon every other series, produces a complexity utterly beyond human grasp. Even in the simplest cases this is so. A servant who puts coals on the fire sees but few effects from the burning of a lump. The man of science, however, knows that there are very many effects. He knows that the combustion establishes numerous atmospheric currents, and through them moves thousands of cubic feet of air inside the house and out. He knows that the heat diffused causes expansions and subsequent contractions of all bodies within its range. He knows that the persons warmed are affected in their rate of respiration and their waste of tissue; and that these physiological changes must have various secondary results. He knows that, could he trace to their ramified consequences all the forces disengaged, mechanical, chemical, thermal, electric—could he enumerate all the subsequent effects of the evaporation caused, the gases generated, the light evolved, the heat radiated; volume would scarcely suffice to enter them. If, now, from a simple inorganic change such numerous and complex results arise, how infinitely multiplied and involved must be the ultimate consequences of any force brought to bear upon society. Wonderfully constructed as it is—mutually dependent as are its members for the satisfaction of their wants—affected as each unit of it is by his fellows, not only as to his safety and prosperity, but in his health, his temper, his culture; the social organism cannot be dealt with in any one part, without all other parts being influenced in ways which cannot be foreseen. You put a duty on paper, and by-and-by find that, through the medium of the jacquard-cards employed, you have inadvertently taxed figured silk, sometimes to the extent of several shillings per piece. On removing the impost from bricks, you discover that its existence had increased the dangers of mining, by preventing shafts from being lined and workings from being tunnelled. By the excise on soap, you have, it turns out, greatly encouraged the use of caustic washing-powders;

and so have unintentionally entailed an immense destruction of clothes. In every case you perceive, on careful inquiry, that besides acting upon that which you sought to act upon, you have acted upon many other things, and each of these again on many others; and so have propagated a multitude of changes in all directions. We need feel no surprise, then, that in their efforts to cure specific evils, legislators have continually caused collateral evils they never looked for. No Carlyle's wisest man, nor any body of such, could avoid causing them. Though their production is explicable enough after it has occurred, it is never anticipated. When, under the new Poor-Law, provision was made for the accommodation of vagrants in the union-houses,* it was hardly expected that a body of tramps would be thereby called into existence, who would spend their time in walking from union to union throughout the kingdom. It was little thought by those who in past generations assigned parish-pay for the maintenance of illegitimate children, that, as a result, a family of such would by-and-by be considered a small fortune, and the mother of them a desirable wife; nor did the same statesmen see that, by the law of settlement, they were organizing a disastrous inequality of wages in different districts, and entailing a system of clearing away cottages, which would result in the crowding of bedrooms, and in a consequent moral and physical deterioration. The English tonnage-law was enacted simply with a view to regulate the mode of measurement. Its framers overlooked the fact that they

---

* Workhouses supported by the Union of several communities. In Scotland they are called "combination poorhouses."

were practically providing "for the effectual and compulsory construction of bad ships"; and that "to cheat
the law, that is, to build a tolerable ship in spite of it, was
the highest achievement left to an English builder."
Greater commercial security was alone aimed at by the
partnership-law. We now find, however, that the unlimited liability it insists upon is a serious hindrance to
progress; it practically forbids the association of small
capitalists; it is found a great obstacle to the building of
improved dwellings for the people; it prevents a better
relationship between artisans and employers; and by
withholding from the working-classes good investments
for their savings, it checks the growth of provident habits
and encourages drunkenness. Thus on all sides are well-
meant measures producing unforeseen mischiefs; a li-
censing-law that promotes the adulteration of beer; a
ticket-of-leave system that encourages men to commit
crime; a police-regulation that forces street-huxters into
the workhouse. And then, in addition to the obvious
and proximate evils, come the remote and less distinguishable ones, which, could we estimate their accumulated result, we should probably find even more
serious.

IV

But the thing to be discussed is, not so much whether,
by any amount of intelligence, it is *possible* for a government to work out the various ends consigned to it, as
whether its fulfillment of them is *probable*. It is less a
question of *can* than a question of *will*. Granting the ab-

solute competence of the State, let us consider what
hope there is of getting from it satisfactory performance.
Let us look at the moving force by which the legislative
machine is worked, and then inquire whether this force
is thus employed as economically as it would otherwise
be.

Manifestly, as desire of some kind is the invariable
stimulus to action in the individual, every social agency,
of what nature soever, must have some aggregate of desires for its motive power. Men in their collective capacity can exhibit no result but what has its origin in some
appetite, feeling, or taste common among them. Did not
they like meat, there could be no cattle-graziers, no
Smithfield, no distributing organization of butchers.
Operas, philharmonic societies, song-books, and street
organ-boys, have all been called into being by our love
of music. Look through the trades' directory; take up a
guide to the London sights; read the index of Bradshaw's
time-tables, the reports of the learned societies, or the
advertisements of new books; and you see in the publication itself, and in the things it describes, so many
products of human activities, stimulated by human desires. Under this stimulus grow up agencies alike the
most gigantic and the most insignificant, the most complicated and the most simple—agencies for national defence and for the sweeping of crossings; for the daily
distribution of letters, and for the collection of bits of
coal out of the Thames mud; agencies that subserve all
ends, from the preaching of Christianity to the protection of ill-treated animals; from the production of bread

for a nation to the supply of groundsel for caged singing-birds. The accumulated desires of individuals being, then, the moving power by which every social agency is worked, the question to be considered is, Which is the most economical kind of agency? The agency having no power in itself, but being merely an instrument, our inquiry must be for the most efficient instrument; the instrument that costs least, and wastes the smallest amount of the moving power; the instrument least liable to get out of order, and most readily put right again when it goes wrong. Of the two kinds of social mechanism exemplified above, the spontaneous and the governmental, which is the best?

From the form of this question will be readily foreseen the intended answer, that is the best mechanism which contains the fewest parts. The common saying, "What you wish well done you must do yourself," embodies a truth equally applicable to political life as to private life. The experience that farming by bailiff entails loss, while tenant-farming pays, is an experience still better illustrated in national history than in a landlord's account-books. This transference of power from constituencies to members of Parliament, from these to the executive, from the executive to a board, from the board to inspectors, and from inspectors through their subs down to the actual workers—this operating through a series of levers, each of which absorbs in friction and inertia part of the moving force; is as bad, in virtue of its complexity, as the direct employment by society of individuals, private companies, and spontaneously-formed institutions, is good in virtue of its simplicity. Fully to appreciate the contrast, we must compare in detail the working of the two systems.

Officialism is habitually slow. When non-governmental agencies are dilatory, the public has its remedy: it ceases to employ them and soon finds quicker ones. Under this discipline all private bodies are taught promptness. But for delays in State-departments there is no such easy cure. Lifelong Chancery suits must be patiently borne; Museum-catalogues must be wearily waited for. While, by the people themselves, a Crystal Palace is designed, erected, and filled, in the course of a few months, the legislature takes twenty years to build itself a new house. While, by private persons, the debates are daily printed and dispersed over the kingdom within a few hours of their utterance, the Board of Trade tables are regularly published a month, and sometimes more, after date. And so throughout. Here is a Board of Health which, since 1849, has been about to close the metropolitan graveyards, but has not done it yet; and which has so long dawdled over projects for cemeteries, that the London Necropolis Company has taken the matter out of its hands. Here is a patentee who has had fourteen years' correspondence with the Horse Guards, before getting a definite answer respecting the use of his improved boot for the Army. Here is a Plymouth port-admiral who delays sending out to look for the missing boats of the *Amazon* until ten days after the wreck.

Again, officialism is stupid. Under the natural course of things each citizen tends towards his fittest function. Those who are competent to the kind of work they undertake, succeed, and, in the average of cases, are advanced in proportion to their efficiency; while the incompetent, society soon finds out, ceases to employ, forces to try something easier, and eventually turns to use. But it is quite otherwise in State-organizations. Here, as every one knows, birth, age, backstairs intrigue, and sycophancy, determine the selections rather than merit. The "fool of the family" readily finds a place in the Church, if "the family" have good connections. A youth too ill-educated for any profession does very well for an officer in the Army. Grey hair, or a title, is a far better guarantee of naval promotion than genius is. Nay, indeed, the man of capacity often finds that, in government offices, superiority is a hindrance—that his chiefs hate to be pestered with his proposed improvements, and are offended by his implied criticisms. Not only, therefore, is legislative machinery complex, but it is made of inferior materials. Hence the blunders we daily read of; the supplying to the dockyards from the royal forests of timber unfit for use; the administration of relief during the Irish famine in such a manner as to draw laborers from the field, and diminish the subsequent harvest by one-fourth; the filing of patents at three different offices and keeping an index at none. Everywhere does this bungling show itself, from the elaborate failure of House of Commons ventilation down to the publication of *The London Gazette*, which invariably comes out wrongly folded.

A further characteristic of officialism is its extravagance. In its chief departments, Army, Navy, and Church, it employs far more officers than are needful, and pays some of the useless ones exorbitantly. The work done by the Sewers Commission has cost, as Sir B. Hall tells us, from 300 to 400 per cent. over the contemplated outlay; while the management charges have reached thirty-five, forty, and forty-five per cent. on the expenditure. The trustees of Ramsgate Harbor—a harbor, by the way, that has taken a century to complete—are spending £18,000 a year in doing what £5,000 has been proved sufficient for. The Board of Health is causing new surveys to be made of all the towns under its control—a proceeding which, as Mr. Stephenson states, and as every tyro in engineering knows, is, for drainage purposes, a wholly needless expense. These public agencies are subject to no such influence as that which obliges private enterprise to be economical. Traders and mercantile bodies succeed by serving society cheaply. Such of them as cannot do this are continually supplanted by those who can. They cannot saddle the nation with the results of their extravagance, and so are prevented from being extravagant. On works that are to return a profit it does not answer to spend forty-eight per cent. of the capital in superintendence, as in the engineering department of the Indian Government; and Indian railway companies, knowing this, manage to keep their superintendence charges within eight per cent. A shopkeeper leaves out of his accounts no item analogous to that £6,000,000 of its revenues, which Parliament allows to be deducted on the way to the Exchequer. Walk through a manufactory, and you see that the stern alternatives, carefulness or ruin, dictate the saving of every penny; visit one of the national dockyards, and the comments you make on any glaring wastefulness are carelessly met by the slang phrase, "Nunky* pays."

The unadaptiveness of officialism is another of its vices. Unlike private enterprise which quickly modifies its actions to meet emergencies; unlike the shopkeeper who promptly finds the wherewith to satisfy a sudden demand; unlike the railway-company which doubles its trains to carry a special influx of passengers; the law-made instrumentality lumbers on under all varieties of circumstances through its ordained routine at its habitual rate. By its very nature it is fitted only for average requirements, and inevitably fails under unusual requirements. You cannot step into the street without having the contrast thrust upon you. Is it summer? You see the water-carts going their prescribed rounds with scarcely any regard to the needs of the weather—to-day sprinkling afresh the already moist roads; to-morrow bestowing their showers with no greater liberality upon roads cloudy with dust. Is it winter? You see the scavengers do not vary in number and activity according to the quantity of mud; and if there comes a heavy fall of snow, you find the thoroughfares remaining for nearly a week in a scarcely passable state, without an effort being made, even in the heart of London, to meet the exigency. The late snow-storm, indeed, supplied a neat antithesis between the two orders of agencies in the effects it respectively produced on omnibuses and cabs. Not being under a law-fixed tariff, the omnibuses put on

---

* "Nunky" diminutive of "uncle." As we would say, "Uncle Sam pays."

extra horses and raised their fares. The cabs, on the contrary, being limited in their charges by an Act of Parliament which, with the usual shortsightedness, never contemplated such a contingency as this, declined to ply, deserted the stands and the stations, left luckless travellers to stumble home with their luggage as best they might, and so became useless at the very time of all others when they were most wanted! Not only by its unsusceptibility of adjustment does officialism entail serious inconveniences, but it likewise entails great injustices. In this case of cabs, for example, it has resulted since the late change of law, that old cabs, which were before saleable at £10 and £12 each, are now unsaleable and have to be broken up; and thus legislation has robbed cab-proprietors of part of their capital. Again, the recently-passed Smoke-Bill for London, which applies only within certain prescribed limits, has the effect of taxing one manufacturer while leaving untaxed his competitor working within a quarter of a mile; and so, as we are credibly informed, gives one an advantage of £1,500 a year over another. These typify the infinity of wrongs, varying in degrees of hardship, which legal regulations necessarily involve. Society, a living, growing organism, placed within apparatuses of dead, rigid, mechanical formulas, cannot fail to be hampered and pinched. The only agencies which can efficiently serve it are those through which its pulsations hourly flow, and which change as it changes.

How invariably officialism becomes corrupt every one knows. Exposed to no such antiseptic as free competition—not dependent for existence, as private unendowed organizations are, on the maintenance of a vigorous vitality; all law-made agencies fall into an inert, over-fed state, from which to disease is a short step. Salaries flow in irrespective of the activity with which duty is performed; continue after duty wholly ceases; become rich prizes for the idle well-born; and prompt to perjury, to bribery, to simony. East India directors are elected not for any administrative capacity they have; but they buy votes by promised patronage—a patronage alike asked and given in utter disregard of the welfare of a hundred millions of people. Registrars of wills not only get many thousands a year each for doing work which their miserably paid deputies leave half done; but they, in some cases, defraud the revenue, and that after repeated reprimands. Dockyard promotion is the result not of efficient services, but of political favoritism. That they may continue to hold rich livings, clergymen preach what they do not believe; bishops make false returns of their revenues; and at their elections to fellowships, well-to-do priests severally make oath that they are *pauper, pius et doctus*. From the local inspector whose eyes are shut to an abuse by a contractor's present, up to the prime minister who finds lucrative berths for his relations, this venality is daily illustrated; and that in spite of public reprobation and perpetual attempts to prevent it. As we once heard said by a State-official of twenty-five years' standing, "Wherever there is government there is villainy." It is the inevitable result of destroying the direct connection between the profit obtained and the work performed. No incompetent person hopes, by offering a *douceur* in *The Times*, to get a permanent place in a mercantile office. But where, as under government, there is no employer's self-interest to forbid; where the appointment is made by some one on whom inefficiency entails no loss; there a *douceur* is operative. In hospitals, in public charities, in endowed schools, in all social agencies in which duty done and income gained do not go hand in hand, the like corruption is found; and is great in proportion as the dependence of income upon duty is remote. In State-organizations, therefore, corruption is unavoidable. In trading-organizations it rarely makes its appearance, and when it does, the instinct of self-preservation soon provides a remedy.

To all which broad contrasts add this, that while private bodies are enterprising and progressive, public bodies are unchanging, and, indeed, obstructive. That officialism should be inventive nobody expects. That it should go out of its easy mechanical routine to introduce improvements, and this at a considerable expense of thought and application, without the prospect of profit, is not to be supposed. But it is not simply stationary; it resists every amendment either in itself or in anything with which it deals. Until now that county courts are taking away their practice, all agents of the law have doggedly opposed law-reform. The universities have maintained an old *curriculum* for centuries after it ceased to be fit; and are now struggling to prevent a threatened reconstruction. Every postal improvement has been vehemently protested against by the postal authorities. Mr. Whiston can say how pertinacious is the conservatism of Church grammar-schools. Not even the gravest consequences in view preclude official resistance: witness the fact that though, as already mentioned, Professor Barlow reported in 1820, of the Admiralty compasses then in store, that "at least one-half were mere lumber," yet notwithstanding the constant risk of shipwrecks thence arising, "very little amelioration in this state of things appears to have taken place until 1838 to 1840." Nor is official obstructiveness to be readily overborne even by a powerful public opinion: witness the fact that though, for generations, nine-tenths of the nation have disapproved this ecclesiastical system which pampers the drones and starves the workers, and though commissions have been appointed to rectify it, it still remains substantially as it was: witness again the fact that though, since 1818, there have been a score of attempts to rectify the scandalous maladministration of charitable trusts—though ten times in ten successive years remedial measures have been brought before Parliament—the abuses still continue in all their grossness. Not only do these legal instrumentalities resist reforms in themselves, but they hinder reforms in other things. In defending their vested interests the clergy delay the closing of town burial-grounds. As Mr. Lindsay can show, government emigration-agents are checking the use of iron for sailing-vessels. Excise officers prevent improvements in the processes they have to overlook. That organic conservatism which is visible in the daily conduct of all men is an obstacle which in private life self-interest slowly overcomes. The prospect of profit does, in the end, teach farmers that deep draining is good; though it takes long to do this. Manufacturers do, ultimately, learn the most economical speed at which to work their steam-engines;

though precedent has long misled them. But in the public service, where there is no self-interest to overcome it, this conservatism exerts its full force; and produces results alike disastrous and absurd. For generations after bookkeeping had become universal the Exchequer accounts were kept by notches cut on sticks. In the estimates for the current year appears the item, "Trimming the oil-lamps at the Horse-Guards."

Between these law-made agencies and the spontaneously-formed ones, who then can hesitate? The one class are slow, stupid, extravagant, unadaptive, corrupt, and obstructive: can any point out in the other, vices that balance these? It is true that trade has its dishonesties, speculation its follies. These are evils inevitably entailed by the existing imperfections of humanity. It is equally true, however, that these imperfections of humanity are shared by State-functionaries; and that being unchecked in them by the same stern discipline, they grow to far worse results. Given a race of men having a certain proclivity to misconduct, and the question is, whether a society of these men shall be so organized that ill-conduct directly brings punishment, or whether it shall be so organized that punishment is but remotely contingent on ill-conduct? Which will be the most healthful community—that in which agents who perform their functions badly, immediately suffer by the withdrawal of public patronage; or that in which such agents can be made to suffer only through an apparatus of meetings, petitions, polling-booths, parliamentary divisions, cabinet-councils, and red-tape documents? Is it not an absurdly utopian hope that men will behave better when correction is far removed and uncertain than when it is near at hand and inevitable? Yet this is the hope which most political schemers unconsciously cherish. Listen to their plans, and you find that just what they propose to have done, they assume the appointed agents will do. That functionaries are trustworthy is their first postulate. Doubtless could good officers be ensured, much might be said for officialism; just as despotism would have its advantages could we ensure a good despot.

If, however, we would duly appreciate the contrast between the artificial modes and the natural modes of achieving social desiderata, we must look not only at the vices of the one but at the virtues of the other. These are many and important. Consider first how immediately every private enterprise is dependent on the need for it; and how impossible it is for it to continue if there be no need. Daily are new trades and new companies established. If they subserve some existing public want, they take root and grow. If they do not, they die of inanition. It needs no agitation, no act of Parliament, to put them down. As with all natural organizations, if there is no function for them no nutrient comes to them, and they dwindle away. Moreover, not only do the new agencies disappear if they are superfluous, but the old ones cease to be when they have done their work. Unlike public instrumentalities; unlike heralds' offices, which are maintained for ages after heraldy has lost all value; unlike ecclesiastical courts, which continue to flourish for generations after they have become an abomination; these private instrumentalities dissolve when they become needless. A widely ramified coaching-system ceases to exist as soon as a more efficient railway-system comes into being. And not simply does it cease to exist, and to abstract funds, but the materials of which it was made are absorbed and turned to use. Coachmen, guards, and the rest, are employed to profit elsewhere; do not continue for twenty years a burden, like the compensated officials of some abolished department of the State. Consider, again, how necessarily these unordained agencies fit themselves to their work. It is a law of all organized things that efficiency presupposes apprenticeship. Not only is it true that the young merchant must begin by carrying letters to the post, that the way to be a successful innkeeper is to commence as waiter; not only is it true that in the development of the intellect there must come first the preceptions of identity and duality, next of number, and that without these, arithmetic, algebra, and the infinitesimal calculus, remain impracticable; but it is true that there is no part of an organism but begins in some simple form with some insignificant function, and passes to its final stage through successive phases of complexity. Every heart is at first a mere pulsatile sac; every brain begins as a slight enlargement of the spinal cord. This law equally extends to the social organism. An instrumentality that is to work well must not be designed and suddenly put together by legislators, but must grow gradually from a germ; each successive addition must be tried and proved good by experience before another addition is made; and by this tentative process only, can an efficient instrumentality be produced. From a trustworthy man who receives deposits of money, insensibly grows up a vast banking-system, with its notes, checks, bills, its complex transactions, and its clearing-house. Pack-horses, then wagons, then coaches, then steam-carriages on common roads, and, finally, steam-carriages on roads made for them—such has been the slow genesis of our present means of communication. Not a trade in the directory but has formed itself an apparatus of manufacturers, brokers, travellers, and retailers, in so gradual a way that no one can trace the steps. And so with organizations of another order. The Zoological Gardens began as the private collection of a few naturalists. The best working-class school known—that at Price's factory—commenced with half-a-dozen boys sitting among the candle-boxes, after hours, to teach themselves writing with worn-out pens. Mark, too, that as a consequence of their mode of growth, these spontaneously-formed agencies expand to any extent required. The same stimulus which brought them into being makes them send their ramifications wherever they are needed. But supply does not thus readily follow demand in governmental agencies. Appoint a board and a staff, fix their duties, and let the apparatus have a generation or two to consolidate, and you cannot get it to fulfil larger requirements without some Act of Parliament obtained only after long delay and difficulty.

Were there space, much more might be said upon the superiority of what naturalists would call the *exogenous* order of institutions over the *endogenous* one. But, from the point of view indicated, the further contrasts between their characteristics will be sufficiently visible.

Hence then the fact, that while the one order of means

is ever failing, making worse, or producing more evils than it cures, the other order of means is ever succeeding, ever improving. Strong as it looks at the outset, State-agency perpetually disappoints every one. Puny as are its first stages, private effort daily achieves results that astound the world. It is not only that joint-stock companies do so much; it is not only that by them a whole kingdom is covered with railways in the same time that it takes the Admiralty to build a hundred-gun ship; but it is that public instrumentalities are outdone even by individuals. The often quoted contrast between the Academy whose forty members took fifty-six years to compile the French dictionary, while Dr. Johnson alone compiled the English one in eight—a contrast still marked enough after making due set-off for the difference in the works—is by no means without parallel. That great sanitary desideratum—the bringing of the New River to London*—which the wealthiest corporation in the world attempted and failed, Sir Hugh Myddleton achieved single-handed. The first canal in England—a work of which government might have been thought the fit projector, and the only competent executor—was undertaken and finished as the private speculation of one man, the Duke of Bridgewater. By his own unaided exertions, William Smith completed that great achievement, the geological map of Great Britain; meanwhile, the Ordnance Survey—a very accurate and elaborate one, it is true—has already occupied a large staff for some two generations, and will not be completed before

---

* The political Corporation of London; not a private corporation.—Ed.

the lapse of another. Howard and the prisons of Europe; Bianconi and Irish travelling; Waghorn and the Overland route; Dargan and the Dublin Exhibition—do not these suggest startling contrasts? While private gentlemen like Mr. Denison build model lodging-houses in which the deaths are greatly below the average, the State builds barracks in which the deaths are greatly above the average, even of the much-pitied town-populations; barracks which, though filled with picked men under medical supervision, show an annual mortality per thousand of 13.6, 17.9 and even 20.4; though among civilians of the same age in the same places, the mortality per thousand is but 11.9. While the State has laid out large sums at Parkhurst in the effort to reform juvenile criminals, who are *not* reformed, Mr. Ellis takes fifteen of the worst young thieves in London—thieves considered by the police irreclaimable—and reforms them all. Side by side with the Emigration Board, under whose management hundreds die of fever from close packing, and under whose licence sail vessels which, like the *Washington*, are the homes of fraud, brutality, tyranny, and obscenity, stands Mrs. Chisholm's Family Colonization Loan Society, which does not provide worse accommodation than ever before but much better; which does not demoralize by promiscuous crowding but improves by mild discipline; which does not pauperize by charity but encourages providence; which does not increase our taxes, but is self-supporting. Here are lessons for the lovers of legislation. The State outdone by a working shoe-maker! The State beaten by a woman!

Stronger still becomes this contrast between the re-

sults of public action and private action, when we remember that the one is constantly eked out by the other,
even doing the things unavoidably left to it. Passing over
military and naval departments, in which much is done
by contractors and not by men receiving goverment
pay—passing over the Church, which is constantly extended not by law but by voluntary effort—passing over
the universities, where the efficient teaching is given not
by the appointed officers but by private tutors; let us
look at the mode in which our judicial system is worked.
Lawyers perpetually tell us that codification is impossible; and some are simple enough to believe them. Merely
remarking, in passing, that what government and all its
employés cannot do for the Acts of Parliament in general, was done for the 1,500 Customs acts in 1825 by the
energy of one man—Mr. Deacon Hume—let us see how
the absence of a digested system of law is made good.
In preparing themselves for the bar, and finally the
bench, law-students, by years of research, have to gain
an acquaintance with this vast mass of unorganized legislation; and that organization which it is held impossible
for the State to effect, it is held possible (sly sarcasm on
the State!) for each student to effect for himself. Every
judge can privately codify, though "united wisdom"
cannot. But how is each judge enabled to codify? By the
private enterprise of men who have prepared the way
for him; by the partial codifications of Blackstone, Coke,
and others; by the digests of partnership-law, bankruptcy-law, law of patents, laws affecting women, and
the rest that daily issue from the press; by abstracts of
cases, and volumes of reports—every one of them un-

official products. Sweep away all these fractional codifications made by individuals, and the State would be in utter ignorance of its own laws! Had not the bunglings of legislators been made good by private enterprise, the administration of justice would have been impossible!

Where, then, is the warrant for the constantly proposed extensions of legislative action? If, as we have seen in a large class of cases, government measures do not remedy the evils they aim at; if, in another large class, they make these evils worse instead of remedying them; and if, in a third large class, while curing some evils they entail others, and often greater ones; if, as we lately saw, public action is continually outdone in efficiency by private action; and if, as just shown, private action is obliged to make up for the shortcomings of public action, even in fulfilling the vital functions of the State; what reason is there for wishing more public administrations? The advocates of such may claim credit for philanthropy, but not for wisdom; unless wisdom is shown by disregarding experience.

V

"Much of this argument is beside the question," will rejoin our opponents. "The true point at issue is, not whether individuals and companies outdo the State when they come in competition with it, but whether there are not certain social wants which the State alone can satisfy. Admitting that private enterprise does much, and does it well, it is nevertheless true that we have daily thrust upon our notice many desiderata which it has not achieved and is not achieving. In these cases its incompetency is obvious; and in these cases, therefore, it behooves the State to make up for its deficiencies: doing this, if not well, yet as well as it can."

Not to fall back upon the many experiences already quoted, showing that the State is likely to do more harm than good in attempting this; nor to dwell upon the fact that, in most of the alleged cases, the apparent insufficiency of private enterprise is a *result* of previous State-interferences, as may be conclusively shown; let us deal with the proposition on its own terms. Though there would have been no need for a Mercantile Marine Act to prevent the unseaworthiness of ships and the ill-treatment of sailors, had there been no Navigation Laws to produce these; and though were all like cases of evils and shortcomings directly or indirectly produced by law, taken out of the category, there would probably remain but small basis for the plea above put; yet let it be granted that, every artificial obstacle having been removed, there would still remain many desiderata unachieved, which there was no seeing how spontaneous effort could achieve. Let all this, we say, be granted; the propriety of legislative action may yet be rightly questioned.

For the said plea involves the unwarrantable assumption that social agencies will continue to work only as they are now working; and will produce no results but those they seem likely to produce. It is the habit of this school of thinkers to make a limited human intelligence the measure of phenomena which it requires omniscience to grasp. That which it does not see the way to, it does not believe will take place. Though society has, generation after generation, been growing to developments which none foresaw, yet there is no practical belief in unforeseen developments in the future. The Parliamentary debates constitute an elaborate balancing of probabilities, having for data things as they are. Meanwhile every day adds new elements to things as they are, and seemingly improbable results constantly occur. Who, a few years ago, expected that a Leicester Square refugee would shortly become Emperor of the French? Who looked for free trade from a landlords' Ministry? Who dreamed that Irish over-population would spontaneously cure itself, as it is now doing? So far from social changes arising in likely ways, they usually arise in ways which, to common sense, appear unlikely. A barber's shop was not a probable-looking place for the germination of the cotton-manufacture. No one supposed that important agricultural improvements would come from a Leadenhall Street tradesman. A farmer would have been the last man thought of to bring to bear the screw-propulsion of steamships. The invention of a new species of architecture we should have hoped from any one rather than a gardener. Yet while the most unexpected changes are daily wrought out in the strangest ways, legislation daily assumes that things will go just as human foresight thinks they will go. Though by the trite exclamation, "What would our forefathers have said!" there is a frequent acknowledgment of the fact that wonderful results have been achieved in modes wholly unforeseen, yet there seems no belief that this will be again. Would it not be wise to admit such a probability into our politics? May we not rationally infer that, as in the past, so in the future?

This strong faith in State-agencies is, however, accompanied by so weak a faith in natural agencies (the two being antagonistic), that, in spite of past experience, it will by many be thought absurd to rest in the conviction that existing social needs will be spontaneously met, though we cannot say how they will be met. Nevertheless, illustrations exactly to the point are now transpiring before their eyes. Instance the scarcely credible phenomenon lately witnessed in the midland counties. Every one has heard of the distress of the stockingers; a chronic evil of some generation or two's standing. Repeated petitions have prayed Parliament for remedy; and legislation has made attempts, but without success. The disease seemed incurable. Two or three years since, however, the circular knitting machine was introduced; a machine immensely outstripping the old stocking-frame in productiveness, but which can make only the legs of stockings, not the feet. Doubtless, the Leicester and Nottingham artisans regarded this new engine with alarm, as likely to intensify their miseries. On the contrary, it has wholly removed them. By cheapening production it has so enormously increased consumption, that the old stocking-frames, which were before too many by half for the work to be done, are now all employed in putting feet to the legs which the new machines make. How insane would he have been thought who anticipated cure from such a cause! If from the unforeseen removal of evils we turn to the unforeseen achievement of desiderata, we find like cases. No one recognized in Oersted's electromagnetic discovery the germ of a new agency for the catching of criminals and the facilitation of commerce. No one expected railways to become agents for the diffusion of cheap literature, as they now are. No one supposed when the Society of Arts was planning an international exhibition of manufacturers in Hyde Park, that the result would be a place for popular recreation and culture at Sydenham.

But there is yet a deeper reply to the appeals of impatient philanthropists. It is not simply that social vitality may be trusted by-and-by to fulfil each much-exaggerated requirement in some quiet spontaneous way—it is not simply that when thus naturally fulfilled it will be fulfilled efficiently, instead of being botched as when attempted artificially; but it is that until thus naturally fulfilled it ought not to be fulfilled at all. A startling paradox, this, to many; but one quite justifiable, as we hope shortly to show.

It was pointed out some distance back, that the force which produces and sets in motion every social mechanism—governmental, mercantile, or other—is some accumulation of personal desires. As there is no individual action without a desire, so, it was urged, there can be no social action without an aggregate of desires. To which there here remains to add, that as it is a general law of the individual that the intenser desires—those corresponding to all-essential functions—are satisfied first, and if need be to the neglect of the weaker and less important ones; so, it must be a general law of society that the chief requisites of social life—those necessary to popular existence and multiplication—will, in the natural order of things, be subserved before those of a less pressing kind. As the private man first ensures himself food; then clothing and shelter; these being secured, takes a wife; and, if he can afford it, presently supplies himself with carpeted rooms, and a piano, and wines, hires servants and gives dinner-parties; so, in the evolution of society, we see first a combination for defence against enemies, and for the better pursuit of game; by-and-by come such political arrangements as are needed to maintain this combination; afterwards, under a demand for more food, more clothes, more houses, arises division of labor; and when satisfaction of the animal wants has been provided for, there slowly grow up literature, science, and the arts. Is it not obvious that these successive evolutions occur in the order of their importance? Is it not obvious, that, being each of them produced by an aggregate of desires, they *must* occur in the order of their importance, if it be a law of the individual that the strongest desires correspond to the most needful actions? Is it not, indeed, obvious that the order of relative importance will be more uniformly followed in social action than in individual action; seeing that the personal idiosyncrasies which disturb that order in the latter case are *averaged* in the former? If any one does not see this, let him take up a book describing life at the gold-diggings. There he will find the whole process exhibited in little. He will read that as the diggers must eat, they are compelled to offer such prices for food that it pays better to keep a store than to dig. As the store-keepers must get supplies, they give enormous sums for carriage from the nearest town; and some men, quickly seeing they can get rich at that, make it their business. This brings drays and horses into demand; the high rates draw these from all quarters; and, after them, wheel-wrights and harness-makers. Blacksmiths to sharpen pickaxes, doctors to cure fevers, get pay exorbitant in proportion to the need for them; and are so brought flocking in proportionate numbers. Presently commod-ities become scarce; more must be fetched from abroad; sailors must have increased wages to prevent them from deserting and turning miners; this necessitates higher charges for freight; higher freights quickly bring more ships; and so there rapidly develops an organization for supplying goods from all parts of the world. Every phase of this evolution takes place in the order of its necessity; or, as we say, in the order of the intensity of the desires subserved. Each man does that which he finds pays best; that which pays best is that for which other men will give most; that for which they will give most is that which, under the circumstances, they most desire. Hence the succession must be throughout from the most important to the less important. A requirement which at any period remains unfulfilled, must be one for the ful-filment of which men will not pay so much as to make it worth any one's while to fulfil it—must be a *less* re-quirement than all the others for the fulfilment of which they will pay more; and must wait until other more need-ful things are done. Well, is it not clear that the same law holds good in every community? Is it not true of the latter phases of social evolution, as of the earlier, that when things are let alone the smaller desiderata will be postponed to the greater?

Hence, then, the justification of the seeming paradox, that until spontaneously fulfilled, a public want should not be fulfilled at all. It must, on the average, result in our complex state, as in simpler ones, that the thing left undone is a thing by doing which citizens cannot gain so much as by doing other things; is therefore a thing which society does not want done so much as it wants these other things done; and the corollary is, that to effect a neglected thing by artificially employing citizens to do it, is to leave undone some more important thing which they would have been doing; is to sacrifice the greater requisite to the smaller.

"But," it will perhaps be objected, "if the things done by a government, or at least by a representative government, are also done in obedience to some aggregate desire, why may we not look for this normal subordination of the more needful to the less needful in them too?" The reply is, that though they have a certain tendency to follow this order; though those primal desires for public defence and personal protection, out of which government originates, were satisfied through its instrumentality in proper succession; though, possibly, some other early and simple requirements may have been so too; yet, when the desires are not few, universal and intense, but, like those remaining to be satisfied in the latter stages of civilization, numerous, partial, and moderate, the judgment of a government is no longer to be trusted. To select out of an immense number of minor wants, physical, intellectual, and moral, felt in different degrees by different classes, and by a total mass varying in every case, the want that is most pressing, is a task which no legislature can accomplish. No man or men by inspecting society can *see* what it most needs; society must be left to *feel* what it most needs. The mode of solution must be experimental, not theoretical. When left, day after day, to experience evils and dissatisfactions of various kinds, affecting them in various degrees, citizens gradually acquire repugnance to these proportionate to their greatness, and corresponding desires to get rid of them, which by spontaneously fostering remedial agencies are likely to end in the worst inconvenience being first removed. And however irregular this process may be (and we admit that men's habits and prejudices produce many anomalies, or seeming anomalies, in it) it is a process far more trustworthy than are legislative judgments. For those who question this, there are instances; and, that the parallel may be the more conclusive, we will take a case in which the ruling power is deemed specially fit to decide. We refer to our means of communication.

Do those who maintain that railways would have been better laid out and constructed by government, hold that the order of importance would have been as uniformly followed as it has been by private enterprise? Under the stimulus of an enormous traffic—a traffic too great for the then existing means—the first line sprung up between Liverpool and Manchester. Next came the Grand Junction and the London and Birmingham (now merged in the London and Northwestern); afterwards the Great Western, the Southwestern, the Southeastern, the Eastern Counties, the Midland. Since then subsidiary lines and branches have occupied our capitalists. As they were quite certain to do, companies made first the most needed, and therefore the best paying, lines; under the

same impulse that a laborer chooses high wages in preference to low. That government would have adopted a
better order can hardly be, for the best has been followed; but that it would have adopted a worse, all the
evidence we have goes to show. In default of materials
for a direct parallel, we might cite from India and the
colonies, cases of injudicious road-making. Or, as ex-
emplifying State-efforts to facilitate communication, we
might dwell on the fact that while our rulers have sacrificed hundreds of lives and spent untold treasure in
seeking a Northwest passage, which would be useless
if found, they have left the exploration of the Isthmus of
Panama, and the making of railways and canals through
it, to private companies. But, not to make much of this
indirect evidence, we will content ourselves with the one
sample of a State-made channel for commerce, which
we have at home—the Caledonian Canal. Up to the present time (1853), this public work has cost upwards of
£1,100,000. It has now been open for many years, and
salaried emissaries have been constantly employed to
get traffic for it. The results, as given in its forty-seventh
annual report, issued in 1852, are—receipts during the
year, £7,909; expenditure ditto, £9,261; loss, £1,352. Has
any such large investment been made with such a pitiful
result by a private canal company?

And if a government is so bad a judge of the relative
importance of social requirements, when these requirements are *of the same kind,* how worthless a judge must
it be when they are of different kinds. If, where a fair
share of intelligence might be expected to lead them
right, legislators and their officers go so wrong, how

terribly will they err where no amount of intelligence would suffice them,—where they must decide among hosts of needs, bodily, intellectual, and moral, which admit of no direct comparisons; and how disastrous must be the results if they act out their erroneous decisions. Should any one need this bringing home to him by an illustration, let him read the following extract from the last of the series of letters some time since published in the *Morning Chronicle,* on the state of agriculture in France. After expressing the opinion that French farming is some century behind English farming, the writer goes on to say:

> There are two causes principally chargeable with this. In the first place, strange as it may seem in a country in which two-thirds of the population are agriculturists, agriculture is a very unhonoured occupation. Develop in the slightest degree a Frenchman's mental faculties, and he flies to a town as surely as steel filings fly to a loadstone. He has no rural tastes, no delight in rural habits. A French amateur farmer would indeed be a sight to see. Again, this national tendency is directly encouraged by the centralizing system of government—by the multitude of the officials, and by the payment of all functionaries. From all parts of France, men of great energy and resource struggle up, and fling themselves on the world of Paris. There they try to become great functionaries. Through every department* of the eighty-four, men of less energy and resource struggle up to the *chef-lieu*—the provincial capital. There they try to become little functionaries. Go still lower—deal with a still smaller scale—and the result will be the same. As is the department to France, so is the arrondissement to the department, and the commune to the arrondissement. All who have,

---

* The departments are political subdivisions, created by redistricting the old provinces of France.—Ed.

or think they have, heads on their shoulders, struggle into towns to fight for office. All who are, or are deemed by themselves or others, too stupid for anything else, are left at home to till the fields, and breed the cattle, and prune the vines, as their ancestors did for generations before them. Thus there is actually no intelligence left in the country. The whole energy, and knowledge, and resource of the land are barreled up in the towns. You leave one city, and in many cases you will not meet an educated or cultivated individual until you arrive at another; all between is utter intellectual barrenness.

To what end now is this constant abstraction of able men from rural districts? To the end that there may be enough functionaries to achieve those many desiderata which French Governments have thought ought to be achieved—to provide amusements, to manage mines, to construct roads and bridges, to erect numerous buildings; to print books, encourage the fine arts, control this trade, and inspect that manufacture; to do all the hundred-and-one things which the State does in France. That the army of officers needed for this may be maintained, agriculture must go unofficered. That certain social conveniences may be better secured, the chief social necessity is neglected. The very basis of the national life is sapped, to gain a few non-essential advantages. Said we not truly, then, that until a requirement is spontaneously fulfilled, it should not be fulfilled at all?

VI

And here indeed we may recognize the close kinship between the fundamental fallacy involved in these State-meddlings and the fallacy lately exploded by the free-trade agitation. These various law-made instrumentalities for effecting ends which might otherwise not yet be effected, all embody a subtler form of the protectionist hypothesis. The same short-sightedness which, looking at commerce, prescribed bounties and restrictions, looking at social affairs in general, prescribes these multiplied administrations; and the same criticism applies alike to all its proceedings.

For was not the error that vitiated every law aiming at the artificial maintenance of a trade, substantially that which we have just been dwelling upon; namely this overlooking of the fact that, in setting people to do one thing, some other thing is inevitably left undone? The statesmen who thought it wise to protect home-made silks against French silks, did so under the impression that the manufacture thus secured constituted a pure gain to the nation. They did not reflect that the men employed in this manufacture would otherwise have been producing something else; a something else which, as they could produce it without legal help, they could more profitably produce. Landlords who have been so anxious to prevent foreign wheat from displacing their own wheat, have never duly realized the fact that if their fields would not yield wheat so economically as to prevent the feared displacement, it simply proved that they were growing unfit crops in place of fit crops; and so working their land at a relative loss. In all cases where, by restrictive duties, a trade has been upheld that would otherwise not have existed, capital has been turned into a channel less productive than some other into which it would naturally have flowed. And so, to pursue certain State-patronized occupations, men have been drawn from more advantageous occupations.

Clearly then, as above alleged, the same oversight runs through all these interferences; be they with commerce, or be they with other things. In employing people to achieve this or that desideratum, legislators have not perceived that they were thereby preventing the achievement of some other desideratum. They have habitually assumed that each proposed good would, if secured, be a pure good, instead of being a good purchasable only by submission to some evil which would else have been remedied; and, making this error, have injuriously diverted men's labor. As in trade, so in other things, labor will spontaneously find out, better than any government can find out for it, the things on which it may best expend itself. Rightly regarded, the two propositions are identical. This division into commercial and non-commercial affairs is quite a superficial one. All the actions going on in society come under the generalization: human effort ministering to human desire. Whether the ministration be effected through a process of buying and selling, or whether in any other way, matters not so far as the general law of it is concerned. In all cases it must be true that the stronger desires will get themselves satisfied before the weaker ones; and in all cases it must be true that to get satisfaction for the weaker ones before they would naturally have it, is to deny satisfaction to the stronger ones.

VII

To the immense positive evils entailed by over-legislation have to be added the equally great negative evils;
evils which, notwithstanding their greatness, are
scarcely at all recognized, even by the far-seeing. While
the State does those things which it ought not to do, *as
an inevitable consequence,* it leaves undone those things
which it ought to do. Time and activity being limited, it
necessarily follows that legislators' sins of *commission*
entail sins of *omission.* Mischievous meddling involves
disastrous neglect; and until statesmen are ubiquitous
and omnipotent, must ever do so. In the very nature of
things an agency employed for two purposes must fulfil
both imperfectly; partly because while fulfilling the one
it cannot be fulfilling the other, and partly, because its
adaptation to both ends implies incomplete fitness for
either. As has been well said *à propos* of this point, "A
blade which is designed both to shave and to carve, will
certainly not shave so well as a razor or carve so well as
a carving-knife. An academy of painting, which should
also be a bank, would in all probability exhibit very bad
pictures and discount very bad bills. A gas-company,
which should also be an infant-school society, would,
we apprehend, light the streets ill, and teach the children
ill." And if an institution undertakes, not two functions
but a score; if a government, whose office it is to defend
citizens against aggressors, foreign and domestic, en-
gages also to disseminate Christianity, to administer
charity, to teach children their lessons, to adjust prices

of food, to inspect coal-mines, to regulate railways, to superintend house-building, to arrange cab-fares, to look into people's stink-traps, to vaccinate their children, to send out emigrants, to prescribe hours of labor, to examine lodging-houses, to test the knowledge of mercantile captains, to provide public libraries, to read and authorize dramas, to inspect passenger-ships, to see that small dwellings are supplied with water, to regulate endless things from a banker's issues down to the boat-fares on the Serpentine; is it not manifest that its primary duty must be ill-discharged in proportion to the multiplicity of affairs it busies itself with? Must not its time and energies be frittered away in schemes, and inquiries, and amendments, in discussions, and divisions, to the neglect of its essential business? And does not a glance over the debates make it clear that this is the fact? and that, while Parliament and public are alike occupied with these mischievous interferences, these utopian hopes, the one thing needful is left almost undone?

See here, then, the proximate cause of our legal abominations. We drop the substance in our efforts to catch shadows. While our firesides and clubs and taverns are filled with talk about corn-law questions, and church questions, and education questions, and poor-law questions—all of them raised by over-legislation—the justice-question gets scarcely any attention; and we daily submit to be oppressed, cheated, robbed. This institution which should succor the man who has fallen among thieves, turns him over to solicitors, barristers, and a legion of law-officers; drains his purse for writs, briefs, affidavits, subpœnas, fees of all kinds and expenses innumerable;

involves him in the intricacies of common courts, chancery-courts, suits, counter-suits, and appeals; and often ruins where it should aid. Meanwhile, meetings are called and leading articles written and votes asked and societies formed and agitations carried on, not to rectify these gigantic evils, but partly to abolish our ancestors' mischievous meddlings and partly to establish meddlings of our own. Is it not obvious that this fatal neglect is a result of this mistaken officiousness? Suppose that external and internal protection had been the sole recognized functions of the ruling powers: is it conceivable that our administration of justice would have been as corrupt as now? Can any one believe that had Parliamentary elections been habitually contested on questions of legal reform, our judicial system would still have been what Sir John Romilly calls it, "a technical system invented for the creation of costs"?* Does any one suppose that, if the efficient defence of person and property had been the constant subject-matter of hustings pledges, we should yet be waylaid by a Chancery court which has now more than two hundred millions of property in its clutches; which keeps suits pending fifty years, until all the funds are gone in fees; which swallows in costs two millions annually? Dare any one assert that had constituencies been always canvassed on principles of law-reform versus law-conservatism, ecclesiastical courts would have continued for centuries fattening on the goods of widows and orphans? The questions are next to absurd. A child may see that with the general

---

* Campaign promises.—Ed.

knowledge people have of legal corruptions and the universal detestation of legal atrocities, an end would long since have been put to them, had the administration of justice always been *the* political topic. Had not the public mind been constantly preoccupied, it could never have been tolerated that a man neglecting to file an answer to a bill in due course, should be imprisoned fifteen years for contempt of court, as Mr. James Taylor was. It would have been impossible that, on the abolition of their sinecures, the sworn-clerks should have been compensated by the continuance of their exorbitant incomes, not only till death, but for seven years after, at a total estimated cost of £700,000. Were the State confined to its defensive and judicial functions, not only the people but legislators themselves would agitate against abuses. The sphere of activity and the opportunities for distinction being narrowed, all the thought and industry and eloquence which members of Parliament now expend on impracticable schemes and artificial grievances, would be expended in rendering justice pure, certain, prompt, and cheap. The complicated follies of our legal verbiage, which the uninitiated cannot understand and which the initiated interpret in various senses, would be quickly put an end to. We should no longer frequently hear of Acts of Parliament so bunglingly drawn up that it requires half a dozen actions and judges' decisions under them, before even lawyers can say how they apply. There would be no such stupidly-designed measures as the Railway Winding-up Act, which, though passed in 1846 to close the accounts of the bubble-schemes* of the

---

* A mania of speculation in railway stocks.—Ed.

mania, leaves them still unsettled in 1854; which, even with funds in hand, withholds payment from creditors whose claims have been years since admitted. Lawyers would no longer be suffered to maintain and to complicate the present absurd system of land-titles, which, besides the litigation and loss it perpetually causes, lowers the value of estates, prevents the ready application of capital to them, checks the development of agriculture, and thus hinders the improvement of the peasantry and the prosperity of the country. In short, the corruptions, follies, and terrors of law would cease; and that which men now shrink from as an enemy they would come to regard as what it purports to be—a friend.

How vast then is the negative evil which, in addition to the positive evils before enumerated, this meddling policy entails on us! How many are the grievances men bear, from which they would otherwise be free! Who is there that has not submitted to injuries rather than run the risk of heavy law-costs? Who is there that has not abandoned just claims rather than "throw good money after bad"? Who is there that has not paid unjust demands rather than withstand the threat of an action? This man can point to property that has been alienated from his family from lack of funds or courage to fight for it. That man can name several relations ruined by a lawsuit. Here is a lawyer who has grown rich on the hard earnings of the needy and the savings of the oppressed. There is a once-wealthy trader who has been brought by legal iniquities to the workhouse or the lunatic asylum. The badness of our judicial system vitiates our whole social life: renders almost every family poorer than it would otherwise be; hampers almost every business transaction; inflicts daily anxieties on every trader. And all this loss of property, time, temper, comfort, men quietly submit to from being absorbed in the pursuit of schemes which eventually bring on them other mischiefs.

Nay, the case is even worse. It is distinctly provable that many of these evils about which outcries are raised, and to cure which special Acts of Parliament are loudly invoked, are themselves *produced* by our disgraceful judicial system. For example, it is well known that the horrors out of which our sanitary agitators make political capital, are found in their greatest intensity on properties that have been for a generation in Chancery; are distinctly traceable to the ruin thus brought about; and would never have existed but for the infamous corruptions of law. Again, it has been shown that the long-drawn miseries of Ireland, which have been the subject of endless legislation, have been mainly produced by inequitable land-tenure and the complicated system of entail: a system which wrought such involvements as to prevent sales; which practically negatived all improvement; which brought landlords to the workhouse; and which required an Incumbered Estates Act to cut its Gordian knots and render the proper cultivation of the soil possible. Judicial negligence, too, is the main cause of railway-accidents. If the State would fulfil its true function, by giving passengers an easy remedy for breach of contract when trains are behind time, it would do more to prevent accidents than can be done by the minutest inspection or the most cunningly-devised regulations; for it is notorious that the majority of accidents are primarily caused by irregularity. In the case of bad house-building, also, it is obvious that a cheap, rigorous, and certain administration of justice, would make Building Acts needless. For is not the man who erects a house of bad materials ill put together, and, concealing these with papering and plaster, sells it as a substantial dwelling, guilty of fraud? And should not the law recognize this fraud as it does in the analogous case of an unsound horse? And if the legal remedy were easy, prompt, and sure, would not builders cease transgressing? So is it in other cases; the evils which men perpetually call on the State to cure by superintendence, themselves arise from non-performance of its original duty.

See then how this vicious policy complicates itself. Not only does meddling legislation fail to cure the evils it aims at; not only does it make many evils worse; not only does it create new evils greater than the old; but while doing this it entails on men the oppressions, robberies, ruin, which flow from the non-administration of justice. And not only to the positive evils does it add this vast negative one, but this again, by fostering many social abuses that would not else exist, furnishes occasions for more meddlings which again act and react in the same way. And thus as ever, "things bad begun make strong themselves by ill."

VIII

After assigning reasons, thus fundamental, for condemning all State-action save that which universal experience has proved to be absolutely needful, it would

seem superfluous to assign subordinate ones. Were it
called for, we might, taking for text Mr. Lindsay's work
on *Navigation and Mercantile Marine Law,* say much upon
the complexity to which this process of adding regulation to regulation—each necessitated by foregoing
ones—ultimately leads: a complexity which, by the mis-
understandings, delays, and disputes it entails, greatly
hampers our social life. Something, too, might be added
upon the perturbing effects of the "gross delusion," as
M. Guizot calls it, "a belief in the sovereign power of
political machinery"—a delusion to which he partly as-
cribes the late revolution in France; and a delusion which
is fostered by every new interference. But, passing over
these, we would dwell for a short space upon the national enervation which this State-superintendence
produces.

The enthusiastic philanthropist, urgent for some Act
of Parliament to remedy this evil or secure the other
good, thinks it a trivial and far-fetched objection that the
people will be morally injured by doing things for them
instead of leaving them to do things themselves. He viv-
idly conceives the benefit he hopes to get achieved,
which is a positive and readily-imaginable thing. He
does not conceive the diffused, invisible, and slowly-
accumulating effect wrought on the popular mind, and
so does not believe in it; or, if he admits it, thinks it
beneath consideration. Would he but remember, however, that all national character is gradually produced by
the daily action of circumstances, of which each day's
result seems so insignificant as not to be worth mention-
ing, he would perceive that what is trifling when viewed

in its increments may be formidable when viewed in its total. Or if he would go into the nursery, and watch how repeated actions—each of them apparently unimportant,—create, in the end, a habit which will affect the whole future life, he would be reminded that every influence brought to bear on human nature tells, and, if continued, tells seriously. The thoughtless mother who hourly yields to the requests, "Mamma, tie my pinafore," "Mamma, button my shoe," and the like, cannot be persuaded that each of these concessions is detrimental; but the wiser spectator sees that if this policy be long pursued, and be extended to other things, it will end in inaptitude. The teacher of the old school who showed his pupil the way out of every difficulty, did not perceive that he was generating an attitude of mind greatly militating against success in life. The modern teacher, however, induces his pupil to solve his difficulties himself; believes that in so doing he is preparing him to meet the difficulties which, when he goes into the world, there will be no one to help him through; and finds confirmation for this belief in the fact that a great proportion of the most successful men are self-made. Well, is it not obvious that this relationship between discipline and success holds good nationally? Are not nations made of men; and are not men subject to the same laws of modification in their adult years as in their early years? Is it not true of the drunkard, that each carouse adds a thread to his bonds? of the trader, that each acquisition strengthens the wish for acquisitions? of the pauper, that the more you assist him the more he wants? of the busy man, that the more he has to do the more he can do? And does it not follow that if every individual is subject to this process of adaptation to conditions, a whole nation must be so; that just in proportion as its members are little helped by extraneous power they will become self-helping, and in proportion as they are much helped they will become helpless? What folly is it to ignore these results because they are not direct and not immediately visible. Though slowly wrought out, they are inevitable. We can no more elude the laws of human development than we can elude the law of gravitation; and so long as they hold true must these effects occur.

If we are asked in what special directions this alleged helplessness, entailed by much state-superintendence, shows itself, we reply that it is seen in a retardation of all social growths requiring self-confidence in the people; in a timidity that fears all difficulties not before encountered; in a thoughtless contentment with things as they are. Let any one, after duly watching the rapid evolution going on in England, where men have been comparatively little helped by governments—or better still, after contemplating the unparalleled progress of the United States, which is peopled by self-made men, and the recent descendants of self-made men—let such an one, we say, go on to the Continent, and consider the relatively slow advance which things are there making; and the still slower advance they would make but for English enterprise. Let him go to Holland and see that though the Dutch early showed themselves good mechanics, and have had abundant practice in hydraulics, Amsterdam has been without any due supply of water until now that works are being established by an English company. Let him go to Berlin and there be told that, to give that city a water-supply such as London has had for generations, the project of an English firm is about to be executed by English capital, under English superintendence. Let him go to Vienna and learn that it, in common with other continental cities, is lighted by an English gas-company. Let him go on the Rhone, on the Loire, on the Danube, and discover that Englishmen established steam navigation on those rivers. Let him inquire concerning the railways in Italy, Spain, France, Sweden, Denmark, how many of them are English projects, how many have been largely helped by English capital, how many have been executed by English contractors, how many have had English engineers. Let him discover, too, as he will, that where railways have been government-made, as in Russia, the energy, the perseverance, and the practical talent developed in England and the United States have been called in to aid. And then if these illustrations of the progressiveness of a self-dependent race, and the torpidity of paternally-governed ones, do not suffice him, he may read Mr. Laing's successive volumes of European travel, and there study the contrast in detail. What, now, is the cause of this contrast? In the order of nature, a capacity for self-help must in every case have been brought into existence by the practice of self-help; and, other things equal, a lack of this capacity must in every case have arisen from the lack of demand for it. Do not these two antecedents and their two consequents agree with the facts as presented in England and Europe? Were not the inhabitants of the two, some centuries ago, much upon a par in point of enterprise?

Were not the English even behind in their manufactures, in their colonization, in their commerce? Has not the immense relative change the English have undergone in this respect, been coincident with the great relative self-dependence they have been since habituated to? And has not the one been caused by the other? Whoever doubts it, is asked to assign a more probable cause. Whoever admits it, must admit that the enervation of a people by perpetual State-aids is not a trifling consideration, but the most weighty consideration. A general arrest of national growth he will see to be an evil greater than any special benefits can compensate for. And, indeed, when, after contemplating this great fact, the over-spreading of the earth by the English, he remarks the absence of any parallel achievement by continental race; when he reflects how this difference must depend chiefly on difference of character, and how such difference of character has been mainly produced by difference of discipline; he will perceive that the policy pursued in this matter may have a large share in determining a nation's ultimate fate.

IX

We are not sanguine, however, that argument will change the convictions of those who put their trust in legislation. With men of a certain order of thought the foregoing reasons will have weight. With men of another order of thought they will have little or none; nor would any accumulation of such reasons affect them. The truth that experience teaches has its limits. The experiences which teach must be experiences which can be appreciated; and experiences exceeding a certain degree of complexity become inappreciable to the majority. It is thus with most social phenomena. If we remember that for these two thousand years and more, mankind have been making regulations for commerce, which have all along been strangling some trades and killing others with kindness, and that though the proofs of this have been constantly before their eyes, they have only just discovered that they have been uniformly doing mischief; if we remember that even now only a small portion of them see this; we are taught that perpetually-repeated and ever-accumulating experiences will fail to teach, until there exist the mental conditions required for the assimilation of them. Nay, when they are assimilated, it is very imperfectly. The truth they teach is only half understood, even by those supposed to understand it best. For example, Sir Robert Peel, in one of his last speeches, after describing the immensely increased consumption consequent on free trade, goes on to say:

> If, then, you can only continue that consumption; if, *by your legislation,* under the favor of Providence, *you can maintain the demand for labor and make your trade and manufactures prosperous;* you are not only increasing the sum of human happiness, but are giving the agriculturists of this country the best chance of that increased demand which must contribute to their welfare. —*The Times,* Feb. 22, 1850.

Thus the prosperity really due to the abandonment of all legislation, is ascribed to a particular kind of legislation. *"You* can maintain the demand," he says; *"you* can make trade and manufactures prosperous"; whereas, the facts he quotes prove that they can do this only by doing nothing. The essential truth of the matter—that law had been doing immense harm, and that this prosperity resulted not from law but from the absence of law—is missed; and his faith in legislation in general, which should, by this experience, have been greatly shaken, seemingly remains as strong as ever. Here, again, is the House of Lords, apparently not yet believing in the relationship of supply and demand, adopting within these few weeks the standing order—

> That before the first reading of any bill for making any work in the construction of which compulsory power is sought to take thirty houses or more, inhabited by the labouring classes in any one parish or place, the promoters be required to deposit in the office of the clerk of the Parliaments a statement of the number, description, and situation of the said houses, the number (so far as they can be estimated) of persons to be displaced, *and whether any, and what, provision is made in the bill for remedying the inconvenience likely to arise from such displacements.*

If, then, in the comparatively simple relationships of trade, the teachings of experience remain for so many ages unperceived, and are so imperfectly apprehended when they are perceived, it is scarcely to be hoped that where all social phenomena—moral, intellectual, and physical—are involved, any due appreciation of the truths displayed will presently take place. The facts cannot yet get recognized as facts. As the alchemist attributed his successive disappointments to some disproportion in the ingredients, some inpurity, or some too great temperature, and never to the futility of his process or the impossibility of his aim; so, every failure of State-regulations the law-worshipper explains away as being caused by this trifling oversight, or that little mistake: all which oversights and mistakes he assures you will in future be avoided. Eluding the facts as he does after this fashion, volley after volley of them produce no effect.

Indeed this faith in governments is in a certain sense organic; and can diminish only by being outgrown. From the time when rulers were thought demi-gods, there has been a gradual decline in men's estimates of their power. This decline is still in progress, and has still far to go. Doubtless, every increment of evidence furthers it in *some* degree, though not to the degree that at first appears. Only in so far as it modifies character does it produce a permanent effect. For while the mental type remains the same, the removal of a special error is inevitably followed by the growth of other errors of the same genus. All superstitions die hard; and we fear that this belief in government-omnipotence will form no exception.

REPRESENTATIVE GOVERNMENT—WHAT IS IT GOOD FOR? (1857)

Shakespeare's simile for adversity—

> Which, like the toad, ugly and venomous,
> Wears yet a precious jewel in his head,

might fitly be used also as a simile for a disagreeable truth. Repulsive as is its aspect, the hard fact which dissipates a cherished illusion, is presently found to contain the germ of a more salutary belief. The experience of every one furnishes instances in which an opinion long shrunk from as seemingly at variance with all that is good, but finally accepted as irresistible, turns out to be fraught with benefits. It is thus with self-knowledge: much as we dislike to admit our defects, we find it better

---

This essay was first published in The Westminster Review *for October 1857 and was reprinted in Spencer's* Essays: Scientific, Political and Speculative *(London and New York, 1892, in three volumes).*

to know and guard against than to ignore them. It is thus with changes of creed: alarming as looks the reasoning by which superstitions are overthrown, the convictions to which it leads prove to be healthier ones than those they superseded. And it is thus with political enlightenment: men eventually see cause to thank those who pull to pieces their political air-castles, hateful as they once seemed. Moreover, not only is it always better to believe truth than error; but the repugnant-looking facts are ever found to be parts of something far better than the ideal which they dispelled. To the many illustrations of this which might be cited, we shall presently add another.

It is a conviction almost universally entertained here in England, that our method of making and administering laws possesses every virtue. Prince Albert's unlucky saying that "Representative Government is on its trial," is vehemently repudiated: we consider that the trial has long since ended in our favour on all the counts. Partly from ignorance, partly from the bias of education, partly from that patriotism which leads the men of each nation to pride themselves in their own institutions, we have an unhesitating belief in the entire superiority of our form of political organization. Yet unfriendly critics can point out vices that are manifestly inherent. And if we may believe the defenders of despotism, these vices are fatal to its efficiency.

Now instead of denying or blinking these allegations, it would be wiser candidly to inquire whether they are true; and if true, what they imply. If, as most of us are so confident, government by representatives is better than any other, we can afford to listen patiently to all adverse remarks: believing that they are either invalid, or that if valid they do not essentially tell against its merits. If our political system is well founded, this crucial criticism will serve but to bring out its worth more clearly than ever; and to give us higher conceptions of its nature, its meaning, its purpose. Let us, then, banishing for the nonce all prepossessions, and taking up a thoroughly antagonistic point of view, set down without mitigation its many flaws, vices, and absurdities.

Is it not manifest that a ruling body made up of many individuals, who differ in character, education, and aims, who belong to classes having antagonistic ideas and feelings, and who are severally swayed by the special opinions of the districts deputing them, must be a cumbrous apparatus for the management of public affairs? When we devise a machine we take care that its parts are as few as possible; that they are adapted to their respective ends; that they are properly joined with one another; and that they work smoothly to their common purpose. Our political machine, however, is constructed upon directly opposite principles. Its parts are extremely numerous: multiplied, indeed, beyond all reason. They are not severally chosen as specially qualified for particular functions. No care is taken that they shall fit well together: on the contrary, our arrangements are such that they are certain not to fit. And that, as a consequence, they do not and cannot act in harmony, is a fact nightly demonstrated to all the world. In truth, had the problem been to find an appliance for the slow and bungling transaction of business, it could scarcely have been better solved. Immense hindrance results from the mere multiplicity of parts; a further immense hindrance results from their incongruity; yet another immense hindrance results from the frequency with which they are changed; while the greatest hindrance of all results from the want of subordination of the parts to their functions—from the fact that the personal welfare of the legislator is not bound up with the efficient performance of his political duty.

These defects are inherent in the very nature of our institutions; and they cannot fail to produce disastrous mismanagement. If proofs be needed, they may be furnished in abundance, both from the current history of our central representative government, and from that of local ones, public and private. Let us, before going on to comtemplate these evils as displayed on a great scale in our legislature, glance at some of them in their simpler and smaller manifestations.

We will not dwell on the comparative inefficiency of deputed administration in mercantile affairs. The untrustworthiness of directorial management might be afresh illustrated by the recent joint-stock-bank catastrophies: the recklessness and dishonesty of rulers whose interests are not one with those of the concern they control, being in these cases conspicuously displayed. Or we could enlarge on the same truth as exhibited in the doings of railway-boards: instancing the malversations proved against their members; the carelessness which has permitted Robson and Redpath frauds; the rashness perseveringly shown in making unprofitable branches and extensions. But facts of this kind are sufficiently familiar.

Let us pass, then, to less notorious examples. Mechanics' Institutions will supply our first. The theory of these is plausible enough. Artisans wanting knowledge, and benevolent middle-class people wishing to help them to it, constitute the raw material. By uniting their means they propose to obtain literary and other advantages, which else would be beyond their reach. And it is concluded that, being all interested in securing the proposed objects, and the governing body being chosen out of their number, the results cannot fail to be such as were intended. In most cases, however, the results are quite otherwise. Indifference, stupidity, party-spirit, and religious dissension, nearly always thwart the efforts of the promoters. It is thought good policy to select as president some local notability; probably not distinguished for wisdom, but whose donation or prestige more than counterbalances his defect in this respect. Vice-presidents are chosen with the same view: a clergyman or two; some neighbouring squires, if they can be had; an ex-mayor; several aldermen; half a dozen manufacturers and wealthy tradesmen; and a miscellaneous complement. While the committee, mostly elected more because of their position or popularity than their intelligence or fitness for cooperation, exhibit similar incongruities. Causes of dissension quickly arise. A book much wished for by the mass of the members, is tabooed, because ordering it would offend the clerical party in the institution. Regard for the prejudices of certain magistrates and squires who figure among the vice-presidents, forbids the engagement of an otherwise desirable and popular lecturer, whose political and religious opinions are somewhat extreme. The selection of newspapers and magazines for the reading-room, is a fruitful source of disputes. Should some, thinking it would be a great boon to those for whom the institution was established, propose to open the reading-room on Sundays, there arises a violent fight; ending, perhaps, in the secession of some of the defeated party. The question of amusements, again, furnishes a bone of contention. Shall the institution exist solely for instruction, or shall it add gratification? The refreshment-question, also, is apt to be raised, and to add to the other causes of difference. In short, the stupidity, prejudice, party-spirit, and squabbling, are such as eventually to drive away in disgust those who should have been the administrators; and to leave the control in the hands of a clique, who pursue some humdrum middle course, satisfying nobody. Instead of that prosperity which would probably have been achieved under the direction of one good man-of-business, whose welfare was bound up with its success, the institution loses its prestige, and dwindles away; ceases almost entirely to be what was intended—a *mechanics'* institution; and becomes little more than a middle-class lounge, kept up not so much by the permanent adhesion of its members, as by the continual addition of new ones in place of the old ones constantly falling off. Meanwhile, the end originally proposed is fulfilled, so far as it gets fulfilled at all, by private enterprise. Cheap newspapers and cheap periodicals, provided by publishers having in view the pockets and tastes of the working-classes; coffee-shops and penny reading-rooms, set up by men whose aim is profit; are the instruments of the chief proportion of such culture as is going on.

In higher-class institutions of the same order—in Literary Societies and Philosophical Societies, etc.—the like inefficiency of representative government is generally displayed. Quickly following the vigour of early enthusiasm, come class and sectarian differences, the final supremacy of a party, bad management, apathy. Subscribers complain they cannot get what they want; and one by one desert to private book-clubs or to Mudie.

Turning from non-political to political institutions, we might, had we space, draw illustrations from the doings of the old poor-law authorities, or from those of modern boards of guardians; but omitting these and other such, we will, among local governments, confine ourselves to the reformed municipal corporations.

If, leaving out of sight all other evidences, and forgetting that they are newly-organized bodies into which corruption has scarcely had time to creep, we were to judge of these municipal corporations by the town-improvements they have effected, we might pronounce them successful. But, even without insisting on the fact that such improvements are more due to the removal of obstructions, and to that same progressive spirit which has established railways and telegraphs, than to the positive virtues of these civic governments; it is to be remarked that the execution of numerous public works is by no means an adequate test. With power of raising funds limited only by a rebellion of ratepayers, it is easy in prosperous, increasing towns, to make a display of efficiency. The proper questions to be asked are: Do municipal elections end in the choice of the fittest men who are to be found? Does the resulting administrative body, perform well and economically the work which devolves on it? And does it show sound judgement in refraining from needless or improper work? To these questions the answers are by no means satisfactory.

Town-councils are not conspicuous for either intelligence or high character. There are competent judges who think that, on the average, their members are inferior to those of the old corporations they superseded. As all the world knows, the elections turn mainly on political opinions. The first question respecting any candidate is, not whether he has great knowledge, judgement, or business-faculty—not whether he has any special aptitude for the duty to be discharged; but whether he is Whig or Tory. Even supposing his politics to be unobjectionable, his nomination still does not depend chiefly on his proved uprightness or capacity, but much more on his friendly relations with the dominant clique. A number of the town magnates, habitually meeting probably at the chief hotel, and there held together as much by the brotherhood of conviviality as by that of opinion, discuss the merits of all whose names are before the public, and decide which are the most suitable. This gin-and-water caucus it is which practically determines the choice of candidates; and, by consequence, the elections. Those who will succumb to leadership—those who will merge their private opinions in the policy of their party, of course have the preference. Men too independent for this—too far-seeing to join in the shibboleth of the hour, or too refined to mix with the "jolly good fellows" who thus rule the town, are shelved; notwithstanding that they are, above all others, fitted for office. Partly from this underhand influence, and partly from the consequent disgust which leads them to decline standing if asked, the best men are generally not in the governing body. It is notorious that in London the most respectable merchants will have nothing to do with the local government. And in New York, "the exertions of its better citizens are still exhausted in private accumulation, while the duties of administration are left to other hands." It cannot then be asserted that in town-government, the representative system succeeds in bringing the ablest and most honourable men to the top.

The efficient and economical discharge of duties is, of course, hindered by this inferiority of the deputies chosen; and it is further hindered by the persistent action of party and personal motives. Not whether he knows well how to handle a level, but whether he voted for the popular candidate at the last parliamentary election, is the question on which may, and sometimes does, hang the choice of a town-surveyor; and if sewers are ill laid out, it is a natural consequence. When, a new public edifice having been decided on, competition designs are advertised for; and when the designs, ostensibly anonymous but really identifiable, have been sent in; T. Square, Esq., who has an influential relative in the corporation, makes sure of succeeding, and is not disappointed: albeit his plans are not those which would have been chosen by any one of the judges, had the intended edifice been his own. Brown, who has for many years been on the town-council and is one of the dominant clique, has a son who is a doctor; and when, in pursuance of an Act of Parliament, an officer of health is to be appointed, Brown privately canvasses his fellow-councillors, and succeeds in persuading them to elect his son; though his son is by no means the fittest man the place can furnish. Similarly with the choice of tradesmen to execute work for the town. A public clock which is frequently getting out of order, and Board-of-Health water-closets which disgust those who have them (we state facts), sufficiently testify that stupidity, favouritism, or some sinister influence, is ever causing mismanagement. The choice of inferior representatives, and by them of inferior *employés*, joined with private interest and divided responsibility, inevitably prevent the discharge of duties from being satisfactory.

Moreover, the extravagance which is now becoming a notorious vice of municipal bodies, is greatly increased by the practice of undertaking things which they ought not to undertake; and the incentive to do this is, in many cases, traceable to the representative origin of the body. The system of compounding with landlords for municipal rates, leads the lower class of occupiers into the erroneous belief that town-burdens do not fall in any degree on them; and they therefore approve of an expenditure which seemingly gives them gratis advantages while it creates employment. As they form the mass of the constituency, lavishness becomes a popular policy; and popularity-hunters vie with one another in bringing forward new and expensive projects. Here is a councillor who, having fears about his next election, proposes an extensive scheme for public gardens—a scheme which many who disapprove do not oppose, because they, too, bear in mind the next election. There is another councillor, who keeps a shop, and who raises and agitates the question of baths and wash-houses; very well knowing that his trade is not likely to suffer from such course. And so in other cases: the small direct interest which each member of the corporation has in economical administration, is antagonized by so many indirect interests of other kinds, that he is not likely to be a good guardian of the public purse.

Thus, neither in respect of the deputies chosen, nor the efficient performance of their work, nor the avoidance of unfit work, can the governments of our towns be held satisfactory. And if in these recently-formed bodies the defects are so conspicuous, still more conspicuous are they where they have had time to grow to their full magnitude: witness the case of New York. According to *The Times* correspondent in that city, the New York people pay "over a million and half sterling, for which they have badly-paved streets, a police by no means as efficient as it should be, though much better than formerly, the greatest amount of dirt north of Italy, the poorest cab-system of any metropolis in the world, and only unsheltered wooden piers for the discharge of merchandise."

And now, having glanced at the general bearings of

the question in these minor cases, let us take the major case of our central government; and, in connexion with it, pursue the inquiry more closely. Here the inherent faults of the representative system are much more clearly displayed. The greater multiplicity of rulers involves greater cumbrousness, greater confusion, greater delay. Differences of class, of aims, of prejudices, are both larger in number and wider in degree; and hence arise dissensions still more multiplied. The direct effect which each legislator is likely to experience from the working of any particular measure, is usually very small and re-mote; while the indirect influences which sway him are, in this above all other cases, numerous and strong; whence follows a marked tendency to neglect public welfare for private advantage. But let us set out from the beginning—with the constituencies.

The representative theory assumes that if a number of citizens, deeply interested as they all are in good gov-ernment, are endowed with political power, they will choose the wisest and best men for governors. Seeing how greatly they suffer from bad administration of pub-lic affairs, it is considered self-evident that they must have the *will* to select proper representatives; and it is taken for granted that average common sense gives the *ability* to select proper representatives. How does expe-rience bear out these assumptions? Does it not to a great degree negative them?

Several considerable classes of electors have little or no *will* in the matter. Not a few of those on the register pique themselves on taking no part in politics—claim credit for having the sense not to meddle with things which they say do not concern them. Many others there are whose interest in the choice of a member of Parliament is so slight, that they do not think it worth while to vote. A notable proportion, too, shopkeepers especially, care so little about the result, that their votes are determined by their wishes to please their chief patrons or to avoid offending them. In the minds of a yet larger class, small sums of money, or even *ad libitum* supplies of beer, outweigh any desires they have to use their political powers independently. Those who adequately recognize the importance of honestly exercising their judgements in the selection of legislators, and who give conscientious votes, form but a minority; and the election usually hangs less upon their wills than upon the illegitimate influences which sway the rest. Here, therefore, the theory fails.

Then, again, as to intelligence. Even supposing that the mass of electors have a sufficiently decided *will* to choose the best rulers, what evidence have we of their *ability?* Is picking out the wisest man among them, a task within the range of their capacities? Let any one listen to the conversation of a farmer's market-table, and then answer how much he finds of that wisdom which is required to discern wisdom in others. Or let him read the clap-trap speeches made from the hustings with a view of pleasing constituents, and then estimate the penetration of those who are to be thus pleased. Even among the higher order of electors he will meet with gross political ignorance—with notions that Acts of Parliament can do whatever it is thought well they should do; that the value of gold can be fixed by law; that distress can be cured by poor-laws; and so forth. If he descends a step, he will find in the still-prevalent ideas that machinery is injurious to the working-classes, and that extravagance is "good for trade," indices of a yet smaller insight. And in the lower and larger class, formed by those who think that their personal interest in good government is not worth the trouble of voting, or is outbalanced by the loss of a customer, or is of less value than a bribe, he will perceive an almost hopeless stupidity. Without going the length of Mr. Carlyle, and defining the people as "twenty-seven millions, mostly fools," he will confess that they are but sparely gifted with wisdom.

That these should succeed in choosing the fittest governors, would be strange; and that they do not so succeed is manifest. Even as judged by the most common-sense tests, their selections are absurd, as we shall shortly see.

It is a self-evident truth that we may most safely trust those whose interests are identical with our own; and that it is very dangerous to trust those whose interests are antagonistic to our own. All the legal securities we take in our transactions with one another, are so many recognitions of this truth. We are not satisfied with *professions*. If another's position is such that he must be liable to motives at variance with the promises he makes, we take care, by introducing an artificial motive (the dread of legal penalties), to make it his interest to fulfil these promises. Down to the asking for a receipt, our daily business-habits testify that, in consequence of the prevailing selfishness, it is extremely imprudent to expect men to regard the claims of others equally with their own: all asseverations of good faith notwithstanding. Now it might have been thought that even the modicum of sense possessed by the majority of electors, would have led them to recognize this fact in the choice of their representatives. But they show a total disregard of it. While the theory of our Constitution, in conformity with this same fact, assumes that the three divisions composing the Legislature will severally pursue each its own ends—while our history shows that Monarch, Lords, and Commons, *have* all along more or less conspicuously done this; our electors manifest by their votes, the belief that their interests will be as well cared for by members of the titled class as by members of their own class. Though, in their determined opposition to the Reform-Bill, the aristocracy showed how greedy they were, not only of their legitimate power but of their illegitimate power—though, by the enactment and pertinacious maintenance of the Corn-Laws, they proved how little popular welfare weighed in the scale against their own profits—though they have ever displayed a watchful jealousy even of their smallest privileges, whether equitable or inequitable (as witness the recent complaint in the House of Lords, that the Mercantile Marine Act calls on lords of manors to show their titles before they can claim the wrecks thrown on the shores of their estates, which before they had always done by prescription)—though they have habitually pursued that self-seeking policy which men so placed were sure to pursue; yet constituencies have decided that members of the aristocracy may fitly be chosen as representatives of the people. Our present House of Commons contains 98 Irish peers and sons of English peers; 66 blood-relations of peers; and 67 connexions of peers by marriage; in all, 231 members whose interests, or sympathies, or both, are with the nobility rather than the commonalty. We are quite prepared to hear the doctrine implied in this criticism condemned by rose-water politicians as narrow and prejudiced. To such we simply reply that they and their friends fully recognize this doctrine when it suits them to do so. Why do they wish to prevent the town-constituencies from predominating over the county-ones; if they do not believe that each division of the community will consult its own welfare? Or what plea can there be for Lord John Russell's proposal to represent minorities, unless it be the plea that those who have the opportunity will sacrifice the interests of others to their own? Or how shall we explain the anxiety of the upper class, to keep a tight rein on the growing power of the lower class, save from their consciousness that *bona fide* representatives of the lower class would be less regardful of their privileges than they are themselves? If there be any reason in the theory of the Constitution, then, while the members of the House of Peers should belong to the peerage, the members of the House of Commons should belong to the commonalty. Either the constitutional theory is sheer nonsense, or else the choice of lords as representatives of the people proves the folly of constituencies.

But this folly by no means ends here; it works out other results quite as absurd. What should we think of a man giving his servants equal authority with himself over the affairs of his household? Suppose the share-holders in a railway-company were to elect, as members of their board of directors, the secretary, engineer, superintendent, traffic-manager, and others such. Should we not be astonished at their stupidity? Should we not prophesy that the private advantage of officials would frequently override the welfare of the company? Yet our parliamentary electors commit a blunder of just the same kind. For what are military and naval officers but servants of the nation; standing to it in a relation like that in which the officers of a railway-company stand to the company? Do they not perform public work? Do they not take public pay? And do not their interests differ from those of the public, as the interests of the employed from those of the employer? The impropriety of admitting executive agents of the State into the Legislature, has over and over again thrust itself into notice; and in minor cases has been prevented by sundry Acts of Parliament. Enumerating those disqualified for the House of Commons, Blackstone says:

> No persons concerned in the management of any duties or taxes created since 1692, except the commissioners of the treasury, nor any of the officers following, viz, commissioners of prizes, transports, sick and wounded, wine licences, navy, and victualling; secretaries or receivers of prizes; comptrollers of the army accounts; agents for regiments; governors of plantations, and their deputies; officers of Minorca or Gibraltar; officers of the excise and customs; clerks and deputies in the several offices of the treasury, exchequer, navy, victualling, admiralty, pay of the army and navy, secretaries of state, salt, stamps,

appeals, wine licences, hackney coaches, hawkers and pedlars, nor any persons that hold any new office under the crown created since 1705, are capable of being elected, or sitting as members.

In which list naval and military officers would doubtless have been included, had they not always been too powerful a body and too closely identified with the dominant classes. Glaring, however, as is the impolicy of appointing public servants to make the laws; and clearly as this impolicy is recognized in the above-specified exclusions from time to time enacted; the people at large seem totally oblivious of it. At the last general election they returned 9 naval officers, 46 military officers, and 51 retired military officers, who, in virtue of education, friendship, and *esprit de corps*, take the same views with their active comrades—in all 106: not including 64 officers of militia and yeomanry, whose sympathies and ambitions are in a considerable degree the same. If any one thinks that this large infusion of officialism is of no consequence, let him look in the division-lists. Let him inquire how much it has had to do with the maintenance of the purchase-system. Let him ask whether the almost insuperable obstacles to the promotion of the private soldier, have not been strengthened by it. Let him see what share it had in keeping up those worn-out practices, and forms, and mis-arrangements, which entailed the disasters of our late war. Let him consider whether the hushing-up of the Crimean Inquiry and the whitewashing of delinquents were not aided by it. Yet, though abundant experience thus confirms what common sense would beforehand have predicted; and though, notwithstanding the late disasters, exposures, and public outcry for army-reform, the influence of the military caste is so great that the reform has been staved-off; our constituencies are stupid enough to send to Parliament as many military officers as ever!

Not even now have we reached the end of these impolitic selections. The general principle on which we have been insisting, and which is recognized by expounders of the constitution when they teach that the legislative and executive divisions of the Government should be distinct—this general principle is yet further sinned against; though not in so literal a manner. For though they do not take State-pay, and are not nominally Government-officers, yet, practically, lawyers are members of the executive organization. They form an important part of the apparatus for the administration of justice. By the working of this apparatus they make their profits; and their welfare depends on its being so worked as to bring them profits, rather than on its being so worked as to administer justice. Exactly as military officers have interests distinct from, and often antagonistic to, the efficiency of the army; so, barristers and solicitors have interests distinct from, and often antagonistic to, the cheap and prompt enforcement of the law. And that they are habitually swayed by these antagonistic interest, is notorious. So strong is the bias, as sometimes even to destroy the power of seeing from any other than the professional stand-point. We have ourselves heard a lawyer declaiming on the damage which the County-Courts-Act had done to the profession; and expecting his non-professional hearers to join him in condemning it there for! And if, as all the world knows, the legal conscience is not of the tenderest, is it wise to depute lawyers to frame the laws which they will be concerned in carrying out; and the carrying out of which must affect their private incomes? Are barristers, who constantly take fees for work which they do not perform, and attorneys, whose bills are so often exorbitant that a special office has been established for taxing them—are these, of all others, to be trusted in a position which would be trying even to the most disinterested? Nevertheless, the towns and counties of England have returned to the present House of Commons 98 lawyers— some 60 of them in actual practice, and the rest retired, but doubtless retaining those class-views acquired during their professional careers.

These criticisms on the conduct of constituencies do not necessarily commit us to the assertion that *none* belonging to the official and aristocratic classes ought to be chosen. Though it would be safer to carry out, in these important cases, the general principle which, as above shown, Parliament has itself recognized and enforced in unimportant cases; yet we are not prepared to say that occasional exceptions might not be made, on good cause being shown. All we aim to show is the gross impolicy of selecting so large a proportion of representatives from classes having interests different from those of the general public. That in addition to more than a third taken from the dominant class, who already occupy one division of the Legislature, the House of Commons should contain nearly another third taken from the naval, military, and legal classes, whose policy, like that of the dominant class, is to maintain things as they are; we consider a decisive proof of electoral misjudgement. That out of the 654 members, of which the People's House now consists, there should be but 250 who, as considered from a class point of view, are eligible, or tolerably eligible (for we include a considerable number who are more or less objectionable), is significant of anything but popular good sense. That into an assembly established to protect their interests, the commonalty of England should have sent one-third whose interests are the same as their own, and two-thirds whose interests are at variance with their own, proves a scarcely credible lack of wisdom; and seems an awkward fact for the representative theory.

If the intelligence of the mass is thus not sufficient even to choose out men who by position and occupation are fit representatives, still less is it sufficient to choose men who are the fittest in character and capacity. To see who will be liable to the bias of private advantage is a very easy thing: to see who is wisest is a very difficult thing; and those who do not succeed in the first must necessarily fail in the last. The higher the wisdom the more incomprehensible does it become by ignorance. It is a manifest fact that the popular man or writer, is always one who is but little in advance of the mass, and consequently understandable by them: never the man who is far in advance of them and out of their sight. Appreciation of another implies some community of thought. "Only the man of worth can recognize worth in men. . . . The worthiest, if he appealed to universal suffrage, would have but a poor chance. . . . Alas! Jesus

Christ, asking the Jews what *he* deserved—was not the answer, Death on the gallows!" And though men do not now-a-days stone the prophet, they, at any rate, ignore him. As Mr. Carlyle says in his vehement way:

> If of ten men nine are recognisable as fools, which is a common calculation, how, . . . in the name of wonder, will you ever get a ballot-box to grind you out a wisdom from the votes of these ten men? . . . I tell you a million blockheads looking authoritatively into one man of what you call genius, or noble sense, will make nothing but nonsense out of him and his qualities, and his virtues and defects, if they look till the end of time.

So that, even were electors content to choose the man proved by general evidence to be the most far-seeing, and refrained from testing him by the coincidence of his views with their own, there would be small chance of their hitting on the best. But judging on him, as they do, by asking him whether he thinks this or that crudity which they think, it is manifest that they will fix on one far removed from the best. Their deputy will be truly representative;—representative, that is, of the average stupidity.

And now let us look at the assembly of representatives thus chosen. Already we have noted the unfit composition of this assembly as respects the interests of its members; and we have just seen what the representative theory itself implies as to their intelligence. Let us now, however, consider them more nearly under this last head.

And first, what is the work they undertake? Observe, we do not say the work which they *ought* to do, but the work which they *propose* to do, and *try* to do. This comprehends the regulation of nearly all actions going on throughout society. Besides devising measures to prevent the aggression of citizens on one another, and to secure each the quiet possession of his own; and besides assuming the further function, also needful in the present state of mankind, of defending the nation as a whole against invaders; they unhesitatingly take on themselves to provide for countless wants, to cure countless ills, to oversee countless affairs. Out of the many beliefs men have held respecting God, Creation, the Future, etc., they presume to decide which are true; and authorize an army of priests to perpetually repeat them to the people. The distress resulting from improvidence, they undertake to remove: they settle the minimum which each ratepayer shall give in charity, and how the proceeds shall be administered. Judging that emigration will not naturally go on fast enough, they provide means for carrying off some of the labouring classes to the colonies. Certain that social necessities will not cause a sufficiently rapid spread of knowledge, and confident that they know what knowledge is most required, they use public money for the building of schools and paying of teachers; they print and publish State-school-books; they employ inspectors to see that their standard of education is conformed to. Playing the part of doctor, they insist that every one shall use their specific, and escape the danger of small-pox by submitting to an attack of cow-pox. Playing the part of moralist, they decide which dramas are fit to be acted and which are not. Playing the part of artist, they prompt the setting up of drawing-schools, provide masters and models; and, at Marlborough House, enact what shall be considered good taste and what bad. Through their lieutenants, the corporations of towns, they furnish appliances for the washing of peoples' skins and clothes; they, in some cases, manufacture gas and put down water-pipes; they lay out sewers and cover over cesspools; they establish public libraries and make public gardens. Moreover, they determine how houses shall be built, and what is a safe construction for a ship; they take measures for the security of railway-travelling; they fix the hour after which public-houses may not be open; regulate the prices chargeable by vehicles plying in the London streets; they inspect lodging-houses; they arrange for burial-grounds; they fix the hours of factory hands. If some social process does not seem to them to be going on fast enough, they stimulate it; where the growth is not in the direction which they think most desirable, they alter it; and so they seek to realize some undefined ideal community.

Such being the task undertaken, what, let us ask, are the qualifications for discharging it? Supposing it possible to achieve all this, what must be the knowledge and capacities of those who shall achieve it? Successfully to prescribe for society, it is needful to know the structure of society—the principles on which it is organized—the natural laws of its progress. If there be not a true understanding of what constitutes social development, there must necessarily be grave mistakes made in checking these changes and fostering those. If there be lack of insight respecting the mutual dependence of the many functions which, taken together, make up the national

life, unforeseen disasters will ensue from not perceiving
how an interference with one will affect the rest. That is
to say, there must be a due acquaintance with the social
science—the science involving all others; the science
standing above all others in complexity.

And now, how far do our legislators possess this qualification? Do they in any moderate degree display it? Do
they make even a distant approximation to it? That many
of them are very good classical scholars is beyond doubt:
not a few have written first-rate Latin verses, and can
enjoy a Greek play; but there is no obvious relation between a memory well stocked with the words spoken
two thousand years ago, and an understanding disciplined to deal with modern society. That in learning the
languages of the past they have learnt some of its history,
is true; but considering that this history is mainly a
narrative of battles and plots and negotiations and
treacheries, it does not throw much light on social philosophy—not even the simplest principles of political
economy have ever been gathered from it. We do not
question, either, that a moderate percentage of members
of Parliament are fair mathematicians; and that mathematical discipline is valuable. As, however, political
problems are not susceptible of mathematical analysis,
their studies in this direction cannot much aid them in
legislation. To the large body of military officers who sit
as representatives, we would not for a moment deny a
competent knowledge of fortification, of strategy, of reg-
imental discipline; but we do not see that these throw
much light on the causes and cure of national evils. Indeed, considering that war fosters anti-social senti-

ments, and that the government of soldiers is necessarily despotic, military education and habits are more likely to unfit than to fit men for regulating the doings of a free people. Extensive acquaintance with the laws, may doubtless be claimed by the many barristers chosen by our constituencies; and this seems a kind of information having some relation to the work to be done. Unless, however, this information is more than technical— unless it is accompanied by knowledge of the ramified consequences which laws have produced in times past and are producing now (which nobody will assert), it cannot give much insight into Social Science. A familiarity with laws is no more a preparation for rational legislation, than would a familiarity with all the nostrums men have ever used be a preparation for the rational practice of medicine. Nowhere, then, in our representative body, do we find appropriate culture. Here is a clever novelist, and there a successful maker of railways; this member has acquired a large fortune in trade, and that member is noted as an agricultural improver; but none of these achievements imply fitness for controlling and adjusting social processes. Among the many who have passed through the public school and university *curriculum*—including though they may a few Oxford double-firsts and one or two Cambridge wranglers—there are none who have received the discipline required by the true legislator. None have that competent knowledge of Science in general, culminating in the Science of Life, which can alone form a basis for the Science of Society. For it is one of those open secrets which seem the more secret because they are so open, that all phenomena displayed by a nation are phenomena of Life, and are dependent on the laws of Life. There is no growth, decay, evil, improvement, or change of any kind, going on the body politic, but what has its cause in the actions of human beings; and there are no actions of human beings but what conform to the laws of Life in general, and cannot be truly understood until those laws are understood.

See, then, the immense incongruity between the end and the means. See on the one hand the countless difficulties of the task; and on the other hand the almost total unpreparedness of those who undertake it. Need we wonder that legislation is ever breaking down? Is it not natural that complaint, amendment, and repeal, should form the staple business of every session? Is there anything more than might be expected in the absurd Jack-Cadeisms which disgrace the debates? Even without setting up so high a standard of qualification as that above specified, the unfitness of most representatives for their duties is abundantly manifest. You need but glance over the miscellaneous list of noblemen, baronets, squires, merchants, barristers, engineers, soldiers, sailors, railway-directors, etc., and then ask what training their previous lives have given them for the intricate business of legislation, to see at once how extreme must be the incompetence. One would think that the whole system had been framed on the sayings of some political Dogberry: "The art of healing is difficult; the art of government easy. The understanding of arithmetic comes by study; while the understanding of society comes by instinct. Watchmaking requires a long apprenticeship;

but there needs none for the making of institutions. To manage a shop properly requires teaching; but the management of a people may be undertaken without preparation." Were we to be visited by some wiser Gulliver, or, as in the "Micromegas" of Voltaire, by some inhabitant of another sphere, his account of our political institutions might run somewhat as follows:

"I found that the English were governed by an assembly of men, said to embody the 'collective wisdom.' This assembly, joined with some other authorities which seem practically subordinate to it, has unlimited power. I was much perplexed by this. With us it is customary to define the office of any appointed body; and, above all things, to see that it does not defeat the ends for which it was appointed. But both the theory and the practice of this English Government imply that it may do whatever it pleases. Though, by their current maxims and usages, the English recognize the right of property as sacred—though the infraction of it is considered by them one of the gravest crimes—though the laws profess to be so jealous of it as to punish even the stealing of a turnip; yet their legislators suspend it at will. They take the money of citizens for any project which they choose to undertake; though such project was not in the least contemplated by those who gave them authority—nay, though the greater part of the citizens from whom the money is taken had no share in giving them such authority. Each citizen can hold property only so long as the 654 deputies do not want it. It seemed to me that an exploded doctrine once current among them of 'the divine right of kings,' had simply been changed into the divine right of Parliaments.

"I was at first inclined to think that the constitution of things on the Earth was totally different from what it is with us; for the current political philosophy here, implies that acts are not right or wrong in themselves but are made one or the other by the votes of law-makers. In our world it is considered manifest that if a number of beings live together, there must, in virtue of their natures, be certain primary conditions on which only they can work satisfactorily in concert; and we infer that the conduct which breaks through these conditions is bad. In the English legislature, however, a proposal to regulate conduct by any such abstract standard would be held absurd. I asked one of their members of Parliament whether a majority of the House could legitimize murder. He said, No. I asked him whether it could sanctify robbery. He thought not. But I could not make him see that if murder and robbery are intrinsically wrong, and not to be made right by decisions of statesmen, that similarly *all* actions must be either right or wrong, apart from the authority of the law; and that if the right and wrong of the law are not in harmony with this intrinsic right and wrong, the law itself is criminal. Some, indeed, among the English think as we do. One of their remarkable men (*not* included in their Assembly of Notables) writes thus:

> To ascertain better and better what the will of the Eternal was and is with us, what the laws of the Eternal are, all Parliaments, Ecumenic Councils, Congresses, and other Collective Wis-

doms, have had this for their object. . . . Nevertheless, in the inexplicable universal votings and debatings of these Ages, an idea or rather a dumb presumption to the contrary has gone idly abroad; and at this day, over extensive tracts of the world, poor human beings are to be found, whose practical belief it is that if we "vote" this or that, so this or that will thenceforth be. . . . Practically, men have come to imagine that the Laws of this Universe, like the laws of constitutional countries, are decided by voting. . . . It is an idle fancy. The Laws of this Universe, of which if the Laws of England are not an exact transcript, they should passionately study to become such, are fixed by the everlasting congruity of things, and are not fixable or changeable by voting!

"But I find that, contemptuously disregarding all such protests, the English legislators persevere in their hyperatheistic notion, that an Act of Parliament duly enforced by State-officers, will work out any object: no question being put whether Laws of Nature permit. I forgot to ask whether they considered that different kinds of food could be made wholesome or unwholesome by State-decree.

"One thing that struck me was the curious way in which the members of their House of Commons judge of one another's capacities. Many who expressed opinions of the crudest kinds, or trivial platitudes, or worn-out superstitions, were civilly treated. Follies as great as that but a few years since uttered by one of their ministers, who said that free-trade was contrary to common sense, were received in silence. But I was present when one of their number, who, as I thought, was speaking very rationally, made a mistake in his pronunciation— made what they call a wrong quantity; and immediately there arose a shout of derision. It seemed quite tolerable that a member should know little or nothing about the business he was there to transact; but quite *in*-tolerable that he should be ignorant of a point of no moment.

"The English pique themselves on being especially practical—have a great contempt for theorizers, and profess to be guided exclusively by facts. Before making or altering a law it is the custom to appoint a committee of inquiry, who send for men able to give information concerning the matter in hand, and ask them some thousands of questions. These questions, and the answers given to them, are printed in large books, and distributed among the members of the Houses of Parliament; and I was told that they spent about £100,000 a year in thus collecting and distributing evidence. Nevertheless, it appeared to me that the ministers and representatives of the English people, pertinaciously adhere to theories long ago disproved by the most conspicuous facts. They pay great respect to petty details of evidence, but of large truths they are quite regardless. Thus, the experience of age after age has shown that their state-management is almost invariably bad. The national estates are so miserably administered as often to bring loss instead of gain. The government ship-yards are uniformly extravagant and inefficient. The judicial system works so ill that most citizens will submit to serious losses rather than run risks of being ruined by law-suits. Countless facts prove the Government to be the worst owner, the worst manufacturer, the worst trader: in fact, the worst manager, be the thing managed what it may. But though the evidence of this is abundant and conclusive—though, during a recent war, the bunglings of officials were as glaring and multitudinous as ever; yet the belief that any proposed duties will be satisfactorily discharged by a new public department appointed to them, seems not a whit the weaker. Legislators, thinking themselves practical, cling to the plausible theory of an officially-regulated society, spite of overwhelming evidence that official regulation perpetually fails.

"Nay, indeed, the belief seems to gain strength among these fact-loving English statesmen, notwithstanding the facts are against it. Proposals for State-control over this and the other, have been of late more rife than ever. And, most remarkable of all, their representative assembly lately listened with grave faces to the assertion, made by one of their high authorities, that State-workshops are more economical than private workshops. Their prime minister, in defending a recently-established arms-factory, actually told them that, at one of their arsenals, certain missiles of war were manufactured not only better than by the trade, but at about one-third the price; and added, *'so it would be in all things.'* The English being a trading people, who must be tolerably familiar with the usual rates of profit among manufacturers, and the margin for possible economy, the fact that they should have got for their chief representative one so utterly in the dark on these matters, struck me as a wonderful result of the representative system.

"I did not inquire much further, for it was manifest that if these were really their wisest men, the English were not a wise people."

Representative government, then, cannot be called a success, in so far as the choice of men is concerned.

Those it puts into power are the fittest neither in respect of their interests, nor their culture, nor their wisdom. And as a consequence, partly of this and partly of its complex and cumbrous nature, representative government is anything but efficient for administrative purposes. In these respects it is manifestly inferior to monarchical government. This has the advantage of simplicity, which is always conducive to efficiency. And it has the further advantage that the power is in the hands of one who is directly concerned in the good management of national affairs; seeing that the continued maintenance of his power—nay, often his very life—depends on this. For his own sake a monarch chooses the wisest councillors he can find, regardless of class-distinctions. His interest in getting the best help is too great to allow of prejudices standing between him and a far-seeing man. We see this abundantly illustrated. Did not the kings of France take Richelieu, and Mazarin, and Turgot to assist them? Had not Henry VIII his Wolsey, Elizabeth her Burleigh, James his Bacon, Cromwell his Milton? And were not these men of greater calibre than those who hold the reins under out constitutional régime? So strong is the motive of an autocrat to make use of ability wherever it exists, that he will, like Louis XI, take even his barber into council if he finds him a clever fellow. Besides choosing them for ministers and advisers, he seeks out the most competent men for other offices. Napoleon raised his marshals from the ranks; and owed his military success in great part to the readiness with which he saw and availed himself of merit wherever found. We have recently seen in Russia how prompt was the recognition and promotion of engineering talent in the case

of Todleben; and know to our cost how greatly the prolonged defence of Sebastopol was due to this. In the
marked contrast to these cases supplied by our own
army, in which genius is ignored while muffs are hon-
oured—in which wealth and caste make the advance of
plebeian merit next to impossible—in which jealousies
between Queen's service and Company's service render
the best generalship almost unavailable; we see that the
representative system fails in the officering of its executive, as much as in the officering of its legislative. A
striking antithesis between the actions of the two forms
of government, is presented in the evidence given before
the Sebastopol Committee respecting the supply of huts
to the Crimean army—evidence showing that while, in
his negotiations with the English Government, the contractor for the huts met with nothing but vacillation,
delay, and official rudeness, the conduct of the French
Government was marked by promptitude, decision,
sound judgement, and great civility. Everything goes to
show that for administrative efficiency, autocratic power
is the best. If your aim is a well-organized army—if you
want to have sanitary departments, and educational departments, and charity-departments, managed in a busi-
ness-like way—if you would have society actively
regulated by staffs of State-agents; then by all means
choose that system of complete centralization which we
call despotism.

Probably, notwithstanding the hints dropped at the
outset, most have read the foregoing pages with surprise. Very likely some have referred to the cover of the

Review, to see whether they have not, in mistake, taken up some other than the *"Westiminster"*; while some may, perhaps, have accompanied their perusal by a running commentary of epithets condemnatory of our seeming change of principles. Let them not be alarmed. We have not in the least swerved from the confession of faith set forth in our prospectus. On the contrary, as we shall shortly show, our adhesion to free institutions is as strong as ever—nay, has even gained strength through this apparently antagonistic criticism.

The subordination of a nation to a man, is not a wholesome but a vicious state of things: needful, indeed, for a vicious humanity; but to be outgrown as fast as may be. The instinct which makes it possible is anything but a noble one. Call it "hero-worship," and it looks respectable. Call it what it is—a blind awe and fear of power, no matter of what kind, but more especially of the brutal kind; and it is by no means to be admired. Watch it in early ages deifying the cannibal chief; singing the praises of the successful thief; commemorating the most bloodthirsty warriors; speaking with reverence of those who had shown undying revenge; and erecting altars to such as carried furthest the vices which disgrace humanity; and the illusion disappears. Read how, where it was strongest, it immolated crowds of victims at the tomb of the dead king—how, at the altars raised to its heroes, it habitually sacrificed prisoners and children to satisfy their traditional appetite for human flesh—how it produced that fealty of subjects to rulers which made possible endless aggressions, battles, massacres, and horrors innumerable—how it has mercilessly slain those who would not lick the dust before its idols;—read all this, and the feeling no longer seems so worthy an one. See it in later days idealizing the worst as well as the best monarchs; receiving assassins with acclamation; hurrahing before successful treachery; rushing to applaud the processions and shows and ceremonies wherewith effete power stengthens itself; and it looks far from laudable. Autocracy presupposes inferiority of nature on the part of both ruler and subject: on the one side a cold, unsympathetic sacrificing of other's wills to self-will; on the other side a mean, cowardly abandonment of the claims of manhood. Our very language bears testimony to this. Do not *dignity, independence,* and other words of approbation, imply a nature at variance with this relation? Are not *tyrannical, arbitrary, despotic,* epithets of reproach? and are not *truckling, fawning, cringing,* epithets of contempt? Is not *slavish* a condemnatory term? Does not *servile,* that is, serf-like, imply littleness, meanness? And has not the word *villain,* which originally meant bondsman, come to signify everything which is hateful? That language should thus inadvertently embody dislike for those who most display the instinct of subordination, is alone sufficient proof that this instinct is associated with evil dispositions. It has been the parent of countless crimes. It is answerable for the torturing and murder of the noble-minded who would not submit—for the horrors of Bastiles and Siberias. It has ever been the represser of knowledge, of free thought, of true progress. In all times it has fostered the vices of courts, and made those vices fashionable throughout nations. With a George IV on the throne, it weekly tells ten thousand lies, in the shape of prayers for a "most religious and gracious king." Whether you read the annals of the far past—whether you look at the various uncivilized races dispersed over the globe—or whether you contrast the existing nations of Europe; you equally find that submission to authority decreases as morality and intelligence increase. From ancient warrior-worship down to modern flunkeyism, the sentiment has ever been strongest where human nature has been vilest.

This relation between barbarism and loyalty, is one of those beneficent arrangements which "the servant and interpreter of nature" everywhere meets with. The subordination of many to one, is a form of society needful for men so long as their natures are savage, or anti-social; and that it may be maintained, it is needful that they should have an extreme awe of the one. Just in proportion as their conduct to one another is such as to breed perpetual antagonism, endangering social union: just in that proportion must there be a reverence for the strong, determined, cruel ruler, who alone can repress their explosive natures and keep them from mutual destruction. Among such a people any form of free government is an impossibility. There must be a despotism as stern as the people are savage; and, that such a despotism may exist, there must be a superstitious worship of the despot. But as fast as the discipline of social life modifies character—as fast as, through lack of use, the old predatory instincts dwindle—as fast as the sympathetic feelings grow; so fast does this hard rule become less necessary; so fast does the authority of the ruler diminish; so fast does the awe of him disappear. From being originally god, or demi-god, he comes at length to be a very ordinary person; liable to be criticized, ridiculed, caricatured. Various influences conspire to this result. Accumulating knowledge gradually divests the ruler of those supernatural attributes at first ascribed to him. The conceptions which developing science gives of the grandeur of creation, as well as the constancy and irresistibleness of its Omnipresent Cause, make all feel the comparative littleness of human power; and the awe once felt for the great man is, by degrees, transferred to that Universe of which the great man is seen to form but an insignificant part. Increase of population, with its average percentage of great men, involves the comparative frequency of such; and the more numerous they are the less respect can be given to each: they dwarf one another. As society becomes settled and organized, its welfare and progress become more and more independent of any one. In a primitive society the death of a chief may alter the whole course of things; but in a society like ours, things go on much as before, no matter who dies. Thus, many influences combine to diminish autocratic power, whether political or other. It is true, not only in the sense in which Tennyson writes it, but also in a higher sense, that:

. . . the individual withers, and world is more and more.

Further, it is to be noted that while the unlimited authority of the greatest man ceases to be needful; and while the superstitious awe which upholds that unlimited authority decreases; it at the same time becomes impossible to get the greatest man to the top. In a rude social state, where might is right, where war is the business of life, where the qualities required in the ruler, alike for controlling his subjects and defeating his enemies, are bodily strength, courage, cunning, will, it is easy to pick out the best; or rather—he picks himself out. The qualities which make him the fittest governor for the barbarians around him, are the qualities by which he gets the mastery over them. But in an advanced, complex, and comparatively peaceful state like ours, these are not the qualities needed; and even were they needed, the firmly-organized arrangements of society do not allow the possessor of them to break through to the top. For the rule of a settled, civilized community, the characteristics required are—not a love of conquest but a desire for the general happiness; not undying hate of enemies but a calm dispassionate equity; not artful manoeuvring but philosophic insight. How is the man most endowed with these to be found? In no country is he ordinarily born heir to the throne; and that he can be chosen out of thirty millions of people none will be foolish enough to think. The incapacity for recognizing the greatest worth, we have already seen illustrated in our parliamentary elections. And if the few thousands forming a constituency cannot pick out from among themselves their wisest man, still less can the millions forming a nation do it. Just as fast as society becomes populous, complex, peaceful; so fast does the political supremacy of the best become impossible.

But even were the relation of autocrat and slave a morally wholesome one; and even were it possible to find the fittest man to be autocrat; we should still contend that such a form of government is bad. We should not contend this simply on the ground that self-government is a valuable educator. But we should take the ground that no human being, however wise and good, is fit to be sole ruler over the doings of an involved society; and that, with the best intentions, a benevolent despot is very likely to produce the most terrible mischiefs which would else have been impossible. We will take the case of all others the most favourable to those who would give supreme power to the best. We will instance Mr. Carlyle's model hero—Cromwell. Doubtless there was much in the manners of the times when Puritanism arose, to justify its disgust. Doubtless the vices and follies bequeathed by effete Catholicism still struggling for existence, were bad enough to create a reactionary asceticism. It is in the order of Nature, however, that men's habits and pleasures are not to be changed suddenly. For any *permanent* effect to be produced it must be produced slowly. Better tastes, higher aspirations, must be developed; not enforced from without. Disaster is sure to result from the withdrawal of lower gratifications before higher ones have taken their places; for gratification of some kind is a condition to healthful existence. Whatever ascetic morality, or rather immorality, may say, pleasures and pains are the incentives and restraints by which Nature keeps her progeny from destruction. No contemptuous title of "pig-philosophy" will alter the eternal fact that Misery is the highway to Death; while Happiness is added Life and the giver of Life. But indignant Puritanism could not see this truth; and with the extravagance of fanaticism sought to abolish pleasure in general. Getting into power, it put down not only questionable amusements but all others along with them. And for these repressions Cromwell, either as enacting, maintaining, or allowing them, was responsible. What, now, was the result of this attempt to dragoon men into virtue? What came when the strong man who thought he was thus "helping God to mend all," died? A dreadful reaction brought in one of the most degraded periods of our history. Into the newly-garnished house entered "seven other spirits more wicked than the first". For generations the English character was lowered. Vice was gloried in, virtue was ridiculed; dramatists made marriage the stock-subject of laughter; profaneness and obscenity flourished; high aspirations ceased; the whole age was corrupt. Not until George III reigned was there a better standard of living. And for this century of demoralization we have, in great measure, to thank Cromwell. Is it, then, so clear that the domination of one man, righteous though he may be, is a blessing?

Lastly, it is to be remarked that when the political supremacy of the greatest no longer exists in an overt form, it still continues in a disguised and more beneficent form. For is it not manifest that in these latter days the wise man eventually gets his edicts enforced by others, if not by himself. Adam Smith, from his chimney-corner, dictated greater changes than prime ministers do. A General Thompson who forges the weapons with which the Anti-Corn-Law battle is fought—a Cobden and a Bright who add to and wield them, forward civilization much more than those who hold sceptres. Repugnant as the fact may be to statesmen, it is yet one not to be gainsayed. Whoever, to the great effects already produced by Free-trade, joins the far greater effects which will be hereafter produced, must see that the revolution initiated by these men is far wider than has been initiated by any potentate of modern times. As Mr. Carlyle very well knows, those who elaborate new truths and teach them to their fellows, are now-a-days the real rulers—"the unacknowledged legislators"—the virtual kings. Thus we have the good which great men can do us, while we are saved from the evil.

No; the old régime has passed away. For ourselves at least, the subordination of the many to the one has become alike needless, repugnant, and impossible. Good for its time, bad for ours, the ancient "hero-worship" is dead; and happily no declamations, be they never so eloquent, can revive it.

Here seem to be two irreconcileable positions—two mutually-destructive arguments. First, a condemnatory criticism on representative government, and then a still more condemnatory criticism on monarchical government: each apparently abolishing the other.

Nevertheless, the paradox is easily explicable. It is quite possible to say all that we have said concerning the defects of representative government, and still to hold that it is the best form of government. Nay, it is quite possible to derive a more profound conviction of its superiority from the very evidence which appears so unfavourable to it.

For nothing that we have urged tells against its good-ness as a means of securing justice between man and man, or class and class. Abundant evidence shows that the maintenance of equitable relations among its sub-jects, which forms the essential business of a ruling power, is surest when the ruling power is of popular origin; notwithstanding the defects to which such a rul-ing power is liable. For discharging the true function of a government, representative government is shown to be the best, alike by its *origin*, its *theory*, and its *results*. Let us glance at the facts under these three heads.

Alike in Spain, in England, and in France, popular power embodied itself as a check upon kingly tyranny, that is—kingly injustice. The earliest accounts we have of the Spanish Cortes, say that it was their office to ad-vise the King; and to follow their advice was his duty. They petitioned, remonstrated, complained of griev-ances, and supplicated for redress. The King, having acceded to their requirements, swore to observe them; and it was agreed that any act of his incontravention of the statutes thus established, should be "respected as the King's commands, but not executed, as contrary to the rights and privileges of the subject." In all which we see very clearly that the special aim of the Cortes was to get rectified the injustices committed by the King or oth-ers; that the King was in the habit of breaking the prom-ises of amendment he made to them; and that they had to adopt measures to enforce the fulfilment of his prom-ises. In England we trace analogous facts. The Barons who bridled the tyranny of King John, though not for-mally appointed, were virtually impromptu representatives of the nation; and in their demand that justice should neither be sold, denied, nor delayed, we discern the social evils which led to this taking of the power into their own hands. In early times the knights and burgesses, summoned by the King with the view of getting supplies from them, had for their especial business to obtain from him the redress of grievances, that is—the execution of justice; and in their eventually-obtained and occasionally-exercised power of withholding supplies until justice was granted, we see both the need there was for remedying the iniquities of autocracy, and the adaptation of representative institutions to this end. And the further development of popular power latterly obtained, originated from the demand for fairer laws— for less class-privilege, class-exemption, class-injustice: a fact which the speeches of the Reform-Bill agitation abundantly prove. In France, again, representative government grew into a definite form under the stimulus of unbearable oppression. When the accumulated extortion of centuries had reduced the mass of the people to misery—when millions of haggard faces were seen throughout the land—when starving complainants were hanged on "a gallows forty feet high"—when the exactions and cruelties of good-for-nothing kings and vampire-nobles had brought the nation to the eye of dissolution; there came, as a remedy, an assembly of men elected by the people.

That, considered *a priori*, representative government is fitted for establishing just laws, is implied by the unanimity with which Spanish, English, and French availed themselves of it to this end; as well as by the endeavours latterly made by other European nations to do the like. The *rationale* of the matter is simple enough. Manifestly, on the average of cases, a man will protect his own interests more solicitously than others will protect them for him. Manifestly, where regulations have to be made affecting the interests of several men, they are most likely to be equitably made when all those concerned are present, and have equal shares in the making of them. And manifestly, where those concerned are so numerous and so dispersed, that it is physically impossible for them all to take part in the framing of such regulations, the next best thing is for the citizens in each locality to appoint one of their number to speak for them, to care for their claims, to be their representative. The general principle is that the welfare of all will be most secure when each looks after his own welfare; and the principle is carried out as directly as the circumstances permit. It is inferable, alike from human nature and from history, that a single man cannot be trusted with the interests of a nation of men, where his real or imagined interests clash with theirs. It is similarly inferable from human nature and from history, that no small section of a nation, as the nobles, can be expected to consult the welfare of the people at large in preference to their own. And it is further inferable that only in a general diffusion of political power, is there a safeguard for the general welfare. This has all along been the conviction under which representative government has been advocated, maintained, and extended. From the early writs summoning the members of the House of Commons—writs which declared it to be a most equitable rule that the laws which concerned all should be approved of by all—down to the reasons now urged by the unenfranchised for a participation in political power, this is the implied theory. Observe, nothing is said about wisdom or administrative ability. From the beginning, the end in view has been *justice*. Whether we consider the question in the abstract, or whether we examine the opinions men have entertained upon it from old times down to the present day, we equally see the theory of representative government to be, that it is the best means of insuring equitable social relations.

And do not the results justify the theory? Did not our early Parliaments, after long-continued struggles, succeed in curbing the licentious exercise of royal power, and in establishing the rights of the subject? Are not the comparative security and justice enjoyed under our form of government, indicated by the envy with which other nations regard it? Was not the election of the French Constituent Assembly followed by the sweeping away of the grievous burdens that weighed down the people—by the abolition of tithes, seignorial dues, gabelle, excessive preservation of game—by the withdrawal of numerous feudal privileges and immunities—by the manumission of the slaves in the French colonies? And has not that extension of our own electoral system embodied in the Reform-Bill, brought about more equitable arrangements?—as witness the repeal of the Corn-Laws, and the equalization of probate and legacy duties. The proofs are undeniable. It is clear, both *a priori* and *a posteriori*, that representative government is especially adapted for the establishment and maintenance of just laws.

And now mark that the objections to representative government awhile since urged, scarcely tell against it at all, so long as it does not exceed this comparatively limited function. Though its mediocrity of intellect makes it incompetent to oversee and regulate the count-less involved processes which make up the national life; it nevertheless has quite enough intellect to enact and enforce those simple principles of equity which underlie the right conduct of citizens to one another. These are such that the commonest minds can understand their chief applications. Stupid as may be the average elector, he can see the propriety of such regulations as shall pre-vent men from murdering and robbing; he can under-stand the fitness of laws which enforce the payment of debts; he can perceive the need of measures to prevent the strong from tyrannizing over the weak; and he can feel the rectitude of a judicial system that is the same for rich and poor. The average representative may be but of small capacity, but he is competent, under the leadership of his wiser fellows, to devise appliances for carrying out these necessary restraints; or rather—he is competent to uphold the set of appliances slowly elaborated by the many generations of his predecessors, and to do some-thing towards improving and extending them in those directions where the need is most manifest. It is true that even these small demands upon electoral and senatorial wisdom are but imperfectly met. But though constituen-cies are blind to the palpable truth that if they would

escape laws which favour the nobility at the expense of
the commonalty, they must cease to choose representatives from among the nobility; yet when the injustice of
this class-legislation is glaring—as in the case of the
Corn-Laws—they have sense enough to use means for
getting it abolished. And though most legislators have
not sufficient penetration to perceive that the greater
part of the evils which they attempt to cure by official
inspection and regulation would disappear were there
a certain, prompt, and cheap administration of justice;
yet the County-Courts-Act and other recent law-
reforms, show that they do eventually recognize the importance of more efficient judicial arrangements. While,
therefore, the lower average of intelligence which necessarily characterizes representative government, unfits
it for discharging the complex business of regulating the
entire national life; it does not unfit it for discharging the
comparatively simple duties of protector. Again, in respect of this all-essential function of a government, there
is a much clearer identity of interest between representative and citizen, than in respect of the multitudinous
other functions which governments undertake. Though
it is generally of but little consequence to the member
of Parliament whether state-teachers, state-preachers,
state-officers of health, state-dispensers of charity, etc.,
do their work well, it is of great consequence to him that
life and property should be secure; and hence he is more
likely to care for the efficient administration of justice
than for the efficient administration of anything else.
Moreover, the complexity, incongruity of parts, and general cumbrousness which deprive a representative

government of that activity and decision required for paternally-superintending the affairs of thirty millions of citizens; do not deprive it of the ability to establish and maintain the regulations by which these citizens are prevented from trespassing against one another. For the principles of equity are permanent as well as simple; and once having been legally embodied in their chief outlines, all that devolves on a government is to develop them more perfectly, and improve the appliances for enforcing them: an undertaking for which the slow and involved action of a representative government does not unfit it. So that while by its origin, theory, and results, representative government is shown to be the best for securing justice between class and class, as well as between man and man, the objections which so strongly tell against it in all its other relations to society, do not tell against it in this fundamental relation.

Thus, then, we reach the solution of the paradox. Here is the reconciliation between the two seemingly-contradictory positions awhile since taken. To the question— What is representative government good for? our reply is—It is good, especially good, good above all others, for doing the thing which a government should do. It is bad, especially bad, bad above all others, for doing the things which a government should not do.

One point remains. We said, some distance back, that not only may representative government be the best, notwithstanding its many conspicuous deficiencies; but that it is even possible to discern in these very deficiencies further proofs of its superiority. The conclusion just arrived at, implying, as it does, that these deficiencies tend to hinder it from doing the things which no government should do, has already furnished a key to this strange-looking assertion. But it will be well here to make a more specific justification of it. This brings us to the pure science of the matter.

The ever-increasing complexity which characterizes advancing societies, is a complexity that results from the multiplication of different parts performing different duties. The doctrine of the division of labour is now-a-days understood by most to some extent; and most know that by this division of labour each operative, each manufacturer, each town, each district, is constantly more and more restricted to one kind of work. Those who study the organization of living bodies find the uniform process of development to be, that each organ gradually acquires a definite and limited function; there arises, step by step, a more perfect "physiological division of labour." And in an article on "Progress: its Law and Cause," published in our April number, we pointed out that this increasing specialization of functions which goes on in all organized bodies, social as well as individual; is one of the manifestations of a still more general process pervading creation, inorganic as well as organic.

Now this specialization of functions, which is the law of all organization, has a twofold implication. At the same time that each part grows adapted to the particular duty it has to discharge, it grows unadapted to all other duties. The becoming especially fit for one thing, is a becoming less fit than before for everything else. We have not space here to exemplify this truth. Any modern work on physiology, however, will furnish the reader with abundant illustrations of it, as exhibited in the evolution of living creatures; and as exhibited in the evolution of societies, it may be studied in the writings of political economists. All which we wish here to point out is, that the governmental part of the body politic exemplifies this truth equally with its other parts. In virtue of this universal law, a government cannot gain ability to perform its special work without losing such ability as it had to perform other work.

This then is, as we say, the pure science of the matter. The original and essential office of a government is that of protecting its subjects against aggression external and internal. In low, undeveloped forms of society, where yet there is but little differentiation of parts, and little specialization of functions, this essential work, discharged with extreme imperfection, is joined with endless other work: the government has a controlling action over all conduct, individual and social—regulates dress, food, ablutions, prices, trade, religion—exercises unbounded power. In becoming so constituted as to discharge better its essential function, the government becomes more limited alike in the power and the habit of doing other things. Increasing ability to perform its true duty, involves decreasing ability to perform all other kinds of actions. And this conclusion, deducible from the universal law of organization, is the conclusion to which inductive reasoning has already led us. We have seen that, whether considered in theory or practice, representative government is the best for securing justice. We have also seen that, whether considered in theory or

practice, it is the worst for all other purposes. And here
we find that this last characteristic is a necessary accompaniment of the first. These various incapacities, which
seem to tell so seriously against the goodness of representative government, are but the inevitable consequences of its more complete adaptation to its proper
work; and, so understood, are themselves indications
that it is the form of government natural to a more
highly-organized and advanced social state.

We do not expect this consideration to weigh much
with those whom it most concerns. Truths of so abstract
a character find no favour with senates. The metamorphosis we have described is not mentioned in Ovid.
History, as at present written, makes no comments on
it. There is nothing about it to be found in blue-books
and committee-reports. Neither is it proved by statistics.
Evidently, then, it has but small chance of recognition
by the "practical" legislator. But to the select few who
study the Social Science, properly so called, we commend this general fact as one of the highest significance.
Those who know something of the general laws of life,
and who perceive that these general laws of life underlie
all social phenomena, will see that this dual change in
the character of advanced governments, involves an answer to the first of all political questions. They will see
that this specialization in virtue of which an advanced
government gains power to perform one function, while
it loses power to perform others, clearly indicates the
true limitations of State-duty. They will see that, even
leaving out all other evidence, this fact alone shows conclusively what is the proper sphere of legislation.

THE SOCIAL ORGANISM (1860)

Sir James Macintosh got great credit for the saying, that "constitutions are not made, but grow". In our day, the most significant thing about this saying is, that it was ever thought so significant. As from the surprise displayed by a man at some familiar fact, you may judge of his general culture; so from the admiration which an age accords to a new thought, its average degree of enlightenment may be inferred. That this apophthegm of Macintosh should have been quoted and requoted as it has, shows how profound has been the ignorance of social science. A small ray of truth has seemed brilliant, as a distant rushlight looks like a star in the surrounding darkness.

This essay was first published in The Westminster Review *for January 1860 and was reprinted in Spencer's* Essays: Scientific, Political and Speculative *(London and New York, 1892, in three volumes).*

383

Such a conception could not, indeed, fail to be startling when let fall in the midst of a system of thought to which it was utterly alien. Universally in Macintosh's day, things were explained on the hypothesis of manufacture, rather than that of growth; as indeed they are, by the majority, in our own day. It was held that the planets were severally projected round the Sun from the Creator's hand, with just the velocity required to balance the Sun's attraction. The formation of the Earth, the separation of sea from land, the production of animals, were mechanical works from which God rested as a labourer rests. Man was supposed to be moulded after a manner somewhat akin to that in which a modeller makes a clay-figure. And of course, in harmony with such ideas, societies were tacitly assumed to be arranged thus or thus by direct interposition of Providence; or by the regulations of law-makers; or by both.

Yet that societies are not artificially put together, is a truth so manifest, that it seems wonderful men should ever have overlooked it. Perhaps nothing more clearly shows the small value of historical studies, as they have been commonly pursued. You need but to look at the changes going on around, or observe social organization in its leading traits, to see that these are neither supernatural, nor are determined by the wills of individual men, as by implication the older historians teach; but are consequent on general natural causes. The one case of the division of labour suffices to prove this. It has not been by command of any ruler that some men have become manufacturers, while others have remained cultivators of the soil. In Lancashire, millions have devoted themselves to the making of cotton-fabrics; in Yorkshire, another million lives by producing woollens; and the pottery of Staffordshire, the cutlery of Sheffield, the hardware of Birmingham, severally occupy their hundreds of thousands. These are large facts in the structure of English society; but we can ascribe them neither to miracle, nor to legislation. It is not by "the hero as king," any more than by "collective wisdom," that men have been segregated into producers, wholesale distributors, and retail distributors. Our industrial organization, from its main outlines down to its minutest details, has become what it is, not simply without legislative guidance, but, to a considerable extent, in spite of legislative hindrances. It has arisen under the pressure of human wants and resulting activities. While each citizen has been pursuing his individual welfare, and none taking thought about division of labour, or conscious of the need of it, division of labour has yet been ever becoming more complete. It has been doing this slowly and silently: few having observed it until quite modern times. By steps so small, that year after year the industrial arrangements have seemed just what they were before— by changes as insensible as those through which a seed passes into a tree; society has become the complex body of mutually-dependent workers we now see. And this economic organization, mark, is the all-essential organization. Through the combination thus spontaneously evolved, every citizen is supplied with daily necessaries; while he yields some product or aid to others. That we are severally alive today, we owe to the regular working of this combination during the past week; and could it be suddenly abolished, multitudes would be dead before another week ended. If these most conspicuous and vital arrangements of our social structure have arisen not by the devising of any one, but through the individual efforts of citizens to satisfy their own wants; we may be tolerably certain that the less important arrangements have similarly arisen.

"But surely," it will be said, "the social changes directly produced by law, cannot be classed as spontaneous growths. When parliaments or kings order this or that thing to be done, and appoint officials to do it, the process is clearly artificial; and society to this extent becomes a manufacture rather than a growth." No, not even these changes are exceptions, if they be real and permanent changes. The true sources of such changes lie deeper than the acts of legislators. To take first the simplest instance. We all know that the enactments of representative governments ultimately depend on the national will: they may for a time be out of harmony with it, but eventually they must conform to it. And to say that the national will finally determines them, is to say that they result from the average of individual desires; or, in other words—from the average of individual natures. A law so initiated, therefore, really grows out of the popular character. In the case of a Government representing a dominant class, the same thing holds, though not so manifestly. For the very existence of a class monopolizing all power, is due to certain sentiments in the commonalty. Without the feeling of loyalty on the part of retainers, a feudal system could not exist. We see in the protest of the Highlanders against the abolition of heritable jurisdictions, that they preferred that kind of local rule. And if to the popular nature must be ascribed the growth of an irresponsible ruling class; then to the popular nature must be ascribed the social arrangements which that class creates in the pursuit of its own ends. Even where the Government is despotic, the doctrine still holds. The character of the people is, as before, the original source of this political form; and, as we have abundant proof, other forms suddenly created will not act, but rapidly retrograde to the old form. Moreover, such regulations as a despot makes, if really operative, are so because of their fitness to the social state. His acts being very much swayed by general opinion—by precedent, by the feeling of his nobles, his priesthood, his army—are in part immediate results of the national character; and when they are out of harmony with the national character, they are soon practically abrogated. The failure of Cromwell permanently to establish a new social condition, and the rapid revival of suppressed institutions and practices after his death, show how powerless is a monarch to change the type of society he governs. He may disturb, he may retard, or he may aid the natural process of organization; but the general course of this process is beyond his control. Nay, more than this is true. Those who regard the histories of societies as the histories of their great men, and think that these great men shape the fates of their societies, overlook the truth that such great men are the products of their societies. Without certain antecedents—without a certain average national character, they neither could have been generated nor could have had the culture which formed them. If their society is to some extent re-moulded by them, they were, both before and after birth, moulded by their society—were the results of all those influences which fostered the ancestral character they inherited, and gave their own early bias, their creed, morals, knowledge, aspirations. So that such social changes as are immediately traceable to individuals of unusual power, are still remotely traceable to the social causes which produced these individuals; and hence, from the highest point of view, such social changes also, are parts of the general developmental process.

Thus that which is so obviously true of the industrial structure of society, is true of its whole structure. The fact that "constitutions are not made, but grow," is simply a fragment of the much larger fact, that under all its aspects and through all its ramifications, society is a growth and not a manufacture.

A perception that there exists some analogy between the body politic and a living individual body, was early reached; and has from time to time re-appeared in literature. But this perception was necessarily vague and more or less fanciful. In the absence of physiological science, and especially of those comprehensive generalizations which it has but lately reached, it was impossible to discern the real parallelisms.

The central idea of Plato's model Republic, is the correspondence between the parts of a society and the faculties of the human mind. Classifying these faculties under the heads of Reason, Will, and Passion, he classifies the members of his ideal society under what he regards as three analogous heads:—councillors, who are to exercise government; military or executive, who are to fulfil their behests; and the commonalty, bent on gain and selfish gratification. In other words, the ruler, the warrior, and the craftsman, are, according to him, the analogues of our reflective, volitional, and emotional powers. Now even were there truth in the implied assumption of a parallelism between the structure of a society and that of a man, this classification would be indefensible. It might more truly be contended that, as the military power obeys the commands of the Government, it is the Government which answers to the Will; while the military power is simply an agency set in motion by it. Or, again, it might be contended that whereas the Will is a product of predominant desires, to which the Reason serves merely as an eye, it is the craftsmen, who, according to the alleged analogy, ought to be the moving power of the warriors.

Hobbes sought to establish a still more definite parallelism: not, however, between a society and the human mind, but between a society and the human body. In the introduction to the work in which he develops this conception, he says:

> For by art is created that great LEVIATHAN called a COMMON-WEALTH, or STATE, in Latin CIVITAS, which is but an artificial man; though of greater stature and strength than the natural, for whose protection and defence it was intended, and in which the *sovereignty* is an artificial *soul,* as giving life and motion to the whole body; the *magistrates* and other *officers* of judicature and execution, artificial *joints; reward* and *punishment,* by which, fastened to the seat of the sovereignty, every joint and member is moved to perform his duty, are the *nerves,* that do the same

in the body natural; the *wealth* and *riches* of all the particular members are the *strength; salus populi,* the *people's safety,* its *business; counsellors,* by whom all things needful for it to know are suggested unto it, are the *memory; equity* and *laws* an artificial *reason* and *will; concord, health; sedition, sickness;* and *civil war, death.*

And Hobbes carries this comparison so far as actually to give a drawing of the Leviathan—a vast human-shaped figure, whose body and limbs are made up of multitudes of men. Just noting that these different analogies asserted by Plato and Hobbes serve to cancel each other (being, as they are, so completely at variance), we may say that on the whole those of Hobbes are the more plausible. But they are full of inconsistencies. If the sovereignty is the *soul* of the body-politic, how can it be that magistrates, who are a kind of deputy-sovereigns, should be comparable to *joints?* Or, again, how can the three mental functions, memory, reason, and will, be severally analogous, the first to counsellors, who are a class of public officers, and the other two to equity and laws, which are not classes of officers, but abstractions? Or, once more, if magistrates are the artificial joints of society, how can reward and punishment be its nerves? Its nerves must surely be some class of persons. Reward and punishment must in societies, as in individuals, be *conditions* of the nerves, and not the nerves themselves.

But the chief errors of these comparisons made by Plato and Hobbes, lie much deeper. Both thinkers assume that the organization of a society is comparable, not simply to the organization of a living body in general, but to the organization of the human body in particular. There is no warrant whatever for assuming this. It is in no way implied by the evidence; and is simply one of those fancies which we commonly find mixed up with the truths of early speculation. Still more erroneous are the two conceptions in this, that they construe a society as an artificial structure. Plato's model republic—his ideal of a healthful body-politic—is to be consciously put together by men, just as a watch might be; and Plato manifestly thinks of societies in general as thus originated. Quite specifically does Hobbes express a like view. "For by *art*," he says, "is created that great LEVIATHAN called a COMMONWEALTH." And he even goes so far as to compare the supposed social contract, from which a society suddenly originates, to the creation of a man by the divine fiat. Thus they both fall into the extreme inconsistency of considering a community as similar in structure to a human being, and yet as produced in the same way as an artificial mechanism—in nature, an organism; in history, a machine.

Notwithstanding errors, however, these speculations have considerable significance. That such likenesses, crudely as they are thought out, should have been alleged by Plato and Hobbes and others, is a reason for suspecting that *some* analogy exists. The untenableness of the particular parallelisms above instanced, is no ground for denying an essential parallelism; since early ideas are usually but vague adumbrations of the truth. Lacking the great generalizations of biology, it was, as we have said, impossible to trace out the real relations of social organizations to organizations of another order. We propose here to show what are the analogies which modern science discloses.

Let us set out by succinctly stating the points of similarity and the points of difference. Societies agree with individual organisms in four conspicuous peculiarities:

1. That commencing as small aggregations, they insensibly augment in mass: some of them eventually reaching ten thousand times what they originally were.

2. That while at first so simple in structure as to be considered structureless, they assume, in the course of their growth, a continually-increasing complexity of structure.

3. That though in their early, undeveloped states, there exists in them scarcely any mutual dependence of parts, their parts gradually acquire a mutual dependence; which becomes at last so great, that the activity and life of each part is made possible only by the activity and life of the rest.

4. That the life of a society is independent of, and far more prolonged than, the lives of any of its component units; who are severally born, grow, work, reproduce, and die, while the body-politic composed of them survives generation after generation, increasing in mass, in completeness of structure, and in functional activity.

These four parallelisms will appear the more significant the more we contemplate them. While the points specified, are points in which societies agree with individual organisms, they are also points in which individual organisms agree with one another, and disagree with all things else. In the course of its existence, every plant and animal increases in mass, in a way not paralleled by inorganic objects: even such inorganic objects as crystals, which arise by growth, show us no such definite relation between growth and existence as organisms do. The orderly progress from simplicity to complexity, displayed by bodies-politic in common with living bodies, is a characteristic which distinguishes living bodies from the inanimate bodies amid which they move. That functional dependence of parts, which is scarcely more manifest in animals than in nations, has no counterpart elsewhere. And in no aggregate except an organic or a social one, is there a perpetual removal and replacement of parts, joined with a continued integrity of the whole. Moreover, societies and organisms are not only alike in these peculiarities, in which they are unlike all other things; but the highest societies, like the highest organisms, exhibit them in the greatest degree. We see that the lowest animals do not increase to anything like the sizes of the higher ones; and, similarly, we see that aboriginal societies are comparatively limited in their growths. In complexity, our large civilized nations as much exceed primitive savage tribes, as a mammal does a zoophyte. Simple communities, like simple creatures, have so little mutual dependence of parts, that mutilation or subdivision causes but little inconvenience; but from complex communities, as from complex creatures, you cannot remove any considerable organ without producing great disturbance or death of the rest. And in societies of low type, as in inferior animals, the life of the aggregate, often cut short by division or dissolution, exceeds in length the lives of the component units, very far less than in civilized communities and superior animals; which outlive many generations of their component units.

On the other hand, the leading differences between societies and individual organisms are these:

1. That societies have no specific external forms. This, however, is a point of contrast which loses much of its importance, when we remember that throughout the vegetal kingdom, as well as in some lower divisions of the animal kingdom, the forms are often very indefinite—definiteness being rather the exception than the rule: and that they are manifestly in part determined by surrounding physical circumstances, as the forms of societies are. If, too, it should eventually be shown, as we believe it will, that the form of every species of organism has resulted from the average play of the external forces to which it has been subject during its evolution as a species; then, that the external forms of societies should depend, as they do, on surrounding conditions, will be a further point of community.

2. That though the living tissue whereof an individual organism consists, forms a continuous mass, the living elements of a society do not form a continuous mass; but are more or less widely dispersed over some portion of the Earth's surface. This, which at first sight appears to be an absolute distinction, is one which yet to a great extent fades when we contemplate all the facts. For, in the lower divisions of the animal and vegetal kingdoms, there are types of organization much more nearly allied,

in this respect, to the organization of a society, than might be supposed—types in which the living units essentially composing the mass, are dispersed through an inert substance, that can scarcely be called living in the full sense of the word. It is thus with some of the *Protococci* and with the *Nostoceæ*, which exist as cells imbedded in a viscid matter. It is so, too, with the *Thalassicollæ*—bodies made up of differentiated parts, dispersed through an undifferentiated jelly. And throughout considerable portions of their bodies, some of the *Acalephæ* exhibit more or less this type of structure. Now this is very much the case with a society. For we must remember that though the men who make up a society are physically separate, and even scattered, yet the surface over which they are scattered is not one devoid of life, but is covered by life of a lower order which ministers to their life. The vegetation which clothes a country makes possible the animal life in that country; and only through its animal and vegetal products can such a country support a society. Hence the members of the body-politic are not to be regarded as separated by intervals of dead space, but as diffused through a space occupied by life of a lower order. In our conception of a social organism, we must include all that lower organic existence on which human existence, and therefore social existence, depend. And when we do this, we see that the citizens who make up a community may be considered as highly vitalized units surrounded by substances of lower vitality, from which they draw their nutriment: much as in the cases above instanced.

3. The third difference is that while the ultimate living elements of an individual organism are mostly fixed in their relative positions, those of the social organism are capable of moving from place to place. But here, too, the disagreement is much less than would be supposed. For while citizens are locomotive in their private capacities, they are fixed in their public capacities. As farmers, manufacturers, or traders, men carry on their businesses at the same spots, often throughout their whole lives; and if they go away occasionally, they leave behind others to discharge their functions in their absence. Each great centre of production, each manufacturing town or district, continues always in the same place; and many of the firms in such town or district, are for generations carried on either by the descendants or successors of those who founded them. Just as in a living body, the cells that make up some important organ severally perform their functions for a time and then disappear, leaving others to supply their places; so, in each part of a society the organ remains, though the persons who compose it change. Thus, in social life, as in the life of an animal, the units as well as the larger agencies formed of them, are in the main stationary as respects the places where they discharge their duties and obtain their sustenance. And hence the power of individual locomotion does not practically affect the analogy.

4. The last and perhaps the most important distinction is, that while in the body of an animal only a special tissue is endowed with feeling, in a society all the members are endowed with feeling. Even this distinction, however, is not a complete one. For in some of the lowest

animals, characterized by the absence of a nervous system, such sensitiveness as exists is possessed by all parts. It is only in the more organized forms that feeling is monopolized by one class of the vital elements. And we must remember that societies, too, are not without certain differentiation of this kind. Though the units of a community are all sensitive, they are so in unequal degrees. The classes engaged in laborious occupations are less susceptible, intellectually and emotionally, than the rest; and especially less so than the classes of highest mental culture. Still, we have here a tolerably decided contrast between bodies-politic and individual bodies; and it is one which we should keep constantly in view. For it reminds us that while, in individual bodies, the welfare of all other parts is rightly subservient to the welfare of the nervous system, whose pleasurable or painful activities make up the good or ill of life; in bodies-politic the same thing does not hold, or holds to but a very slight extent. It is well that the lives of all parts of an animal should be merged in the life of the whole, because the whole has a corporate consciousness capable of happiness or misery. But it is not so with a society; since its living units do not and cannot lose individual consciousness, and since the community as a whole has no corporate consciousness. This is an everlasting reason why the welfares of citizens cannot rightly be sacrificed to some supposed benefit of the State, and why, on the other hand, the State is to be maintained solely for the benefit of citizens. The corporate life must here be subservient to the lives of the parts, instead of the lives of the parts being subservient to the corporate life.

Such, then, are the points of analogy and the points
of difference. May we not say that the points of difference serve but to bring into clearer light the points of
analogy? While comparison makes definite the obvious
contrasts between organisms commonly so called, and
the social organism, it shows that even these contrasts
are not so decided as was to be expected. The indefiniteness of form, the discontinuity of the parts, and the
universal sensitiveness, are not only peculiarities of the
social organism which have to be stated with considerable qualifications; but they are peculiarities to which the
inferior classes of animals present approximations. Thus
we find but little to conflict with the all-important analogies. Societies slowly augment in mass; they progress
in complexity of structure; at the same time their parts
become more mutually dependent; their living units are
removed and replaced without destroying their integrity; and the extents to which they display these peculiarities are proportionate to their vital activities. These
are traits that societies have in common with organic
bodies. And these traits in which they agree with organic
bodies and disagree with all other things, entirely subordinate the minor distinctions: such distinctions being
scarcely greater than those which separate one half of
the organic kingdom from the other. The *principles* of
organization are the same, and the differences are simply
differences of application.

Here ending this general survey of the facts which
justify the comparisons of a society with a living body,
let us look at them in detail. We shall find that the par-

allelism becomes the more marked the more closely it is examined.

The lowest animal and vegetal forms—*Protozoa* and *Protophyta*—are chiefly inhabitants of the water. They are minute bodies, most of which are made individually visible only by the microscope. All of them are extremely simple in structure, and some of them, as the *Rhizopods*, almost structureless. Multiplying, as they ordinarily do, by the spontaneous division of their bodies, they produce halves which may either become quite separate and move away in different directions, or may continue attached. By the repetition of this process of fission, aggregations of various sizes and kinds are formed. Among the *Protophyta* we have some classes, as the *Diatomaceæ* and the Yeast-plant, in which the individuals may be either separate or attached in groups of two, three, four, or more; other classes in which a considerable number of cells are united into a thread (*Conferva, Monilia*); others in which they form a network (*Hydrodictyon*); others in which they form plates (*Ulva*); and others in which they form masses (*Laminaria, Agaricus*): all which vegetal forms, having no distinction of root, stem, or leaf, are called *Thallogens*. Among the *Protozoa* we find parallel facts. Immense numbers of *Amœba*-like creatures, massed together in a framework of horny fibres, constitute Sponge. In the *Foraminifera* we see smaller groups of such creatures arranged into more definite shapes. Not only do these almost structureless *Protozoa* unite into regular or irregular aggregations of various sizes, but among some of the more organized ones, as the *Vorticellæ*, there are also produced clusters of individuals united to a common stem. But these little societies of monads, of cells, or whatever else we may call them, are societies only in the lowest sense: there is no subordination of parts among them—no organization. Each of the component units lives by and for itself; neither giving nor receiving aid. The only mutual dependence is that consequent on mechanical union.

Do we not here discern analogies to the first stages of human societies? Among the lowest races, as the Bushmen, we find but incipient aggregation: sometimes single families sometimes two or three families wandering about together. The number of associated units is small and variable, and their union inconstant. No division of labour exists except between the sexes, and the only kind of mutual aid is that of joint attack or defence. We see an undifferentiated group of individuals, forming the germ of a society; just as in the homogeneous groups of cells above described, we see the initial stage of animal and vegetal organization.

The comparison may now be carried a step higher. In the vegetal kingdom we pass from the *Thallogens*, consisting of mere masses of similar cells, to the *Acrogens*, in which the cells are not similar throughout the whole mass; but are here aggregated into a structure serving as leaf and there into a structure serving as root; thus forming a whole in which there is a certain subdivision of functions among the units, and therefore a certain mutual dependence. In the animal kingdom we find analogous progress. From mere unorganized groups of cells, or cell-like bodies, we ascend to groups of such cells arranged into parts that have different duties. The common Polype, from the substance of which may be separated cells that exhibit, when detached, appearances and movements like those of a solitary *Amœba*, illustrates this stage. The component units, though still showing great community of character, assume somewhat diverse functions in the skin, in the internal surface, and in the tentacles. There is a certain amount of "physiological division of labour."

Turning to societies, we find these stages paralleled in most aboriginal tribes. When, instead of such small variable groups as are formed by Bushmen, we come to the larger and more permanent groups formed by savages not quite so low, we find traces of social structure. Though industrial organization scarcely shows itself, except in the different occupations of the sexes; yet there is more or less of governmental organization. While all the men are warriors and hunters, only a part of them are included in the council of chiefs; and in this council of chiefs some one has commonly supreme authority. There is thus a certain distinction of classes and powers; and through this slight specialization of functions is effected a rude cooperation among the increasing mass of individuals, whenever the society has to act in its corporate capacity. Beyond this analogy in the slight extent to which organization is carried, there is analogy in the indefiniteness of the organization. In the *Hydra*, the respective parts of the creature's substance have many functions in common. They are all contractile; omitting the tentacles, the whole of the external surface can give origin to young *hydræ;* and, when turned inside out, stomach performs the duties of skin and skin the duties of stomach. In aboriginal societies such differentiations as exist are similarly imperfect. Notwithstanding distinctions of rank, all persons maintain themselves by their own exertions. Not only do the head men of the tribe, in common with the rest, build their own huts, make their own weapons, kill their own food; but the chief does the like. Moreover, such governmental organization as exists is inconstant. It is frequently changed by violence or treachery, and the function of ruling assumed by some other warrior. Thus between the rudest societies and some of the lowest forms of animal life, there is analogy alike in the slight extent to which organization is carried, in the indefiniteness of this organization, and in its want of fixity.

A further complication of the analogy is at hand. From the aggregation of units into organized groups, we pass to the multiplication of such groups, and their coalescence into compound groups. The *Hydra,* when it has reached a certain bulk, puts forth from its surface a bud which, growing and gradually assuming the form of the parent, finally becomes detached; and by this process of gemmation the creature peoples the adjacent water with others like itself. A parallel process is seen in the multiplication of those lowly-organized tribes above described. When one of them has increased to a size that is either too great for coordination under so rude a structure, or else that is greater than the surrounding country can supply with game and other wild food, there arises a tendency to divide; and as in such communities there often occur quarrels, jealousies, and other causes of division, there soon comes an occasion on which a part of the tribe separates under the leadership of some subordinate chief and migrates. This process being from time to time repeated, an extensive region is at length occupied by numerous tribes descended from a common ancestry. The analogy by no means ends here. Though in the common *Hydra* the young ones that bud out from the parent soon become detached and independent; yet throughout the rest of the class *Hydrozoa*, to which this creature belongs, the like does not generally happen. The successive individuals thus developed continue attached; give origin to other such individuals which also continue attached; and so there results a compound animal. As in the *Hydra* itself we find an aggregation of units which, considered separately, are akin to the lowest *Protozoa*; so here, in a *Zoophyte*, we find an aggregation of such aggregations. The like is also seen throughout the extensive family of *Polyzoa* or *Molluscoida*. The Ascidian Mollusks, too, in their many forms, show us the same thing: exhibiting, at the same time, various degrees of union among the component individuals. For while in the *Salpæ* the component individuals adhere so slightly that a blow on the vessel of water in which they are floating will separate them; in the *Botryllidæ* there exist vascular connexions among them, and a common circulation. Now in these different stages of aggregation, may we not see paralleled the union of groups of connate tribes into nations? Though, in regions where circumstances permit, the tribes descended from some original tribe migrate in all directions, and become far removed and quite separate; yet, where the territory presents barriers to distant migration, this does not happen: the small kindred communities are held in closer contact, and eventually become more or less united into a nation. The contrast between the tribes of American Indians and the Scottish clans, illustrates this. And a glance at our own early history, or the early histories of continental nations, shows this fusion of small simple communities taking place in various ways and to various extents. As says M. Guizot, in his *History of the Origin of Representative Government:*

> By degrees, in the midst of the chaos of the rising society, small aggregations are formed which feel the want of alliance and union with each other. . . . Soon inequality of strength is displayed among neighbouring aggregations. The strong tend to subjugate the weak, and usurp at first the rights of taxation and military service. Thus political authority leaves the aggregations which first instituted it, to take a wider range.

That is to say, the small tribes, clans, or feudal groups, sprung mostly from a common stock, and long held in contact as occupants of adjacent lands, gradually get united in other ways than by kinship and proximity.

A further series of changes begins now to take place, to which, as before, we find analogies in individual organisms. Returning to the *Hydrozoa*, we observe that in the simplest of the compound forms the connected individuals are alike in structure, and perform like functions; with the exception that here and there a bud, instead of developing into a stomach, mouth, and tentacles, becomes an egg-sac. But with the oceanic *Hydrozoa* this is by no means the case. In the *Calycophoridæ* some of the polypes growing from the common germ, become developed and modified into large, long, sacklike bodies, which, by their rhythmical contractions, move through the water, dragging the community of polypes after them. In the *Physophoridæ* a variety of organs similarly arise by transformation of the budding polypes; so that in creatures like the *Physalia*, commonly known as the "Portuguese Man-of-war," instead of that tree-like group of similar individuals forming the original type, we have a complex mass of unlike parts fulfilling unlike duties. As an individual *Hydra* may be regarded as a group of *Protozoa* which have become partially metamorphosed into different organs; so a *Physalia* is, morphologically considered, a group of *Hydræ* of which the individuals have been variously transformed to fit them for various functions.

This differentiation upon differentiation is just what takes place during the evolution of a civilized society. We observed how, in the small communities first formed, there arises a simple political organization: there is a partial separation of classes having different duties. And now we have to observe how, in a nation formed by the fusion of such small communities, the several sections, at first alike in structures and modes of activity, grow unlike in both—gradually become mutually-dependent parts, diverse in their natures and functions.

The doctrine of the progressive division of labour, to which we are here introduced, is familiar to all readers. And further, the analogy between the economical division of labour and the "physiological division of labour," is so striking as long since to have drawn the attention of scientific naturalists: so striking, indeed, that the expression "physiological division of labour," has been suggested by it. It is not needful, therefore, to treat this part of the subject in great detail. We shall content ourselves with noting a few general and significant facts, not manifest on a first inspection.

Throughout the whole animal kingdom, from the *Cœlenterata* upwards, the first stage of evolution is the same. Equally in the germ of a polype and in the human ovum, the aggregated mass of cells out of which the creature is to arise, gives origin to a peripheral layer of cells, slightly differing from the rest which they include; and this layer subsequently divides into two—the inner, lying in contact with the included yelk, being called the mucous layer, and the outer, exposed to surrounding agencies, being called the serous layer: or, in the terms used by Prof. Huxley, in describing the development of the *Hydrozoa*—the endoderm and ectoderm. This primary division marks out a fundamental contrast of parts in the future organism. From the mucous layer, or endoderm, is developed the apparatus of nutrition; while from the serous layer, or ectoderm, is developed the apparatus of external action. Out of the one arise the organs by which food is prepared and absorbed, oxygen imbibed, and blood purified; while out of the other arise the nervous, muscular, and osseous systems, by the combined actions of which the movements of the body as a whole are effected. Though this is not a rigorously-correct distinction, seeing that some organs involve both of these primitive membranes, yet high authorities agree in stating it as a broad general distinction. Well, in the evolution of a society, we see a primary differentiation of analogous kind, which similarly underlies the whole future structure. As already pointed out, the only manifest contrast of parts in primitive societies, is that between the governing and the governed. In the least organized tribes, the council of chiefs may be a body of men distinguished simply by greater courage or experience. In more organized tribes, the chief-class is definitely separated from the lower class, and often regarded as different in nature—sometimes as god-descended. And later, we find these two becoming respectively freemen and slaves, or nobles and serfs. A glance at their respective functions, makes it obvious that the great divisions thus early formed, stand to each other in a relation similar to that in which the primary divisions of the embryo stand to each other. For, from its first appearance, the warrior-class, headed by chiefs, is that by which the external acts of the society are carried on: alike in war, in negotiation, and in migration. Afterwards, while this upper class grows distinct from the lower, and at the same time becomes more and more exclusively regulative and defensive in its functions, alike in the persons of kings and subordinate rulers, priests, and soldiers; the inferior class becomes more and more exclusively occupied in providing the necessaries of life for the community at large. From the soil, with which it comes in most direct contact, the mass of the people takes up, and prepares for use, the food and such rude articles of manufacture as are known; while the overlying mass of superior men, maintained by the working population, deals with circumstances external to the community—circumstances with which, by position, it is more immediately concerned. Ceasing by-and-by to have any knowledge of, or power over, the concerns of the society as a whole, the serf-class becomes devoted to the processes of alimentation; while the noble class, ceasing to take any part in the processes of alimentation, becomes devoted to the coordinated movements of the entire body-politic.

Equally remarkable is a further analogy of like kind. After the mucous and serous layers of the embryo have separated, there presently arises between the two a third, known to physiologists as the vascular layer—a layer out of which are developed the chief blood-vessels. The mucous layer absorbs nutriment from the mass of yelk it encloses; this nutriment has to be transferred to the overlying serous layer, out of which the nervo-muscular system is being developed; and between the two arises a vascular system by which the transfer is effected—a system of vessels which continues ever after to be the transferrer of nutriment from the places where it is absorbed and prepared, to the places where it is needed for growth and repair. Well, may we not trace a parallel step in social progress? Between the governing and the governed, there at first exists no intermediate class; and even in some societies that have reached considerable sizes, there are scarcely any but the nobles and their kindred on the one hand, and the serfs on the other: the social structure being such that transfer of commodities takes place directly from slaves to their masters. But in societies of a higher type, there grows up, between these two primitive classes, another—the trading or middle class. Equally at first as now, we may see that, speaking generally, this middle class is the analogue of the middle layer in the embryo. For all traders are essentially distributors. Whether they be wholesale dealers, who collect into large masses the commodities of various producers; or whether they be retailers, who divide out to those who want them, the masses of commodities thus collected together; all mercantile men are agents of transfer from the places where things are produced to the places where they are consumed. Thus the distributing apparatus in a society, answers to the distributing apparatus in a living body; not only in its functions, but in its intermediate origin and subsequent position, and in the time of its appearance.

Without enumerating the minor differentiations which these three great classes afterwards undergo, we will merely note that throughout, they follow the same general law with the differentiations of an individual organism. In a society, as in a rudimentary animal, we have seen that the most general and broadly contrasted divisions are the first to make their appearance; and of the subdivisions it continues true in both cases, that they arise in the order of decreasing generality.

Let us observe, next, that in the one case as in the other, the specializations are at first very incomplete, and approach completeness as organization progresses. We saw that in primitive tribes, as in the simplest animals, there remains much community of function between the parts which are nominally different—that, for instance, the class of chiefs long remains industrially the same as the inferior class; just as in a *Hydra*, the property of contractility is possessed by the units of the endoderm as well as by those of the ectoderm. We noted also how, as the society advanced, the two great primitive classes partook less and less of each other's functions. And we have here to remark that all subsequent specializations are at first vague and gradually become distinct. "In the infancy of society," says M. Guizot, "everything is confused and uncertain; there is as yet no fixed and precise line of demarcation between the different powers in a state." "Originally kings lived like other landowners, on the incomes derived from their own private estates." Nobles were petty kings; and kings only the most powerful nobles. Bishops were feudal lords and military leaders. The right of coining money was possessed by powerful subjects, and by the Church, as well as by the king. Every leading man exercised alike the functions of landowner, farmer, soldier, statesman, judge. Retainers were now soldiers, and now labourers, as the day required. But by degrees the Church has lost all civil jurisdiction; the State has exercised less and less control over religious teaching; the military class has grown a distinct one; handicrafts have concentrated in towns; and the spinning-wheels of scattered farmhouses, have disappeared before the machinery of manufacturing districts. Not only is all progress from the homogeneous to the heterogeneous, but, at the same time, it is from the indefinite to the definite.

Another fact which should not be passed over, is that in the evolution of a large society out of a cluster of small ones, there is a gradual obliteration of the original lines of separation—a change to which, also, we may see analogies in living bodies. The sub-kingdom *Annulosa*, furnishes good illustrations. Among the lower types the body consists of numerous segments that are alike in nearly every particular. Each has its external ring; its pair of legs, if the creature has legs; its equal portion of intestine, or else its separate stomach; its equal portion of the great blood-vessel, or, in some cases, its separate heart; its equal portion of the nervous cord; and, perhaps, its separate pair of ganglia. But in the highest types, as in the large *Crustacea*, many of the segments are completely fused together; and the internal organs are no longer uniformly repeated in all the segments. Now the segments of which nations at first consist, lose their separate external and internal structures in a similar manner. In feudal times the minor communities, governed by feudal lords, were severally organized in the same rude way, and were held together only by the fealty of their respective rulers to a suzerain. But along with the growth of a central power, the demarcations of these local communities become relatively unimportant, and their separate organizations merge into the general organization. The like is seen on a larger scale in the fusion of England, Wales, Scotland, and Ireland; and, on the Continent, in the coalescence of provinces into kingdoms. Even in the disappearance of law-made divisions, the process is analogous. Among the Anglo-Saxons, England was divided into tithings, hundreds, and counties: there were county-courts, courts of hundred, and courts of tithing. The courts of tithing disappeared first; then the courts of hundred, which have, however, left traces; while the county-jurisdiction still exists. Chiefly, however, it is to be noted, that there eventually grows up an organization which has no reference to these original divisions, but traverses them in various directions, as is the case in creatures belonging to the sub-kingdom just named; and, further, that in both cases it is the sustaining organization which thus traverses old boundaries, while, in both cases, it is the governmental, or coordinating organization in which the original boundaries continue traceable. Thus, in the highest *Annulosa* the exo-skeleton and the muscular system never lose all traces of their primitive segmentation; but throughout a great part of the body, the contained viscera do not in the least conform to the external divisions. Similarly with a nation we see that while, for governmental purposes, such divisions as counties and parishes still exist, the structure developed for carrying on the nutrition of society wholly ignores these boundaries: our great cotton-manufacture spreads out of Lancashire into North Derbyshire; Leicestershire and Nottinghamshire have long divided the stocking-trade between them; one great centre for the production of iron and iron-goods, includes parts of Warwickshire, Staffordshire, and Worcestershire; and those various specializations of agriculture which have made different parts of England noted for different products, show no more respect to county-boundaries than do our growing towns to the boundaries of parishes.

If, after contemplating these analogies of structure, we inquire whether there are any such analogies between the processes of organic change, the answer is—yes. The causes which lead to increase of bulk in any part of the body-politic, are of like nature with those which lead to increase of bulk in any part of an individual body. In both cases the antecedent is greater functional activity consequent on greater demand. Each limb, viscus, gland, or other member of an animal, is developed by exercise—by actively discharging the duties which the body at large requires of it; and similarly, any class of labourers or artisans, any manufacturing centre, or any official agency, begins to enlarge when the community devolves on it more work. In each case, too, growth has its conditions and its limits. That any organ in a living being may grow by exercise, there needs a due supply of blood. All action implies waste; blood brings the materials for repair; and before there can be growth, the quantity of blood supplied must be more than is requisite for repair. In a society it is the same. If to some district which elaborates for the community particular commodities—say the woollens of Yorkshire—there comes an augmented demand; and if, in fulfilment of this demand, a certain expenditure and wear of the manufacturing organization are incurred; and if, in payment for the extra quantity of woollens sent away, there comes back only such quantity of commodities as replaces the expenditure, and makes good the waste of life and machinery; there can clearly be no growth. That there may be growth, the commodities obtained in return must be more than sufficient for these ends; and just in proportion as the surplus is great will the growth be rapid. Whence it is manifest that what in commercial affairs we call *profit*, answers to the excess of nutrition over waste in a living body. Moreover, in both cases when the functional activity is high and the nutrition defective, there results not growth but decay. If in an animal, any organ is worked so hard that the channels which bring blood cannot furnish enough for repair, the organ dwindles: atrophy is set up. And if in the body-politic, some part has been stimulated into great productivity, and cannot afterwards get paid for all its produce, certain of its members become bankrupt, and it decreases in size.

One more parallelism to be here noted, is that the different parts of a social organism, like the different parts of an individual organism, compete for nutriment; and severally obtain more or less of it according as they are discharging more or less duty. If a man's brain be over-excited it abstracts blood from his viscera and stops digestion; or digestion, actively going on, so affects the circulation through the brain as to cause drowsiness; or great muscular exertion determines such a quantity of blood to the limbs as to arrest digestion or cerebral action, as the case may be. So, likewise, in a society, great activity in some one direction causes partial arrests of activity elsewhere by abstracting capital, that is commodities: as instance the way in which the sudden development of our railway-system hampered commercial operations; or the way in which the raising of a large military force temporarily stops the growth of leading industries.

The last few paragraphs introduce the next division of our subject. Almost unawares we have come upon the analogy which exists between the blood of a living body and the circulating mass of commodities in the body-politic. We have now to trace out this analogy from its simplest to its most complex manifestations.

In the lowest animals there exists no blood properly so called. Through the small assemblage of cells which make up a *Hydra*, permeate the juices absorbed from the food. There is no apparatus for elaborating a concentrated and purified nutriment, and distributing it among the component units; but these component units directly imbibe the unprepared nutriment, either from the digestive cavity or from one another. May we not say that this is what takes place in an aboriginal tribe? All its members severally obtain for themselves the necessaries of life in their crude states; and severally prepare them for their own uses as well as they can. When there arises a decided differentiation between the governing and the governed, some amount of transfer begins between those inferior individuals who, as workers, come directly in contact with the products of the earth, and those superior ones who exercise the higher functions—a transfer parallel to that which accompanies the differentiation of the ectoderm from the endoderm. In the one case, as in the other, however, it is a transfer of products that are little if at all prepared; and takes place directly from the unity which obtains to the unit which consumes, without entering into any general current.

Passing to larger organisms—individual and social—we meet the first advance on this arrangement. Where, as among the compound *Hydrozoa*, there is a union of many such primitive groups as form *Hydræ*; or where, as in a *Medusa*, one of these groups has become of great size; there exist rude channels running throughout the substance of the body: not, however, channels for the conveyance of prepared nutriment, but mere prolongations of the digestive cavity, through which the crude chyle-aqueous fluid reaches the remoter parts, and is moved backwards and forwards by the creature's contractions. Do we not find in some of the more advanced primitive communities an analogous condition? When the men, partially or fully united into one society, become numerous—when, as usually happens, they cover a surface of country not everywhere alike in its products—when, more especially, there arise considerable classes which are not industrial; some process of exchange and distribution inevitably arises. Traversing here and there the earth's surface, covered by that vegetation on which human life depends, and in which, as we say, the units of a society are imbedded, there are formed indefinite paths, along which some of the necessaries of life occasionally pass, to be bartered for others which presently come back along the same channels. Note, however, that at first little else but crude commodities are thus transferred—fruits, fish, pigs or cattle, skins, etc.: there are few, if any, manufactured products or articles prepared for consumption. And note also, that such distribution of these unprepared necessaries of life as takes place, is but occasional—goes on with a certain slow, irregular rhythm.

Further progress in the elaboration and distribution of nutriment, or of commodities, is a necessary accompaniment of further differentiation of functions in the individual body or in the body-politic. As fast as each organ of a living animal becomes confined to a special action, it must become dependent on the rest for those materials which its position and duty do not permit it to obtain for itself; in the same way that, as fast as each particular class of a community becomes exclusively occupied in producing its own commodity, it must become dependent on the rest for the other commodities it needs. And, simultaneously, a more perfectly-elaborated blood will result from a highly specialized group of nutritive organs, severally adapted to prepare its different elements; in the same way that the stream of commodities circulating throughout a society, will be of superior quality in proportion to the greater division of labour among the workers. Observe, also, that in either case the circulating mass of nutritive materials, besides coming gradually to consist of better ingredients, also grows more complex. An increase in the number of the unlike organs which add to the blood their waste matters, and demand from it the different materials they severally need, implies a blood more heterogeneous in composition—an *a priori* conclusion which, according to Dr. Williams, is inductively confirmed by examination of the blood throughout the various grades of the animal kingdom. And similarly, it is manifest that as fast as the division of labour among the classes of a community becomes greater, there must be an increasing heterogeneity in the currents of merchandise flowing throughout that community.

The circulating mass of nutritive materials in individual organisms and in social organisms, becoming at once better in the quality of its ingredients and more hetero-

geneous in composition, as the type of structure becomes higher, eventually has added to it in both cases
another element, which is not itself nutritive but facilitates the processes of nutrition. We refer, in the case of
the individual organism, to the blood-discs; and in the
case of the social organism, to money. This analogy has
been observed by Liebig, who in his *Familiar Letters on
Chemistry* says:

> Silver and gold have to perform in the organism of the state,
> the same function as the blood-corpuscles in the human orga-
> nism. As these round discs, without themselves taking an im-
> mediate share in the nutritive process, are the medium, the
> essential condition of the change of matter, of the production
> of the heat and of the force by which the temperature of the
> body is kept up, and the motions of the blood and all the juices
> are determined, so has gold become the medium of all activity
> in the life of the state.

And blood-corpuscles being like coin in their functions, and in the fact that they are not consumed in nutrition, he further points out that the number of them
which in a considerable interval flows through the great
centres, is enormous when compared with their absolute
number; just as the quantity of money which annually
passes through the great mercantile centres, is enormous
when compared with the quantity of money in the kingdom. Nor is this all. Liebig has omitted the significant
circumstance that only at a certain stage of organization
does this element of the circulation make its appearance.
Throughout extensive divisions of the lower animals,
the blood contains no corpuscles; and in societies of low
civilization, there is no money.

Thus far we have considered the analogy between the blood in a living body and the consumable and circulating commodities in the body-politic. Let us now compare the appliances by which they are respectively distributed. We shall find in the developments of these appliances parallelisms not less remarkable than those above set forth. Already we have shown that, as classes, wholesale and retail distributors discharge in a society the office which the vascular system discharges in an individual creature; that they come into existence later than the other two great classes, as the vascular layer appears later than the mucous and serous layers; and that they occupy a like intermediate position. Here, however it remains to be pointed out that a complete conception of the circulating system in a society, includes not only the active human agents who propel the currents of commodities, and regulate their distribution, but includes, also, the channels of communication. It is the formation and arrangement of these to which we now direct attention.

Going back once more to those lower animals in which there is found nothing but a partial diffusion, not of blood, but only of crude nutritive fluids, it is to be remarked that the channels through which the diffusion takes place, are mere excavations through the half-organized substance of the body: they have no lining membranes, but are mere *lacunæ* traversing a rude tissue. Now countries in which civilization is but commencing, display a like condition: there are no roads properly so called; but the wilderness of vegetal life covering the earth's surface is pierced by tracks, through which the distribution of crude commodities takes place. And while, in both cases, the acts of distribution occur only at long intervals (the currents, after a pause, now setting towards a general centre and now away from it), the transfer is in both cases slow and difficult. But among other accompaniments of progress, common to animals and societies, comes the formation of more definite and complete channels of communications. Blood-vessels acquire distinct walls; roads are fenced and gravelled. This advance is first seen in those roads or vessels that are nearest to the chief centres of distribution; while the peripheral roads and peripheral vessels long continue in their primitive states. At a yet later stage of development, where comparative finish of structure is found throughout the system as well as near the chief centres, there remains in both cases the difference that the main channels are comparatively broad and straight, while the subordinate ones are narrow and tortuous in proportion to their remoteness. Lastly, it is to be remarked that there ultimately arise in the higher social organisms, as in the higher individual organisms, main channels of distribution still more distinguished by their perfect structures, their comparative straightness, and the absence of those small branches which the minor channels perpetually give off. And in railways we also see, for the first time in the social organism, a system of double channels conveying currents in opposite directions, as do the arteries and veins of a well-developed animal.

These parallelisms in the evolutions and structures of the circulating systems, introduce us to others in the kinds and rates of the movements going on through them. Through the lowest societies, as through the lowest creatures, the distribution of crude nutriment is by slow gurgitations and regurgitations. In creatures that have rude vascular systems, just as in societies that are beginning to have roads, there is no regular circulation along definite courses; but, instead, periodical changes of the currents—now towards this point and now towards that. Through each part of an inferior mollusc's body, the blood flows for a while in one direction, then stops and flows in the opposite direction; just as through a rudely-organized society, the distribution of merchandise is slowly carried on by great fairs, occurring in different localities, to and from which the currents periodically set. Only animals of tolerably complete organizations, like advanced communities, are permeated by constant currents that are definitely directed. In living bodies, the local and variable currents disappear when there grow up great centres of circulation, generating more powerful currents by a rhythm which ends in a quick, regular pulsation. And when in social bodies there arise great centres of commercial activity, producing and exchanging large quantities of commodities, the rapid and continuous streams drawn in and emitted by these centres subdue all minor and local circulations: the slow rhythm of fairs merges into the faster one of weekly markets, and in the chief centres of distribution, weekly markets merge into daily markets; while in place of the languid transfer from place to place, taking place at first weekly, then twice or thrice a week, we by-and-by get daily transfer, and finally transfer many times a day—the original sluggish, irregular rhythm, becomes a rapid, equable pulse. Mark, too, that in both cases the increased activity, like the greater perfection of structure, is much less conspicuous at the periphery of the vascular system. On main lines of railway, we have, perhaps, a score trains in each direction daily, going at from thirty to fifty miles an hour; as, through the great arteries, the blood moves rapidly in successive gushes. Along high roads, there go vehicles conveying men and commodities with much less, though still considerable, speed, and with a much less decided rhythm; as, in the smaller arteries, the speed of the blood is greatly diminished and the pulse less conspicuous. In parish-roads, narrower, less complete, and more tortuous, the rate of movement is further decreased and the rhythm scarcely traceable; as in the ultimate arteries. In those still more imperfect by-roads which lead from these parish-roads to scattered farmhouses and cottages, the motion is yet slower and very irregular; just as we find it in the capillaries. While along the field-roads, which, in their unformed, unfenced state, are typical of *lacunæ*, the movement is the slowest, the most irregular, and the most infrequent; as it is, not only in the primitive *lacunæ* of animals and societies, but as it is also in those *lacunæ* in which the vascular system ends among extensive families of inferior creatures.

Thus, then, we find between the distributing systems of living bodies and the distributing systems of bodies-politic, wonderfully close parallelisms. In the lowest forms of individual and social organisms, there exist neither prepared nutritive matters nor distributing appliances; and in both, these, arising as necessary accompaniments of the differentiation of parts, approach perfection as this differentiation approaches completeness. In animals, as in societies, the distributing agencies begin to show themselves at the same relative periods, and in the same relative positions. In the one, as in the other, the nutritive materials circulated are at first crude and simple, gradually become better elaborated and more heterogeneous, and have eventually added to them a new element facilitating the nutritive processes. The channels of communication pass through similar phases of development, which bring them to analogous forms. And the directions, rhythms, and rates of circulation, progress by like steps to like final conditions.

We come at length to the nervous system. Having noticed the primary differentiation of societies into the governing and governed classes, and observed its analogy to the differentiation of the two primary tissues which respectively develop into organs of external action and organs of alimentation; having noticed some of the leading analogies between the development of industrial arrangements and that of the alimentary apparatus; and having, above, more fully traced the analogies between the distributing systems, social and individual; we have now to compare the appliances by which a society, as a whole, is regulated, with those by which the movements of an individual creature are regulated. We shall find here parallelisms equally striking with those already detailed.

The class out of which governmental organization originates, is, as we have said, analogous in its relations to the ectoderm of the lowest animals and of embryonic forms. And as this primitive membrane, out of which the nervo-muscular system is evolved, must, even in the first stage of its differentiation, be slightly distinguished from the rest by that greater impressibility and contractility characterizing the organs to which it gives rise; so, in that superior class which is eventually transformed into the directo-executive system of a society (its legislative and defensive appliances), does there exist in the beginning, a larger endowment of the capacities required for these higher social functions. Always, in rude assemblages of men, the strongest, most courageous, and most sagacious, become rulers and leaders; and, in a tribe of some standing, this results in the establishment of a dominant class, characterized on the average by those mental and bodily qualities which fit them for deliberation and vigorous combined action. Thus that greater impressibility and contractility, which in the rudest animal types characterize the units of the ectoderm, characterize also the units of the primitive social stratum which controls and fights; since impressibility and contractility are the respective roots of intelligence and strength.

Again, in the unmodified ectoderm, as we see it in the *Hydra*, the units are all endowed both with impressibility and contractility; but as we ascend to higher types of organization, the ectoderm differentiates into classes of units which divide those two functions between them: some, becoming exclusively impressible, cease to be contractile; while some, becoming exclusively contractile, cease to be impressible. Similarly with societies. In an aboriginal tribe, the directive and executive functions are diffused in a mingled form throughout the whole governing class. Each minor chief commands those under him, and, if need be, himself coerces them into obedience. The council of chiefs itself carries out on the battlefield its own decisions. The head chief not only makes laws, but administers justice with his own hands. In larger and more settled communities, however, the directive and executive agencies begin to grow distinct from each other. As fast as his duties accumulate, the head chief or king confines himself more and more to directing public affairs, and leaves the execution of his will to others: he deputes others to enforce submission, to inflict punishments, or to carry out minor acts of offence and defence; and only on occasions when, perhaps, the safety of the society and his own supremacy are at stake, does he begin to act as well as direct. As this differentiation establishes itself, the characteristics of the ruler begin to change. No longer, as in an aboriginal tribe, the strongest and most daring man, the tendency is for him to become the man of greatest cunning, foresight, and skill in the management of others; for in societies that have advanced beyond the first stage, it is chiefly such qualities that insure success in gaining supreme power, and holding it against internal and external enemies. Thus that member of the governing class who comes to be the chief directing agent, and so plays the same part that a rudimentary nervous centre does in an unfolding organism, is usually one endowed with some superiorities of nervous organization.

In those larger and more complex communities possessing, perhaps, a separate military class, a priesthood, and dispersed masses of population requiring local control, there grow up subordinate governing agents; who, as their duties accumulate, severally become more directive and less executive in their characters. And when, as commonly happens, the king begins to collect round himself advisers who aid him by communicating information, preparing subjects for his judgment, and issuing his orders; we may say that the form of organization is comparable to one very general among inferior types of animals, in which there exists a chief ganglion with a few dispersed minor ganglia under its control.

The analogies between the evolution of governmental structures in societies, and the evolution of governmental structures in living bodies, are, however, more strikingly displayed during the formation of nations by coalescence of tribes—a process already shown to be, in several respects, parallel to the development of creatures that primarily consist of many like segments. Among other points of community between the successive rings which make up the body in the lower *Annulosa*, is the possession of similar pairs of ganglia. These pairs of ganglia, though connected by nerves, are very incompletely dependent on any general controlling power. Hence it results that when the body is cut in two, the hinder part continues to move forward under the propulsion of its numerous legs; and that when the chain of ganglia has been divided without severing the body, the hind limbs may be seen trying to propel the body in one direction while the fore limbs are trying to propel it in another. But in the higher *Annulosa*, called *Articulata*, sundry of the anterior pairs of ganglia, besides growing larger, unite in one mass; and this great cephalic ganglion having become the coordinator of all the creature's movements, there no longer exists much local independence. Now may we not in the growth of a consolidated kingdom out of petty sovereignties or baronies, observe analogous changes? Like the chiefs and primitive rulers above described, feudal lords, exercising supreme power over their respective groups of retainers, discharge functions analogous to those of rudimentary nervous centres. Among these local governing centres there is, in early feudal times, very little subordination. They are in frequent antagonism; they are individually restrained chiefly by the influence of parties in their own class; and they are but irregularly subject to that most powerful member of their order who has gained the position of head-suzerain or king. As the growth and organization of the society progresses, these local directive centres fall more and more under the control of a chief directive centre. Closer commercial union between the several segments is accompanied by closer governmental union; and these minor rulers end in being little more than agents who administer, in their several localities, the laws made by the supreme ruler: just as the local ganglia above described, eventually become agents which enforce, in their respective segments, the orders of the cephalic ganglion. The parallelism holds still further. We remarked above, when speaking of the rise of aboriginal kings, that in proportion as their territories increase, they are obliged not only to perform their executive functions by deputy, but also to gather round themselves advisers to aid in their directive functions; and that thus, in place of a solitary governing unit, there grows up a group of governing units, comparable to a ganglion consisting of many cells. Let us here add that the advisers and chief officers who thus form the rudiment of a ministry, tend from the beginning to exercise some control over the ruler. By the information they give and the opinions they express, they sway his judgement and affect his commands. To this extent he is made a channel through which are communicated the directions originating with them; and in course of time, when the advice of ministers becomes the acknowledged source of his actions, the king assumes the character of an automatic centre, reflecting the impressions made on him from without.

Beyond this complication of governmental structure many societies do not progress; but in some, a further development takes place. Our own case best illustrates this further development and its further analogies. To kings and their ministries have been added, in England, other great directive centres, exercising a control which, at first small, has been gradually becoming predominant: as with the great governing ganglia which especially distinguish the highest classes of living beings. Strange as the assertion will be thought, our Houses of Parliament discharge, in the social economy, functions which are in sundry respects comparable to those discharged by the cerebral masses in a vertebrate animal. As it is in the nature of a single ganglion to be affected only by special stimuli from particular parts of the body; so it is in the nature of a single ruler to be swayed in his acts by exclusive personal or class interests. As it is in the nature of a cluster of ganglia, connected with the primary one, to convey to it a greater variety of influences from more numerous organs, and thus to make its acts conform to more numerous requirements; so it is in the nature of the subsidiary controlling powers surrounding a king to adapt his rule to a greater number of public exigencies. And as it is in the nature of those great and latest-developed ganglia which distinguish the higher animals, to interpret and combine the multiplied and varied impressions conveyed to them from all parts of the system, and to regulate the actions in such way as duly to regard them all; so it is in the nature of those great and latest-developed legislative bodies which distinguish the most advanced societies, to interpret and combine the wishes of all classes and localities, and to make laws in harmony with the general wants. We may describe the office of the brain as that of *averaging* the interests of life, physical, intellectual, moral; and a good brain is one in which the desires answering to these respective interests are so balanced, that the conduct they jointly dictate, sacrifices none of them. Similarly, we may describe the office of a Parliament as that of *averaging* the interests of the various classes in a community; and a good Parliament is one in which the parties answering to these respective interests are so balanced, that their united legislation allows to each class as much as consists with the claims of the rest. Besides being comparable in their duties, these great directive centres, social and individual, are comparable in the processes by which their duties are discharged. The cerebrum is not occupied with direct impressions from without but with the ideas of such impressions. Instead of the actual sensations produced in the body, and directly appreciated by the sensory ganglia, or primitive nervous centres, the cerebrum receives only the representations of these sensations; and its consciousness is called *representative* consciousness, to distinguish it from the original or *presentative* consciousness. Is it not significant that we have hit on the same word to distinguish the function of our House of Commons? We call it a *representative* body, because the interests with which it deals are not directly presented to it, but represented to it by its various members; and a debate is a conflict of representations of the results likely to follow from a proposed course—a description which applies with equal truth to a debate in the individual consciousness. In both cases, too, these great governing masses take no part in the executive functions. As, after a conflict in the cerebrum, those desires which finally predominate act on the subjacent ganglia, and through their instrumentality determine the bodily actions; so the parties which, after a parliamentary struggle, gain the victory, do not themselves carry out their wishes, but get them carried out by the executive divisions of the Government. The fulfilment of all legislative decisions still devolves on the original directive centres: the impulse passing from the Parliament to the Ministers and from the Ministers to the King, in whose name everything is done; just as those smaller, first-developed ganglia, which in the lowest vertebrata are the chief controlling agents, are still, in the brains of the higher vertebrata, the agents through which the dictates of the cerebrum are worked out. Moreover, in both cases these original centres become increasingly automatic. In the developed vertebrate animal, they have little function beyond that of conveying impressions to, and executing the determinations of, the larger centres. In our highly organized government, the monarch has long been lapsing into a passive agent of Parliament; and now, ministries are rapidly falling into the same position. Nay, between the two cases there is a parallelism even in respect of the exceptions to this automatic action. For in the individual creature it happens that under circumstances of sudden alarm, as from a loud sound close at hand, an unexpected object starting up in front, or a slip from insecure footing, the danger is guarded against by some quick involuntary jump, or adjustment of the limbs, which occurs before there is time to consider the impending evil and take deliberate measures to avoid it: the rationale of which is that these violent impressions produced on the senses, are reflected from the sensory ganglia to the spinal cord and muscles, without, as in ordinary cases, first passing through the cerebrum. In like manner on national emergencies calling for prompt action, the King and Ministry, not having time to lay the matter before the great deliberative bodies, themselves issue commands for the requisite movements or precautions; the primitive, and now almost automatic, directive centres, resume for a moment their original uncontrolled power. And then, strangest of all, observe that in either case there is an after-process of approval or disapproval. The individual on recovering from his automatic start, at once contemplates the cause of his fright; and, according to the case, concludes that it was well he moved as he did, or condemns himself for his groundless alarm. In like manner, the deliberative powers of the State discuss, as soon as may be, the unauthorized acts of the executive powers; and, deciding that the reasons were or were not sufficient, grant or withhold a bill of indemnity.[1]

Thus far in comparing the governmental organization of the body-politic with that of an individual body, we have considered only the respective co-ordinating centres. We have yet to consider the channels through which these co-ordinating centres receive information and convey commands. In the simplest societies, as in the simplest organisms, there is no "internuncial apparatus," as Hunter styled the nervous system. Consequently, impressions can be but slowly propagated from unit to unit throughout the whole mass. The same progress, however, which, in animal-organization, shows itself in the establishment of ganglia or directive centres, shows itself also in the establishment of nerve-threads, through which the ganglia receive and convey impressions and so control remote organs. And in societies the like eventually takes place. After a long period during which the directive centres communicate with various

---

[1] It may be well to warn the reader against an error fallen into by one who criticized this essay on its first publication—the error of supposing that the analogy here intended to be drawn, is a specific analogy between the organization of society in England, and the human organization. As said at the outset, no such specific analogy exists. The above parallel is one between the most-developed systems of governmental organization, individual and social; and the vertebrate type is instanced merely as exhibiting this most-developed system. If any specific comparison were made, which it cannot rationally be, it would be made with some much lower vertebrate form than the human.

parts of the society through other means, there at last comes into existence an "internuncial apparatus," analogous to that found in individual bodies. The comparison of telegraph-wires to nerves is familiar to all. It applies, however, to an extent not commonly supposed. Thus, throughout the vertebrate sub-kingdom, the great nerve-bundles diverge from the vertebrate axis side by side with the great arteries; and similarly, our groups of telegraph-wires are carried along the sides of our railways. The most striking parallelism, however, remains. Into each great bundle of nerves, as it leaves the axis of the body along with an artery, there enters a branch of the sympathetic nerve; which branch, accompanying the artery throughout its ramifications, has the function of regulating its diameter and otherwise controlling the flow of blood through it according to local requirements. Analogously, in the group of telegraph-wires running alongside each railway, there is a wire for the purpose of regulating the traffic—for retarding or expediting the flow of passengers and commodities, as the local conditions demand. Probably, when our now rudimentary telegraph-system is fully developed, other analogies will be traceable.

Such, then, is a general outline of the evidence which justifies the comparison of societies to living organisms. That they gradually increase in mass; that they become little by little more complex; that at the same time their parts grow more mutually dependent; and that they continue to live and grow as wholes, while successive generations of their units appear and disappear; are broad peculiarities which bodies-politic display in common with all living bodies; and in which they and living bodies differ from everything else. And on carrying out the comparison in detail, we find that these major analogies involve many minor analogies, far closer than might have been expected. Others might be added. We had hoped to say something respecting the different types of social organization, and something also on social metamorphoses; but we have reached our assigned limits.

SPECIALIZED ADMINISTRATION (1871)

It is contrary to common-sense that fish should be more difficult to get at the sea-side than in London; but it is true, nevertheless. No less contrary to common-sense seems the truth that though, in the West Highlands, oxen are to be seen everywhere, no beef can be had without sending two or three-hundred miles to Glasgow for it. Rulers who, guided by common-sense, tried to suppress certain opinions by forbidding the books containing them, never dreamed that their interdicts would cause the diffusion of these opinions; and rulers who, guided by common-sense, forbade excessive rates of interest, never dreamed that they were thereby making the terms harder for borrowers than before. When print-

---

This essay was first published in The Fortnightly Review *for December 1871 and was reprinted in Spencer's* Essays: Scientific, Political and Speculative *(London and New York, 1892, in three volumes).*

ing replaced copying, any one who had prophesied that the number of persons engaged in the manufacture of books would immensely increase, as a consequence, would have been thought wholly devoid of common-sense. And equally devoid of common-sense would have been thought any one who, when railways were displacing coaches, said that the number of horses employed in bringing passengers and goods to and from railways, would be greater than the number directly displaced by railways. Such cases might be multiplied. Whoso remembers that, among quite simple phenomena, causes produce effects which are sometimes utterly at variance with anticipation, will see how frequently this must happen among complex phenomena. That a balloon is made to rise by the same force which makes a stone fall; that the melting of ice may be greatly retarded by wrapping the ice in a blanket; that the simplest way of setting potassium on fire is to throw it into the water; are truths which those who know only the outside aspect of things would regard as manifest falsehoods. And, if, when the factors are few and simple, the results may be so absolutely opposed to seeming probability, much more will they be often thus opposed when the factors are many and involved. The saying of the French respecting political events, that "it is always the unexpected which happens"—a saying which they have been abundantly re-illustrating of late—is one which legislators, and those who urge on schemes of legislation, should have ever in mind. Let us pause a moment to contemplate a seemingly-impossible set of results which social forces have wrought out.

Up to quite recent days, Language was held to be of supernatural origin. That this elaborate apparatus of symbols, so marvellously adapted for the conveyance of thought from mind to mind, was a miraculous gift, seemed unquestionable. No possible alternative way could be thought of by which there had come into existence these multitudinous assemblages of words of various orders, genera, and species, moulded into fitness for articulating with one another, and capable of being united from moment to moment into ever-new combinations, which represent with precision each idea as it arises. The supposition that, in the slow progress of things, Language grew out of the continuous use of signs—at first mainly mimetic, afterward partly mimetic, partly vocal, and at length almost wholly vocal—was an hypothesis never even conceived by men in early stages of civilization; and when the hypothesis was at length conceived, it was thought too monstrous an absurdity to be even entertained. Yet this monstrous absurdity proves to be true. Already the evolution of Language has been traced back far enough to show that all its particular words, and all its leading traits of structure, have had a natural genesis; and day by day investigation makes it more manifest that its genesis has been natural from the beginning. Not only has it been natural from the beginning, but it has been spontaneous. No language is a cunningly-devised scheme of a ruler or body of legislators. There was no council of savages to invent the parts of speech, and decide on what principles they should be used. Nay, more. Going on without any authority or appointed regulation, this natural process went on without any man observing that it was going on. Solely under pressure of the need for communicating their ideas and feelings—solely in pursuit of their personal interests—men little by little developed speech in absolute unconsciousness that they were doing anything more than pursuing their personal interests. Even now the unconsciousness continues. Take the whole population of the globe, and there is probably not above one in a million who knows that in his daily talk he is carrying on the process by which Language has been evolved.

I commence thus by way of giving the key-note to the argument which follows. My general purpose, in dwelling a moment on this illustration, has been that of showing how utterly beyond the conceptions of common-sense, literally so called, and even beyond the conceptions of cultivated common-sense, are the workings-out of sociological processes—how these workings-out are such that even those who have carried to the uttermost "the scientific use of the imagination," would never have anticipated them. And my more special purpose has been that of showing how marvelous are the results indirectly and unintentionally achieved by the cooperation of men who are severally pursuing their private ends. Let me pass now to the particular topic to be here dealt with.

I have greatly regretted to see Prof. Huxley strengthening, by his deservedly high authority, a school of politicians which can scarcely be held to need strengthening: its opponents being so few. I regret it the more because, thus far, men prepared for the study of Sociology by previous studies of Biology and Psychology, have scarcely expressed any opinions on the question at issue; and that Prof. Huxley, who by both general and special culture is so eminently fitted to judge, should have come to the conclusions set forth in the last number of the *Fortnightly Review,* will be discouraging to the small number who have reached opposite conclusions. Greatly regretting however, though I do, this avowed antagonism of Prof. Huxley to a general political doctrine with which I am identified, I do not propose to make any reply to his arguments at large: being deterred partly by reluctance to dwell on points of difference with one whom I so greatly admire, and partly by the consciousness that what I should say would be mainly a repetition of what I have explicitly or implicitly said elsewhere. But with one point raised I feel obliged to deal. Prof. Huxley tacitly puts to me a question. By so doing he leaves me to choose between two alternatives, neither of which is agreeable to me. I must either, by leaving it unanswered, accept the implication that it is unanswerable, and the doctrine I hold untenable; or else I must give it an adequate answer. Little as I like it, I see that the latter of these alternatives is that which, on public as well as on personal grounds, I must accept.

Had I been allowed to elaborate more fully the Review-article from which Prof. Huxley quotes, this question would possibly not have been raised. That article closes with the following words: "We had hoped to say something respecting the different types of social organization, and something also on social metamorphoses; but we have reached our assigned limits." These further developments of the conception—developments to be hereafter set forth in the *Principles of Sociology*—I must here sketch in outline before my answer can be made intelligible. In sketching them, I must say much that would be needless were my answer addressed to Prof. Huxley only. Bare allusions to general phenomena of organization, with which he is immeasurably more familiar than I am, would suffice. But, as the sufficiency of my answer has to be judged by the general reader, the general reader must be supplied with the requisite data: my presentation of them being under correction from Prof. Huxley if it is inaccurate.

The primary differentiation in organic structures, manifested alike in the history of each organism and in the history of the organic world as a whole, is the differentiation between outer and inner parts—the parts which hold direct converse with the environment and the parts which do not hold direct converse with the environment. We see this alike in those smallest and lowest forms improperly, though suggestively, sometimes called unicellular, and also in the next higher division of creatures which, with considerable reason, are regarded as aggregations of the lower. In these creatures the body is divisible into endoderm and ectoderm, differing very little in their characters, but serving the one to form the digestive sac, and the other to form the outer wall of the body. As Prof. Huxley describes them in his *Oceanic Hydrozoa*, these layers represent respectively the organs of nutrition and the organs of external relation—

generally, though not universally; for there are exceptions, especially among parasites. In the embryos of
higher types, these two layers severally become double
by the splitting of a layer formed between them; and
from the outer double layer is developed the body-wall
with its limbs, nervous system, senses, muscles, etc.;
while from the inner double layer there arise the alimentary canal and its appendages, together with the heart
and lungs. Though in such higher types these two systems of organs, which respectively absorb nutriment
and expend nutriment, become so far connected by ram-
ifying blood-vessels and nerves that this division cannot
be sharply made, still the broad contrast remains. At the
very outset, then, there arises this separation, which implies at once a cooperation and an antagonism—a cooperation, because, while the outer organs secure for the
inner organs the crude food, the inner organs elaborate
and supply to the outer organs the prepared materials
by which they are enabled to do their work; and an antagonism, because each set of organs, living and growing at the cost of these prepared materials, cannot
appropriate any portion of the total supply without diminishing by so much the supply available for the other.
This general cooperation and general antagonism becomes complicated with special cooperations and special
antagonisms, as fast as these two great systems of organs
develop. The originally simple alimentary canal, differ-
entiating into many parts, becomes a congeries of structures which, by cooperation, fulfil better their general
functions, but between which there nevertheless arise
antagonisms; since each has to make good its waste and

to get matter for growth, at the cost of the general supply of nutriment available for them all. Similarly, as fast as the outer system develops into special senses and limbs, there arise among these, also, secondary cooperations and secondary antagonisms. By their variously-combined actions, food is obtained more effectually; and yet the activity of each set of muscles, or each directive nervous structure, entails a draft upon the stock of prepared nutriment which the outer organs receive, and is by so much at the cost of the rest. Thus the method of organization, both in general and in detail, is a simultaneous combination and opposition. All the organs unite in subserving the interests of the organism they form; and yet they have all their special interests, and compete with one another for blood.

A form of government, or control, or coordination develops as fast as these systems of organs develop. Eventually this becomes double. A general distinction arises between the two controlling systems belonging to the two great systems of organs. Whether the inner controlling system is or is not originally derived from the outer, matters not to the argument—when developed it is in great measure independent.[1] If we contemplate

---

[1] Here, and throughout the discussion, I refer to these controlling systems only as they exist in the *Vertebrata*, because their relations are far better known in this great division of the animal kingdom—not because like relations do not exist elsewhere. Indeed, in the great sub-kingdom *Annulosa*, these controlling systems have relations that are extremely significant to us here. For while an inferior annulose animal has only a single set of nervous structures, a superior annulose animal (as a moth) has a set of nervous structures presiding over the viscera, as well as a more conspicuous set presiding over the organs of external relation. And this contrast is analogous to one of the contrasts between undeveloped and developed societies; for, while among the uncivilized and incipiently

their respective sets of functions, we shall perceive the origin of this distinction. That the outer organs may co-operate effectively for the purposes of catching prey, escaping danger, etc., it is needful that they should be under a government capable of directing their combined actions, now in this way and now in that, according as outer circumstances vary. From instant to instant there must be quick adjustments to occasions that are more or less new; and hence there requires a complex and centralized nervous apparatus, to which all these organs are promptly and completely obedient. The government needful for the inner system of organs is a different and much simpler one. When the food obtained by the outer organs has been put into the stomach, the cooperation required of the viscera, though it varies somewhat as the quantity or kind of food varies, has nevertheless a general uniformity; and it is required to go on in much the same way whatever the outer circumstances may be. In each case the food has to be reduced to a pulp, supplied with various solvent secretions, propelled onward, and its nutritive part taken up by absorbent surfaces. That these processes may be effective, the organs which carry them on must be supplied with fit blood; and to this end the heart and the lungs have to act with greater vigour. This visceral cooperation, carried on with this comparative uniformity, is regulated by a nervous system which is to a large extent independent of that higher and more complex nervous system controlling the external organs. The act of swallowing is, indeed, mainly effected by the

---

civilized there is but a single set of directive agencies, there are among the fully civilized, as we shall presently see, two sets of directive agencies, for the outer and inner structures respectively.

higher nervous system; but, being swallowed, the food affects by its presence the local nerves, through them the local ganglia, and indirectly, through nervous connexions with other ganglia, excites the rest of the viscera into cooperative activity. It is true that the functions of the sympathetic or ganglionic nervous system, or "nervous system of organic life," as it is otherwise called, are imperfectly understood. But, since we know positively that some of its plexuses, as the cardiac, are centres of local stimulation and coordination, which can act independently, though they are influenced by higher centres, it is fairly to be inferred that the other and still larger plexuses, distributed among the viscera, are also such local and largely independent centres; especially as the nerves they send into the viscera, to join the many subordinate ganglia distributed through them, greatly exceed in quantity the cerebro-spinal fibres accompanying them. Indeed, to suppose otherwise is to leave unanswered the question—What are their functions? as well as the question—How are these unconscious visceral coordinations effected? There remains only to observe the kind of cooperation which exists between the two nervous systems. This is both a general and a special cooperation. The general cooperation is that by which either system of organs is enabled to stimulate the other to action. The alimentary canal yields through certain nervous connexions the sensation of hunger to the higher nervous system; and so prompts efforts for procuring food. Conversely, the activity of the nervo-muscular system, or, at least, its normal activity, sends inward to the cardiac and other plexuses a gush of stimulus which excites the viscera to action. The special co-operation is one by which it would seem that each system puts an indirect restraint on the other. Fibres from the sympathetic accompany every artery through-out the organs of external relation, and exercise on the artery a constrictive action; and the converse is done by certain of the cerebro-spinal fibres which ramify with the sympathetic throughout the viscera: through the vagus and other nerves, an inhibitory influence is exercised on the heart, intestines, pancreas, etc. Leaving doubtful details, however, the fact which concerns us here is suf-ficiently manifest. There are, for these two systems of organs, two nervous systems, in great measure inde-pendent; and, if it is true that the higher system influ-ences the lower, it is no less true that the lower very powerfully influences the higher. The restrictive action of the sympathetic upon the circulation, throughout the nervo-muscular system, is unquestionable; and it is pos-sibly through this that, when the viscera have much work to do, the nervo-muscular system is incapacitated in so marked a manner.[2]

---

[2] To meet the probable objection that the experiments of Bernard, Lud-wig, and others, show that in the case of certain glands the nerves of the cerebrospinal system are those which set up the secreting process, I would remark that in these cases, and in many others where the relative functions of the cerebro-spinal nerves and the sympathetic nerves have been studied, the organs have been those in which *sensation* is either the stimulus to activity or its accompaniment; and that from these cases no conclusion can be drawn applying to the cases of those viscera which normally perform their functions without sensation. Perhaps it may even be that the functions of those sympathetic fibres which accompany the arteries of the outer organs are simply ancillary to those of the central parts of the sympathetic system, which stimulate and regulate the vis-

The one further fact here concerning us is the contrast
presented in different kinds of animals, between the degrees of development of these two great sets of structures that carry on respectively the outer functions and
the inner functions. There are active creatures in which
the locomotive organs, the organs of sense, together
with the nervous apparatus which combines their actions, bear a large ratio to the organs of alimentation and
their appendages; while there are inactive creatures in
which these organs of external relation bear a very small
ratio to the organs of alimentation. And a remarkable
fact, here especially instructive to us, is that very frequently there occurs a metamorphosis, which has for its
leading trait a great change in the ratio of these two systems—a metamorphosis which accompanies a great
change in the mode of life. The most familiar metamorphosis is variously illustrated among insects. During the
early or larval stage of a butterfly, the organs of alimentation are largely developed, while the organs of external
relation are but little developed; and then, during a
period of quiescence, the organs of external relation
undergo an immense development, making possible the
creature's active and varied adjustments to the surrounding world, while the alimentary system becomes
relatively small. On the other hand, among the lower
invertebrate animals there is a very common metamorphosis of an opposite kind. When young, the creature,

---

cera—ancillary in this sense, that they check the diffusion of blood in
external organs when it is wanted in internal organs: cerebro-spinal inhibition (except in its action on the heart) working the opposite way.
And possibly this is the instrumentality for carrying on that competition
for nutriment which, as we saw, arises at the very outset between these
two great systems of organs.

with scarcely any alimentary system, but supplied with limbs and sense organs, swims about actively. Presently it settles in a *habitat* where food is to be obtained without moving about, loses in great part its organs of external relation, develops its visceral system, and, as it grows, assumes a nature utterly unlike that which it originally had—a nature adapted almost exclusively to alimentation and the propagation of the species.

Let us turn now to the social organism, and the analogies of structure and function which may be traced in it. Of course these analogies between the phenomena presented in a physically coherent aggregate forming an individual, and the phenomena presented in a physically incoherent aggregate of individuals distributed over a wide area, cannot be analogies of a visible or sensible kind; but can only be analogies between the systems, or methods, of organization. Such analogies as exist result from the one unquestionable community between the two organizations: *there is in both a mutual dependence of parts.* This is the origin of all organization; and determines what similarities there are between an individual organism and a social organism. Of course the similarities thus determined are accompanied by transcendent differences, determined, as above said, by the unlikenesses of the aggregates. One cardinal difference is that, while in the individual organism there is but one centre of consciousness capable of pleasure or pain, there are, in the social organism, as many such centres as there are individuals, and the aggregate of them has no consciousness of pleasure or pain—a difference which entirely changes the ends to be pursued.

Bearing in mind this qualification, let us now glance at the parallelisms indicated.

A society, like an individual, has a set of structures fitting it to act upon its environment—appliances for attack and defence, armies, navies, fortified and garrisoned places. At the same time, a society has an industrial organization which carries on all those processes that make possible the national life. Though these two sets of organs for external activity and internal activity do not bear to one another just the same relation which the outer and inner organs of an animal do (since the industrial structures in a society supply themselves with raw materials, instead of being supplied by the external organs), yet they bear a relation otherwise similar. There is at once a cooperation and an antagonism. By the help of the defensive system the industrial system is enabled to carry on its functions without injury from foreign enemies; and by the help of the industrial system, which supplies it with food and materials, the defensive system is enabled to maintain this security. At the same time the two systems are opposed in so far that they both depend for their existence upon the common stock of produce. Further, in the social organism, as in the individual organism, this primary cooperation and antagonism subdivides into secondary cooperations and antagonisms. If we look at the industrial organization, we see that its agricultural part and its manufacturing part aid one another by the exchange of their products, and are yet otherwise opposed to one another; since each takes of the other's products the most it can get in return for its own products. Similarly throughout the manufacturing system itself. Of the total returns secured by Manchester for its goods, Liverpool obtains as much as possible for the raw material, and Manchester gives as little as possible—the two at the same time cooperating in secreting for the rest of the community the woven fabrics it requires, and in jointly obtaining from the rest of the community the largest payment in other commodities. And thus it is in all kinds of direct and indirect ways throughout the industrial structures. Men prompted by their own needs as well as those of their children, and bodies of such men more or less aggregated, are quick to find every unsatisfied need of their fellow-men, and to satisfy it in return for the satisfaction of their own needs; and the working of this process is inevitably such that the strongest need, ready to pay the most for satisfaction, is that which draws most workers to satisfy it, so that there is thus a perpetual balancing of the needs and of the appliances which subserve them.

This brings us to the regulative structures under which these two systems of cooperating parts work. As in the individual organism, so in the social organism, the outer parts are under a rigorous central control. For adjustment to the varying and incalculable changes in the environment, the external organs, offensive and defensive, must be capable of prompt combination; and that their actions may be quickly combined to meet each exigency as it arises, they must be completely subordinated to a supreme executive power: armies and navies must be despotically controlled. Quite otherwise is it with the regulative apparatus required for the industrial system. This, which carries on the nutrition of a society, as the visceral system carries on the nutrition of an individual, has a regulative apparatus in great measure distinct from that which regulates the external organs. It is not by any "order in council" that farmers are determined to grow so much wheat and so much barley, or to divide their land in due proportion between arable and pasture. There requires no telegram from the Home Office to alter the production of woollens in Leeds, so that it may be properly adjusted to the stocks on hand and the forth-coming crop of wool. Staffordshire produces its due quantity of pottery, and Sheffield sends out cutlery with rapidity adjusted to the consumption, without any leg-islative stimulus or restraint. The spurs and checks to production which manufacturers and manufacturing centres receive, have quite another origin. Partly by di-rect orders from distributors and partly by the indirect indications furnished by the market reports throughout the kingdom, they are prompted to secrete actively or to diminish their rates of secretion. The regulative appa-ratus by which these industrial organs are made to co-operate harmoniously, acts somewhat as the sympathetic does in a vertebrate animal. There is a system of com-munications among the great producing and distribut-ing centres, which excites or retards as the circumstances vary. From hour to hour messages pass between all the chief provincial towns, as well as between each of them and London; from hour to hour prices are adjusted, sup-plies are ordered hither or thither, and capital is drafted from place to place, according as there is greater or less need for it. All this goes on without any ministerial overseeing—without any dictation from those executive centres which combine the actions of the outer organs. There is, however, one all-essential influence which these higher centres exercise over the industrial activities—a restraining influence which prevents aggression, direct and indirect. The condition under which only these producing and distributing processes can go on healthfully, is that, wherever there is work and waste, there shall be a proportionate supply of materials for repair. And securing this is nothing less than securing fulfilment of contracts. Just in the same way that a bodily organ which performs function, but is not adequately paid in blood, must dwindle, and the organism as a whole eventually suffer, so an industrial centre which has made and sent out its special commodity, but does not get adequately paid in other commodities, must decay. And when we ask what is requisite to prevent this local innutrition and decay, we find the requisite to be that agreements shall be carried out; that goods shall be paid for at the stipulated prices; that justice shall be administered.

One further leading parallelism must be described— that between the metamorphoses which occur in the two cases. These metamorphoses are analogous in so far that they are changes in the ratios of the inner and outer systems of organs; and also in so far as they take place under analogous conditions. At the one extreme we have that small and simple type of society which a wandering horde of savages presents. This is a type almost wholly predatory in its organization. It consists of little

else than a cooperative structure for carrying on warfare—the industrial part is almost absent, being represented only by the women. When the wandering tribe
becomes a settled tribe, an industrial organization begins
to show itself—especially where, by conquest, there has
been obtained a slave-class that may be forced to labour.
The predatory structure, however, still for a long time
predominates. Omitting the slaves and the women, the
whole body politic consists of parts organized for offence
and defence, and is efficient in proportion as the control
of them is centralized. Communities of this kind, continuing to subjugate their neighbours, and developing
an organization of some complexity, nevertheless retain
a mainly-predatory type, with just such industrial structures as are needful for supporting the offensive and
defensive structures. Of this Sparta furnished a good
example. The characteristics of such a social type are
these—that each member of the ruling race is a soldier;
that war is the business of life; that everyone is subject
to a rigorous discipline fitting him for this business; that
centralized authority regulates all the social activities,
down to the details of each man's daily conduct; that the
welfare of the State is everything, and that the individual
lives for public benefit. So long as the environing societies are such as necessitate and keep in exercise the
militant organization, these traits continue; but when,
mainly by conquest and the formation of large aggregates, the militant activity becomes less constant, and
war ceases to be the occupation of every free man, the
industrial structures begin to predominate. Without trac-
ing the transition, it will suffice to take, as a sample of

the pacific or industrial type, the Northern States of America before the late war. Here military organization had almost disappeared; the infrequent local assemblings of militia had turned into occasions for jollity, and everything martial had fallen into contempt. The traits of the pacific or industrial type are these—that the central authority is relatively feeble; that it interferes scarcely at all with the private actions of individuals; and that the State, instead of being that for the benefit of which individuals exist, has become that which exists for the benefit of individuals.

It remains to add that this metamorphosis, which takes place in societies along with a higher civilization, very rapidly retrogrades if the surrounding conditions become unfavourable to it. During the late war in America, Mr. Seward's boast—"I touch this bell, and any man in the remotest State is a prisoner of the Government" (a boast which was not an empty one, and which was by many of the Republican party greatly applauded)— shows us how rapidly, along with militant activities, there tends to be resumed the needful type of centralized structure; and how there quickly grow up the corresponding sentiments and ideas. Our own history since 1815 has shown a double change of this kind. During the thirty years' peace, the militant organization dwindled, the military sentiment greatly decreased, the industrial organization rapidly developed, the assertion of the individuality of the citizen became more decided, and many restrictive and despotic regulations were got rid of. Conversely, since the revival of militant activities and structures on the Continent, our own offensive and defensive structures have been re-developing; and the tendency toward increase of that centralized control which accompanies such structures has become marked.

And now, closing this somewhat elaborate introduction, I am prepared to deal with the question put to me. Prof. Huxley, after quoting some passages from that essay on the "Social Organism" which I have supplemented in the foregoing paragraphs; and after expressing a qualified concurrence which I greatly value as coming from so highly fitted a judge, proceeds, with characteristic acumen, to comment on what seems an incongruity between certain analogies set forth in that essay, and the doctrine I hold respecting the duty of the State. Referring to a passage in which I have described the function of the individual brain as "that of *averaging* the interests of life, physical, intellectual, moral, social," and have compared it to the function of Parliament as "that of *averaging* the interests of the various classes in a community," adding that "a good Parliament is one in which the parties answering to these respective interests are so balanced that their united legislation concedes to each class as much as consists with the claims of the rest"; Prof. Huxley proceeds to say:

> All this appears to be very just. But if the resemblances between the body physiological and the body politic are any indication, not only of what the latter is, and how it has become what it is, but what it ought to be, and what it is tending to become, I cannot but think that the real force of the analogy is totally opposed to the negative view of State function.
>
> Suppose that, in accordance with this view, each muscle were to maintain that the nervous system had no right to interfere

with its contraction, except to prevent it from hindering the contraction of another muscle; or each gland, that it had a right to secrete, so long as its secretion interfered with no other; suppose every separate cell left free to follow its own "interests," and *laissez-faire* Lord of all, what would become of the body physiological?

On this question the remark I have first to make is, that if I held the doctrine of M. Proudhon, who deliberately named himself an "anarchist," and if along with this doctrine I held the above-indicated theory of social structures and functions, the inconsistency implied by the question put would be clear, and the question would be unanswerable. But since I entertain no such view as that of Proudhon—since I hold that within its proper limits governmental action is not simply legitimate but all-important—I do not see how I am concerned with a question which tacitly supposes that I deny the legitimacy and the importance. Not only do I contend that the restraining power of the State over individuals, and bodies or classes of individuals, is requisite, but I have contended that it should be exercised much more effectually, and carried out much further, than at present.[3] And as the maintenance of this control implies the maintenance of a controlling apparatus, I do not see that I am placed in any difficulty when I am asked what would happen were the controlling apparatus forbidden to interfere. Further, on this general aspect of the question I have to say that, by comparing the deliberative assembly of a nation to the deliberative nervous centre of a ver-

---

[3] See *Social Statics*, chap. xxi., "The Duty of the State." See also essay on "Over-legislation."

tebrate animal, as respectively averaging the interests of the society and of the individual, and as both doing this through processes of representation, I do not mean to *identify* the two sets of interest; for these in a society (or at least a peaceful society) refer mainly to interior actions, while in an individual creature they refer mainly to exterior actions. The "interests" to which I refer, as being averaged by a representative governing body, are the conflicting interests between class and class, as well as between man and man—conflicting interests the balancing of which is nothing but the preventing of aggression and the administration of justice.

I pass now from this general aspect of the question, which does not concern me, to a more special aspect which does concern me. Dividing the actions of governing structures, whether in bodies individual or bodies politic, into the *positively regulative* and the *negatively regulative*, or those which stimulate and direct, as distinguished from those which simply restrain, I may say that if there is raised the question—What will happen when the controlling apparatus does not act? there are quite different replies according as one or other system of organs is referred to. If, in the individual body, the muscles were severally independent of the deliberative and executive centres, utter impotence would result: in the absence of muscular coordination, there would be no possibility of standing, much less of acting on surrounding things, and the body would be a prey to the first enemy. Properly to combine the actions of these outer organs, the great nervous centres must exercise functions that are both positively regulative and negatively regulative—must both command action and arrest action. Similarly with the outer organs of a political body. Unless the offensive and defensive structures can be despotically commanded by a central authority, there cannot be those prompt combinations and adjustments required for meeting the variable actions of external enemies. But if, instead of asking what would happen supposing the outer organs in either case were without control from the great governing centres, we ask what would happen were the inner organs (the industrial and commercial structures in the one case, and the alimentary and distributive in the other) without such control, the answer is quite different. Omitting the respiratory and some minor ancillary parts of the individual organism, to which the social organism has nothing analogous; and limiting ourselves to absorptive, elaborative, and distributive structures, which are found in both; it may, I think, be successfully contended that in neither the one case nor the other do they require the positively regulative control of the great governing centres, but only the negatively regulative. Let us glance at the facts.[4]

Digestion and circulation go on very well in lunatics

---

[4] Lest there should be any misunderstanding of the terms *positively regulative* and *negatively regulative*, let me briefly illustrate them. If a man has land, and I either cultivate it for him, partially or wholly, or dictate any or all of his modes of cultivation, my action is positively regulative; but if, leaving him absolutely unhelped and unregulated in his farming, I simply prevent him from taking his neighbour's crops, or from making approach-roads over his neighbour's land, or from depositing rubbish upon it, my action is negatively regulative. There is a tolerably sharp distinction between the act of securing a citizen's ends for him or interfering with his mode of securing them, and the act of checking him when he interferes with another citizen in the pursuit of his ends.

and idiots, though the higher nervous centres are either deranged or partly absent. The vital functions proceed properly during sleep, though less actively than when the brain is at work. In infancy, while the cerebro-spinal system is almost incapable, and cannot even perform such simple actions as those of commanding the sphincters, the visceral functions are active and regular. Nor in an adult does that arrest of cerebral action shown by insensibility, or that extensive paralysis of the spinal system which renders all the limbs immovable, prevent these functions from being carried on for a considerable time; though they necessarily begin to flag in the absence of the demand which an active system of outer organs makes upon them. These internal organs are, indeed, so little under the positively directive control of the great nervous centres, that their independence is often very inconvenient. No mandate sent into the interior stops an attack of diarrhœa; nor, when an indigestible meal excites the circulation at night, and prevents sleep, will the bidding of the brain cause the heart to pulsate more quietly. It is doubtless true that these vital processes are modified in important ways, both by general stimulation and by inhibition, from the cerebro-spinal system; but that they are mainly independent cannot, I think, be questioned. The facts that peristaltic motion of the intestines can go on when their nervous connexions are cut, and that the heart (in cold-blooded vertebrates, at least) continues to pulsate for some time after being detached from the body, make it manifest that the spontaneous activities of these vital organs subserve the wants of the body at large without direction from its higher governing centres. And this is made even more manifest if it be a fact, as alleged by Schmuleswitsch experimenting under Ludwig's direction, that, under duly-adjusted conditions, the secretion of bile may be kept up for some time when blood is passed through the excised liver of a newly-killed rabbit. There is an answer, not, I think, unsatisfactory, even to the crucial part of the question—"Suppose every separate cell left free to follow its own interests, and *laissez faire* Lord of all, what would become of the body physiological?" Limiting the application of this question in the way above shown to the organs and parts of organs which carry on vital actions, it seems to me that much evidence may be given for the belief that, when they follow their respective "interests" (limited here to growing and multiplying), the general welfare will be tolerably well secured. It was proved by Hunter's experiments on a kite and a sea-gull, that a part of the alimentary canal which has to triturate harder food than that which the creature naturally eats, acquires a thicker and harder lining. When a stricture of the intestine impedes the passage of its contents, the muscular walls of the intestine above, thicken and propel the contents with greater force. When there is somewhere in the course of the circulation a serious resistance to the passage of blood, there habitually occurs hypertrophy of the heart, or thickening of its muscular walls; giving it greater power to propel the blood. And similarly, when the duct through which it discharges its contents is obstructed, the gall-bladder thickens and strengthens. These changes go on without any direction from the brain—without any consciousness that they are

going on. They are effected by the growth, or multiplication, or adaptation, of the local units, be they cells or
fibres, which results from the greater action or modified
action thrown upon them. The only pre-requisite to this
spontaneous adaptive change is, that these local units
shall be supplied with extra blood in proportion as they
perform extra function—a pre-requisite answering to
that secured by the administration of justice in a society;
namely, that more work shall bring more pay. If, however, direct proof be called for that a system of organs
may, by carrying on their several independent activities
uncontrolled, secure the welfare of the aggregate they
form, we have it in that extensive class of creatures
which do not possess any nervous systems at all; and
which nevertheless show, some of them, considerable
degrees of activity. The Oceanic Hydrozoa supply good
examples. Notwithstanding "the multiplicity and complexity of the organs which some of them possess,"
these creatures have no nervous centres—no regulative
apparatus by which the actions of their organs are co-
ordinated. One of their highest kinds is composed of
different parts distinguished as cœnosarc, polypites,
tentacles, hydrocysts, nectocalyces, genocalyces, etc.,
and each of these different parts is composed of many
partially-independent units—thread-cells, ciliated cells,
contractile fibres, etc.; so that the whole organism is a
group of heterogeneous groups, each one of which is
itself a more or less heterogeneous group. And, in the
absence of a nervous system, the arrangement must necessarily be such that these different units, and different
groups of units, severally pursuing their individual lives

without positive direction from the rest, nevertheless do, by virtue of their constitutions, and the relative positions into which they have grown, cooperate for the maintenance of one another and the entire aggregate. And if this can be so with a set of organs that are not connected by nerves, much more can it be so with a set of organs which, like the viscera of a higher animal, have a special set of nervous communications for exciting one another to cooperation.

Let us turn now to the parallel classes of phenomena which the social organism presents. In it, as in the individual organism, we find that while the system of external organs must be rigorously subordinated to a great governing centre which positively regulates it, the system of internal organs needs no such positive regulation. The production and interchange by which the national life is maintained, go on as well while Parliament is not sitting as while it is sitting. When the members of the Ministry are following grouse or stalking deer, Liverpool imports, Manchester manufactures, London distributes, just as usual. All that is needful for the normal performance of these internal social functions is, that the restraining or inhibitory structures shall continue in action: these activities of individuals, corporate bodies, and classes, must be carried on in such ways as not to transgress certain conditions, necessitated by the simultaneous carrying on of other activities. So long as order is maintained, and the fulfilment of contracts is everywhere enforced—so long as there is secured to each citizen, and each combination of citizens, the full return agreed upon for work done or commodities produced;

and so long as each may enjoy what he obtains by labour, without trenching on his neighbour's like ability to enjoy; these functions will go on healthfully—more healthfully, indeed, than when regulated in any other way. Fully to recognize this fact, it is needful only to look at the origins and actions of the leading industrial structures. We will take two of them, the most remote from one another in their natures.

The first shall be those by which food is produced and distributed. In the fourth of his *Introductory Lectures on Political Economy*, Archbishop Whately remarks that:

> Many of the most important objects are accomplished by the joint agency of persons who never think of them, nor have any idea of acting in concert; and that, with a certainty, completeness, and regularity, which probably the most diligent benevolence, under the guidance of the greatest human wisdom, could never have attained.

To enforce this truth he goes on to say:—"Let any one propose to himself the problem of supplying with daily provisions of all kinds such a city as our metropolis, containing above a million of inhabitants." And then he points out the many immense difficulties of the task caused by inconstancy in the arrival of suplies; by the perishable nature of many of the commodities; by the fluctuating number of consumers; by the heterogeneity of their demands; by variations in the stocks, immediate and remote, and the need for adjusting the rate of consumption; and by the complexity in the process of distribution required to bring due quantities of these many commodities to the homes of all citizens. And, having dwelt on these many difficulties, he finishes his picture by saying:

> Yet this object is accomplished far better than it could be by any effort of human wisdom, through the agency of men who think each of nothing beyond his own immediate interest—who, with that object in view, perform their respective parts with cheerful zeal—and combine unconsciously to employ the wisest means for effecting an object, the vastness of which it would bewilder them even to contemplate.

But though the far-spreading and complex organization by which foods of all kinds are produced, prepared, and distributed throughout the entire kingdom, is a natural growth and not a State-manufacture; though the State does not determine where and in what quantities cereals and cattle and sheep shall be reared; though it does not arrange their respective prices so as to make supplies last until fresh supplies can come; though it has done nothing toward causing that great improvement of quality which has taken place in food since early times; though it has not the credit of that elaborate apparatus by which bread, and meat, and milk, come round to our doors with a daily pulse that is as regular as the pulse of the heart; yet the State has not been wholly passive. It has from time to time done a great deal of mischief. When Edward I forbade all towns to harbour forestallers, and when Edward VI made it penal to buy grain for the purpose of selling it again, they were preventing the process by which consumption is adjusted to supply: they were doing all that could be done to insure alternations of abundance and starvation. Similarly with the many legislative attempts since made to regulate one branch or other of the food-industry, down to the corn-law sliding-scale of odious memory. For the marvellous efficiency of this organization we are indebted to private enterprise; while the derangements of it we owe to the positively-regulative action of the Government. Meanwhile, its negatively-regulative action, required to keep this organization in order, Government has not duly performed. A quick and costless remedy for breach of contract, when a trader sells, as the commodity asked for, what proves to be wholly or in part some other commodity, is still wanting.

Our second case shall be the organization which so immensely facilitates commerce by transfers of claims and credits. Banks were not inventions of rulers or their counsellors. They grew up by small stages out of the transactions of traders with one another. Men who for security deposited money with goldsmiths, and took receipts; goldsmiths who began to lend out at interest the moneys left with them, and then to offer interest at lower rates to those who would deposit money; were the founders of them. And when, as presently happened, the receipt-notes became transferable by indorsement, banking commenced. From that stage upward the development, notwithstanding many hindrances, has gone on naturally. Banks have sprung up under the same stimulus which has produced all other kinds of trading bodies. The multiplied forms of credit have been gradually differentiated from the original form; and while the banking system has spread and become complex, it has also become consolidated into a whole by a spontaneous process. The clearing-house, which is a place for carry-

ing on the banking between bankers, arose unobtru-
sively out of an effort to economize time and money.
And when, in 1862, Sir John Lubbock—not in his legislative capacity but in his capacity as banker—succeeded
in extending the privileges of the clearing-house to country banks, the unification was made perfect; so that now
the transactions of any trader in the kingdom with any
other may be completed by the writing off and balancing
of claims in bankers' books. This natural evolution, be
it observed, has reached with us a higher phase than has
been reached where the positively-regulative control of
the State is more decided. They have no clearing-house
in France; and in France the method of making payments
by checks, so dominant among ourselves, is very little
employed and in an imperfect way. I do not mean to
imply that in England the State has been a mere spectator
of this development. Unfortunately, it has from the beginning had relations with banks and bankers: not
much, however, to their advantage, or that of the public.
The first kind of deposit-bank was in some sense a State-
bank: merchants left funds for security at the Mint in the
Tower. But when Charles I appropriated their property
without consent, and gave it back to them only under
pressure, after a long delay, he destroyed their confidence. Similarly, when Charles II, in furtherance of
State-business, came to have habitual transactions with
the richer of the private bankers; and when, having got
nearly a million and a half of their money in the Exchequer, he stole it, ruined a multitude of merchants,
distressed ten thousand depositors, and made some lunatics and suicides, he gave a considerable shock to the

banking system as it then existed. Though the results of State-relations with banks in later times have not been so disastrous in this direct way, yet they have been indirectly disastrous—perhaps even in a greater degree. In return for a loan, the State gave the Bank of England special privileges; and for the increase and continuance of this loan the bribe was the maintenance of these privileges—privileges which immensely hindered the development of banks. The State did worse. It led the Bank of England to the verge of bankruptcy by a forced issue of notes, and then authorized it to break its promises to pay. Nay, worse still, it prevented the Bank of England from fulfilling its promises to pay when it wished to fulfil them. The evils that have arisen from the positively-regulative action of the State on banks are too multitudinous to be here enumerated. They may be found in the writings of Tooke, Newmarch, Fullarton, Macleod, Wilson, J. S. Mill, and others. All we have here to note is, that while the enterprise of citizens in the pursuit of private ends has developed this great trading-process, which so immensely facilitates all other trading-processes, Governments have over and over again disturbed it to an almost fatal extent; and that, while they have done enormous mischief of one kind by their positively-regulative action, they have done enormous mischief of another kind by failing in their negatively-regulative action. They have not done the one thing they had to do: they have not uniformly insisted on fulfilment of contract between the banker and the customer who takes his promise to pay on demand.

Between these two cases of the trade in food and the

trade in money, might be put the cases of other trades: all of them carried on by organizations similarly evolved, and similarly more or less deranged from time to time by State-meddling. Passing over these, however, let us turn from the positive method of elucidation to the comparative method. When it is questioned whether the spontaneous cooperation of men in pursuit of personal benefits will adequately work out the general good, we may get guidance for judgment by comparing the results achieved in countries where spontaneous cooperation has been most active and least regulated, with the results achieved in countries where spontaneous cooperation has been less trusted and State-action more trusted. Two cases, furnished by the two leading nations on the Continent, will suffice.

In France, the École des Ponts et Chaussées was founded in 1747 for educating civil engineers; and in 1795 was founded the École Polytechnique, serving, among other purposes, to give a general scientific training to those who were afterward to be more specially trained for civil engineering. Averaging the two dates, we may say that for a century France has had a State-established and State-maintained appliance for producing skilled men of this class—a double gland, we may call it, to secrete engineering faculty for public use. In England, until quite recently, we have had no institution for preparing civil engineers. Not by intention, but unconsciously, we left the furnishing of engineering faculty to take place under the law of supply and demand—a law which at present seems to be no more recognized as applying to education, than it was recognized as applying to commerce in the days of bounties and restrictions. This, however, by the way. We have here simply to note that Brindley, Smeaton, Rennie, Telford, and the rest, down to George Stephenson, acquired their knowledge, and got their experience, without State-aid or supervision. What have been the comparative results in the two nations? Space does not allow a detailed comparison: the later results must suffice. Railways originated in England, not in France. Railways spread through England faster than through France. Many railways in France were laid out and officered by English engineers. The earlier French railways were made by English contractors; and English locomotives served the French makers as models. The first French work written on locomotive engines, published about 1840 (at least I had a copy at that date), was by the Comte de Pambour, who had studied in England, and who gave in his work nothing whatever but drawings and descriptions of the engines of English makers.

The second illustration is supplied to us by the model nation, now so commonly held up to us for imitation. Let us contrast London and Berlin in respect of an all-essential appliance for the comfort and health of citizens. When, at the beginning of the seventeenth century, the springs and local conduits, supplemented by water-carriers, failed to supply the Londoners; and when the water-famine, for a long time borne, had failed to make the Corporation do more than propose schemes, and had not spurred the central government to do anything; Hugh Myddleton, a merchant citizen, took in hand himself the work of bringing the New River to Islington.

When he had half completed the work, the king came to his help—not, indeed, in his capacity of ruler, but in the capacity of speculator, investing his money with a view to profit: his share being disposed of by his successor after the formation of the New River Company, which finished the distributing system. Subsequently, the formation of other water-companies, utilizing other sources, has given London a water-supply that has grown with its growth. What, meanwhile, happened at Berlin? Did there in 1613, when Hugh Myddleton completed his work, grow up there a like efficient system? Not at all. The seventeenth century passed, the eighteenth century passed, the middle of the nineteenth century was reached, and still Berlin had no water supply like that of London. What happened then? Did the paternal government at length do what had been so long left undone? No. Did the citizens at length unite to secure the desideratum? No. It was finally achieved by the citizens of another nation, more accustomed to cooperate in gaining their own profits by ministering to public needs. In 1845 an English company was formed for giving Berlin an adequate water-supply; and the work was executed by English contractors—Messrs. Fox and Crampton.

Should it be said that great works of ancient nations, in the shape of aqueducts, roads, etc., might be instanced in proof that State agency secures such ends, or should it be said that a comparison between the early growth of inland navigation on the Continent, and its later growth here would be to our disadvantage, I reply that, little as they at first seem so, these facts are con-

gruous with the general doctrine. While the militant social type is dominant, and the industrial organization
but little developed, there is but one coordinating agency
for regulating both sets of activities; just as we saw happens with the lower types of individual organisms. It is
only when a considerable advance has been made in that
metamorphosis which develops the industrial structures
at the expense of the militant structures, and which
brings along with it a substantially-independent coordinating agency for the industrial structures—it is only
then that the efficiency of these spontaneous cooperations for all purposes of internal social life becomes
greater than the efficiency of the central governing
agency.

Possibly it will be said that though, for subserving
material needs, the actions of individuals, stimulated by
necessity and made quick by competition, are demon-
strably adequate, they are not adequate for subserving
other needs. I do not see, however, that the facts justify
this position. We have but to glance around to find in
abundance similarly-generated appliances for satisfying
our higher desires, as well as our lower desires. The fact
that the Fine Arts have not thriven here as much as in
some Continental countries, is ascribable to natural character, to absorption of our energies in other activities,
and to the repressive influence of chronic asceticism,
rather then to the absence of fostering agencies: these
the interests of individuals have provided in abundance.
Literature, in which we are second to none, owes, with
us, nothing to State-aid. The poetry which will live is
poetry which has been written without official prompt-

ing; and though we have habitually had a prize-poet, paid to write loyal verses, it may be said, without disparaging the present one, that a glance over the entire list does not show any benefit derived by poetry from State-patronage. Nor are other forms of literature any more indebted to State-patronage. It was because there was a public liking for fiction that fiction began to be produced; and the continued public liking causes a continued production, including, along with much that is worthless, much that could not have been made better by any academic or other supervision. And the like holds of biographies, histories, scientific books, etc. Or, as a still more striking case of an agency that has grown up to meet a non-material want, take the newspaper press. What has been the genesis of this marvellous appliance, which each day gives us an abstract of the world's life the day before? Under what promptings have there been got together its staffs of editors, sub-editors, article-writers, reviewers; its reporters of parliamentary debates, of public meetings, of law cases and police cases; its critics of music, theatricals, paintings, etc.; its correspondents in all parts of the world? Who devised and brought to perfection this system which at six o'clock in the morning gives the people of Edinburgh a report of the debates that ended at two or three o'clock in the House of Commons, and at the same time tells them of events that occurred the day before in America? It is not a Government invention. It is not a Government suggestion. It has not been in any way improved or developed by legislation. On the contrary, it has grown up in spite of many hindrances from the Government and burdens which the Government has imposed on it. For a long time the reporting of parliamentary debates was resisted; for generations censorships and prosecutions kept newspapers down, and for several subsequent generations the laws in force negatived a cheap press, and the educational benefits accompanying it. From the war-correspondent, whose letters give to the very nations that are fighting their only trustworthy accounts of what is being done, down to the newsboy who brings round the third edition with the latest telegrams, the whole organization is a product of spontaneous cooperation among private individuals, aiming to benefit themselves by ministering to the intellectual needs of their fellows— aiming also, not a few of them, to benefit their fellows by giving them clearer ideas and a higher standard of right. Nay, more than this is true. While the press is not indebted to the Government, the Government is enormously indebted to the press; without which, indeed, it would stumble daily in the performance of its functions. This agency which the State once did its best to put down, and has all along impeded, now gives to the ministers news in anticipation of their dispatches, gives to members of Parliament a guiding knowledge of public opinion, enables them to speak from the House of Commons benches to their constituents, and gives to both legislative chambers a full record of their proceedings.

I do not see, therefore, how there can be any doubt respecting the sufficiency of agencies thus originating. The truth that in this condition of mutual dependence brought about by social life, there inevitably grow up arrangements such that each secures his own ends by

ministering to the ends of others, seems to have been
for a long time one of those open secrets which remain
secret because they are so open; and even now the conspicuousness of this truth seems to cause an imperfect
consciousness of its full meaning. The evidence shows,
however, that even were there no other form of spontaneous cooperation among men than that dictated by
self-interest, it might be rationally held that this, under
the negatively-regulative control of a central power,
would work out, in proper order, the appliances for satisfying all needs, and carrying on healthfully all the essential social functions.

But there is a further kind of spontaneous cooperation,
arising, like the other, independently of State-action,
which takes a large share in satisfying certain classes of
needs. Familiar though it is, this kind of spontaneous
cooperation is habitually ignored in sociological discussions. Alike from newspaper articles and parliamentary
debates, it might be inferred that, beyond the force due
to men's selfish activities, there is no other social force
than the governmental force. There seems to be a deliberate omission of the fact that, in addition to their selfish
interests, men have sympathetic interests, which, acting
individually and cooperatively, work out results scarcely
less remarkable than those which the selfish interests
work out. It is true that, during the earlier phases of
social evolution, while yet the type is mainly militant,
agencies thus produced do not exist: among the Spartans, I suppose, there were few, if any, philanthropic
agencies. But as there arise forms of society leading
toward the pacific type—forms in which the indus-

trial organization develops itself, and men's activities become of a kind that do not perpetually sear their sympathies; these structures which their sympathies generate become many and important. To the egoistic interests, and the cooperations prompted by them, there come to be added the altruistic interests and their co-operations; and what the one set fails to do, the other does. That, in his presentation of the doctrine he opposes, Prof. Huxley did not set down the effects of fellow-feeling as supplementing the effects of self-regarding feelings, surprises me the more, because he displays fellow-feeling himself in so marked a degree, and shows in his career how potent a social agency it becomes. Let us glance rapidly over the results wrought out among ourselves by individual and combined "altruism"—to employ M. Comte's useful word.

Though they show a trace of this feeling, I will not dwell upon the numerous institutions by which men are enabled to average the chances throughout life by insurance societies, which provide against the evils entailed by premature deaths, accidents, fires, wrecks, etc.; for these are mainly mercantile and egoistic in their origin. Nor will I do more than name those multitudinous Friendly Societies that have arisen spontaneously among the working-classes to give mutual aid in time of sickness, and which the Commission now sitting is showing to be immensely beneficial, notwithstanding their defects; for these also, though containing a larger element of sympathy, are prompted chiefly by anticipations of personal benefits. Leaving these, let us turn to the organizations in which altruism is more decided:

taking first that by which religious ministrations are carried on. Throughout Scotland and England, cut away all
that part of it which is not established by law—in Scotland, the Episcopal Church, the Free Church, the United
Presbyterians, and other Dissenting bodies; in England,
the Wesleyans, Independents, and the various minor
sects. Cut off, too, from the Established Church itself, all
that part added in recent times by voluntary zeal, made
conspicuous enough by the new steeples that have been
rising on all sides; and then also take out, from the remainder of the Established Church, that energy which
has during these three generations been infused into it
by competition with the Dissenters: so reducing it to the
degraded, inert state in which John Wesley found it. Do
this, and it becomes manifest that more than half the
organization, and immensely more than half its function, is extra-governmental. Look round, again, at the
multitudinous institutions for mitigating men's ills—the
hospitals, dispensaries, alms-houses, and the like—the
various benevolent and mendicity societies, etc., of
which London alone contains between six and seven
hundred. From our vast St. Thomas's, exceeding the
palace of the Legislature itself in bulk, down to Dorcas
societies and village clothing-clubs, we have charitable
agencies, many in kind and countless in number, which
supplement, perhaps too largely, the legally-established
one; and which, whatever evil they may have done along
with the good, have done far less evil than the Poor-Law
organization did before it was reformed in 1834. Akin to
these are still more striking examples of power in agencies thus originating, such as that furnished by the Anti-

slavery Society, which carried the emancipation of the slaves, notwithstanding the class-opposition so predominant in the Legislature. And if we look for more recent like instances, we have them in the organization which promptly and efficiently dealt with the cotton-famine in Lancashire, and in that which last year ministered to the wounded and distressed in France. Once more, consider our educational system as it existed till within these few years. Such part of it as did not consist of private schools, carried on for personal profit, consisted of schools or colleges set up or maintained by men for the benefit of their fellows, and the posterity of their fellows. Omitting the few founded or partially founded by kings, the numerous endowed schools scattered throughout the kingdom, originated from altruistic feelings (so far, at least, as they were not due to egoistic desires for good places in the other world). And then, after these appliances for teaching the poor had been almost entirely appropriated by the rich, whence came the remedy? Another altruistic organization grew up for educating the poor, struggled against the opposition of the Church and the governing classes, eventually forced these to enter into competition and produce like altruistic organizations, until by school systems, local and general, ecclesiastical, dissenting, and secular, the mass of the people had been brought from a state of almost entire ignorance to one in which nearly all of them possessed the rudiments of knowledge. But for these spontaneously-developed agencies, ignorance would have been universal. Not only such knowledge as the poor now possess—not only the knowledge of the trading-classes—not only the knowledge of those who write books and leading articles; but the knowledge of those who carry on the business of the country as ministers and legislators, has been derived from these extra-governmental agencies, egoistic or altruistic. Yet now, strangely enough, the cultured intelligence of the country has taken to spurning its parent; and that to which it owes both its existence and the consciousness of its own value is pooh-poohed as though it had done, and could do, nothing of importance! One other fact let me add. While such teaching organizations, and their results in the shape of enlightenment, are due to these spontaneous agencies, to such agencies also are due the great improvements in the quality of the culture now happily beginning to take place. The spread of scientific knowledge, and of the scientific spirit, has not been brought about by laws and officials. Our scientific societies have arisen from the spontaneous cooperation of those interested in the accumulation and diffusion of the kinds of truth they respectively deal with. Though the British Association has from time to time obtained certain small subsidies, their results in the way of advancing science have borne but an extremely small ratio to the results achieved without any such aid. If there needs a conclusive illustration of the power of agencies thus arising, we have it in the history and achievements of the Royal Institution. From this, which is a product of altruistic cooperation, and which has had for its successive professors Young, Davy, Faraday, and Tyndall, there has come a series of brilliant discoveries which cannot be paralleled by a series from any State-nurtured institution.

I hold, then, that forced, as men in society are, to seek satisfaction of their own wants by satisfying the wants of others; and led as they also are by sentiments which social life has fostered, to satisfy many wants of others irrespective of their own; they are moved by two sets of forces which, working together, will amply suffice to carry on all needful activities; and I think the facts fully justify this belief. It is true that, *a priori*, one would not have supposed that by their unconscious cooperations men could have wrought out such results, any more than one would have supposed, *a priori*, that by their unconscious cooperation they could have evolved Language. But reasoning *a posteriori*, which it is best to do when we have the facts before us, it becomes manifest that they can do this; that they have done it in very astonishing ways; and perhaps may do it hereafter in ways still more astonishing. Scarcely any scientific generalization had, I think, a broader inductive basis than we have for the belief that these egoistic and altruistic feelings are powers which, taken together, amply suffice to originate and carry on all the activities which constitute healthy national life: the only pre-requisite being, that they shall be under the negatively-regulative control of a central power—that the entire aggregate of individuals, acting through the legislature and executive as its agents, shall put upon each individual, and group of individuals, the restraints needful to prevent aggression, direct and indirect.

And here I might go on to supplement the argument by showing that the immense majority of the evils which government aid is invoked to remedy, are evils which arise immediately or remotely because it does not perform properly its negatively-regulative function. From the waste of, probably, £100,000,000 of national capital in un-productive railways, for which the Legislature is responsible by permitting the original proprietary contracts to be broken,[5] down to the railway accidents and loss of life caused by unpunctuality, which would never have grown to its present height were there an easy remedy for breach of contract between company and passenger; nearly all the vices of railway management have arisen from the non-administration of justice. And everywhere else we shall find that, were the restraining action of the State prompt, effective, and costless to those aggrieved, the pleas put in for positive regulation would nearly all disappear.

I am thus brought naturally to remark on the title given to this theory of State-functions. That "Administrative Nihilism" adequately describes the view set forth by Von Humboldt, may be: I have not read his work. But I cannot see how it adequately describes the doctrine I have been defending; nor do I see how this can be properly expressed by the more positive title, "police-government." The conception suggested by police-government does not include the conception of an organization for external protection. So long as each nation is given to burglary, I quite admit each other nation must keep guards, under the forms of army or navy, or both, to prevent burglars from breaking in. And the title police-government does not, in its ordinary acceptation, com-

---

[5] See Essay on "Railway Morals and Railway Policy."

prehend these offensive and defensive appliances needful for dealing with foreign enemies. At the other extreme, too, it falls short of the full meaning to be expressed. While it duly conveys the idea of an organization required for checking and punishing criminal aggression, it does not convey any idea of the no less important organization required for dealing with civil aggression—an organization quite essential for properly discharging the negatively-regulative function. Though latent police-force may be considered as giving their efficiency to legal decisions on all questions brought into *nisi prius* courts, yet, since here police-force rarely comes into visible play, police-government does not suggest this very extensive part of the administration of justice. Far from contending for a *laissez-faire* policy in the sense which the phrase commonly suggests, I have contended for a more active control of the kind distinguishable as negatively regulative. One of the reasons I have urged for excluding State-action from other spheres, is, that it may become more efficient within its proper sphere. And I have argued that the wretched performance of its duties within its proper sphere continues, because its time is chiefly spent over imaginary duties.[6] The facts that often, in bankruptcy cases, three-fourths and more of the assets go in costs; that creditors are led by the expectation of great delay and a miserable dividend to accept almost any composition offered; and that so the bankruptcy-law offers a premium to roguery; are facts which would long since have ceased to be facts, had

---

[6] See Essay on "Over-Legislation."

citizens been mainly occupied in getting an efficient judicial system. If the due performance by the State of its all-essential function had been the question on which elections were fought, we should not see, as we now do, that a shivering cottager who steals palings for firewood, or a hungry tramp who robs an orchard, gets punishment in more than the old Hebrew measure, while great financial frauds which ruin their thousands bring no punishments. Were the negatively-regulative function of the State in internal affairs dominant in the thoughts of men, within the Legislature and without, there would be tolerated no such treatment as that suffered lately by Messrs Walker, of Cornhill; who, having been robbed of £6,000 worth of property and having spent £950 in rewards for apprehending thieves and prosecuting them, cannot get back the proceeds of their property found on the thieves—who bear the costs of administering justice, while the Corporation of London makes £940 profit out of their loss. It is in large measure because I hold that these crying abuses and inefficiencies, which everywhere characterize the administration of justice, need more than any other evils to be remedied; and because I hold that remedy of them can go on only as fast as the internal function of the State is more and more restricted to the administration of justice; that I take the view which I have been re-explaining. *It is a law illustrated by organizations of every kind, that, in proportion as there is to be efficiency, there must be specialization, both of structure and function—specialization which, of necessity, implies accompanying limitation.* And, as I have elsewhere argued, the development of representative government is the development of a type of government fitted above all others for this negatively-regulative control.[7] This doctrine, that while the negatively-regulative control should be extended and made better, the positively-regulative control should be diminished, and that the one change implies the other, may properly be called the doctrine of Specialized Administration—if it is to be named from its administrative aspect. I regret that my presentation of this doctrine has been such as to lead to misinterpretation. Either it is that I have not adequately explained it, which, if true, surprises me, or else it is that the space occupied in seeking to show what are not the duties of the State is so much greater than the space occupied in defining its duties, that these last make but little impression. In any case, that Prof. Huxley should have construed my view in the way he has done, shows me that it needs fuller exposition; since, had he put upon it the construction I intended, he would not, I think, have included it under the title he has used, nor would he have seen it needful to raise the question I have endeavoured to answer.

POSTSCRIPT—Since the above article was written, a fact of some significance in relation to the question of State-management has come under my notice. There is one department, at any rate, in which the State succeeds well—the Post-Office. And this department is sometimes instanced as showing the superiority of public over private administration.

I am not about to call in question the general satisfactoriness of our postal arrangements; nor shall I con-

---

[7] See Essay on "Representative Government—What is it good for?"

tend that this branch of State-organization, now well-established, could be replaced with advantage. Possibly the type of our social structure had become, in this respect, so far fixed that a radical change would be injurious. In dealing with those who make much of this success, I have contented myself with showing that the developments which have made the Post-Office efficient, have not originated with the Government, but have been thrust upon it from without. I have in evidence cited the facts that the mail-coach system was established by a private individual, Mr. Palmer, and lived down official opposition; that the reform originated by Mr. Rowland Hill had to be made against the wills of *employés;* and, further, I have pointed out that, even as it is, a large part of the work is done by private enterprise—that the Government gets railway-companies to do for it most of the inland carriage, and steam-boat companies the outland carriage: contenting itself with doing the local collection and distribution.

Respecting the general question whether, in the absence of our existing postal system, private enterprise would have developed one as good or better, I have been able to say only that analogies like that furnished by our newspaper-system, with its efficient news-vending organization, warrant us in believing that it would. Recently, however, I have been shown both that private enterprise is capable of this, and that, but for a legal interdict, it would have done long ago what the State has but lately done. Here is the proof:

> To facilitate correspondence between one part of London and another was not originally one of the objects of the Post-Office. But, in the reign of Charles II, an enterprising citizen of Lon-

don, William Dockwray, set up, at great expense, a penny post, which delivered letters and parcels six or eight times a-day in the busy and crowded streets near the Exchange, and four times a-day in the outskirts of the capital. . . . As soon as it became clear that the speculation would be lucrative, the Duke of York complained of it as an infraction of his monopoly, and the courts of law decided in his favour.—*Macaulay, History of England*, 1866, i., pp. 302–3.

Thus it appears that two centuries since, private enterprise initiated a local postal system, similar, in respect both of cheapness and frequency of distribution, to that lately-established one boasted of as a State-success. Judging by what has happened in other cases with private enterprises which had small beginnings, we may infer that the system thus commenced, would have developed throughout the kingdom as fast as the needs pressed and the possibilities allowed. So far from being indebted to the State, we have reason to believe that, but for State-repression, we should have obtained a postal organization like our present one generations ago!

Second Postscript—When the foregoing essay was republished in the third series of my *Essays, Scientific, Political, and Speculative*, I included, in the preface to the volume, some comments upon Prof. Huxley's reply. In the absence of this preface, now no longer appropriate, there seems no other fit place for these comments than this. I therefore here append them.

"On the brief rejoinder to my arguments which Prof. Huxley makes in the preface to his *Critiques and Addresses*, I may here say a few words. The reasons he gives for still thinking that the name 'Administrative Nihilism' fitly indicates the system which I have described as 'negatively regulative,' are, I think, adequately met by asking whether 'Ethical Nihilism' would fitly describe the remnant of the decalogue, were all its positive injunctions omitted. If the eight commandments which, substantially or literally, come under the form 'thou shalt not,' constitute by themselves a set of rules which can scarcely be called nihilistic; I do not see how an administrative system limited to the enforcement of such rules can be called nihilistic: especially if to the punishment of murder, adultery, stealing, and false-witness, it adds the punishment of assault, breach of contract, and all minor aggressions, down to the annoyance of neighbours by nuisances. Respecting the second and essential question, whether limitation of the internal functions of government to those which are negatively regulative, is consistent with that theory of the social organism and its controlling agencies held by me, I may say that the insufficiency of my reply has not, I think, been shown. I was tacitly asked how the analogy I have drawn between those governmental structures by which the parts of the body politic have their actions regulated and those nervous structures which regulate the organic actions of the individual living body, is to be reconciled with my belief that social activities will in the main adjust themselves. My answer was this. I recognized as essential the positively-regulative functions of the State in respect to the offensive and defensive appliances needful for national self-preservation, during the predatory phase of social evolution; and I not only admitted the importance of its negatively-regulative functions in respect to the internal social activities, but insisted that these should be carried out much more efficiently than now. Assuming always, however, that the internal social activities continue subject to that restraining action of the State which consists in preventing aggressions, direct and indirect, I contended that the coordination of these internal social activities is effected by other structures of a different kind. I aimed to show that my two beliefs are not inconsistent, by pointing out that in the individual organism, also, those vital activities which parallel the activities constituting national life, are regulated by a substantially-independent nervous system. Prof. Huxley does, indeed, remind me that recent researches show increasingly the influence of the cerebro-spinal nervous system over the processes of organic life; against which, however, has to be set the growing evidence of the power exercised by the visceral nervous system over the cerebro-spinal. But, recognizing the influence he names (which, indeed, corresponds to that governmental influence I regard as necessary); I think the consistency of my positions is maintainable so long as it is manifest that the viscera, under the control of their own nervous system, can carry on the vital actions when the control of the cerebro-spinal system is substantially arrested by sleep, or by anaesthetics, or by other causes of insensibility; and while it is shown that a considerable degree of coordination may exist among the organs of a creature which has no nervous system at all."

FROM FREEDOM TO BONDAGE (1891)

O f the many ways in which common-sense inferences about social affairs are flatly contradicted by
events (as when measures taken to suppress a book
cause increased circulation of it, or as when attempts to
prevent usurious rates of interest make the terms harder
for the borrower, or as when there is greater difficulty in
getting things at the places of production than elsewhere) one of the most curious is the way in which the
more things improve the louder become the exclama-
tions about their badness.

In days when the people were without any political
power, their subjection was rarely complained of; but

---

*This essay was originally published as the Introduction to a
collection of essays edited by Thomas Mackay under the title*
A Plea for Liberty: An Argument Against Socialism and
Socialistic Legislation *(London and New York, 1891). This
volume was reprinted by Liberty Fund in 1981.*

after free institutions had so far advanced in England that our political arrangements were envied by continental peoples, the denunciations of aristocratic rule grew gradually stronger, until there came a great widening of the franchise, soon followed by complaints that things were going wrong for want of still further widening. If we trace up the treatment of women from the days of savagedom, when they bore all the burdens and after the men had eaten received such food as remained, up through the middle ages when they served the men at their meals, to our own day when throughout our social arrangements the claims of women are always put first, we see that along with the worst treatment there went the least apparent consciousness that the treatment was bad; while now that they are better treated than ever before, the proclaiming of their grievances daily strengthens: the loudest outcries coming from "the paradise of women," America. A century ago, when scarcely a man could be found who was not occasionally intoxicated, and when inability to take one or two bottles of wine brought contempt, no agitation arose against the vice of drunkenness; but now that, in the course of fifty years, the voluntary efforts of temperance societies, joined with more general causes, have produced comparative sobriety, there are vociferous demands for laws to prevent the ruinous effects of the liquor traffic. Similarly again with education. A few generations back, ability to read and write was practically limited to the upper and middle classes, and the suggestion that the rudiments of culture should be given to labourers was never made, or, if made, ridiculed; but when, in the days of our grand-fathers, the Sunday-school system, initiated by a few philanthropists, began to spread and was followed by the establishment of day-schools, with the result that among the masses those who could read and write were no longer the exceptions, and the demand for cheap literature rapidly increased, there began the cry that the people were perishing for lack of knowledge, and that the State must not simply educate them but must force education upon them.

And so is it, too, with the general state of the population in respect of food, clothing, shelter, and the appliances of life. Leaving out of the comparison early barbaric states, there has been a conspicuous progress from the time when most rustics lived on barley bread, rye bread, and oatmeal, down to our own time when the consumption of white wheaten bread is universal—from the days when coarse jackets reaching to the knees left the legs bare, down to the present day when labouring people, like their employers, have the whole body covered, by two or more layers of clothing—from the old era of single-roomed huts without chimneys, or from the fifteenth century when even an ordinary gentleman's house was commonly without wainscot or plaster on its walls, down to the present century when every cottage has more rooms than one and the houses of artisans usually have several, while all have fireplaces, chimneys, and glazed windows, accompanied mostly by paper-hangings and painted doors; there has been, I say, a conspicuous progress in the condition of the people.

And this progress has been still more marked within our own time. Any one who can look back sixty years, when the amount of pauperism was far greater than now and beggars abundant, is struck by the comparative size and finish of the new houses occupied by operatives—by the better dress of workmen, who wear broad-cloth on Sundays, and that of servant girls, who vie with their mistresses—by the higher standard of living which leads to a great demand for the best qualities of food by working people: all results of the double change to higher wages and cheaper commodities, and a distribution of taxes which has relieved the lower classes at the expense of the upper classes. He is struck, too, by the contrast between the small space which popular welfare then occupied in public attention, and the large space it now occupies, with the result that outside and inside Parliament, plans to benefit the millions form the leading topics, and everyone having means is expected to join in some philanthropic effort. Yet while elevation, mental and physical, of the masses is going on far more rapidly than ever before—while the lowering of the death-rate proves that the average life is less trying, there swells louder and louder the cry that the evils are so great that nothing short of a social revolution can cure them. In presence of obvious improvements, joined with that increase of longevity which even alone yields conclusive proof of general amelioration, it is proclaimed, with increasing vehemence, that things are so bad that society must be pulled to pieces and reorganized on another plan. In this case, then, as in the previous cases instanced, in proportion as the evil decreases the denunciation of it increases; and as fast as natural causes are shown to be powerful there grows up the belief that they are powerless.

Not that the evils to be remedied are small. Let no one suppose that, by emphasizing the above paradox, I wish to make light of the sufferings which most men have to bear. The fates of the great majority have ever been, and doubtless still are, so sad that it is painful to think of them. Unquestionably the existing type of social organization is one which none who care for their kind can contemplate with satisfaction; and unquestionably men's activities accompanying this type are far from being admirable. The strong divisions of rank and the immense inequalities of means, are at variance with that ideal of human relations on which the sympathetic imagination likes to dwell; and the average conduct, under the pressure and excitement of social life as at present carried on, is in sundry respects repulsive. Though the many who revile competition strangely ignore the enormous benefits resulting from it—though they forget that most of the appliances and products distinguishing civilization from savagery, and making possible the maintenance of a large population on a small area, have been developed by the struggle for existence—though they disregard the fact that while every man, as producer, suffers from the under-bidding of competitors, yet, as consumer, he is immensely advantaged by the cheapening of all he has to buy—though they persist in dwelling on the evils of competition and saying nothing of its benefits; yet it is not to be denied that the evils are great, and form a large set-off from the benefits. The system under which we at present live fosters dishonesty and lying. It prompts adulterations of countless kinds; it is answerable for the cheap imitations which eventually in many cases thrust the genuine articles out of the market; it leads to the use of short weights and false measures; it introduces bribery, which vitiates most trading relations, from those of the manufacturer and buyer down to those of the shopkeeper and servant; it encourages deception to such an extent that an assistant who cannot tell a falsehood with a good face is blamed; and often it gives the conscientious trader the choice between adopting the malpractices of his competitors, or greatly injuring his creditors by bankruptcy. Moreover, the extensive frauds, common throughout the commercial world and daily exposed in law-courts and newspapers, are largely due to the pressure under which competition places the higher industrial classes; and are otherwise due to that lavish expenditure which, as implying success in the commercial struggle, brings honour. With these minor evils must be joined the major one, that the distribution achieved by the system, gives to those who regulate and superintend, a share of the total produce which bears too large a ratio to the share it gives to the actual workers. Let it not be thought, then, that in saying what I have said above, I under-estimate those vices of our competitive system which, thirty years ago, I described and denounced.[1] But it is not a question of absolute evils; it is a question of relative evils—whether the evils at present suffered are or are not less than the evils which would be suffered under another system—whether ef-

---

[1] See Essay on "The Morals of Trade."

forts for mitigation along the lines thus far followed are not more likely to succeed than efforts along utterly different lines.

This is the question here to be considered. I must be excused for first of all setting forth sundry truths which are, to some at any rate, tolerably familiar, before proceeding to draw inferences which are not so familiar.

Speaking broadly, every man works that he may avoid suffering. Here, remembrance of the pangs of hunger prompts him; and there, he is prompted by the sight of the slave-driver's lash. His immediate dread may be the punishment which physical circumstances will inflict, or may be punishment inflicted by human agency. He must have a master; but the master may be Nature or may be a fellow man. When he is under the impersonal coercion of Nature, we say that he is free; and when he is under the personal coercion of some one above him, we call him, according to the degree of his dependence, a slave, a serf, or a vassal. Of course I omit the small minority who inherit means: an incidental, and not a necessary, social element. I speak only of the vast majority, both cultured and uncultured, who maintain themselves by labour, bodily or mental, and must either exert themselves of their own unconstrained wills, prompted only by thoughts of naturally-resulting evils or benefits, or must exert themselves with constrained wills, prompted by thoughts of evils and benefits artificially resulting.

Men may work together in a society under either of these two forms of control: forms which, though in many cases mingled, are essentially contrasted. Using the word cooperation in its wide sense, and not in that re-stricted sense now commonly given to it, we may say that social life must be carried on by either voluntary cooperation or compulsory cooperation; or, to use Sir Henry Maine's words, the system must be that of *contract* or that of *status*—that in which the individual is left to do the best he can by his spontaneous efforts and get success or failure according to his efficiency, and that in which he has his appointed place, works under coercive rule, and has his apportioned share of food, clothing, and shelter.

The system of voluntary cooperation is that by which, in civilized societies, industry is now everywhere carried on. Under a simple form we have it on every farm, where the labourers, paid by the farmer himself and taking orders directly from him, are free to stay or go as they please. And of its more complex form an example is yielded by every manufacturing concern, in which, under partners, come managers and clerks, and under these, time-keepers and over-lookers, and under these operatives of different grades. In each of these cases there is an obvious working together, or cooperation, of employer and employed, to obtain in the one case a crop and in the other case a manufactured stock. And then, at the same time, there is a far more extensive, though unconscious, cooperation with other workers of all grades throughout the society. For while these particular employers and employed are severally occupied with their special kinds of work, other employers and employed are making other things needed for the carrying on of their lives as well as the lives of all others. This

voluntary cooperation, from its simplest to its most complex forms, has the common trait that those concerned
work together by consent. There is no one to force terms
or to force acceptance. It is perfectly true that in many
cases an employer may give, or an *employé* may accept,
with reluctance: circumstances he says compel him. But
what are the circumstances? In the other case there are
goods ordered, or a contract entered into, which he cannot supply or execute without yielding; and in the other
case he submits to a wage less than he likes because
otherwise he will have no money wherewith to procure
food and warmth. The general formula is not—"Do this,
or I will make you"; but it is—"Do this, or leave your
place and take the consequences."

On the other hand compulsory cooperation is exemplified by an army—not so much by our own army, the
service in which is under agreement for a specified period, but in a continental army, raised by conscription.
Here, in time of peace, the daily duties—cleaning, pa-
rade, drill, sentry work, and the rest—and in time of war
the various actions of the camp and the battle-field, are
done under command, without room for any exercise
of choice. Up from the private soldier through the
non-commissioned officers and the half-dozen or more
grades of commissioned officers, the universal law is
absolute obedience from the grade below to the grade
above. The sphere of individual will is such only as is
allowed by the will of the superior. Breaches of subordination are, according to their gravity, dealt with by
deprivation of leave, extra drill, imprisonment, flogging,
and, in the last resort, shooting. Instead of the under-

standing that there must be obedience in respect of specified duties under pain of dismissal; the understanding
now is—"Obey in everything ordered under penalty of
inflicted suffering and perhaps death."

This form of cooperation, still exemplified in an army,
has in days gone by been the form of cooperation
throughout the civil population. Everywhere, and at all
times, chronic war generates a militant type of structure,
not in the body of soldiers only but throughout the community at large. Practically, while the conflict between
societies is actively going on, and fighting is regarded as
the only manly occupation, the society is the quiescent
army and the army the mobilized society: that part which
does not take part in battle, composed of slaves, serfs,
women, etc., constituting the commissariat. Naturally,
therefore, throughout the mass of inferior individuals
constituting the commissariat, there is maintained a system of discipline identical in nature if less elaborate. The
fighting body being, under such conditions, the ruling
body, and the rest of the community being incapable of
resistance, those who control the fighting body will, of
course, impose their control upon the non-fighting
body; and the régime of coercion will be applied to it
with such modifications only as the different circumstances involve. Prisoners of war become slaves. Those
who were free cultivators before the conquest of their
country, become serfs attached to the soil. Petty chiefs
become subject to superior chiefs; these smaller lords
become vassals to over-lords; and so on up to the highest: the social ranks and powers being of like essential
nature with the ranks and powers throughout the mili-

tary organization. And while for the slaves compulsory cooperation is the unqualified system, a cooperation which is in part compulsory is the system that pervades all grades above. Each man's oath of fealty to his suzerain takes the form—"I am your man."

Throughout Europe, and especially in our own country, this system of compulsory cooperation gradually relaxed in rigour, while the system of voluntary cooperation step by step replaced it. As fast as war ceased to be the business of life, the social structure produced by war and appropriate to it, slowly became qualified by the social structure produced by industrial life and appropriate to it. In proportion as a decreasing part of the community was devoted to offensive and defensive activities, an increasing part became devoted to production and distribution. Growing more numerous, more powerful, and taking refuge in towns where it was less under the power of the militant class, this industrial population carried on its life under the system of voluntary cooperation. Though municipal governments and guild-regulations, partially pervaded by ideas and usages derived from the militant type of society, were in some degree coercive; yet production and distribution were in the main carried on under agreement—alike between buyers and sellers, and between masters and workmen. As fast as these social relations and forms of activity became dominant in urban populations, they influenced the whole community: compulsory cooperation lapsed more and more, through money commutation for services, military and civil; while divisions of rank became less rigid and class-power diminished. Until at length,

restraints exercised by incorporated trades having fallen
into desuetude, as well as the rule of rank over rank,
voluntary cooperation became the universal principle.
Purchase and sale became the law for all kinds of services
as well as for all kinds of commodities.

The restlessness generated by pressure against the
conditions of existence, perpetually prompts the desire
to try a new position. Everyone knows how long-
continued rest in one attitude becomes wearisome—
everyone has found how even the best easy chair, at first
rejoiced in, becomes after many hours intolerable; and
change to a hard seat, previously occupied and rejected,
seems for a time to be a great relief. It is the same with
incorporated humanity. Having by long struggles eman-
cipated itself from the hard discipline of the ancient
régime, and having discovered that the new régime
into which it has grown, though relatively easy, is not
without stresses and pains, its impatience with these
prompts the wish to try another system: which other
system is, in principle if not in appearance, the same as
that which during past generations was escaped from
with much rejoicing.

For as fast as the régime of contract is discarded the
régime of status is of necessity adopted. As fast as voluntary cooperation is abandoned compulsory cooperation must be substituted. Some kind of organization
labour must have; and if it is not that which arises by
agreement under free competition, it must be that which
is imposed by authority. Unlike in appearance and
names as it may be to the old order of slaves and serfs,

working under masters, who were coerced by barons, who were themselves vassals of dukes or kings, the new order wished for, constituted by workers under foremen of small groups, overlooked by superintendents, who are subject to higher local managers, who are controlled by superiors of districts, themselves under a central government, must be essentially the same in principle. In the one case, as in the other, there must be established grades, and enforced subordination of each grade to the grades above. This is a truth which the communist or the socialist does not dwell upon. Angry with the existing system under which each of us takes care of himself, while all of us see that each has fair play, he thinks how much better it would be for all of us to take care of each of us; and he refrains from thinking of the machinery by which this is to be done. Inevitably, if each is to be cared for by all, then the embodied all must get the means— the necessaries of life. What it gives to each must be taken from the accumulated contributions; and it must therefore require from each his proportion—must tell him how much he has to give to the general stock in the shape of production, that he may have so much in the shape of sustentation. Hence, before he can be provided for, he must put himself under orders, and obey those who say what he shall do, and at what hours, and where; and who give him his share of food, clothing, and shelter. If competition is excluded, and with it buying and selling, there can be no voluntary exchange of so much labour for so much produce; but there must be apportionment of the one to the other by appointed officers. This apportionment must be enforced. Without alternative the work must be done, and without alternative the benefit, whatever it may be, must be accepted. For the worker may not leave his place at will and offer himself elsewhere. Under such a system he cannot be accepted elsewhere, save by order of the authorities. And it is manifest that a standing order would forbid employment in one place of an insubordinate member from another place: the system could not be worked if the workers were severally allowed to go or come as they pleased. With corporals and sergeants under them, the captains of industry must carry out the orders of their colonels, and these of their generals, up to the council of the commander-in-chief; and obedience must be required throughout the industrial army as throughout a fighting army. "Do your prescribed duties, and take your apportioned rations," must be the rule of the one as of the other.

"Well, be it so"; replies the socialist. "The workers will appoint their own officers, and these will always be subject to criticisms of the mass they regulate. Being thus in fear of public opinion, they will be sure to act judiciously and fairly; or when they do not, will be deposed by the popular vote, local or general. Where will be the grievance of being under superiors, when the superiors themselves are under democratic control?" And in this attractive vision the socialist has full belief.

Iron and brass are simpler things than flesh and blood, and dead wood than living nerve; and a machine constructed of the one works in more definite ways than an organism constructed of the other,—especially when the machine is worked by the inorganic forces of steam or water, while the organism is worked by the forces of living nerve-centres. Manifestly, then, the ways in which the machine will work are much more readily calculable than the ways in which the organism will work. Yet in how few cases does the inventor foresee rightly the actions of his new apparatus! Read the patent-list, and it will be found that not more than one device in fifty turns out to be of any service. Plausible as his scheme seemed to the inventor, one or other hitch prevents the intended operation, and brings out a widely different result from that which he wished.

What, then, shall we say of these schemes which have to do not with dead matters and forces, but with complex living organisms working in ways less readily foreseen, and which involve the cooperation of multitudes of such organisms? Even the units out of which this re-arranged body politic is to be formed are often incomprehensible. Everyone is from time to time surprised by others' behaviour, and even by the deeds of relatives who are best known to him. Seeing, then, how uncertainly anyone can foresee the actions of an individual, how can he with any certainty foresee the operation of a social structure? He proceeds on the assumption that all concerned will judge rightly and act fairly—will think as they ought to think, and act as they ought to act; and he assumes this regardless of the daily experiences which show him that men do neither the one nor the other, and forgetting that the complaints he makes against the existing system show his belief to be that men have neither the wisdom nor the rectitude which his plan requires them to have.

Paper constitutions raise smiles on the faces of those
who have observed their results; and paper social systems similarly affect those who have contemplated the
available evidence. How little the men who wrought the
French revolution and were chiefly concerned in setting
up the new governmental apparatus, dreamt that one of
the early actions of this apparatus would be to behead
them all! How little the men who drew up the American
Declaration of Independence and framed the republic,
anticipated that after some generations the legislature
would lapse into the hands of wire-pullers; that its
doings would turn upon the contests of office-seekers;
that political action would be everywhere vitiated by the
intrusion of a foreign element holding the balance between parties; that electors, instead of judging for themselves, would habitually be led to the polls in thousands
by their "bosses"; and that respectable men would be
driven out of public life by the insults and slanders of
professional politicians. Nor were there better previsions
in those who gave constitutions to the various other
states of the New World, in which unnumbered revolutions have shown with wonderful persistence the contrasts between the expected results of political systems
and the achieved results. It has been no less thus with
proposed systems of social re-organization, so far as they
have been tried. Save where celibacy has been insisted
on, their history has been everywhere one of disaster;
ending with the history of Cabet's Icarian colony lately
given by one of its members, Madame Fleury Robinson,
in *The Open Court*—a history of splittings, re-splittings
and re-re-splittings, accompanied by numerous individ-

ual secessions and final dissolution. And for the failure of such social schemes, as for the failure of the political schemes, there has been one general cause.

Metamorphosis is the universal law, exemplified throughout the Heavens and on the Earth: especially throughout the organic world; and above all in the animal division of it. No creature, save the simplest and most minute, commences its existence in a form like that which it eventually assumes; and in most cases the unlikeness is great—so great that kinship between the first and the last forms would be incredible were it not daily demonstrated in every poultry-yard and every garden. More than this is true. The changes of form are often several: each of them being an apparently complete transformation—egg, larva, pupa, imago, for example. And this universal metamorphosis, displayed alike in the development of a planet and of every seed which germinates on its surface, holds also of societies, whether taken as wholes or in their separate institutions. No one of them ends as it begins; and the difference between its original structure and its ultimate structure is such that, at the outset, change of the one into the other would have seemed incredible. In the rudest tribe the chief, obeyed as leader in war, loses his distinctive position when the fighting is over; and even where continued warfare has produced permanent chieftainship, the chief, building his own hut, getting his own food, making his own implements, differs from others only by his predominant influence. There is no sign that in course of time, by conquests and unions of tribes, and

consolidations of clusters so formed with other such
clusters, until a nation has been produced, there will
originate from the primitive chief, one who, as czar or
emperor, surrounded with pomp and ceremony, has
despotic power over scores of millions, exercised
through hundreds of thousands of soldiers and
hundreds of thousands of officials. When the early
Christian missionaries, having humble externals and
passing self-denying lives, spread over pagan Europe,
preaching forgiveness of injuries and the returning of
good for evil, no one dreamt that in course of time their
representatives would form a vast hierarchy, possessing
everywhere a large part of the land, distinguished by the
haughtiness of its members grade above grade, ruled by
military bishops who led their retainers to battle, and
headed by a pope exercising supreme power over kings.
So, too, has it been with that very industrial system
which many are now so eager to replace. In its original
form there was no prophecy of the factory-system or
kindred organizations of workers. Differing from them
only as being the head of his house, the master worked
along with his apprentices and a journeyman or two,
sharing with them his table and accommodation, and
himself selling their joint produce. Only with industrial
growth did there come employment of a larger number
of assistants, and a relinquishment, on the part of the
master, of all other business than that of superintendence. And only in the course of recent times did there
evolve the organizations under which the labours of
hundreds and thousands of men receiving wages, are

regulated by various orders of paid officials under a single or multiple head. These originally small, semi-socialistic, groups of producers, like the compound families or house-communities of early ages, slowly dissolved because they could not hold their ground: the larger establishments, with better sub-division of labour, succeeded because they ministered to the wants of society more effectually. But we need not go back through the centuries to trace transformations sufficiently great and unexpected. On the day when £30,000 a year in aid of education was voted as an experiment, the name of idiot would have been given to an opponent who prophesied that in 50 years the sum spent through imperial taxes and local rates would amount to £10,000,000 or who said that the aid to education would be followed by aids to feeding and clothing, or who said that parents and children, alike deprived of all option, would, even if starving, be compelled by fine or imprisonment to conform, and receive that which, with papal assumption, the State calls education. No one, I say, would have dreamt that out of so innocent-looking a germ would have so quickly evolved this tyrannical system, tamely submitted to by people who fancy themselves free.

Thus in social arrangements, as in all other things, change is inevitable. It is foolish to suppose that new institutions set up, will long retain the character given them by those who set them up. Rapidly or slowly they will be transformed into institutions unlike those intended—so unlike as even to be unrecognizable by their devisers. And what, in the case before us, will be the metamorphosis? The answer pointed to by instances above given, and warranted by various analogies, is manifest.

A cardinal trait in all advancing organization is the development of the regulative apparatus. If the parts of a whole are to act together, there must be appliances by which their actions are directed; and in proportion as the whole is large and complex, and has many requirements to be met by many agencies, the directive apparatus must be extensive, elaborate, and powerful. That it is thus with individual organisms needs no saying; and that it must be thus with social organisms is obvious. Beyond the regulative apparatus such as in our own society is required for carrying on national defence and maintaining public order and personal safety, there must, under the régime of socialism, be a regulative apparatus everywhere controlling all kinds of production and distribution, and everywhere apportioning the shares of products of each kind required for each locality, each working establishment, each individual. Under our existing voluntary cooperation, with its free contracts and its competition, production and distribution need no official oversight. Demand and supply, and the desire of each man to gain a living by supplying the needs of his fellows, spontaneously evolve that wonderful system whereby a great city has its food daily brought round to all doors or stored at adjacent shops; has clothing for its citizens everywhere at hand in multitudinous varieties; has its houses and furniture and fuel ready made or stocked in each locality; and has mental pabulum from halfpenny papers hourly hawked round, to weekly shoals of novels, and less abundant books of instruction, furnished without stint for small payments. And throughout the kingdom, production as well as distribution is similarly carried on with the smallest amount of superintendence which proves efficient; while the quantities of the numerous commodities required daily in each locality are adjusted without any other agency than the pursuit of profit. Suppose now that this industrial régime of willinghood, acting spontaneously, is replaced by a régime of industrial obedience, enforced by public officials. Imagine the fast administration required for that distribution of all commodities to all people in every city, town and village, which is now effected by traders! Imagine, again, the still more vast administration required for doing all that farmers, manufacturers, and merchants do; having not only its various orders of local superintendents, but its sub-centres and chief centres needed for apportioning the quantities of each thing everywhere needed, and the adjustment of them to the requisite times. Then add the staffs wanted for working mines, railways, roads, canals; the staffs required for conducting the importing and exporting businesses and the administration of mercantile shipping; the staffs required for supplying towns not only with water and gas but with locomotion by tramways, omnibuses, and other vehicles, and for the distribution of power, electric and other. Join with these the existing postal, telegraphic, and telephonic administrations; and finally those of the police and army, by which the dictates of this immense consolidated regulative system are to be everywhere enforced. Imagine all this and then ask what will be the position of the actual workers! Already on the continent, where governmental organizations are more elaborate and coercive than here, there are chronic complaints of the tyranny of bureaucracies—the *hauteur* and brutality of their members. What will these become when not only the more public actions of citizens are controlled, but there is added this far more extensive control of all their respective daily duties? What will happen when the various divisions of this vast army of officials, united by interests common to officialism—the interests of the regulators *versus* those of the regulated— have at their command whatever force is needful to suppress insubordination and act as "saviours of society?" Where will be the actual diggers and miners and smelters and weavers, when those who order and superintend, everywhere arranged class above class, have come, after some generations, to inter-marry with those of kindred grades, under feelings such as are operative in existing classes; and when there have been so produced a series of castes rising in superiority; and when all these, having everything in their own power, have arranged modes of living for their own advantage: eventually forming a new aristocracy far more elaborate and better organized than the old? How will the individual worker fare if he is dissatisfied with his treatment—thinks that he has not an adequate share of the products, or has more to do than can rightly be demanded, or wishes to undertake a function for which he feels himself fitted but which is not thought proper for him by his superiors, or desires to make an independent career for himself? This dissatisfied unit in the immense machine will be told he must submit or go. The mildest penalty for disobedience will be industrial excommunication. And if an international organization of labour is formed as proposed, exclusion in one country will mean exclusion in all others—industrial excommunication will mean starvation.

That things must take this course is a conclusion reached not by deduction only, nor only by induction from those experiences of the past instanced above, nor only from consideration of the analogies furnished by organisms of all orders; but it is reached also by observation of cases daily under our eyes. The truth that the regulative structure always tends to increase in power, is illustrated by every established body of men. The history of each learned society, or society for other purpose, shows how the staff, permanent or partially permanent, sways the proceedings and determines the actions of the society with but little resistance, even when most members of the society disapprove: the repugnance to anything like a revolutionary step being ordinarily an efficient deterrent. So is it with joint-stock companies— those owning railways for exmple. The plans of a board of directors are usually authorized with little or no discussion; and if there is any considerable opposition, this is forthwith crushed by an overwhelming number of proxies sent by those who always support the existing administration. Only when the misconduct is extreme does the resistance of shareholders suffice to displace the ruling body. Nor is it otherwise with societies formed of working men and having the interests of labour especially at heart—the trades-unions. In these, too, the regulative agency becomes all powerful. Their members, even when they dissent from the policy pursued, habitually yield to the authorities they have set up. As they cannot secede without making enemies of their fellow workmen, and often losing all chance of employment, they succumb. We are shown, too, by the late congress, that already, in the general organization of trades-unions so recently formed, there are complaints of "wire-pullers" and "bosses" and "permanent officials." If, then, this supremacy of the regulators is seen in bodies of quite modern origin, formed of men who have, in many of the cases instanced, unhindered powers of asserting their independence, what will the supremacy of the regulators become in long-established bodies, in bodies which have become vast and highly organized, and in bodies which, instead of controlling only a small part of the unit's life, control the whole of his life?

Again there will come the rejoinder—"We shall guard against all that. Everybody will be educated; and all, with their eyes constantly open to the abuse of power, will be quick to prevent it." The worth of these expectations would be small even could we not identify the causes which will bring disappointment; for in human affairs the most promising schemes go wrong in ways which no one anticipated. But in this case the going wrong will be necessitated by cases which are conspicuous. The working of institutions is determined by men's characters; and the existing defects in their characters will inevitably bring about the results above indicated. There is no adequate endowment of those sentiments required to prevent the growth of a despotic bureaucracy.

Were it needful to dwell on indirect evidence, much might be made of that furnished by the behaviour of the so-called Liberal party—a party which, relinquishing the original conception of a leader as a mouthpiece for a known and accepted policy, thinks itself bound to accept a policy which its leader springs upon it without consent or warning—a party so utterly without the feeling and idea implied by liberalism, as not to resent this trampling on the right of private judgement, which constitutes the root of liberalism—nay, a party which vilifies as renegade liberals, those of its members who refuse to surrender their independence! But without occupying space with indirect proofs that the mass of men have not the natures required to check the development of tyrannical officialism, it will suffice to contemplate the direct proofs furnished by those classes among whom the socialistic idea most predominates, and who think themselves most interested in propagating it—the operative classes. These would constitute the great body of the socialistic organization, and their characters would determine its nature. What, then, are their characters as displayed in such organizations as they have already formed?

Instead of the selfishness of the employing classes and the selfishness of competition, we are to have the unselfishness of a mutually-aiding system. How far is this unselfishness now shown in the behaviour of working men to one another? What shall we say to the rules limiting the numbers of new hands admitted into each trade, or to the rules which hinder ascent from inferior classes of workers to superior classes? One does not see in such regulations any of that altruism by which socialism is to be pervaded. Contrariwise, one sees a pursuit of private interests no less keen than among traders. Hence, unless we suppose that men's natures will be suddenly exalted, we must conclude that the pursuit of private interests will sway the doings of all the component classes in a socialistic society.

With passive disregard of others' claims goes active encroachment on them. "Be one of us or we will cut off your means of living," is the usual threat of each trades-union to outsiders of the same trade. While their members insist on their own freedom to combine and fix the rates at which they will work (as they are perfectly justified in doing), the freedom of those who disagree with them is not only denied but the assertion of it is treated as a crime. Individuals who maintain their rights to make their own contracts are vilified as "blacklegs" and "traitors," and meet with violence which would be merciless were there no legal penalties and no police. Along with this trampling on the liberties of men of their own class, there goes peremptory dictation to the employing class: not prescribed terms and working arrangements only shall be conformed to, but none save those belonging to their body shall be employed—nay, in some cases, there shall be a strike if the employer carries on transactions with trading bodies that give work to non-union men. Here, then, we are variously shown by trades-unions, or at any rate by the newer trades-unions, a determination to impose their regulations without regard to the rights of those who are to be coerced. So complete is the inversion of ideas and sentiments that maintenance of these rights is regarded as vicious and trespass upon them as virtuous.[2]

Along with this aggressiveness in one direction there goes submissiveness in another direction. The coercion of outsiders by unionists is paralleled only by their subjection to their leaders. That they may conquer in the struggle they surrender their individual liberties and individual judgements, and show no resentment however dictatorial may be the rule exercised over them. Everywhere we see such subordination that bodies of workmen unanimously leave their work or return to it as their authorities order them. Nor do they resist when taxed all round to support strikers whose acts they may or may not approve, but instead, ill-treat recalcitrant members of their body who do not subscribe.

---

[2] Marvellous are the conclusions men reach when once they desert the simple principle, that each man should be allowed to pursue the objects of life, restrained only by the limits which the similar pursuits of their objects by other men impose. A generation ago we heard loud assertions to "the right to labour," that is, the right to have labour provided; and there are still not a few who think the community bound to find work for each person. Compare this with the doctrine current in France at the time when the monarchical power culminated; namely, that "the right of working is a royal right which the prince can sell and the subjects must buy." This contrast is startling enough; but a contrast still more startling is being provided for us. We now see a resuscitation of the despotic doctrine, differing only by the substitution of Trades-Unions for kings. For now that Trades-Unions are becoming universal, and each artisan has to pay prescribed monies to one or another of them, with the alternative of being a non-unionist to whom work is denied by force, it has come to this, that the right to labour is a Trade-Union right, which the Trade-Union can sell and the individual worker must buy!

The traits thus shown must be operative in any new social organization, and the question to be asked is— What will result from their operation when they are relieved from all restraints? At present the separate bodies of men displaying them are in the midst of a society partially passive, partially antagonistic; are subject to the criticisms and reprobations of an independent press; and are under the control of law, enforced by police. If in these circumstances these bodies habitually take courses which override individual freedom, what will happen when, instead of being only scattered parts of the community, governed by their separate sets of regulators, they constitute the whole community, governed by a consolidated system of such regulators; when functionaries of all orders, including those who officer the press, form parts of the regulative organization; and when the law is both enacted and administered by this regulative organization? The fanatical adherents of a social theory are capable of taking any measures, no matter how extreme, for carrying out their views: holding, like the merciless priesthoods of past times, that the end justifies the means. And when a general socialistic organization has been established, the vast, ramified, and consolidated body of those who direct its activities, using without check whatever coercion seems to them needful in the interests of the system (which will practically become their own interests) will have no hesitation in imposing their rigorous rule over the entire lives of the actual workers; until, eventually, there is developed an official oligarchy, with its various grades, exercising a tyranny more gigantic and more terrible than any which the world has seen.

Let me again repudiate an erroneous inference. Any one who supposes that the foregoing argument implies contentment with things as they are, makes a profound mistake. The present social state is transitional, as past social states have been transitional. There will, I hope and believe, come a future social state differing as much from the present as the present differs from the past with its mailed barons and defenceless serfs. In *Social Statics,* as well as in *The Study of Sociology* and in *Political Institutions,* is clearly shown the desire for an organization more conducive to the happiness of men at large than that which exists. My opposition to socialism results from the belief that it would stop the progress to such a higher state and bring back a lower state. Nothing but the slow modification of human nature by the discipline of social life can produce permanently advantageous changes.

A fundamental error pervading the thinking of nearly all parties, political and social, is that evils admit of immediate and radical remedies. "If you will but do this, the mischief will be prevented." "Adopt my plan and the suffering will disappear." "The corruption will unquestionably be cured by enforcing this measure." Everywhere one meets with beliefs, expressed or implied, of these kinds. They are all ill-founded. It is possible to remove causes which intensify the evils; it is possible to change the evils from one form into another;

and it is possible, and very common, to exacerbate the evils by the efforts made to prevent them; but anything like immediate cure is impossible. In the course of thousands of years mankind have, by multiplication, been forced out of that original savage state in which small numbers supported themselves on wild food, into the civilized state in which the food required for supporting great numbers can be got only by continuous labour. The nature required for this last mode of life is widely different from the nature required for the first; and long-continued pains have to be passed through in re-moulding the one into the other. Misery has necessarily to be borne by a constitution out of harmony with its conditions; and a constitution inherited from primitive men is out of harmony with the conditions imposed on existing men. Hence it is impossible to establish forthwith a satisfactory social state. No such nature as that which has filled Europe with millions of armed men, here eager for conquest and there for revenge—no such nature as that which prompts the nations called Christian to vie with one another in filibustering expeditions all over the world, regardless of the claims of aborigines, while their tens of thousands of priests of the religion of love look on approvingly—no such nature as that which, in dealing with weaker races, goes beyond the primitive rule of life for life, and for one life takes many lives—no such nature, I say, can, by any device, be framed into a harmonious community. The root of all well-ordered social action is a sentiment of justice, which at once insists on personal freedom and is solicitous for the like freedom of others; and there at present exists but a very inadequate amount of this sentiment.

Hence the need for further long continuance of a social discipline which requires each man to carry on his activities with due regard to the like claims of others to carry on their activities; and which, while it insists that he shall have all the benefits his conduct naturally brings, insists also that he shall not saddle on others the evils his conduct naturally brings: unless they freely undertake to bear them. And hence the belief that endeavours to elude this discipline, will not only fail, but will bring worse evils than those to be escaped.

It is not, then, chiefly in the interests of the employing classes that socialism is to be resisted, but much more in the interests of the employed classes. In one way or other production must be regulated; and the regulators, in the nature of things, must always be a small class as compared with the actual producers. Under voluntary cooperation as at present carried on, the regulators, pursuing their personal interests, take as large a share of the produce as they can get; but, as we are daily shown by trades-union successes, are restrained in the selfish pursuit of their ends. Under that compulsory cooperation which socialism would necessitate, the regulators, pursuing their personal interests with no less selfishness, could not be met by the combined resistance of free workers; and their power, unchecked as now by refusals to work save on prescribed terms, would grow and ramify and consolidate till it became irresistible. The ultimate result, as I have before pointed out, must be a

society like that of ancient Peru, dreadful to contemplate, in which the mass of the people, elaborately reg-
imented in groups of 10, 50, 100, 500, and 1000, ruled by
officers of corresponding grades, and tied to their districts, were superintended in their private lives as well
as in their industries, and toiled hopelessly for the support of the governmental organization.

INDEX

519

The Palatino typeface used in this volume is the work of Hermann Zapf, the noted European type designer and master calligrapher. Palatino is basically an "old style" letterform, yet, it is strongly endowed with Zapf's distinctive exquisiteness. With concern not solely for the individual letter but also for the working visual relationship in a page of text, Zapf's edged pen has given this type a brisk, natural motion.

This book is printed on paper that is acid-free and meets the requirements of the American National Standard for Permanence of Paper for Printed Library Materials, Z39.48-1992. ∞

Book design by JMH Corporation, Indianapolis, Indiana
Cover design by Erin Kirk New, Watkinsville, Georgia
Typography by Weimer Typesetting Company, Indianapolis, Indiana
Printed and bound by Edwards Brothers, Inc., Ann Arbor, Michigan